Rosario + Vampire

Monster Mamas

9

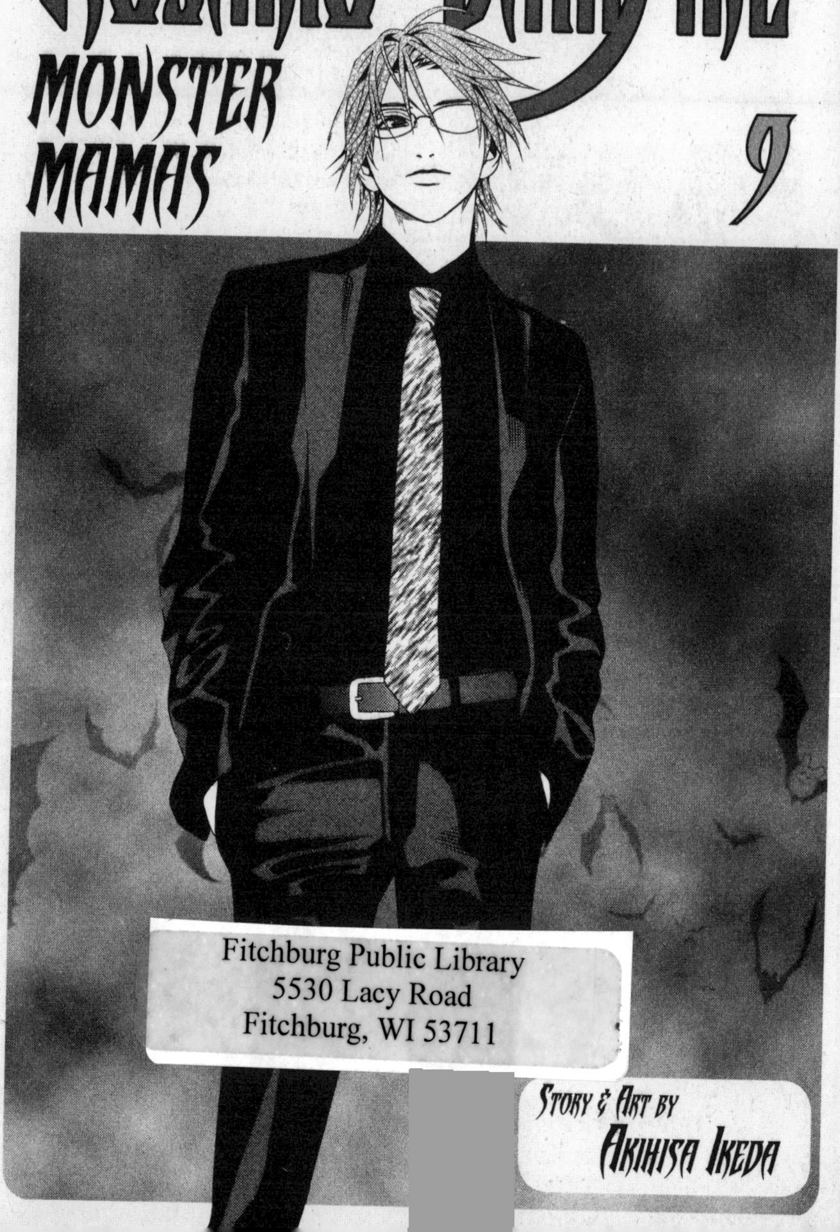

Story & Art by
Akihisa Ikeda

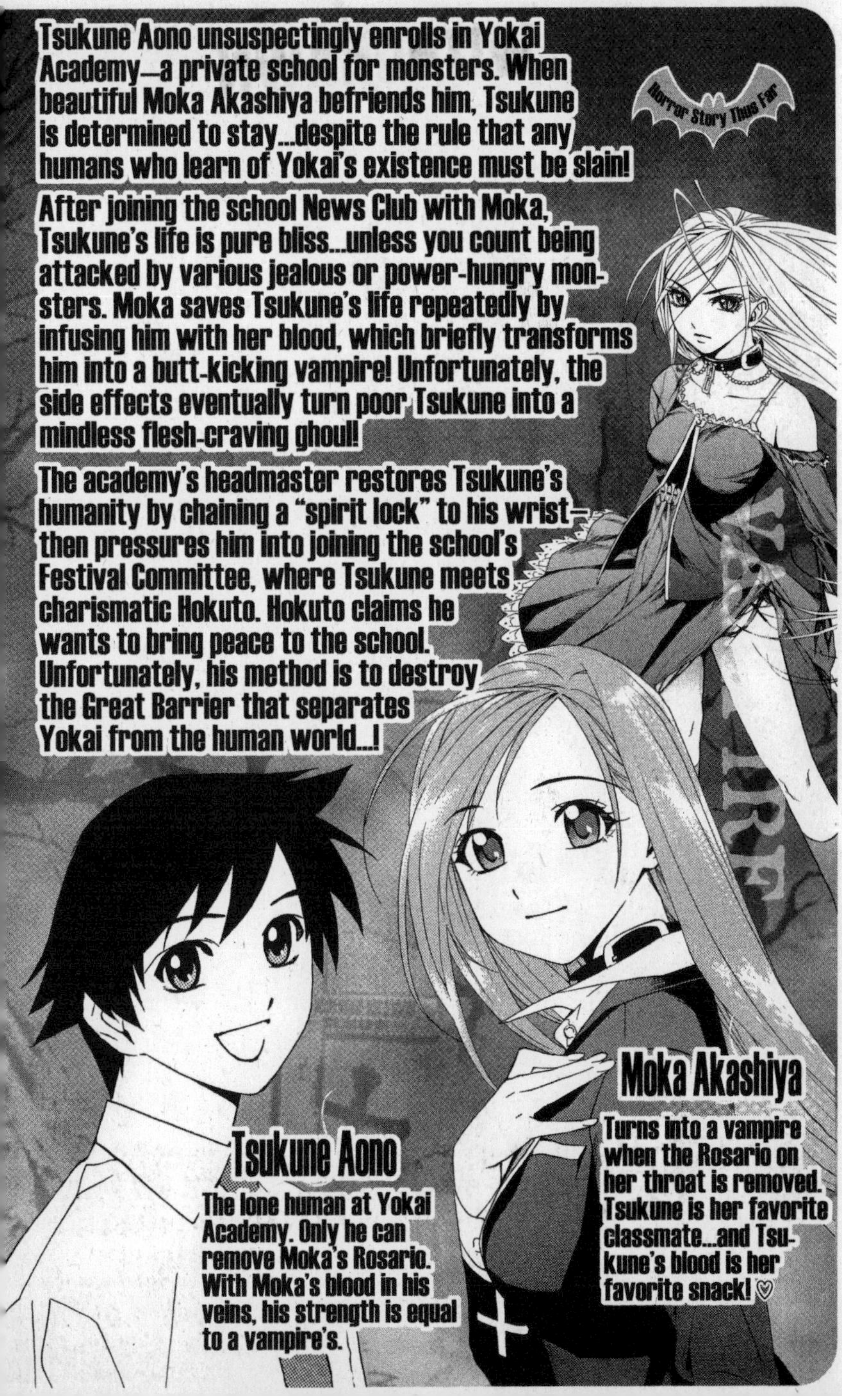

Horror Story Thus Far

Tsukune Aono unsuspectingly enrolls in Yokai Academy—a private school for monsters. When beautiful Moka Akashiya befriends him, Tsukune is determined to stay...despite the rule that any humans who learn of Yokai's existence must be slain!

After joining the school News Club with Moka, Tsukune's life is pure bliss...unless you count being attacked by various jealous or power-hungry monsters. Moka saves Tsukune's life repeatedly by infusing him with her blood, which briefly transforms him into a butt-kicking vampire! Unfortunately, the side effects eventually turn poor Tsukune into a mindless flesh-craving ghoul!

The academy's headmaster restores Tsukune's humanity by chaining a "spirit lock" to his wrist—then pressures him into joining the school's Festival Committee, where Tsukune meets charismatic Hokuto. Hokuto claims he wants to bring peace to the school. Unfortunately, his method is to destroy the Great Barrier that separates Yokai from the human world...!

Moka Akashiya

Turns into a vampire when the Rosario on her throat is removed. Tsukune is her favorite classmate...and Tsukune's blood is her favorite snack! ♡

Tsukune Aono

The lone human at Yokai Academy. Only he can remove Moka's Rosario. With Moka's blood in his veins, his strength is equal to a vampire's.

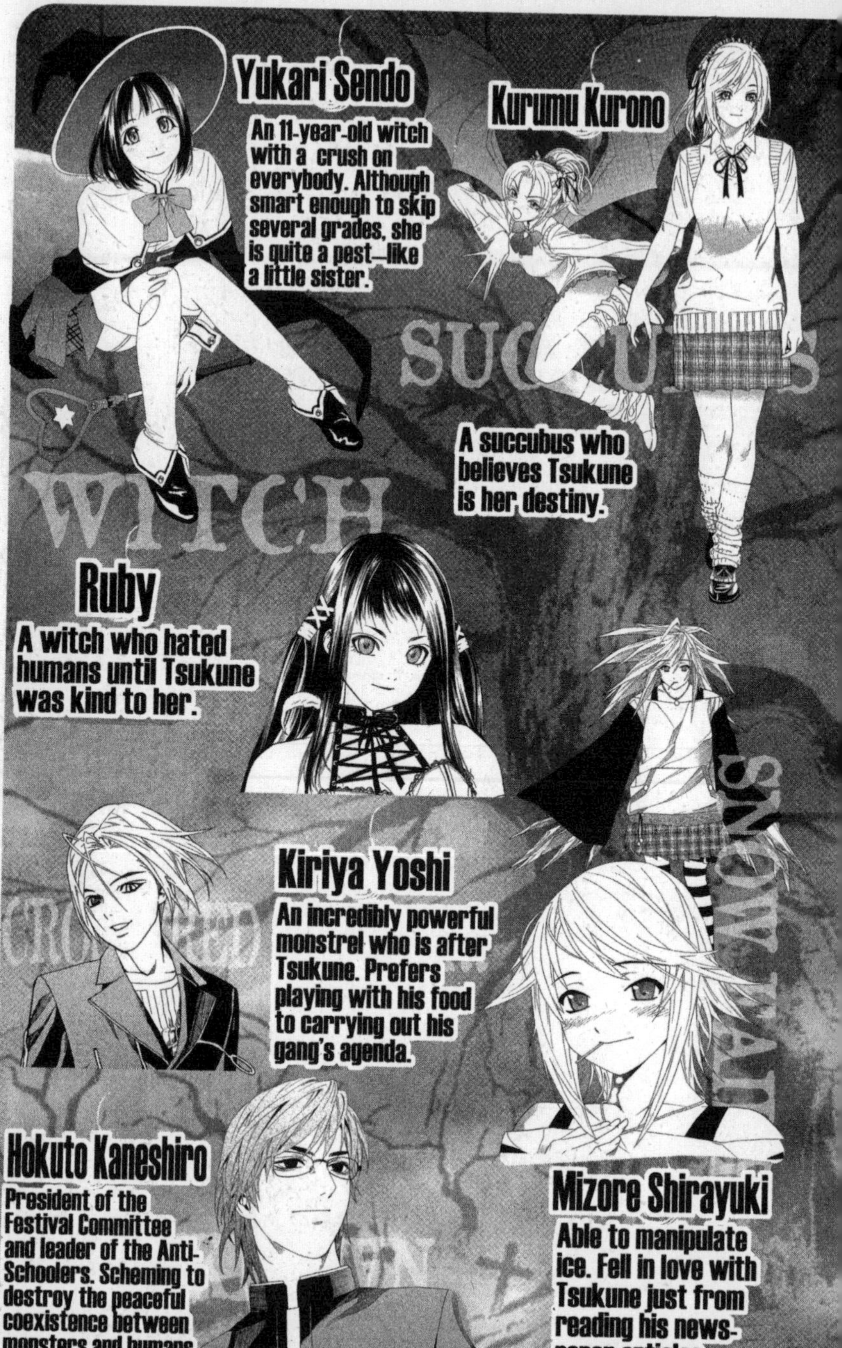
Yukari Sendo
An 11-year-old witch with a crush on everybody. Although smart enough to skip several grades, she is quite a pest—like a little sister.
Kurumu Kurono
A succubus who believes Tsukune is her destiny.
WITCH
Ruby
A witch who hated humans until Tsukune was kind to her.
Kiriya Yoshi
An incredibly powerful monstrel who is after Tsukune. Prefers playing with his food to carrying out his gang's agenda.
Hokuto Kaneshiro
President of the Festival Committee and leader of the Anti-Schoolers. Scheming to destroy the peaceful coexistence between monsters and humans.
Mizore Shirayuki
Able to manipulate ice. Fell in love with Tsukune just from reading his news-paper articles.

CONTENTS

Volume 9: Monster Mamas

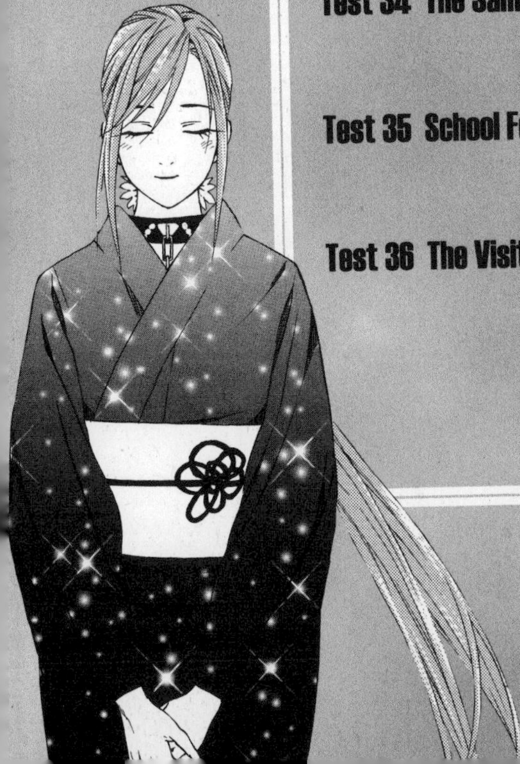

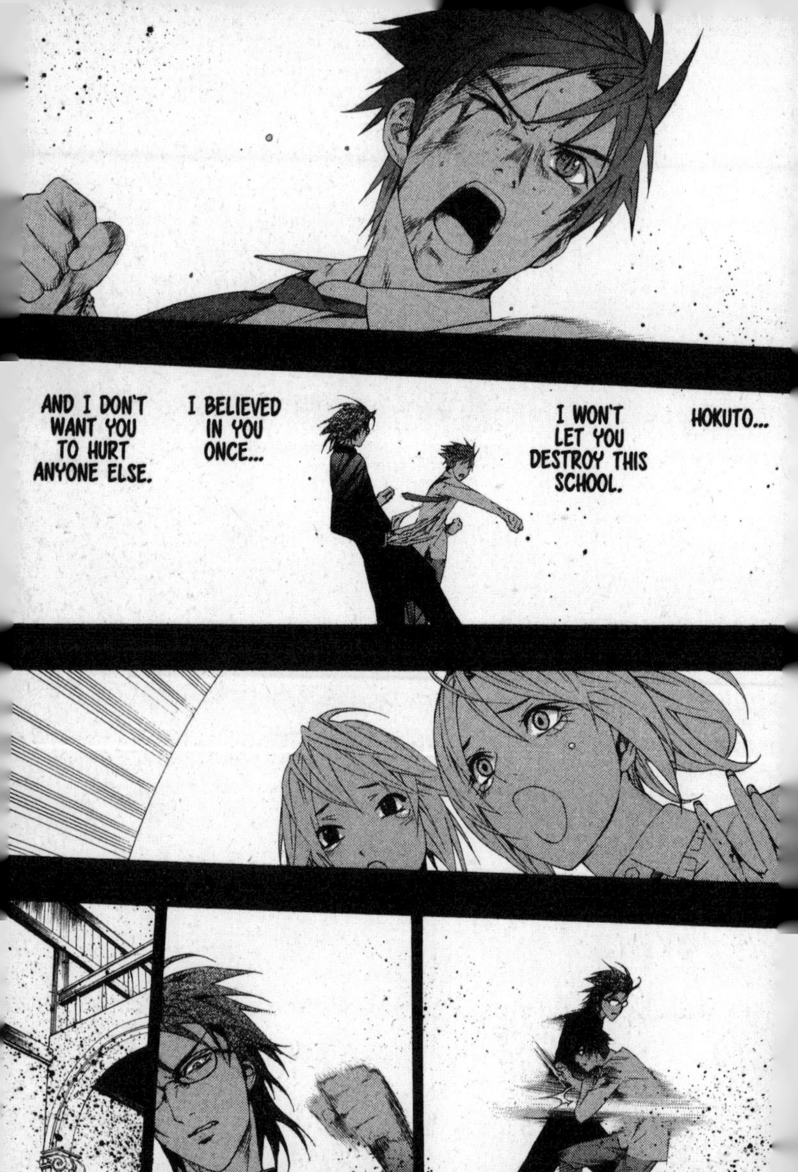
HOKUTO...
I WON'T LET YOU DESTROY THIS SCHOOL.
I BELIEVED IN YOU ONCE...
AND I DON'T WANT YOU TO HURT ANYONE ELSE.

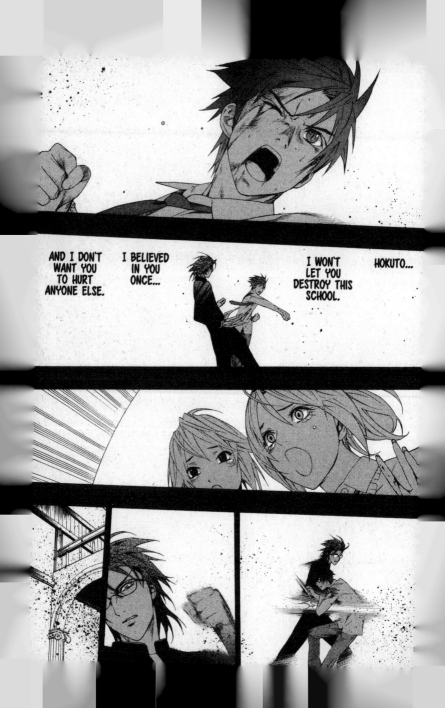

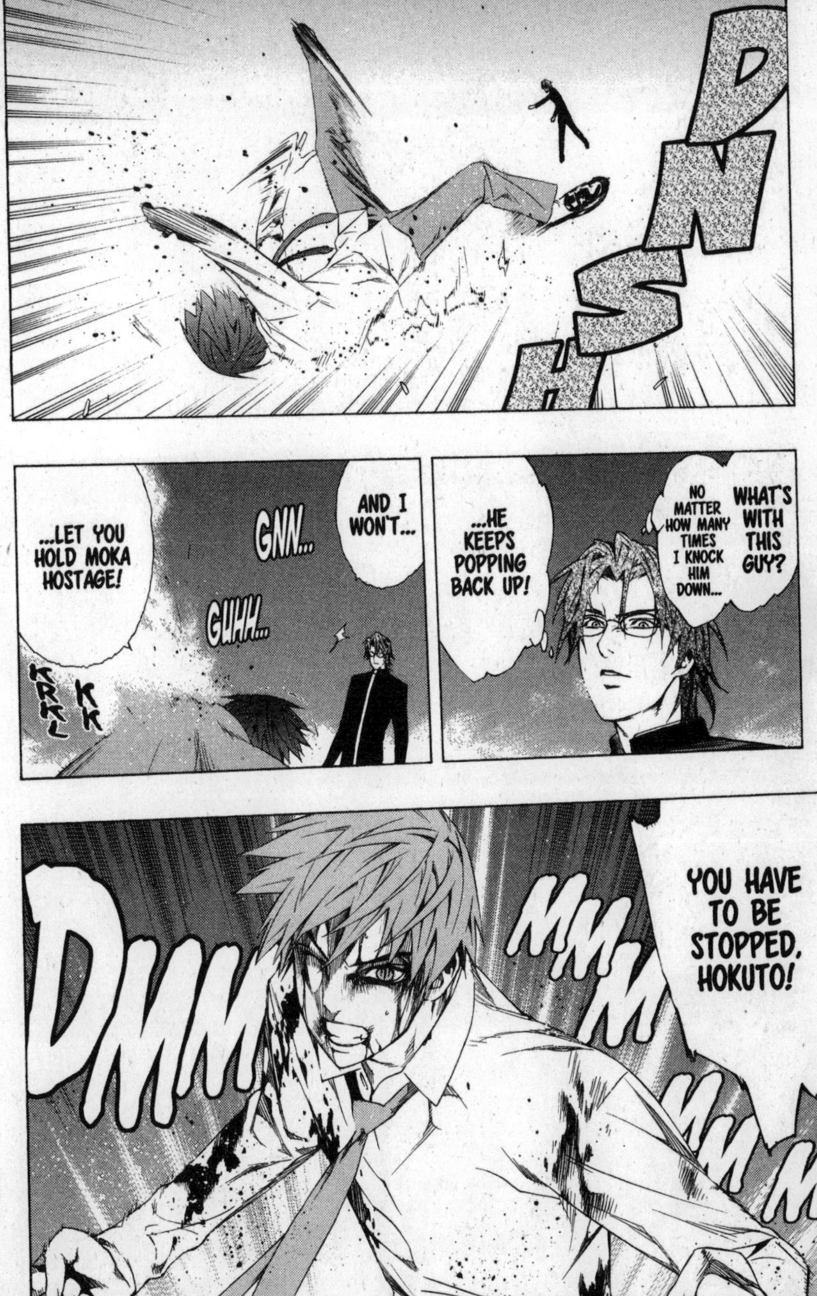
DNSH
WHAT'S WITH THIS GUY?
NO MATTER HOW MANY TIMES I KNOCK HIM DOWN...
...HE KEEPS POPPING BACK UP!
AND I WON'T...
GNN...
GUHH...
...LET YOU HOLD MOKA HOSTAGE!
KRKL KK
YOU HAVE TO BE STOPPED, HOKUTO!
DMMMMMMMMMMM

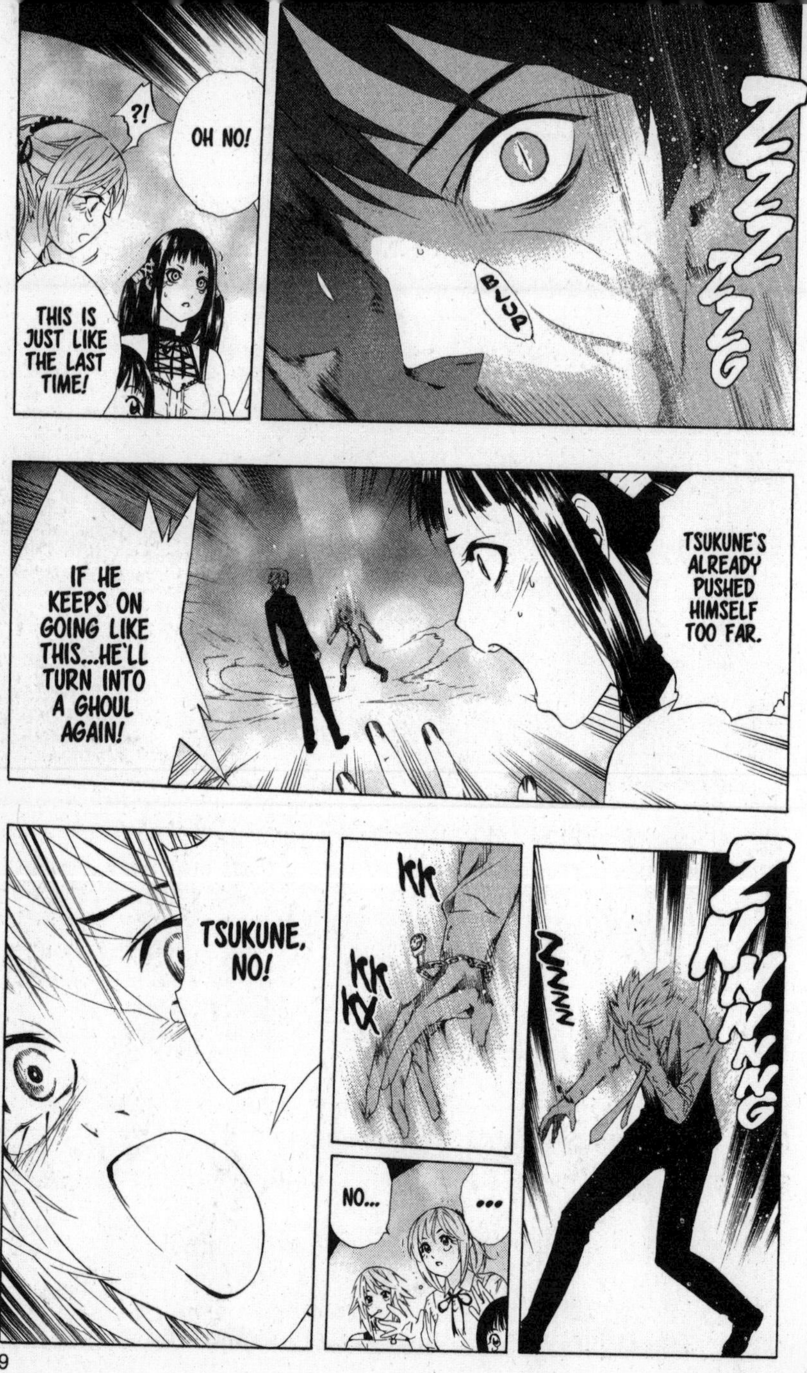
ZZZZZG
BLUP
?!
OH NO!
THIS IS JUST LIKE THE LAST TIME!
TSUKUNE'S ALREADY PUSHED HIMSELF TOO FAR.
IF HE KEEPS ON GOING LIKE THIS...HE'LL TURN INTO A GHOUL AGAIN!
ZNNNNG
ZNNN
KK
KK KX
...
NO...
TSUKUNE, NO!

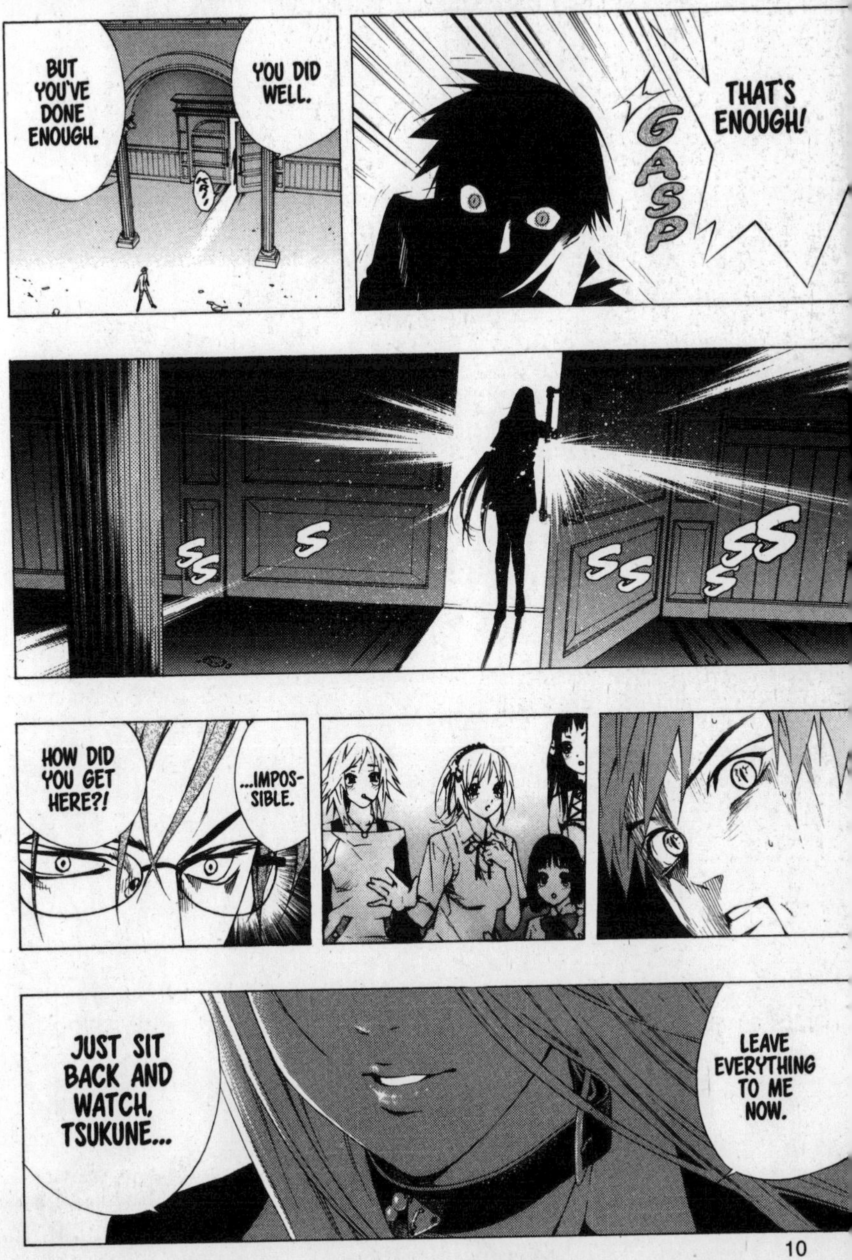

THAT'S ENOUGH!
GASP
YOU DID WELL.
BUT YOU'VE DONE ENOUGH.
SSS
SS
S
SS
...IMPOSSIBLE.
HOW DID YOU GET HERE?!
LEAVE EVERYTHING TO ME NOW.
JUST SIT BACK AND WATCH, TSUKUNE...

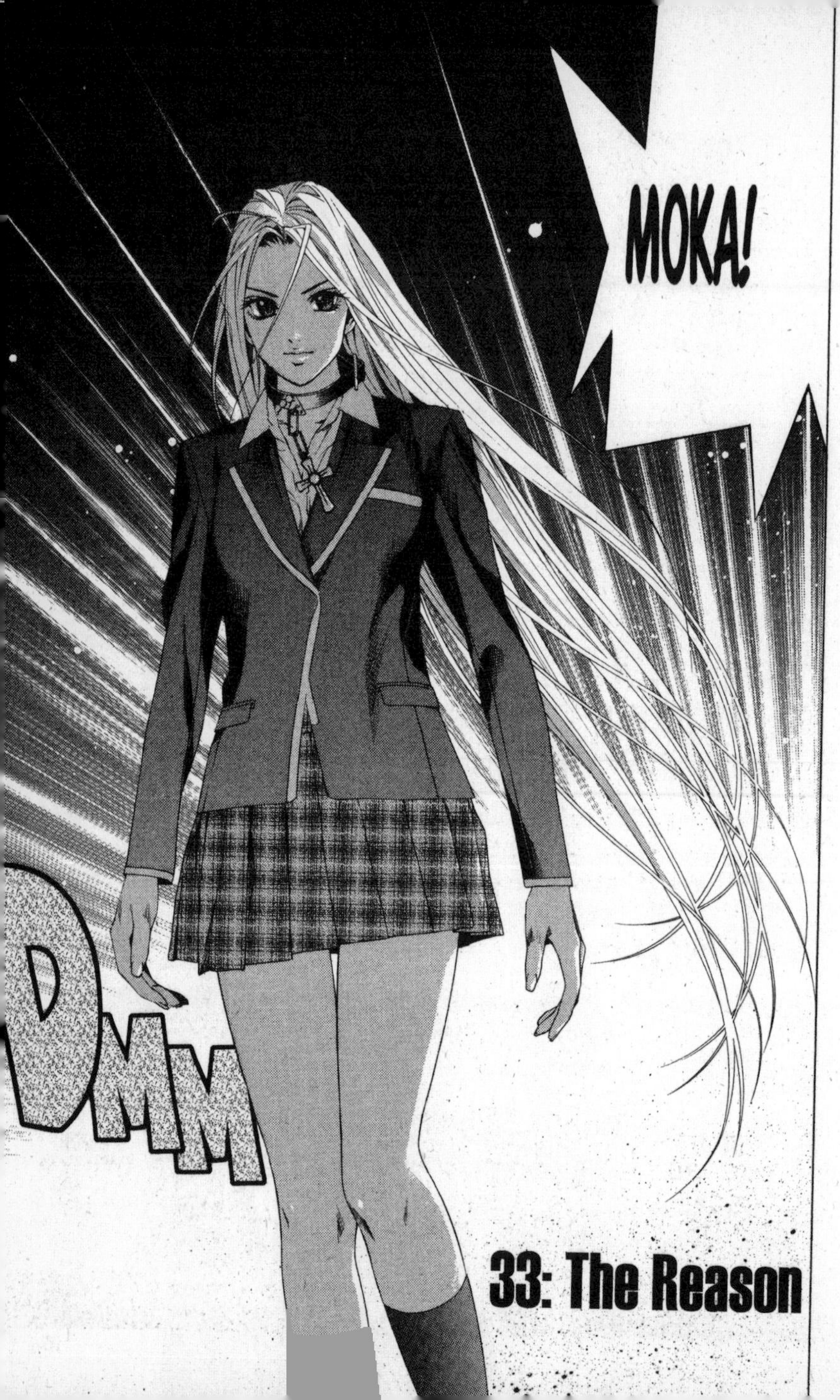
MOKA!
DMMM
33: The Reason

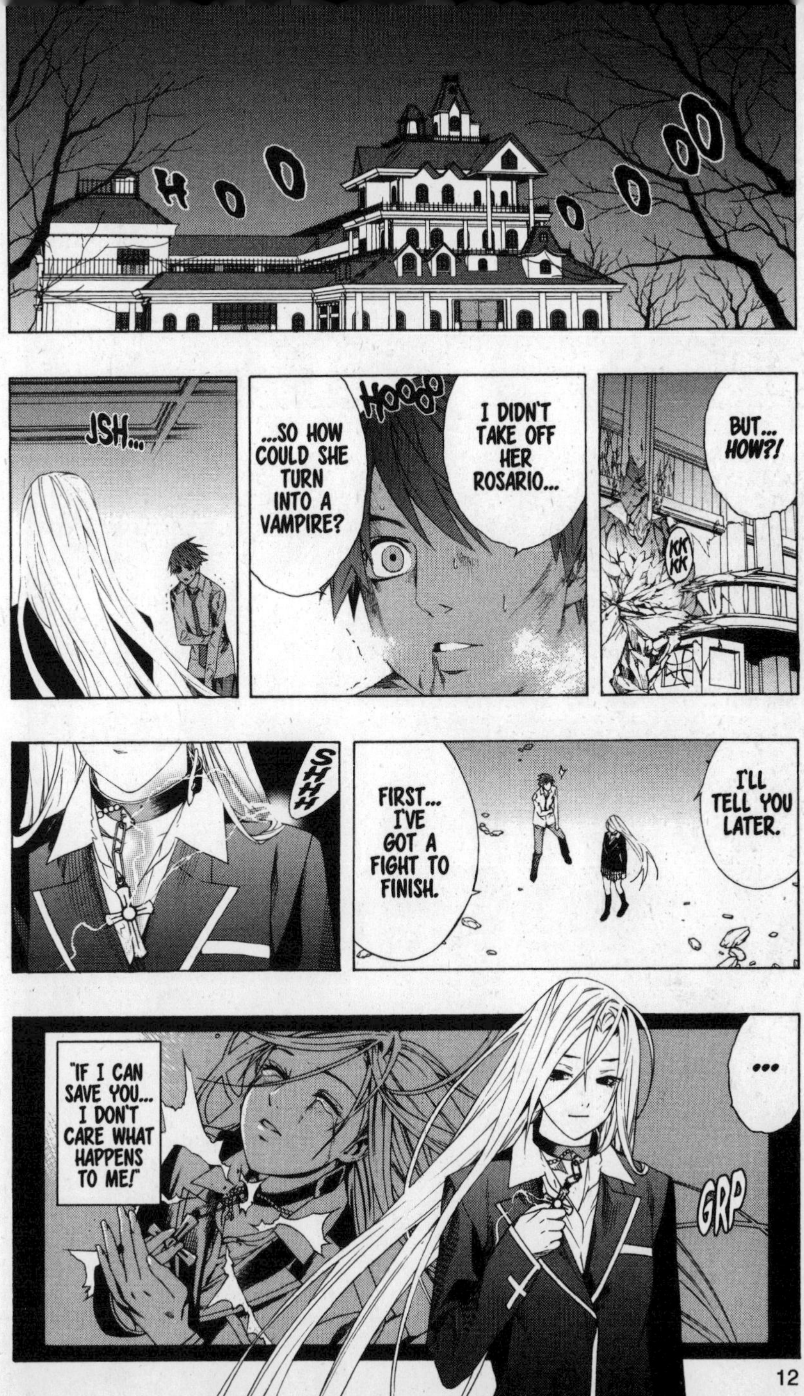
HOOOOOOO
BUT... HOW?!
KKKK
I DIDN'T TAKE OFF HER ROSARIO...
HOOO
...SO HOW COULD SHE TURN INTO A VAMPIRE?
JSH...
I'LL TELL YOU LATER.
FIRST... I'VE GOT A FIGHT TO FINISH.
SHHH
...
GRP
"IF I CAN SAVE YOU... I DON'T CARE WHAT HAPPENS TO ME!"

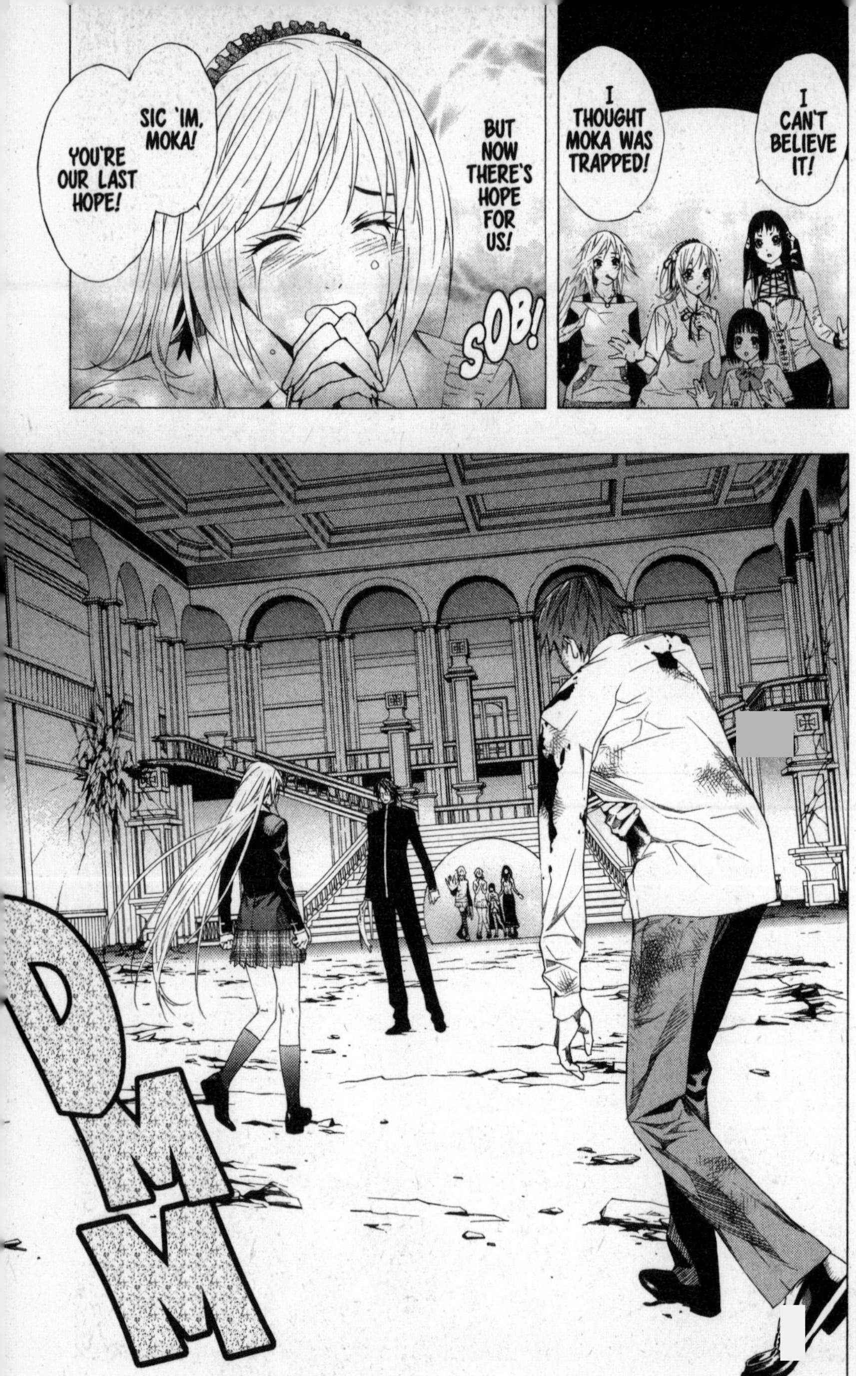
I CAN'T BELIEVE IT!
I THOUGHT MOKA WAS TRAPPED!
BUT NOW THERE'S HOPE FOR US!
SIC 'IM, MOKA! YOU'RE OUR LAST HOPE!
SOB!
DMM

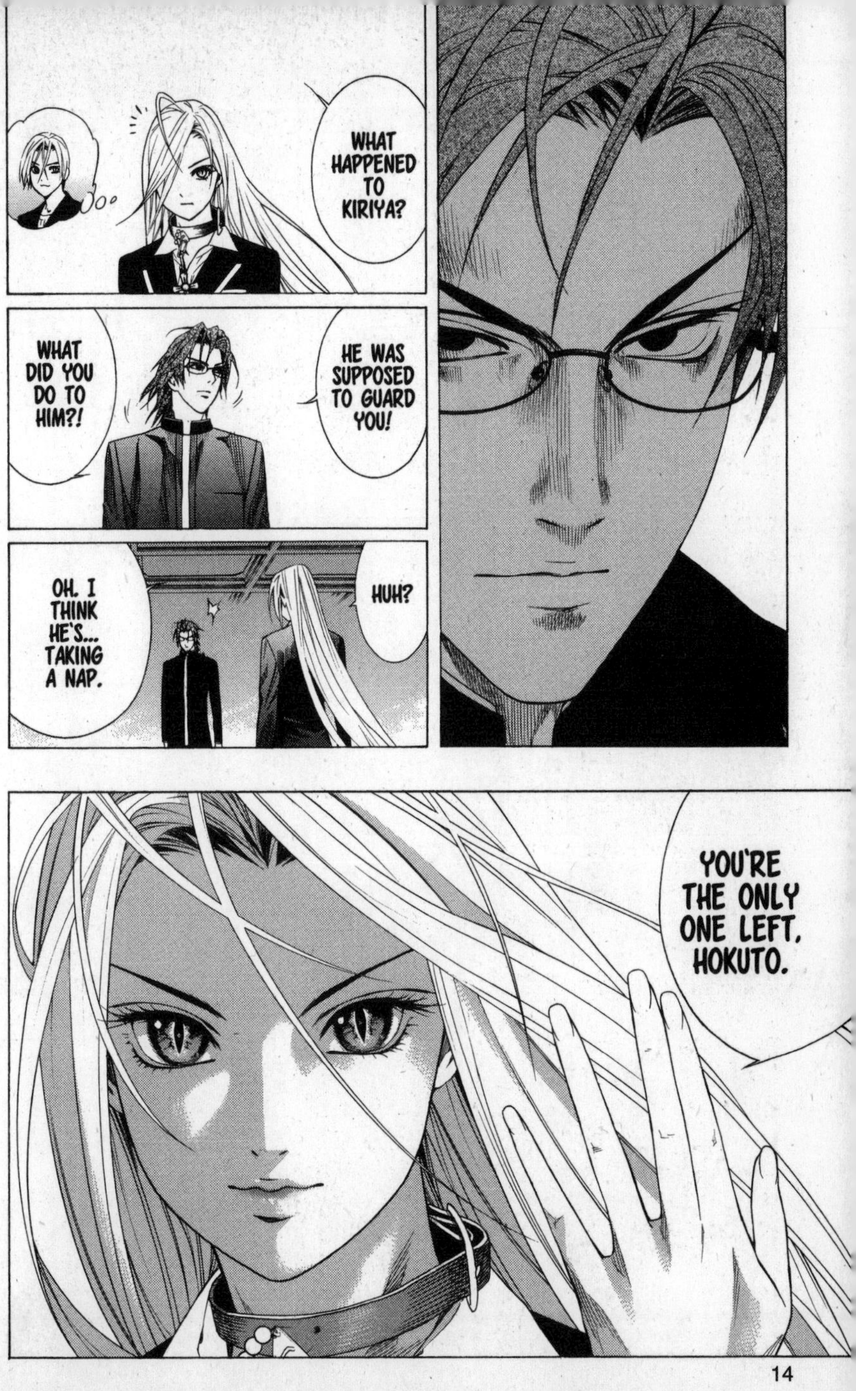
WHAT HAPPENED TO KIRIYA?
HE WAS SUPPOSED TO GUARD YOU!
WHAT DID YOU DO TO HIM?!
HUH?
OH. I THINK HE'S... TAKING A NAP.
YOU'RE THE ONLY ONE LEFT, HOKUTO.

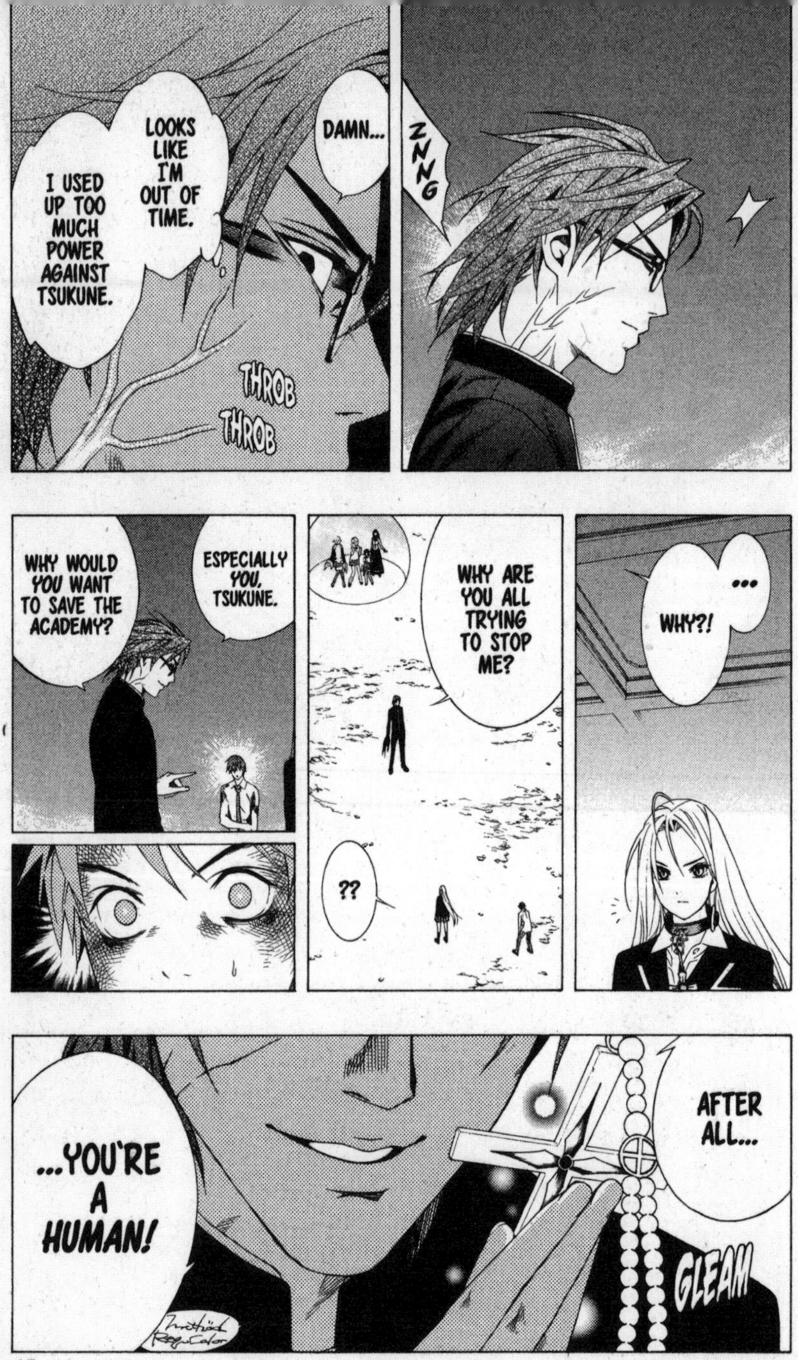
ZNNG
DAMN...
LOOKS LIKE I'M OUT OF TIME.
I USED UP TOO MUCH POWER AGAINST TSUKUNE.
THROB
THROB
...
WHY?!
WHY ARE YOU ALL TRYING TO STOP ME?
??
ESPECIALLY YOU, TSUKUNE.
WHY WOULD YOU WANT TO SAVE THE ACADEMY?
AFTER ALL...
...YOU'RE A HUMAN!
GLEAM

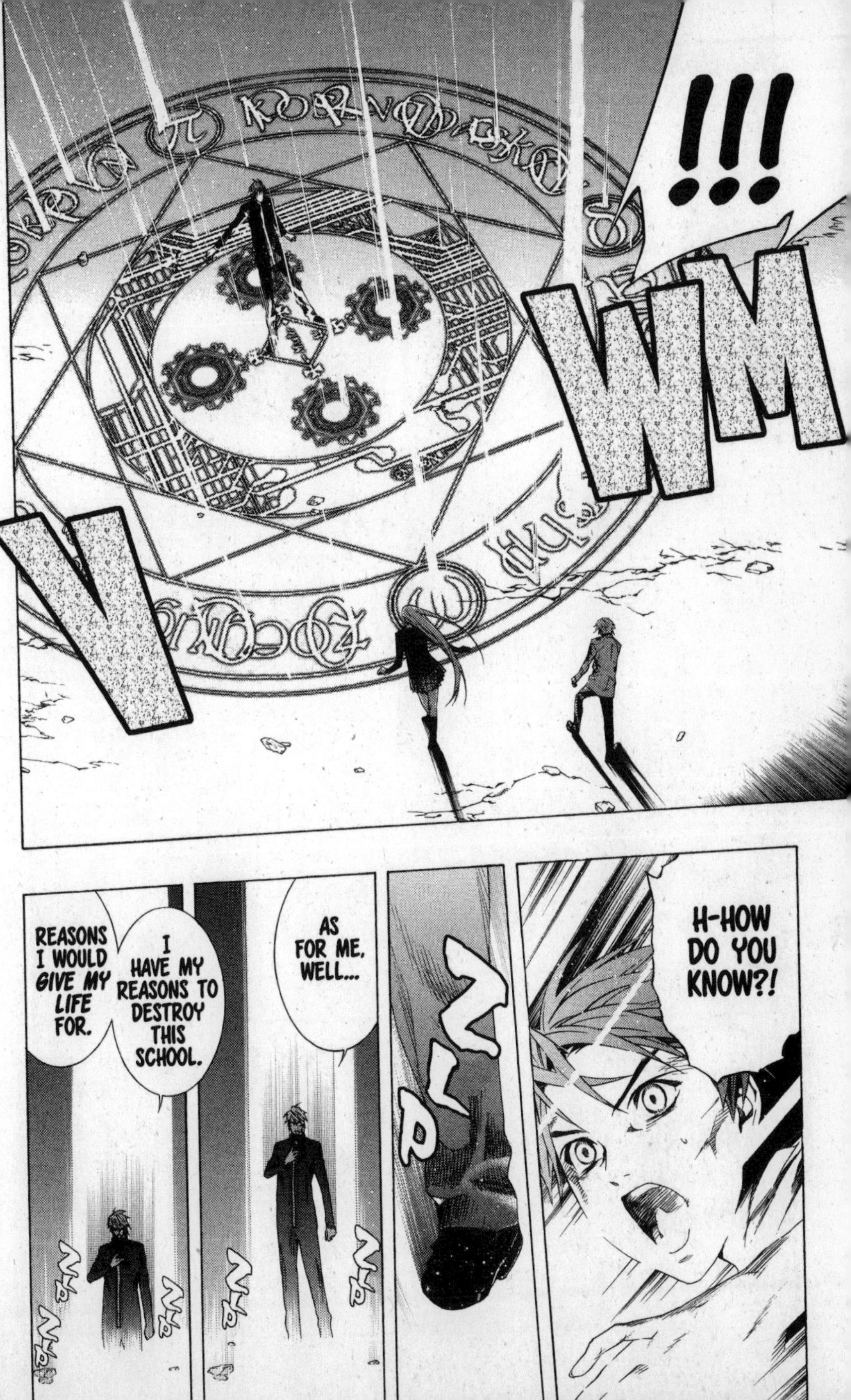
!!!
VWM
H-HOW DO YOU KNOW?!
AS FOR ME, WELL...
I HAVE MY REASONS TO DESTROY THIS SCHOOL.
REASONS I WOULD GIVE MY LIFE FOR.

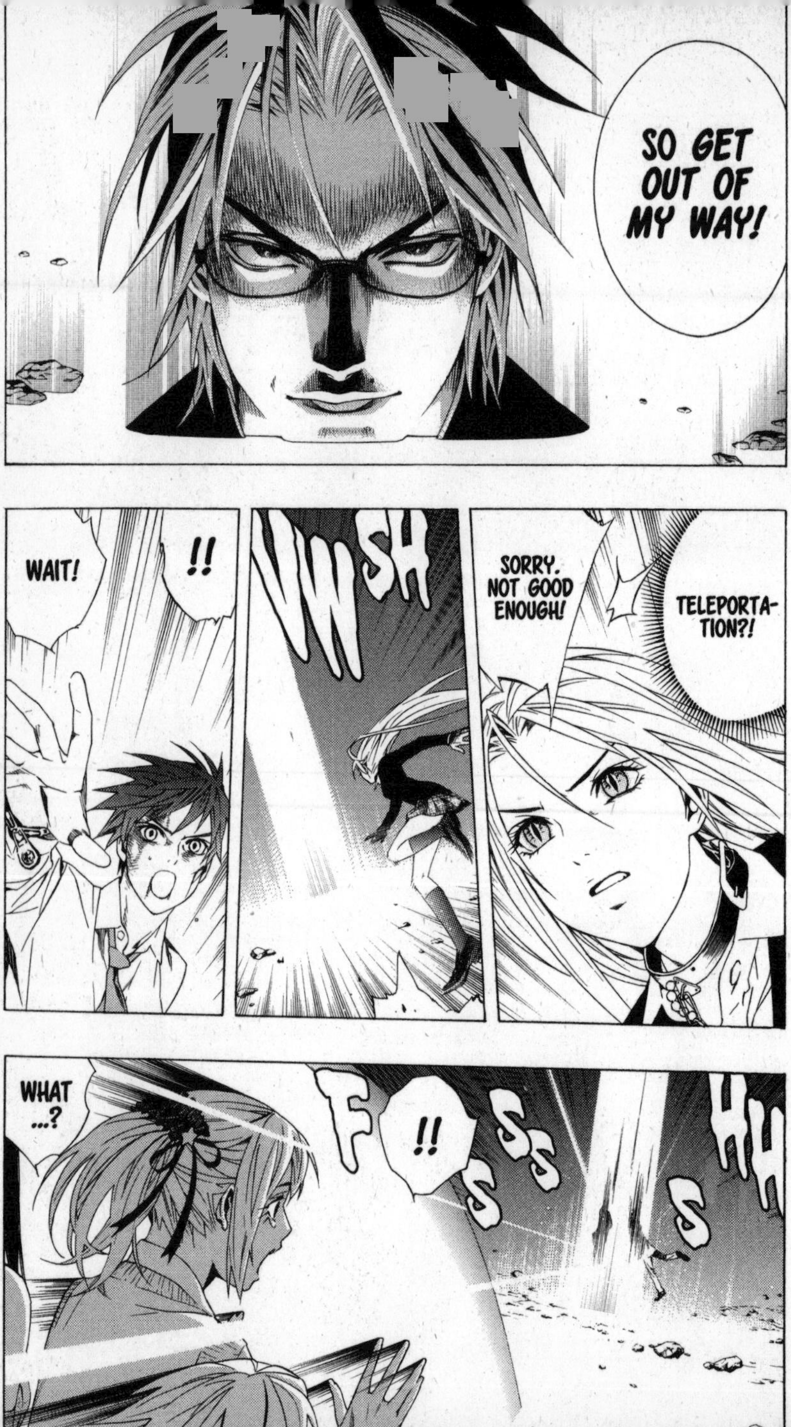
SO GET OUT OF MY WAY!
TELEPORTA-TION?!
SORRY. NOT GOOD ENOUGH!
VWSH
!!
WAIT!
FSSSSHH
!!
WHAT ...?

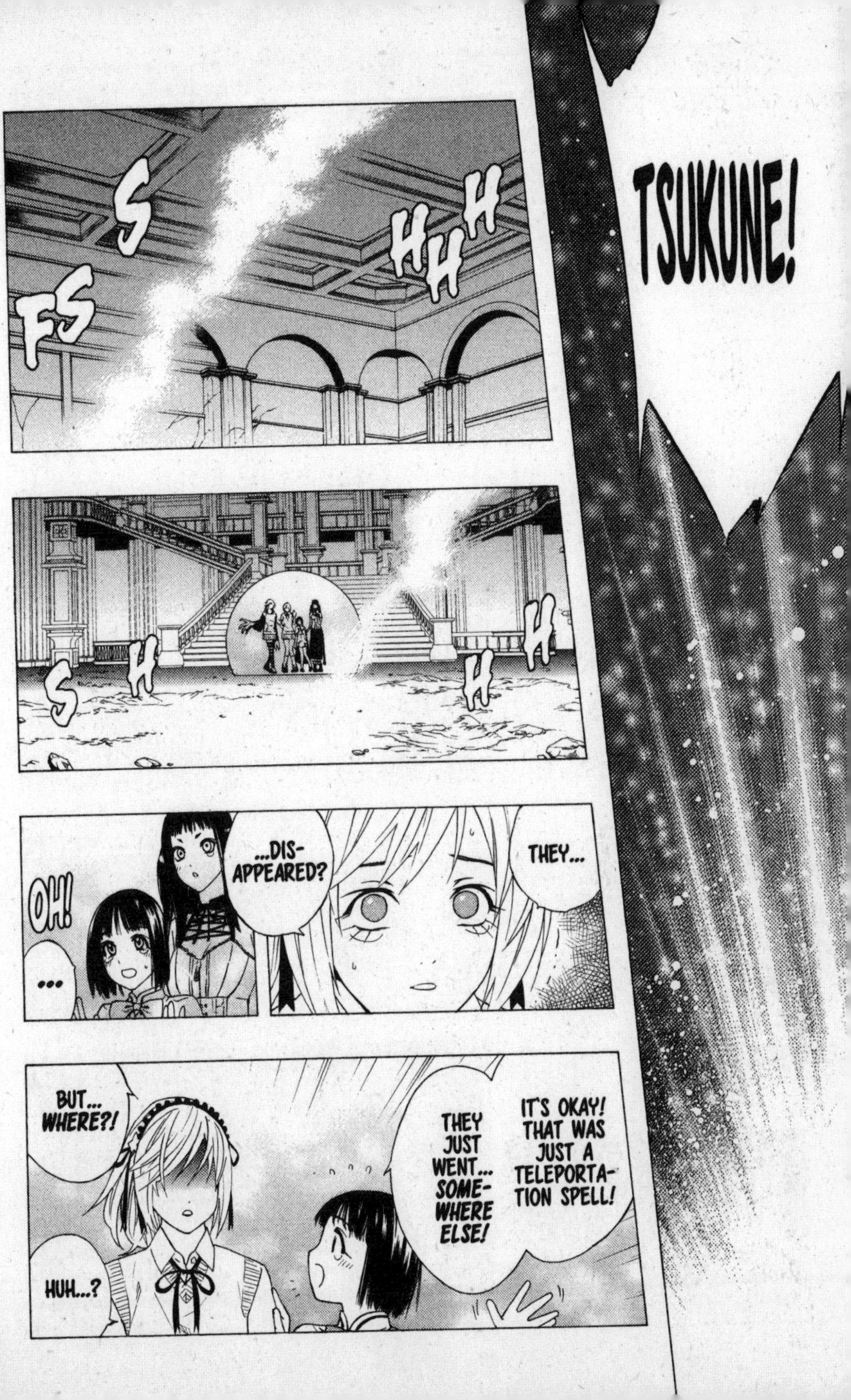

TSUKUNE!
HHHH
S
FS
HH
SH
THEY...
...DIS-APPEARED?
OH!
...
IT'S OKAY! THAT WAS JUST A TELEPORTA-TION SPELL!
THEY JUST WENT... SOME-WHERE ELSE!
BUT... WHERE?!
HUH...?

READ THIS WAY

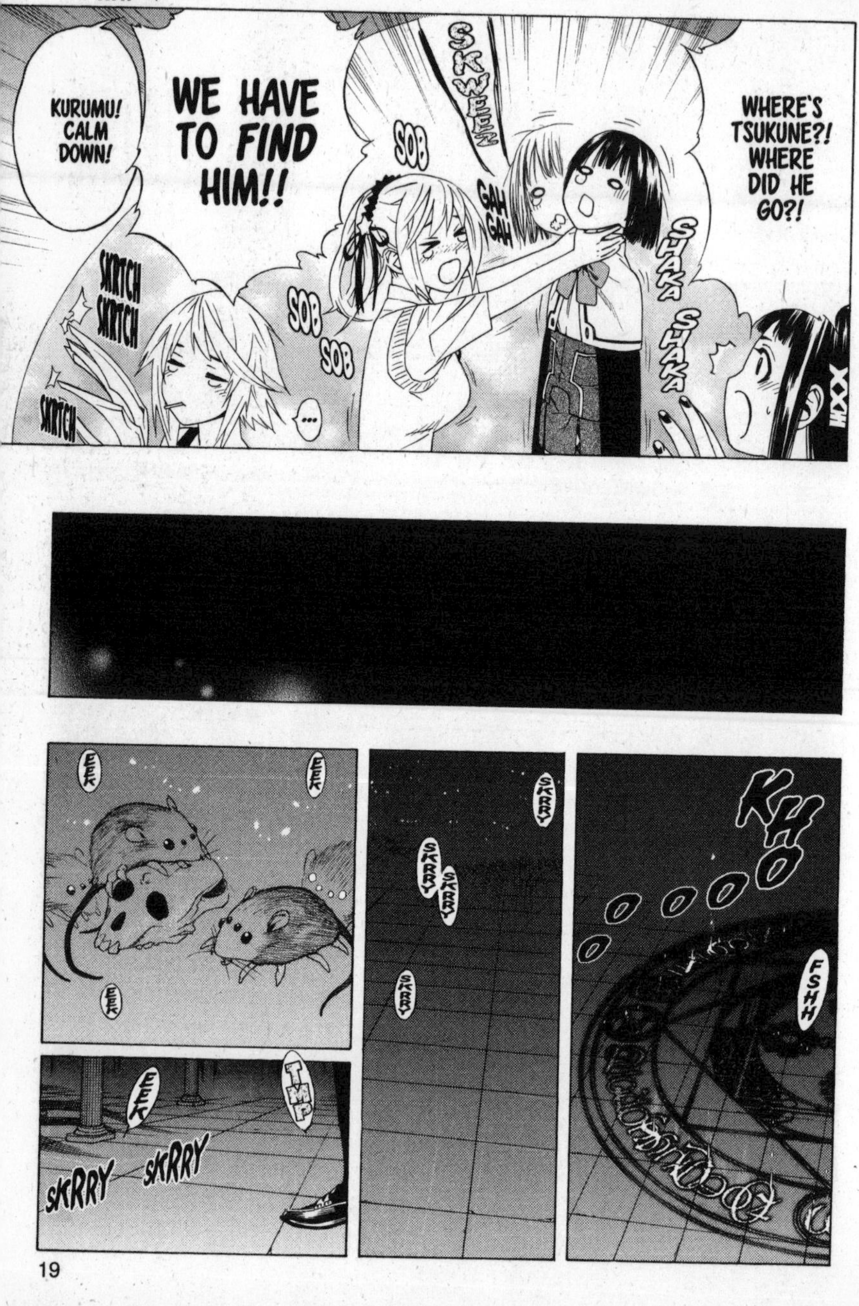

WHERE'S TSUKUNE?! WHERE DID HE GO?!
SHAKA SHAKA
SKWEEZ
GAH GAH
SOB
WE HAVE TO FIND HIM!!
KURUMU! CALM DOWN!
SOB SOB
...
SKRTCH SKRTCH
SKRTCH
KHO
FSHHH
SKRRY
SKRRY SKRRY
SKRRY
EEK
EEK
EEK
TMP
EEK
SKRRY
SKRRY

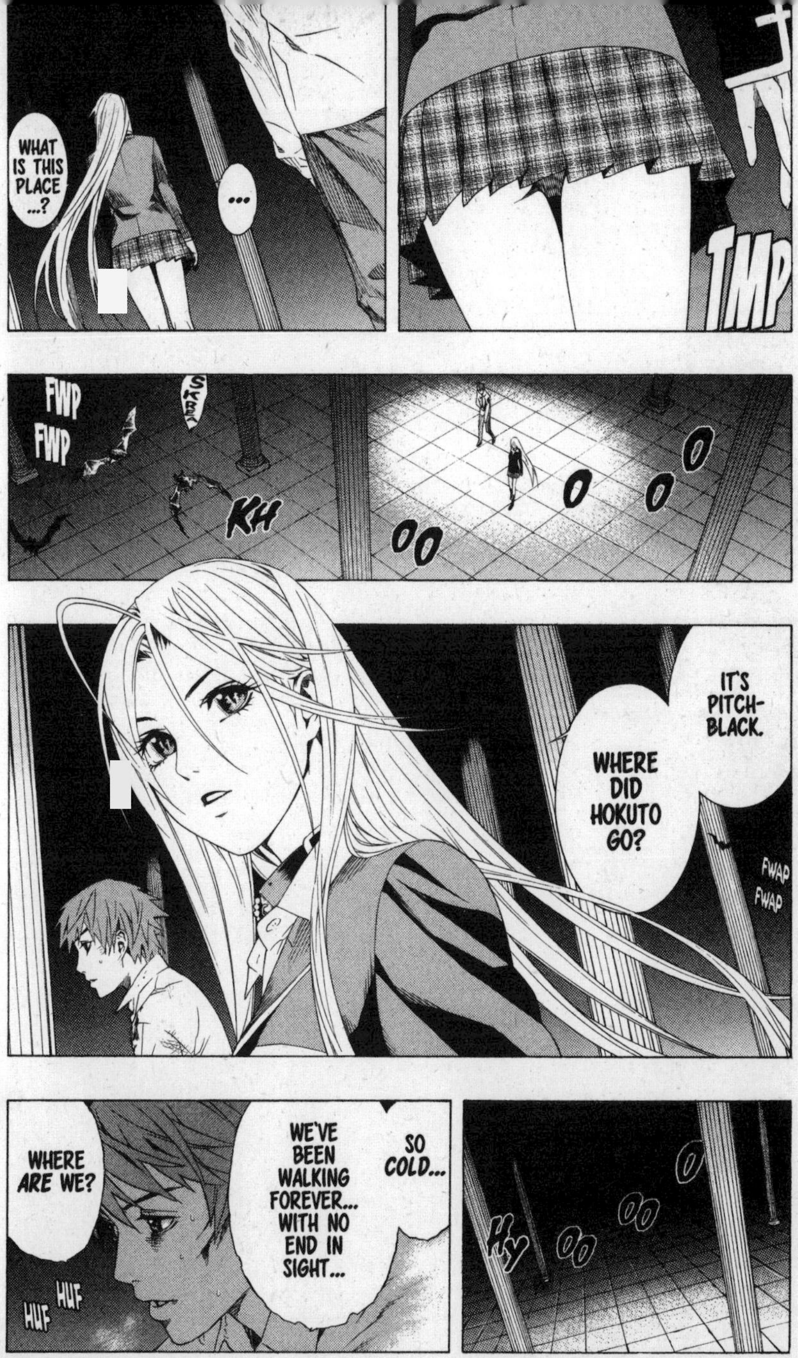
TMP
...
WHAT IS THIS PLACE ...?
KH
FWP
FWP
IT'S PITCH-BLACK.
WHERE DID HOKUTO GO?
FWAP
FWAP
Hy
SO COLD...
WE'VE BEEN WALKING FOREVER... WITH NO END IN SIGHT...
WHERE ARE WE?
HUF
HUF

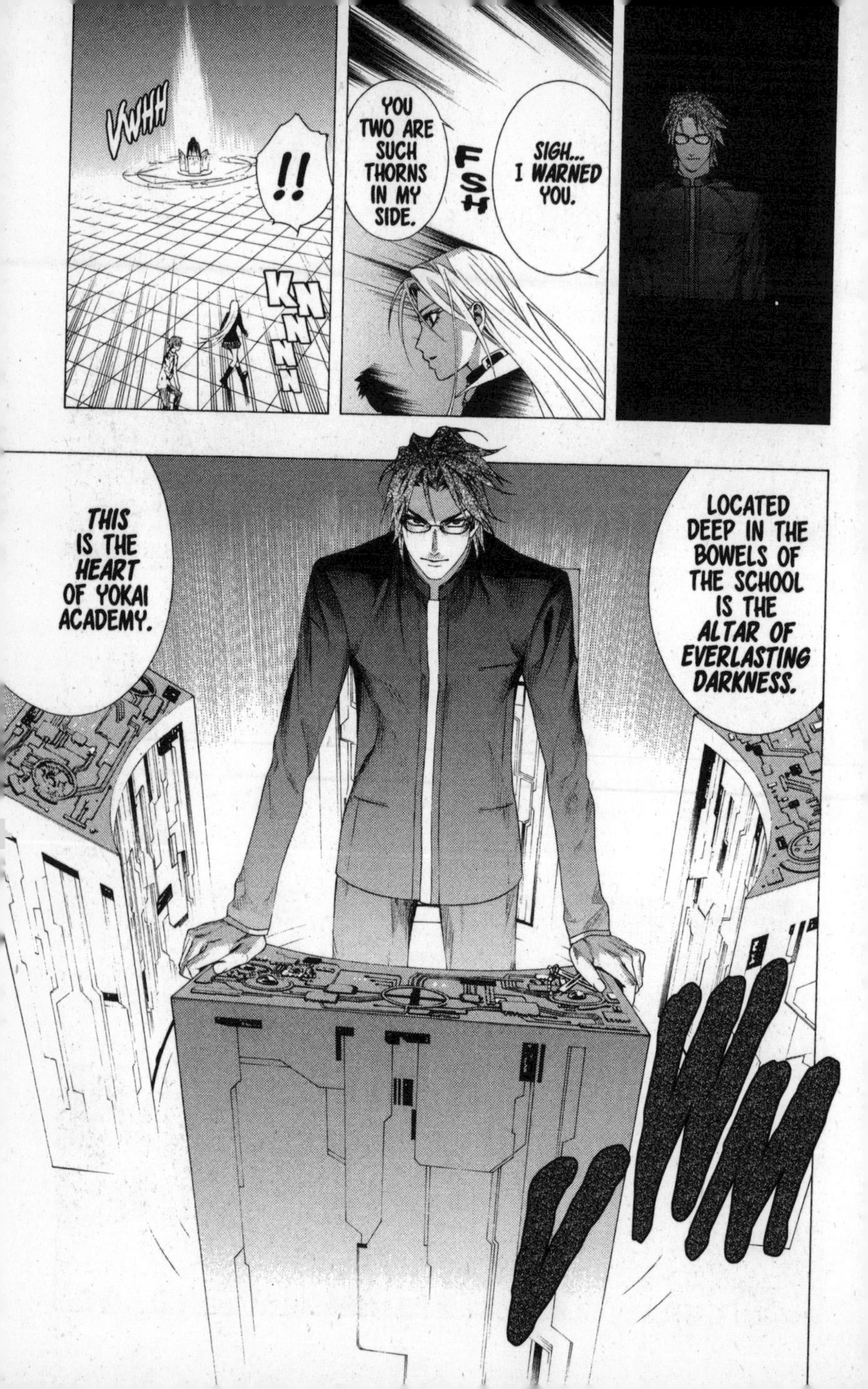
SIGH... I WARNED YOU.
FSH
YOU TWO ARE SUCH THORNS IN MY SIDE.
!!
VWHH
KNNNN
LOCATED DEEP IN THE BOWELS OF THE SCHOOL IS THE ALTAR OF EVERLASTING DARKNESS.
THIS IS THE HEART OF YOKAI ACADEMY.

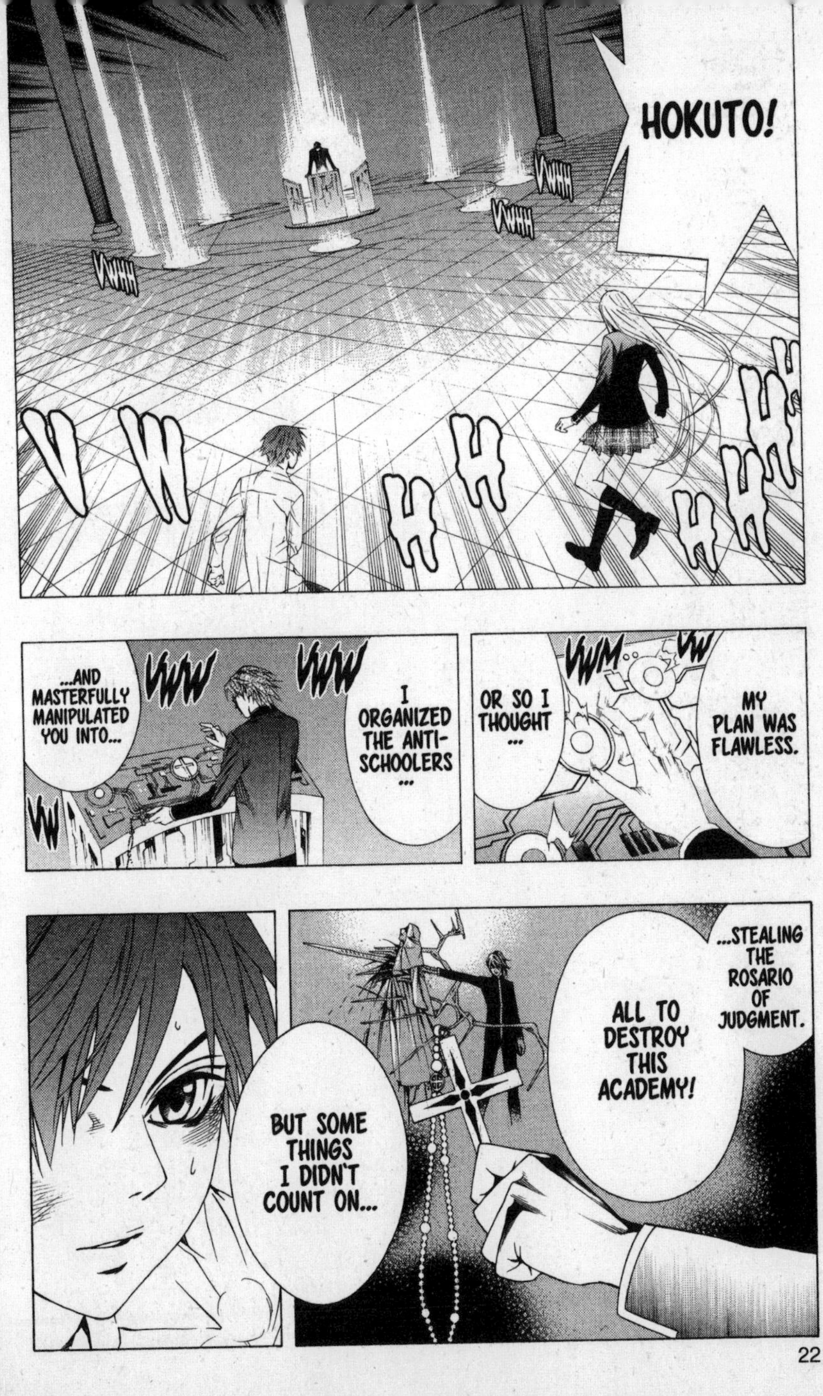
HOKUTO!
VWHH
VWHH
VWHH
VWHHHHH
MY PLAN WAS FLAWLESS.
OR SO I THOUGHT...
VWM
VW
I ORGANIZED THE ANTI-SCHOOLERS...
...AND MASTERFULLY MANIPULATED YOU INTO...
VWW
VWW
VW
...STEALING THE ROSARIO OF JUDGMENT.
ALL TO DESTROY THIS ACADEMY!
BUT SOME THINGS I DIDN'T COUNT ON...

READ THIS WAY

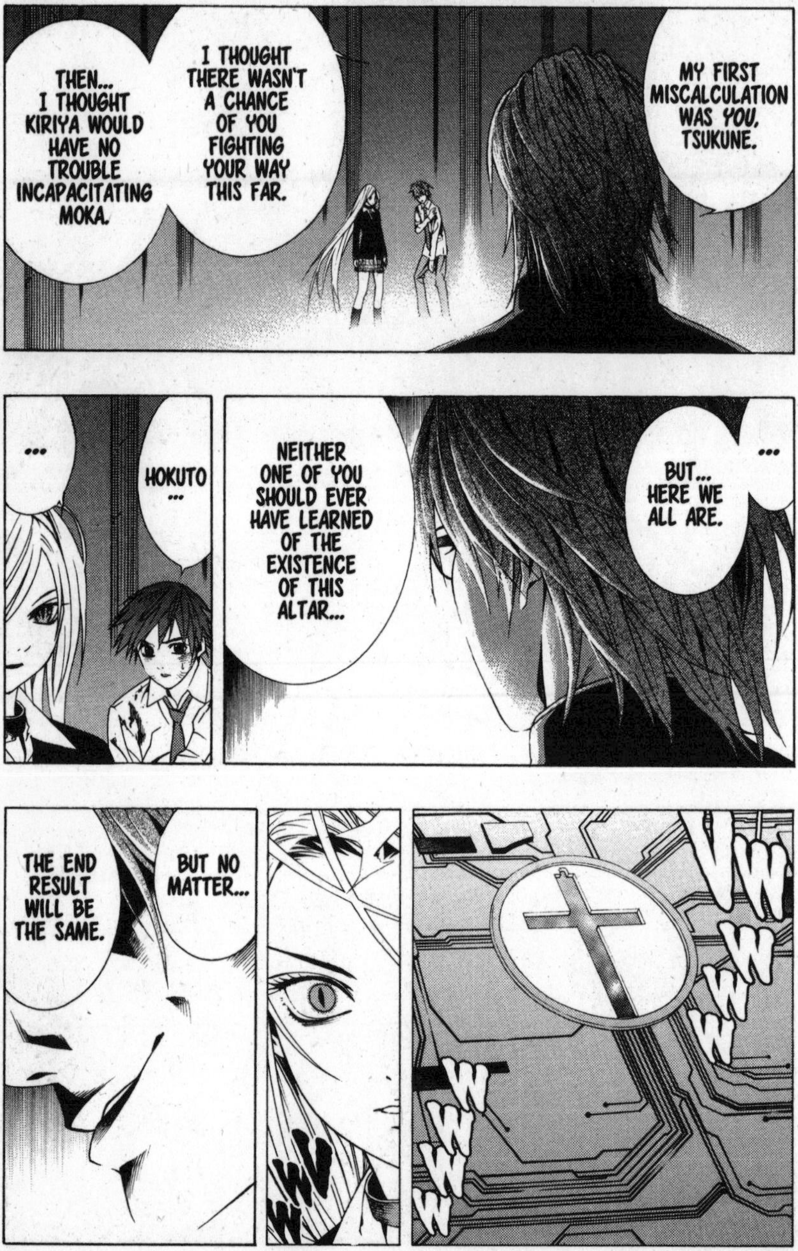
MY FIRST MISCALCULATION WAS YOU, TSUKUNE.
I THOUGHT THERE WASN'T A CHANCE OF YOU FIGHTING YOUR WAY THIS FAR.
THEN... I THOUGHT KIRIYA WOULD HAVE NO TROUBLE INCAPACITATING MOKA.
...
BUT... HERE WE ALL ARE.
NEITHER ONE OF YOU SHOULD EVER HAVE LEARNED OF THE EXISTENCE OF THIS ALTAR...
HOKUTO ...
...
BUT NO MATTER...
THE END RESULT WILL BE THE SAME.

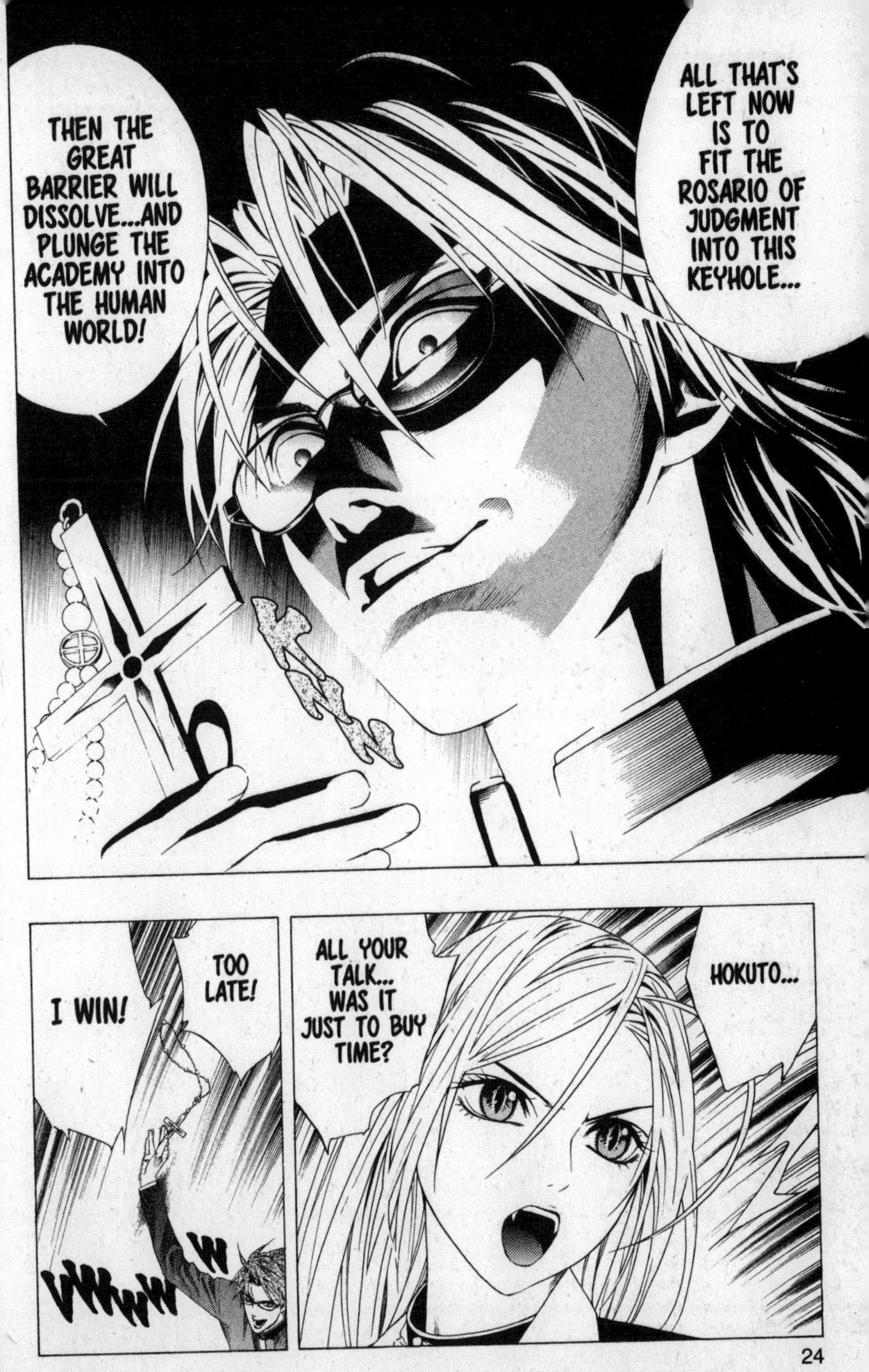
ALL THAT'S LEFT NOW IS TO FIT THE ROSARIO OF JUDGMENT INTO THIS KEYHOLE...
THEN THE GREAT BARRIER WILL DISSOLVE...AND PLUNGE THE ACADEMY INTO THE HUMAN WORLD!
HOKUTO...
ALL YOUR TALK... WAS IT JUST TO BUY TIME?
TOO LATE!
I WIN!

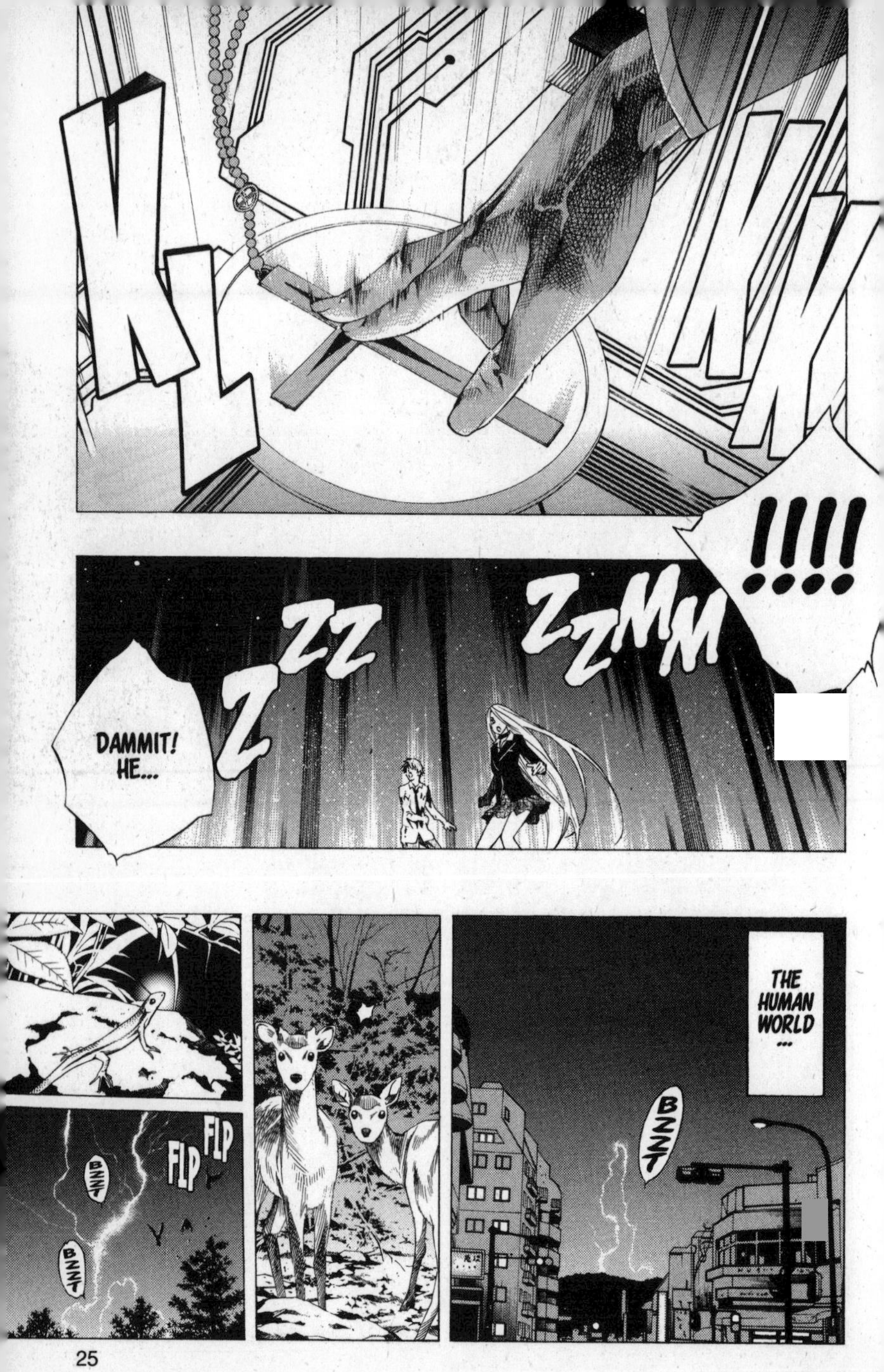
KL
NK
!!!!
ZZMM
ZZZ
DAMMIT! HE...
THE HUMAN WORLD ...
BZZT
FLP FLP
BZZT
BZZT

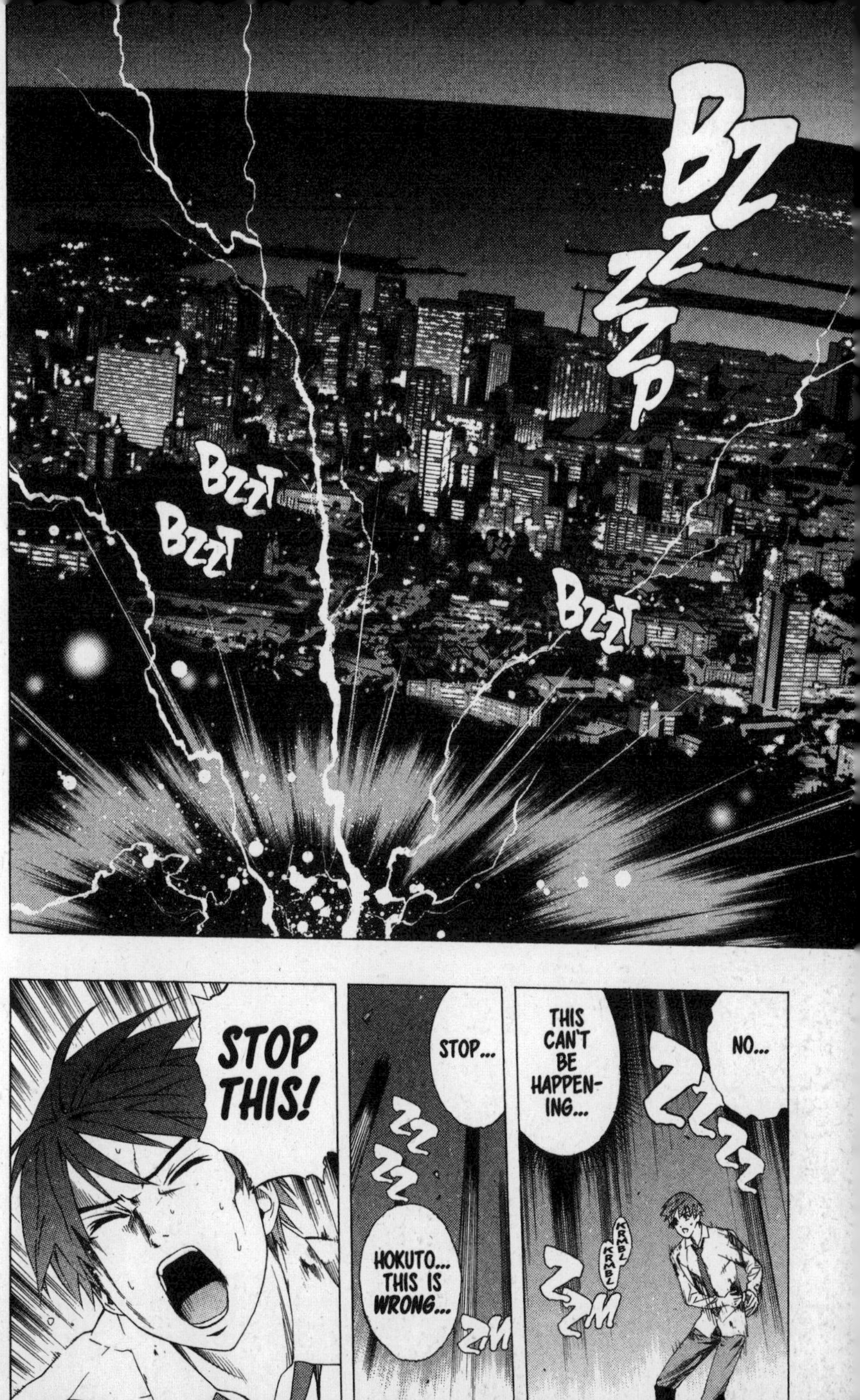
BZZZZP
BZZT
BZZT
BZZT
NO...
THIS CAN'T BE HAPPEN-ING...
ZZZZZ
KRMBL
KRMBL
ZZZM
STOP...
ZZZZ
HOKUTO... THIS IS WRONG...
STOP THIS!

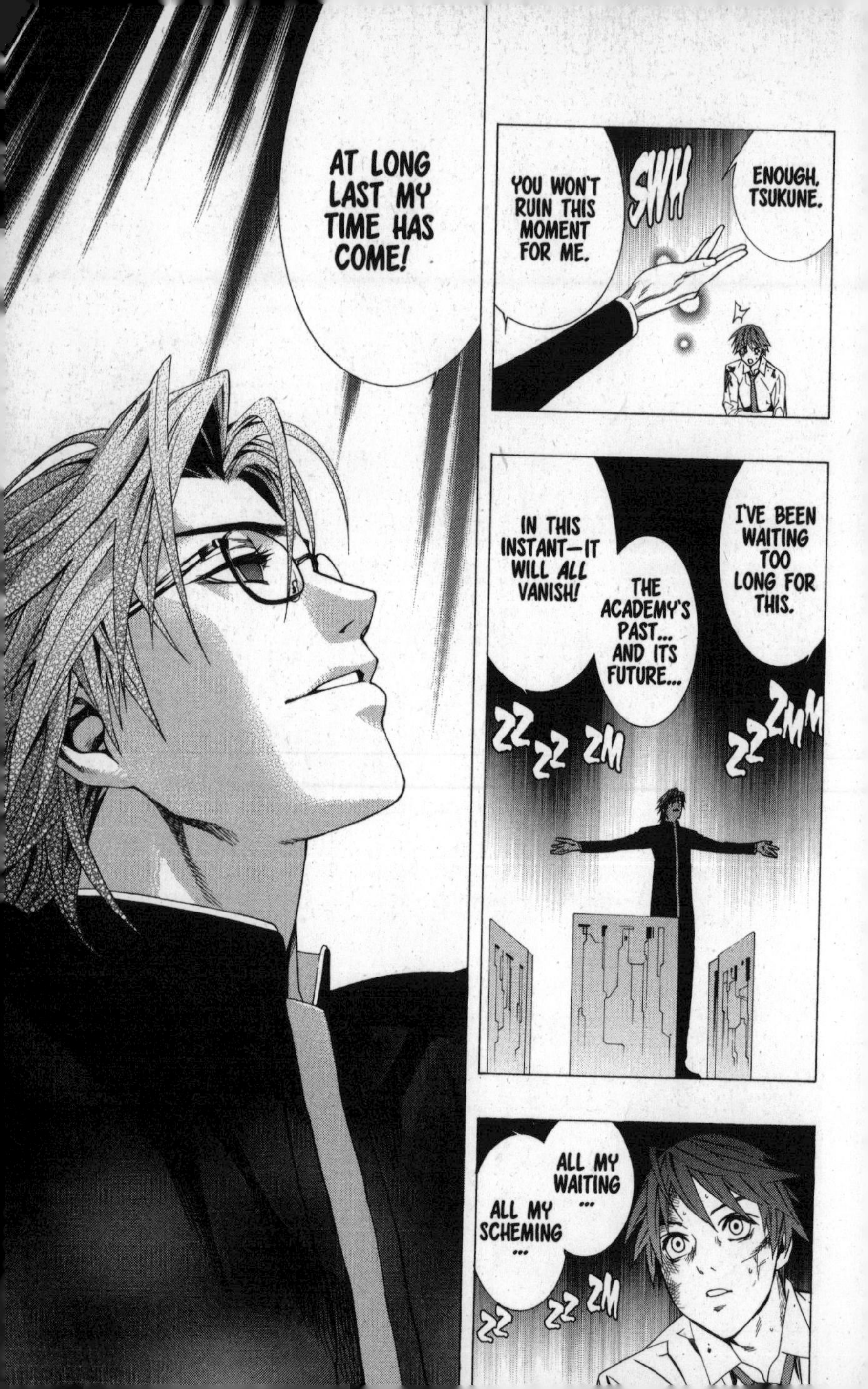
ENOUGH, TSUKUNE.
SWH
YOU WON'T RUIN THIS MOMENT FOR ME.
I'VE BEEN WAITING TOO LONG FOR THIS.
THE ACADEMY'S PAST... AND ITS FUTURE...
IN THIS INSTANT—IT WILL *ALL* VANISH!
ZZZMM
ZZZZ ZM
ALL MY WAITING...
ALL MY SCHEMING...
ZZZ ZM
AT LONG LAST MY TIME HAS COME!

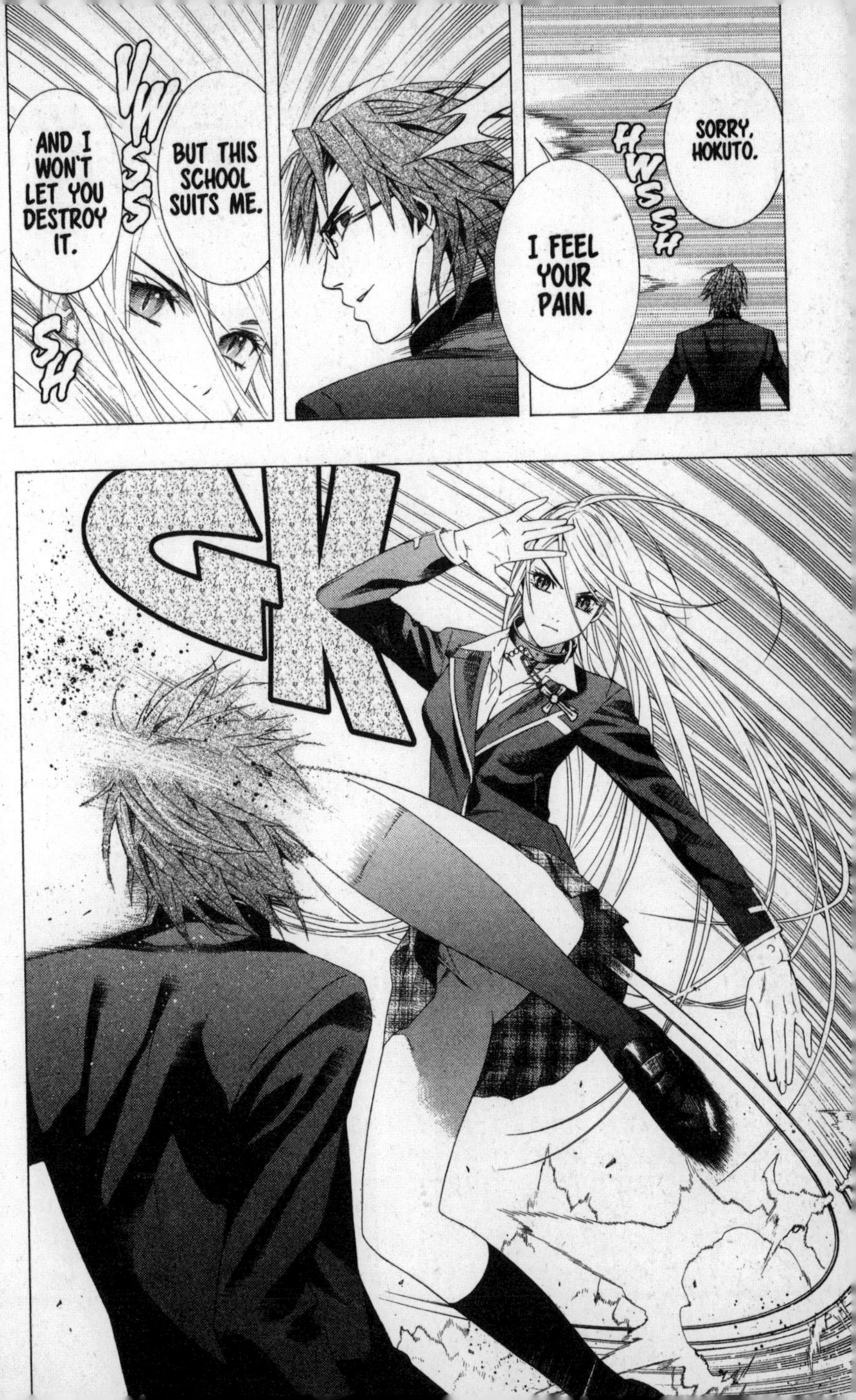
SORRY, HOKUTO.
HWSSH
I FEEL YOUR PAIN.
BUT THIS SCHOOL SUITS ME.
VWSS
AND I WON'T LET YOU DESTROY IT.
SH
GK

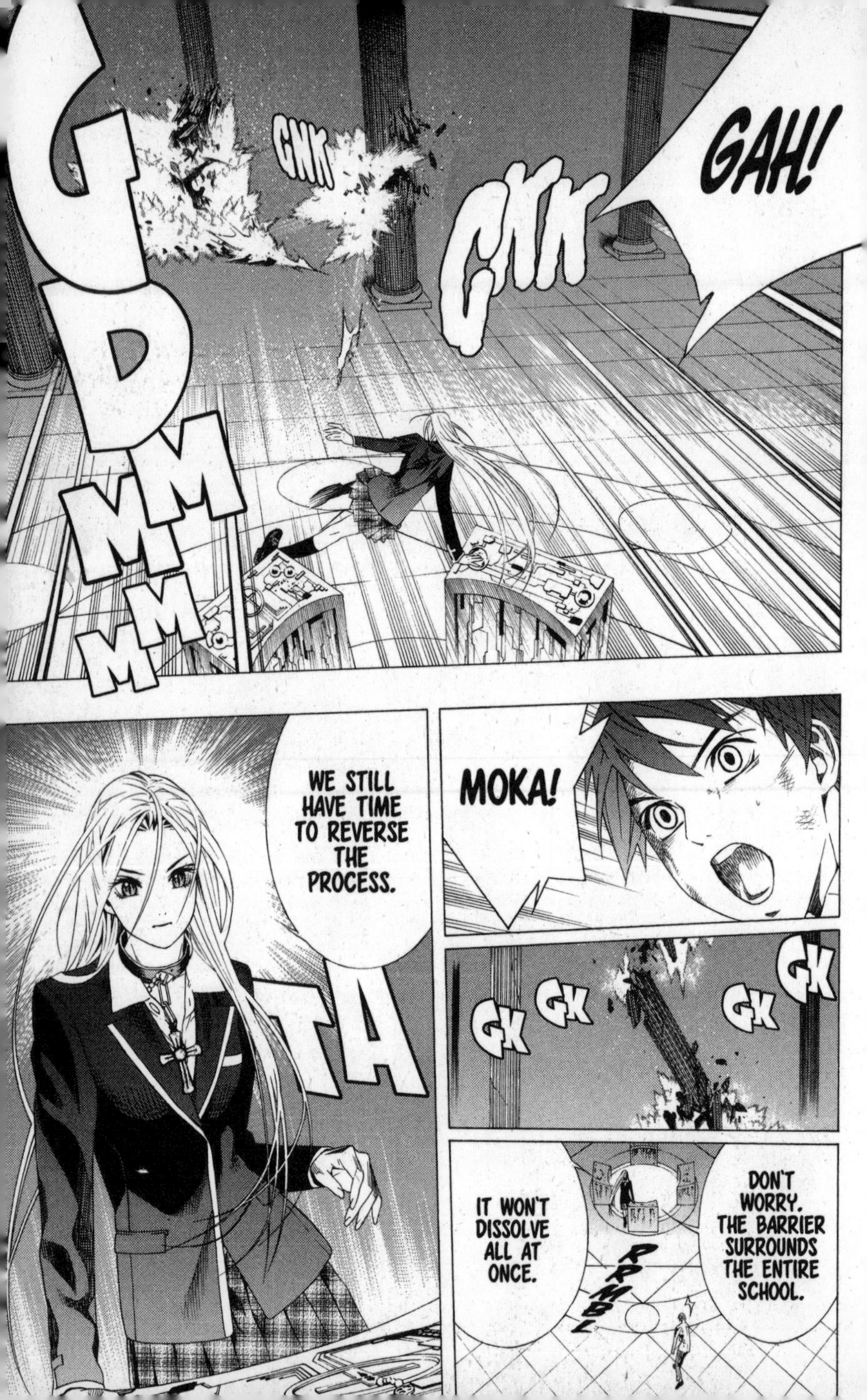
GAH!
GNK
GNK
GDMMMMM
MOKA!
GK GK
GK GK
DON'T WORRY. THE BARRIER SURROUNDS THE ENTIRE SCHOOL.
RRMBL
IT WON'T DISSOLVE ALL AT ONCE.
WE STILL HAVE TIME TO REVERSE THE PROCESS.
TA

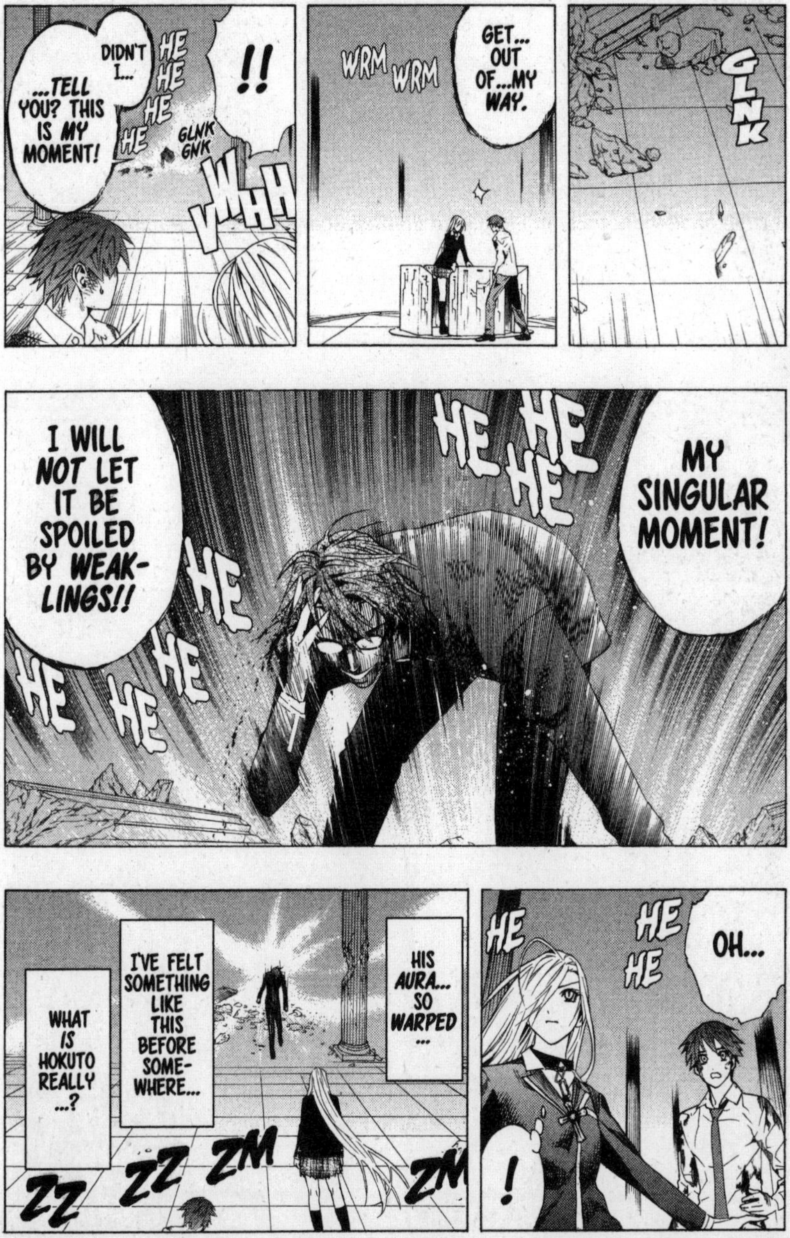
GLNK
WRM WRM
GET... OUT OF...MY WAY.
!!
DIDN'T I...
...TELL YOU? THIS IS MY MOMENT!
HE HE HE HE
GLNK GNK
VWHH
MY SINGULAR MOMENT!
HE HE HE
I WILL NOT LET IT BE SPOILED BY WEAK-LINGS!!
HE HE HE HE
OH...
HE HE
HE
!
HIS AURA... SO WARPED ...
I'VE FELT SOMETHING LIKE THIS BEFORE SOME-WHERE...
WHAT IS HOKUTO REALLY ...?
ZM ZZ ZM ZZ

READ THIS WAY

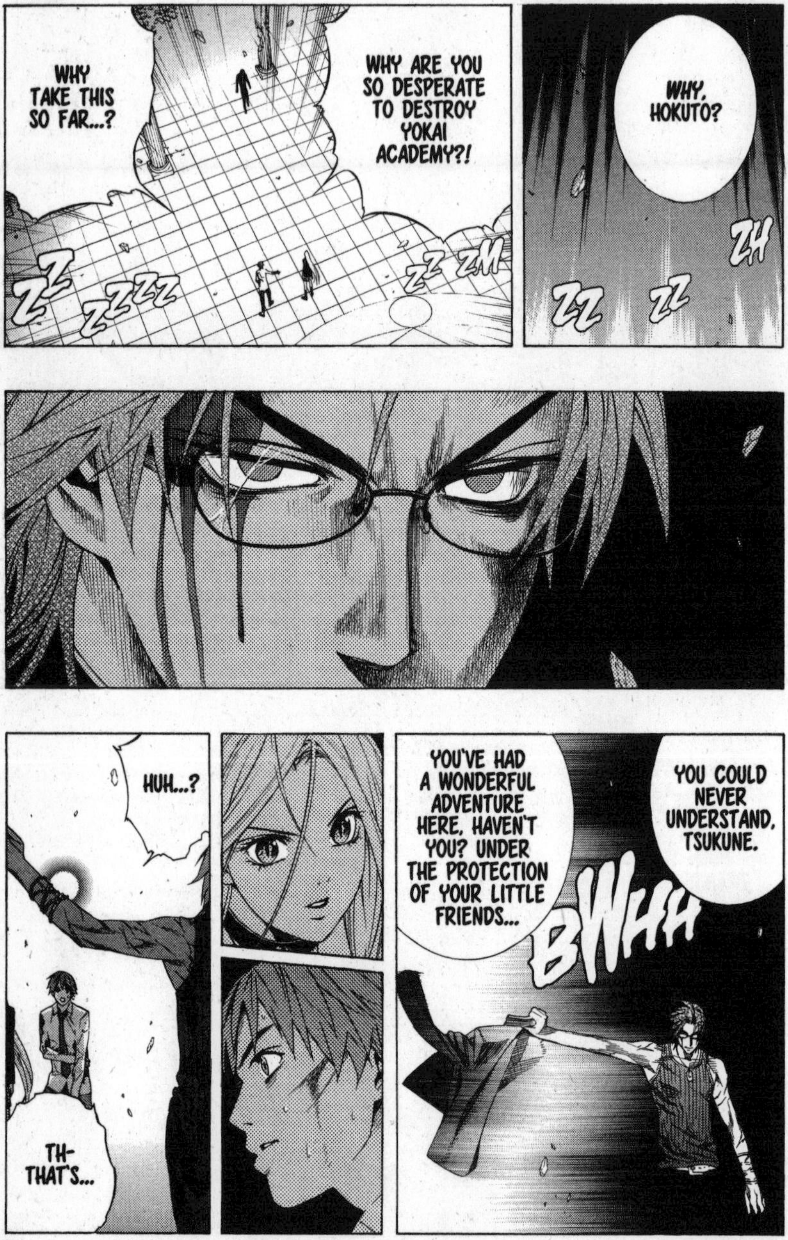
WHY, HOKUTO?
ZH
ZZ
ZZ
WHY ARE YOU SO DESPERATE TO DESTROY YOKAI ACADEMY?!
WHY TAKE THIS SO FAR...?
ZZ ZM
ZZ
ZZZZZ
YOU COULD NEVER UNDERSTAND, TSUKUNE.
YOU'VE HAD A WONDERFUL ADVENTURE HERE, HAVEN'T YOU? UNDER THE PROTECTION OF YOUR LITTLE FRIENDS...
BWHH
HUH...?
TH- THAT'S...

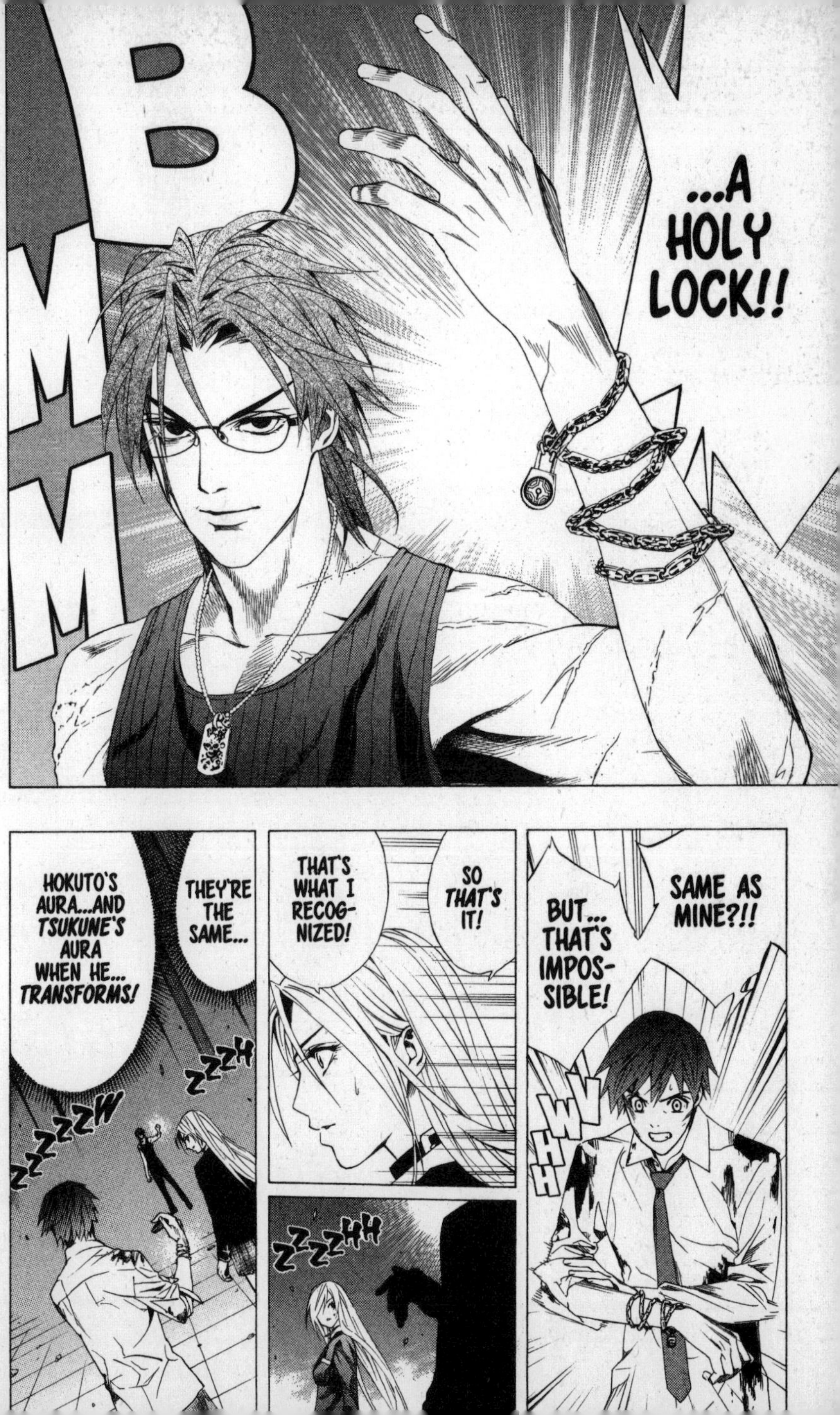
...A HOLY LOCK!!
BMMM
SAME AS MINE?!!
BUT... THAT'S IMPOS-SIBLE!
WWHHH
SO THAT'S IT!
THAT'S WHAT I RECOG-NIZED!
ZZZZHH
THEY'RE THE SAME...
HOKUTO'S AURA...AND TSUKUNE'S AURA WHEN HE... TRANSFORMS!
ZZZZH
ZZZZZW

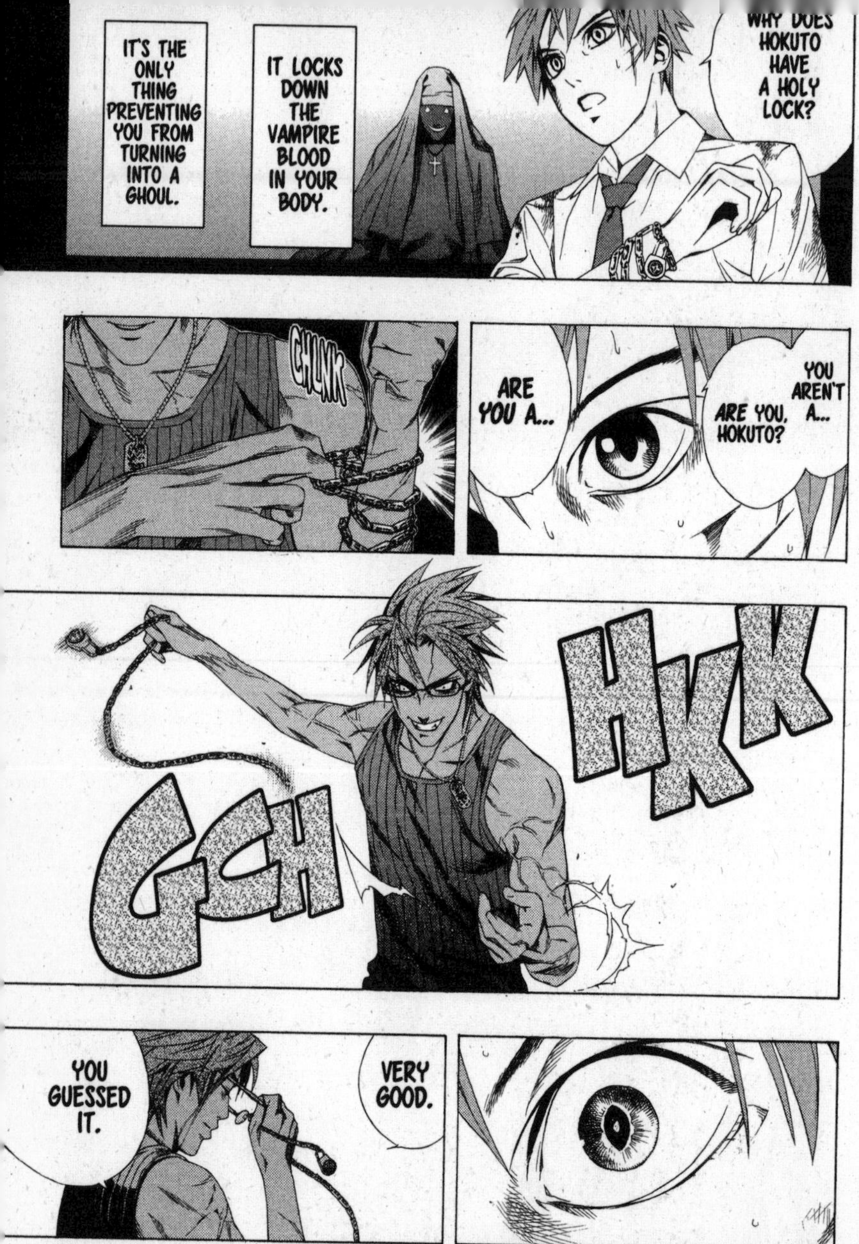

WHY DOES HOKUTO HAVE A HOLY LOCK?
IT LOCKS DOWN THE VAMPIRE BLOOD IN YOUR BODY.
IT'S THE ONLY THING PREVENTING YOU FROM TURNING INTO A GHOUL.
YOU AREN'T A...
ARE YOU, HOKUTO?
ARE YOU A...
CHLNK
HKK
GCH
VERY GOOD.
YOU GUESSED IT.

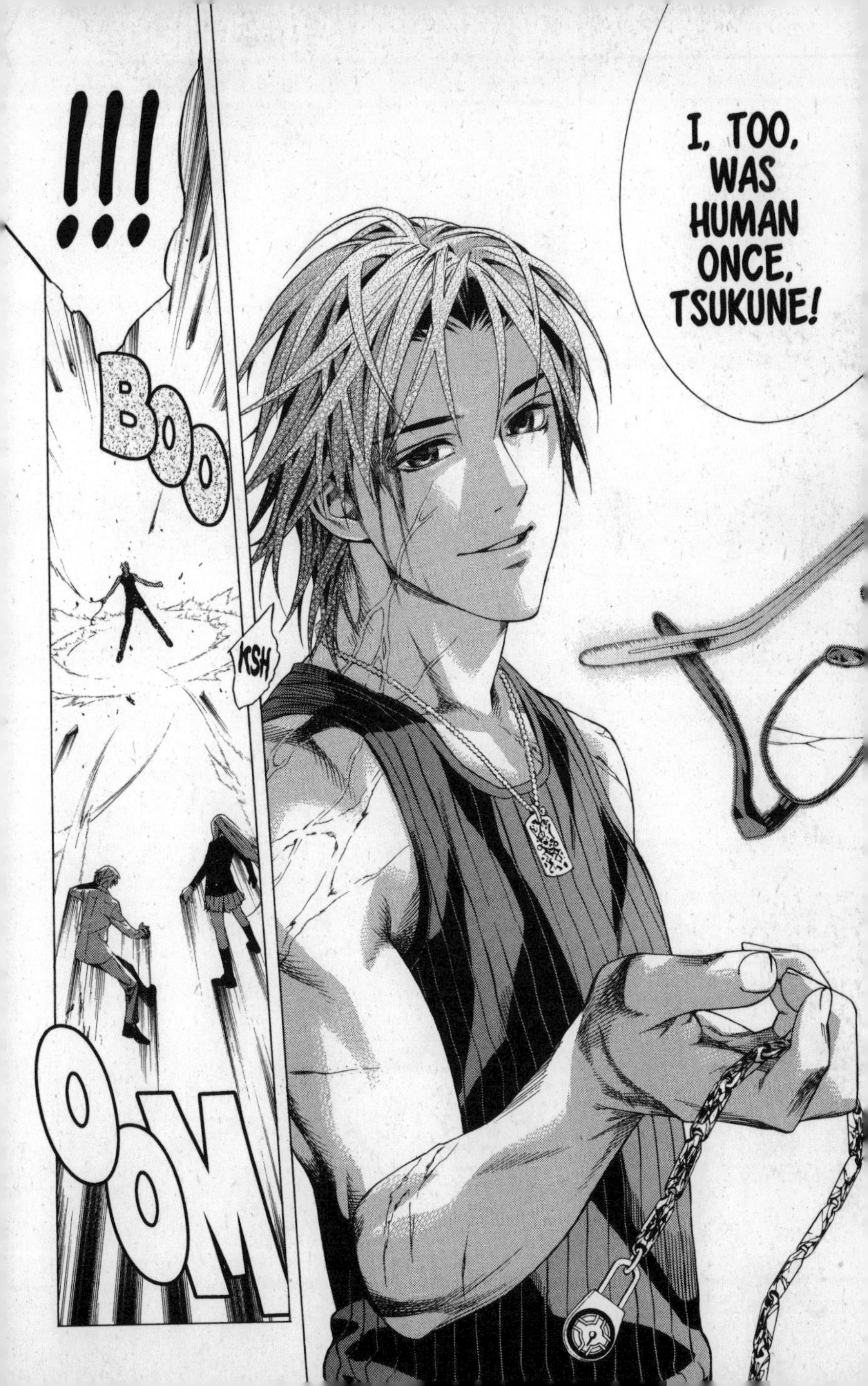
I, TOO, WAS HUMAN ONCE, TSUKUNE!
KSH
!!!
BOOO
OOM

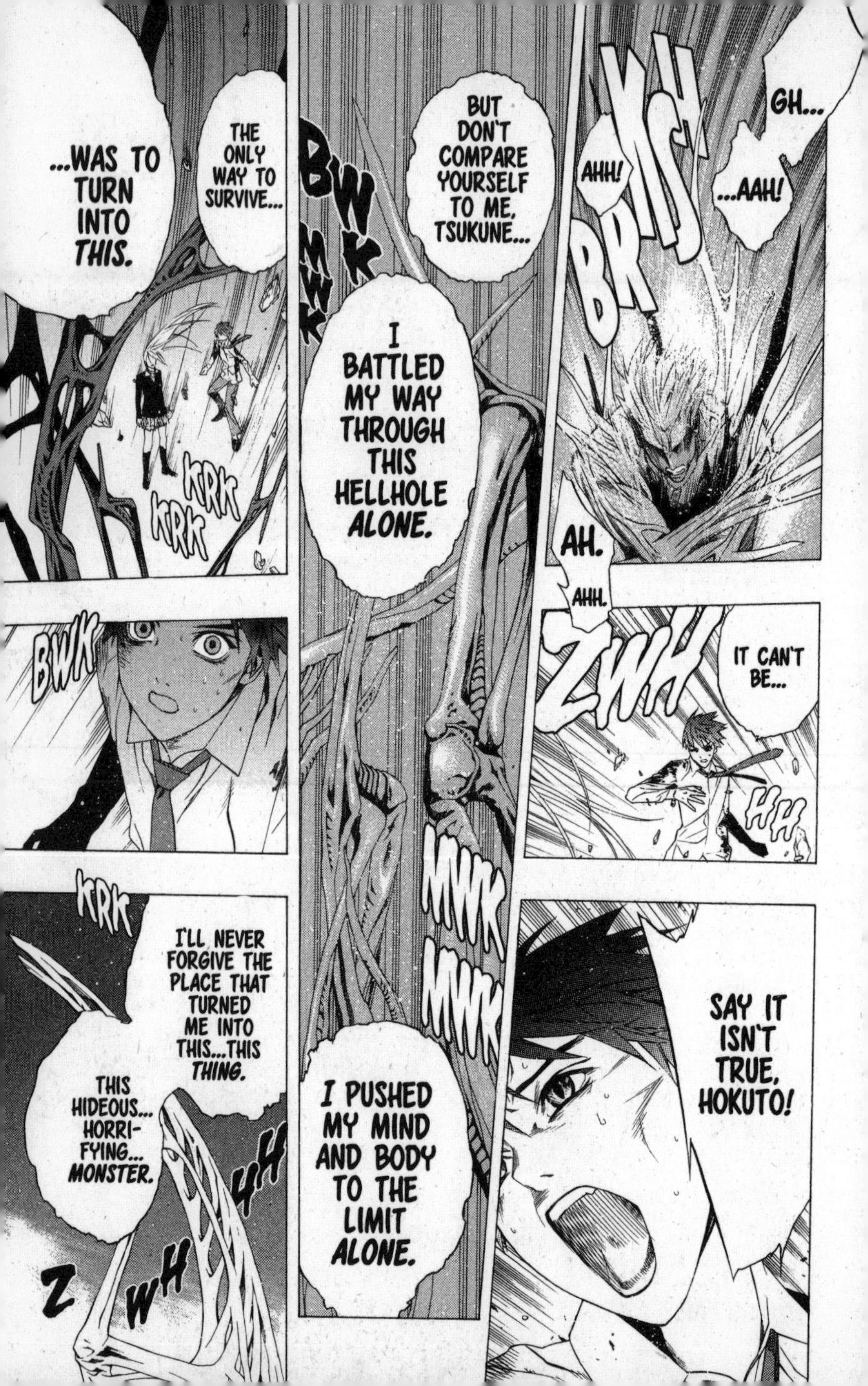
GH...
...AAH!
AHH!
BRISH
AH.
AHH.
IT CAN'T BE...
ZWH
HH
SAY IT ISN'T TRUE, HOKUTO!
BUT DON'T COMPARE YOURSELF TO ME, TSUKUNE...
BWMK
I BATTLED MY WAY THROUGH THIS HELLHOLE ALONE.
MWK
MWK
I PUSHED MY MIND AND BODY TO THE LIMIT ALONE.
THE ONLY WAY TO SURVIVE...
...WAS TO TURN INTO THIS.
KRK
KRK
BWK
KRK
I'LL NEVER FORGIVE THE PLACE THAT TURNED ME INTO THIS...THIS THING.
THIS HIDEOUS... HORRI-FYING... MONSTER.
ZWH
HH

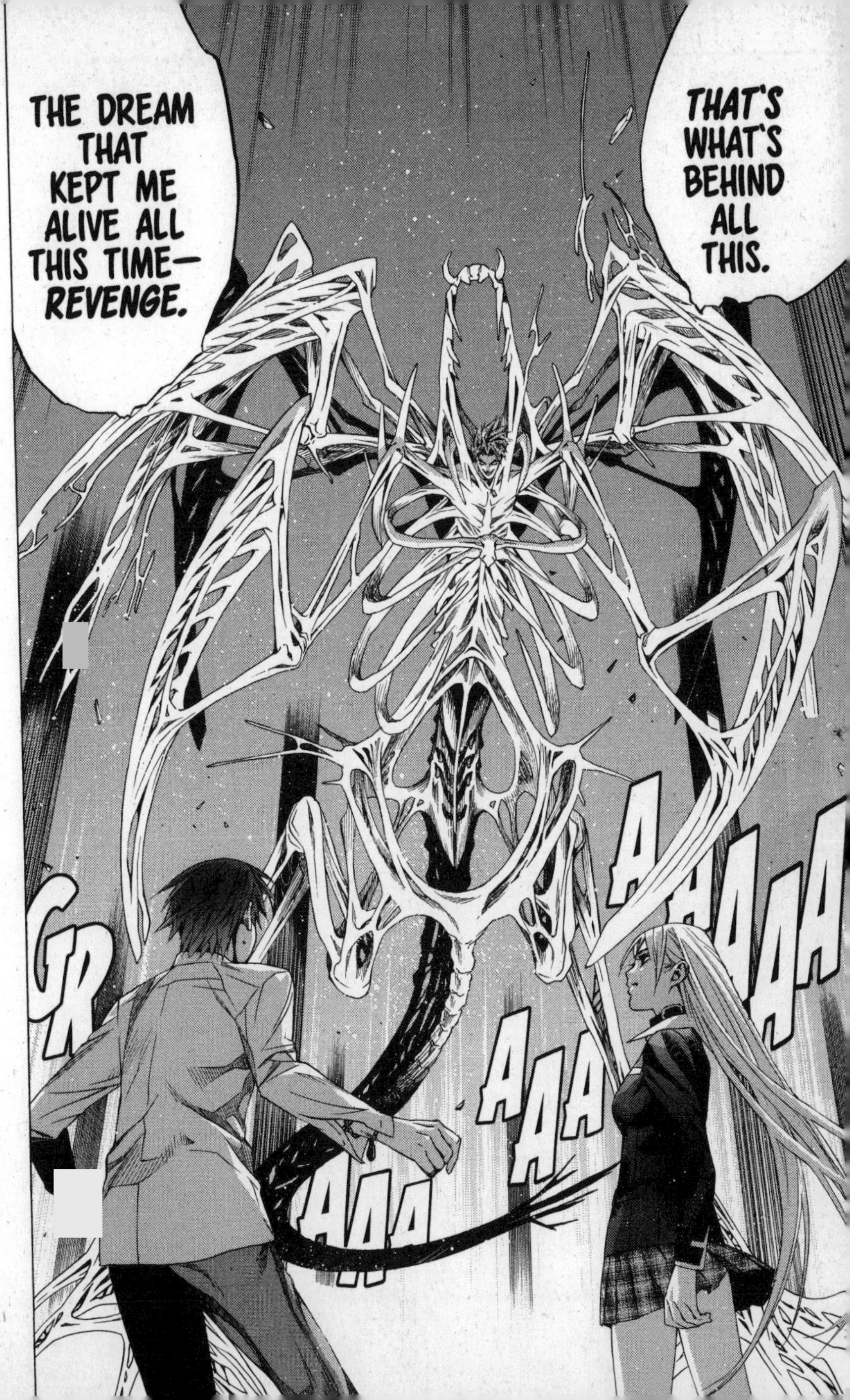
THAT'S WHAT'S BEHIND ALL THIS.
THE DREAM THAT KEPT ME ALIVE ALL THIS TIME—REVENGE.
AAAAA
AAAAA
GR
AAAA

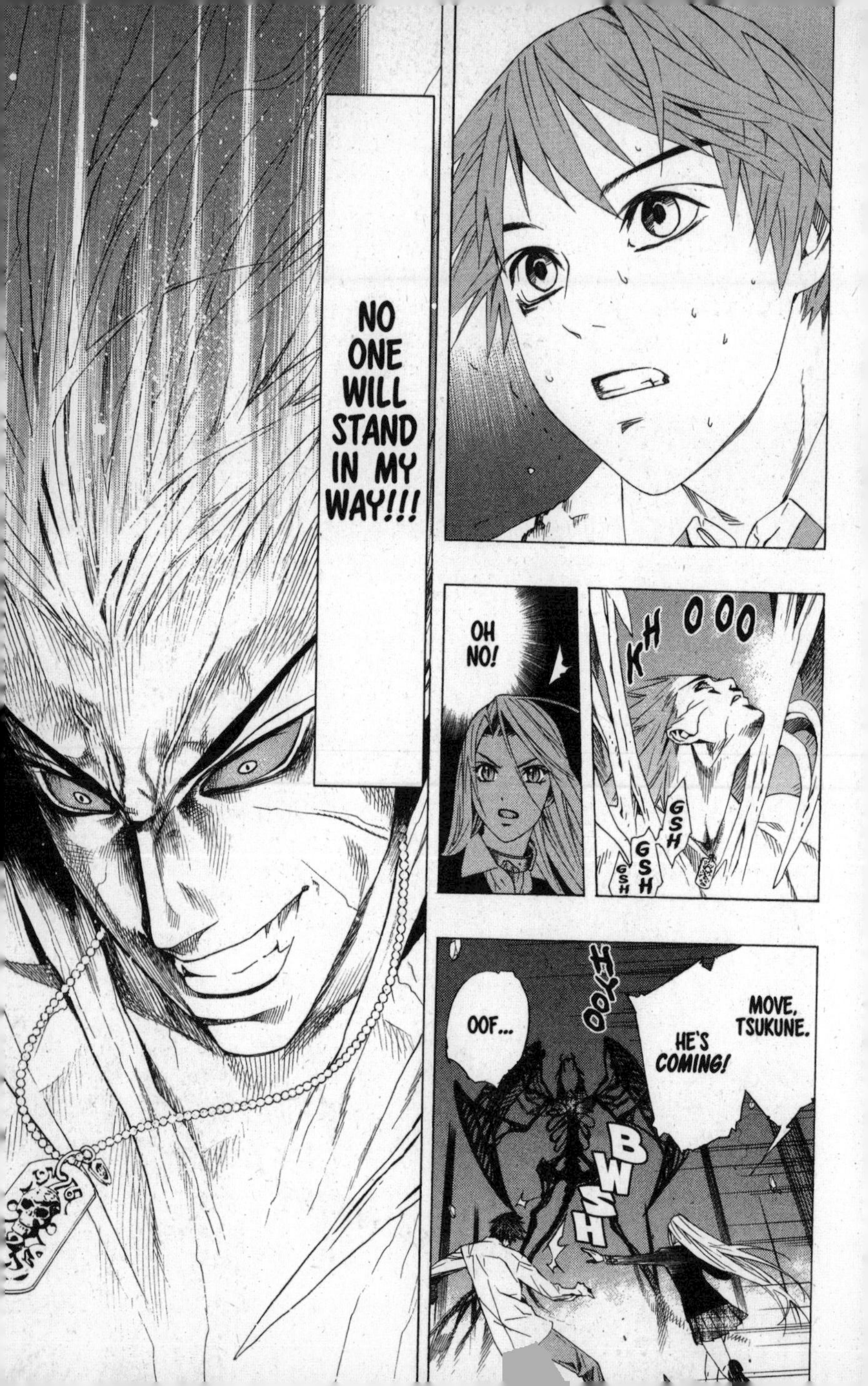
KHOOO
GSH
GSH
GSH
OH NO!
MOVE, TSUKUNE.
HE'S COMING!
HYOOO
OOF...
BWSH
NO ONE WILL STAND IN MY WAY!!!

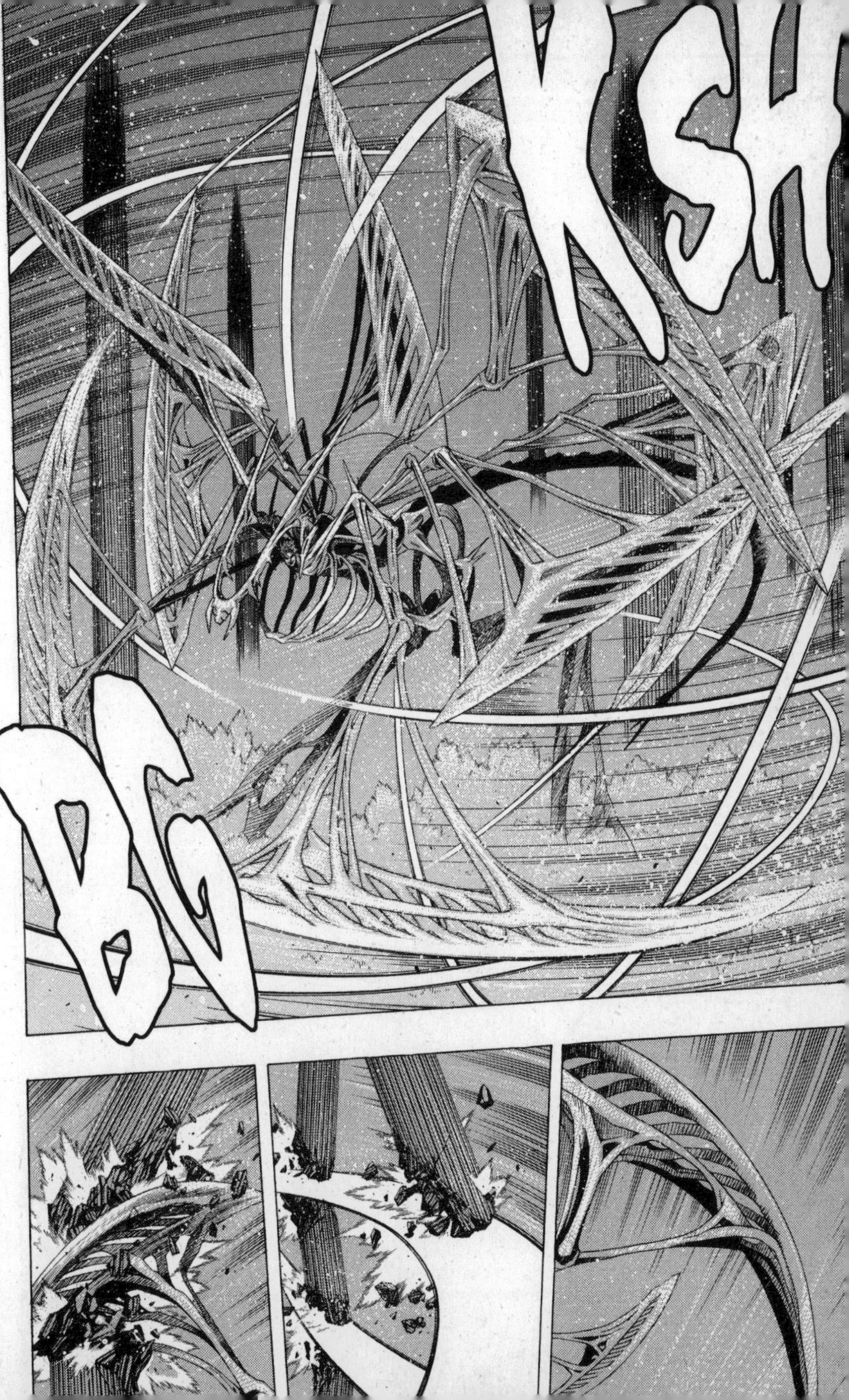
KSH
BG

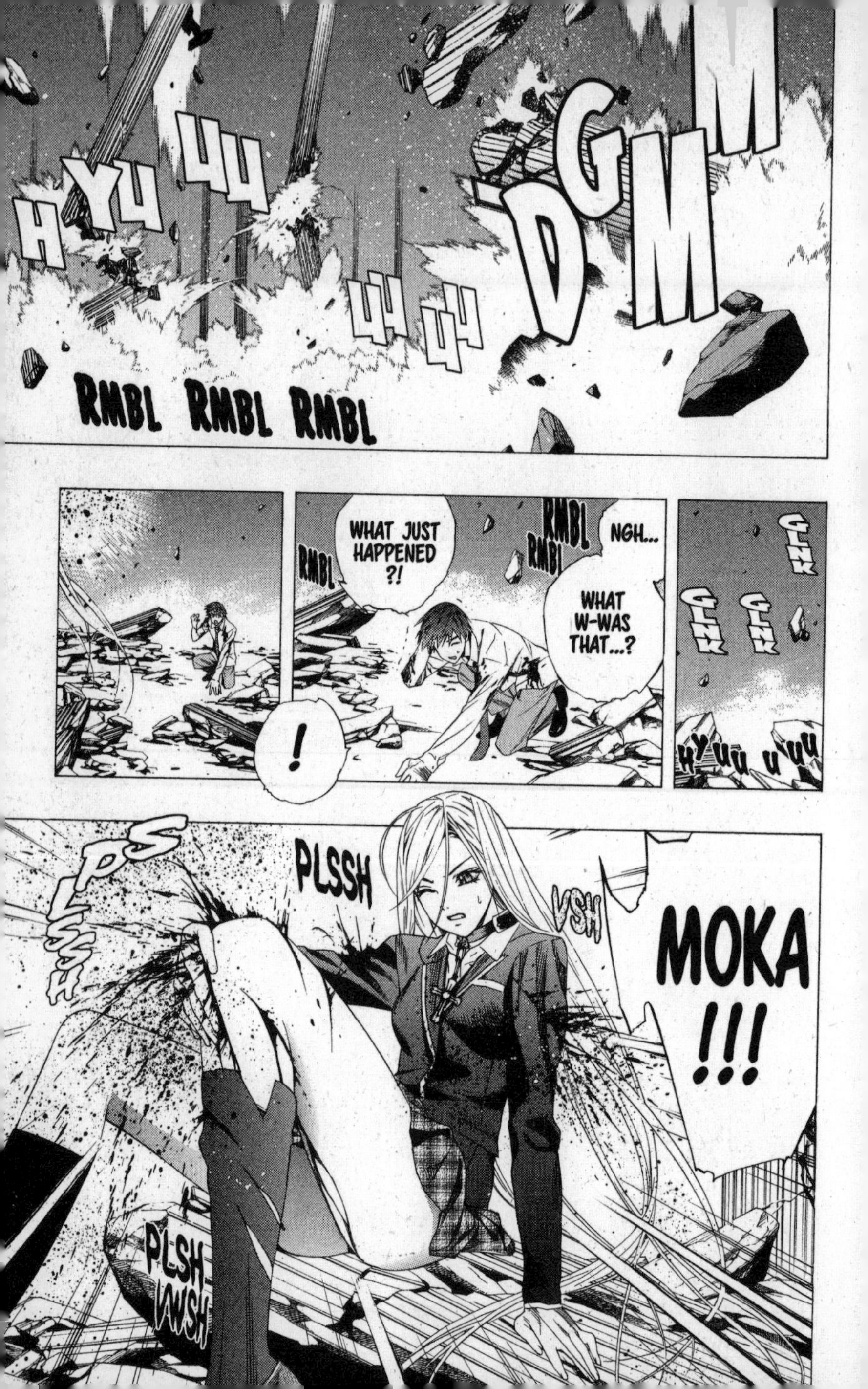
DGMMM
HYUUUU
UUUU
RMBL RMBL RMBL
GLNK
GLNK GLNK
HYUUU UUU
RMBL
RMBL
NGH...
WHAT W-WAS THAT...?
WHAT JUST HAPPENED ?!
RMBL
!
MOKA !!!
VSH
PLSSH
PSPLSSH
PLSH-VWSH

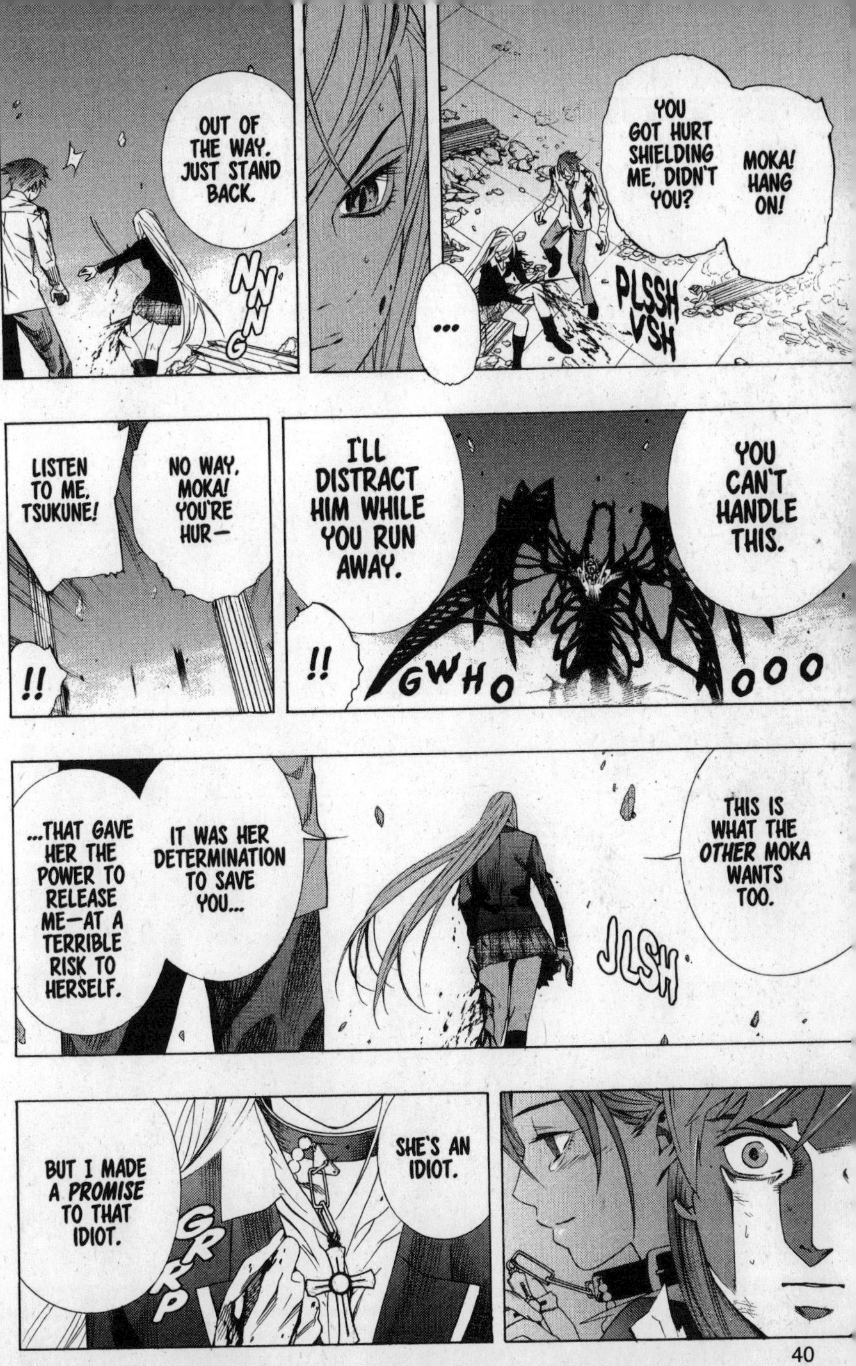
MOKA! HANG ON!
YOU GOT HURT SHIELDING ME, DIDN'T YOU?
PLSSH VSH
...
OUT OF THE WAY. JUST STAND BACK.
NNNNG
YOU CAN'T HANDLE THIS.
I'LL DISTRACT HIM WHILE YOU RUN AWAY.
GWHOOOO
!!
NO WAY, MOKA! YOU'RE HUR—
LISTEN TO ME, TSUKUNE!
!!
THIS IS WHAT THE *OTHER* MOKA WANTS TOO.
JLSH
IT WAS HER DETERMINATION TO SAVE YOU...
...THAT GAVE HER THE POWER TO RELEASE ME—AT A TERRIBLE RISK TO HERSELF.
SHE'S AN IDIOT.
BUT I MADE A *PROMISE* TO THAT IDIOT.
GRKP

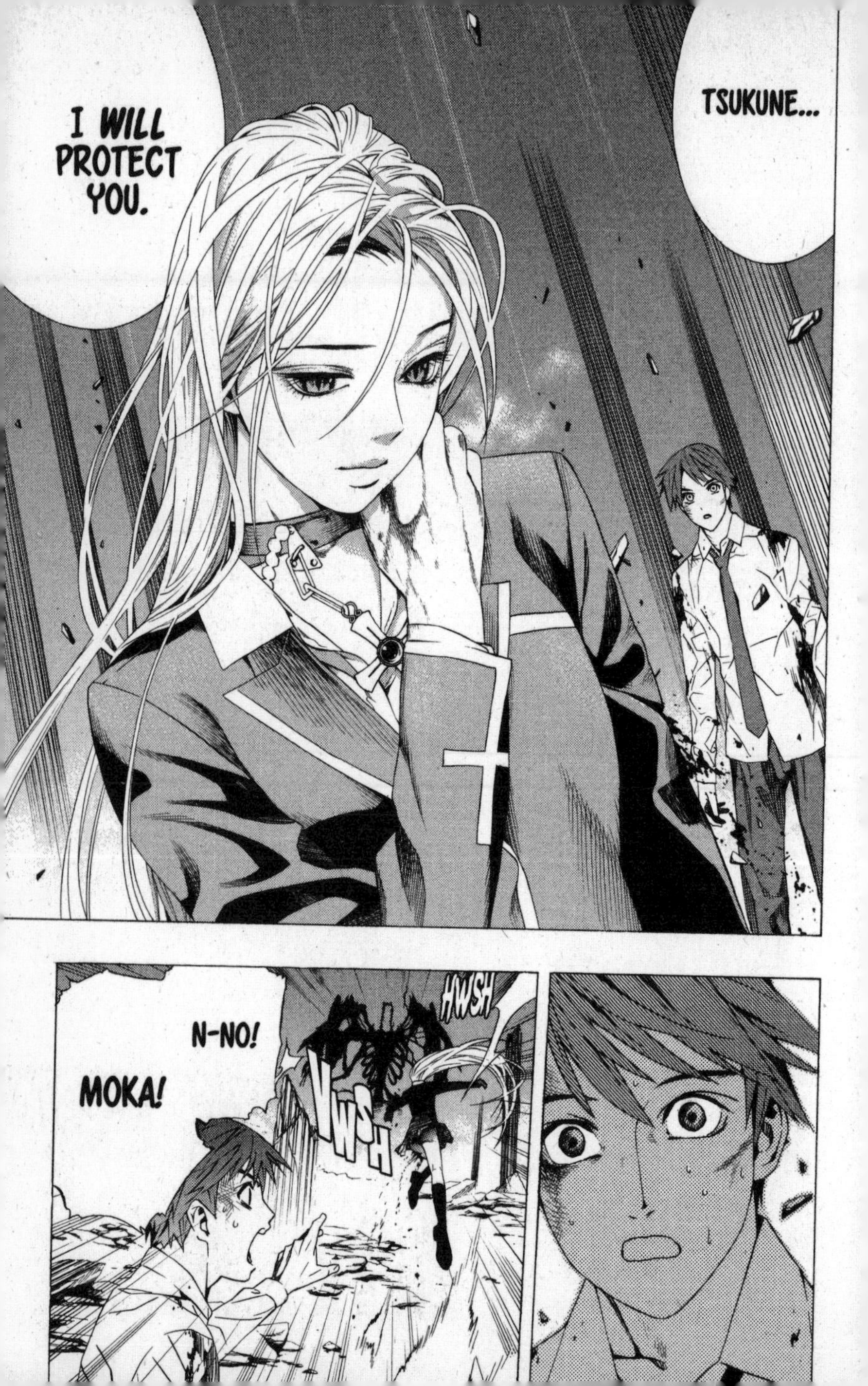
TSUKUNE...
I WILL PROTECT YOU.
HWSH
N-NO!
MOKA!
VWSH

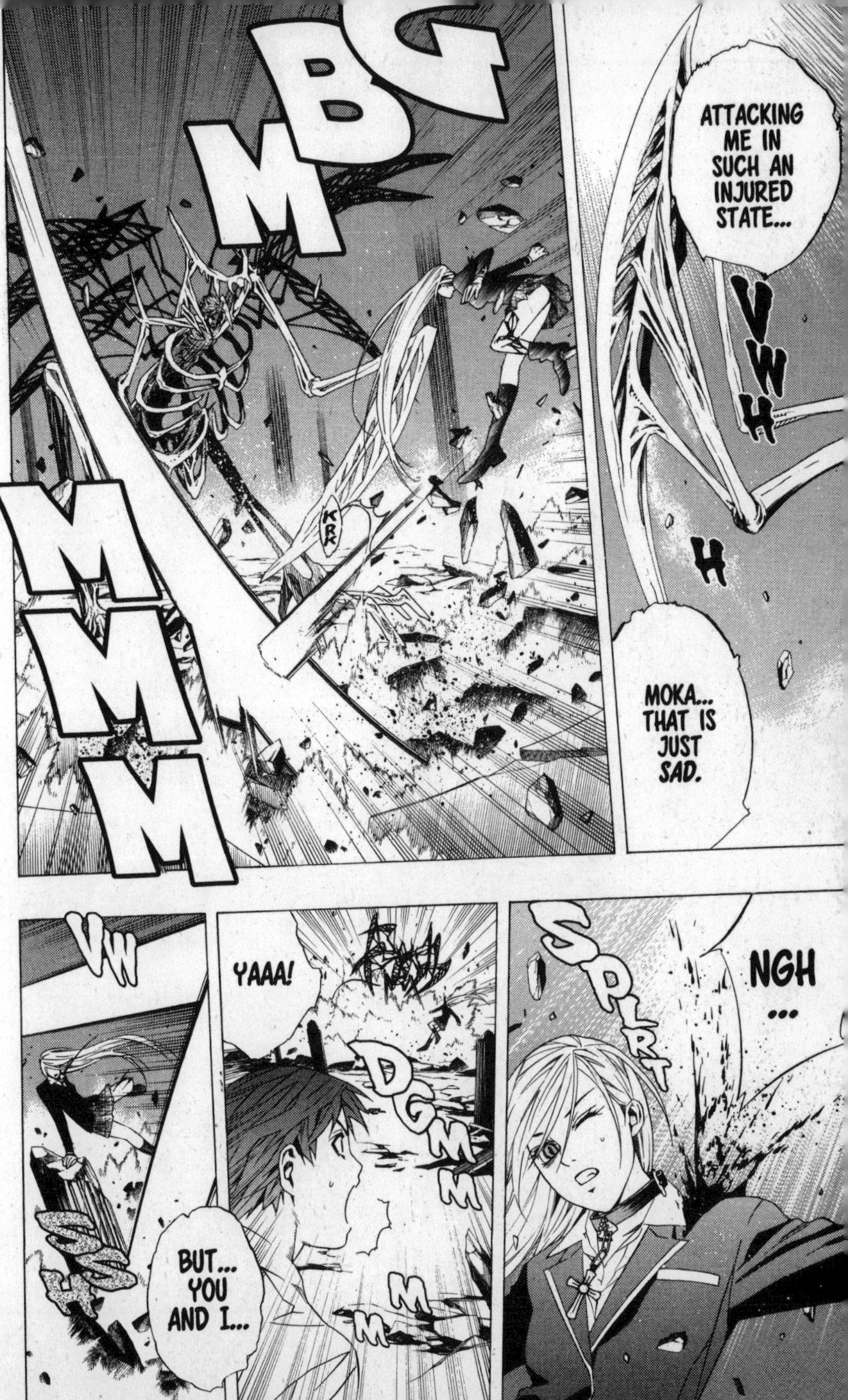

ATTACKING ME IN SUCH AN INJURED STATE...
VWH
H
MOKA... THAT IS JUST SAD.
BG
M
KRK
MMMM
SPLRT
NGH ...
YAAA!
DGMM
BUT... YOU AND I...
M
M
VW

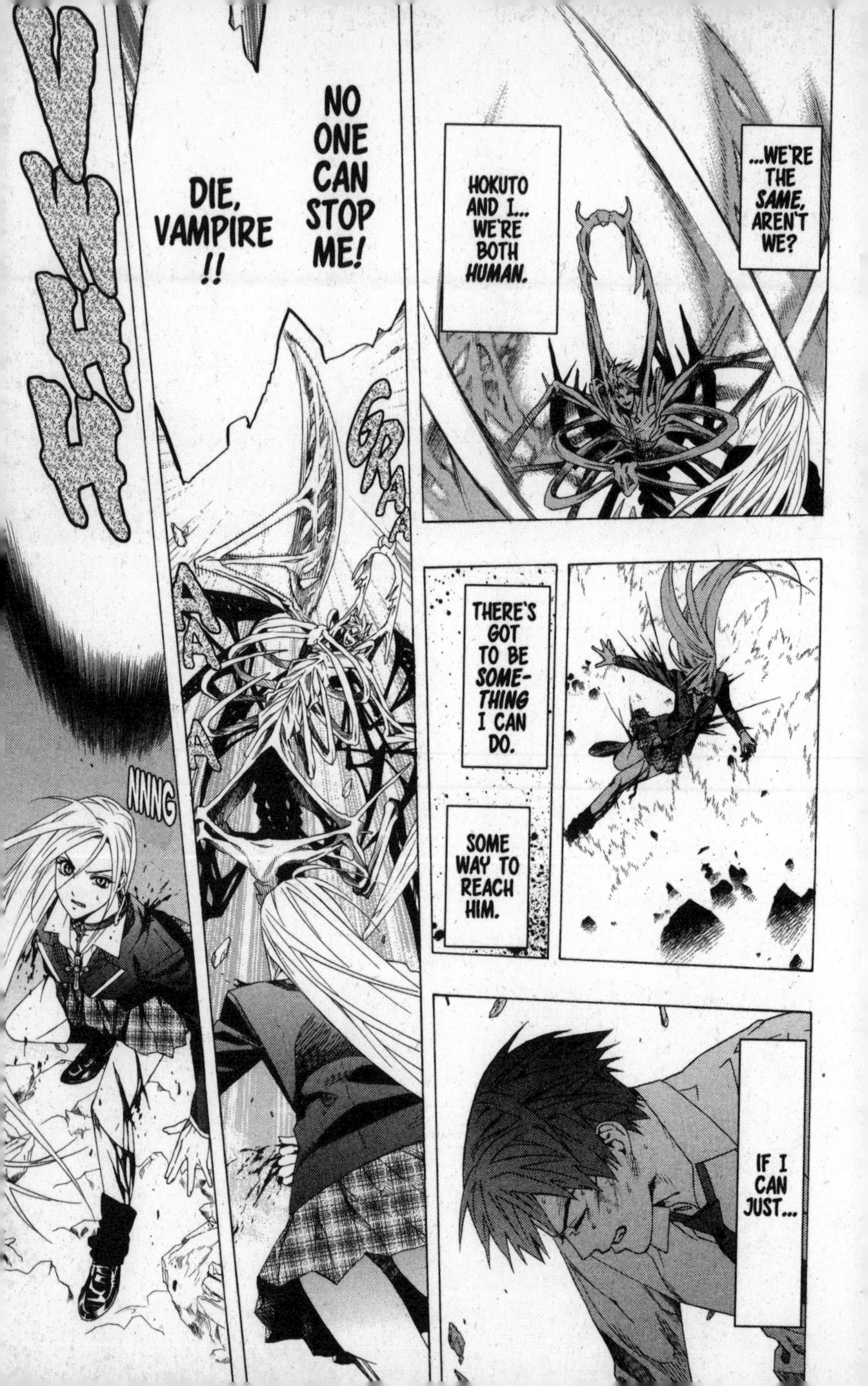
...WE'RE THE SAME, AREN'T WE?
HOKUTO AND I... WE'RE BOTH HUMAN.
THERE'S GOT TO BE SOMETHING I CAN DO.
SOME WAY TO REACH HIM.
IF I CAN JUST...
NO ONE CAN STOP ME!
DIE, VAMPIRE!!
GRAAAA
NNNG

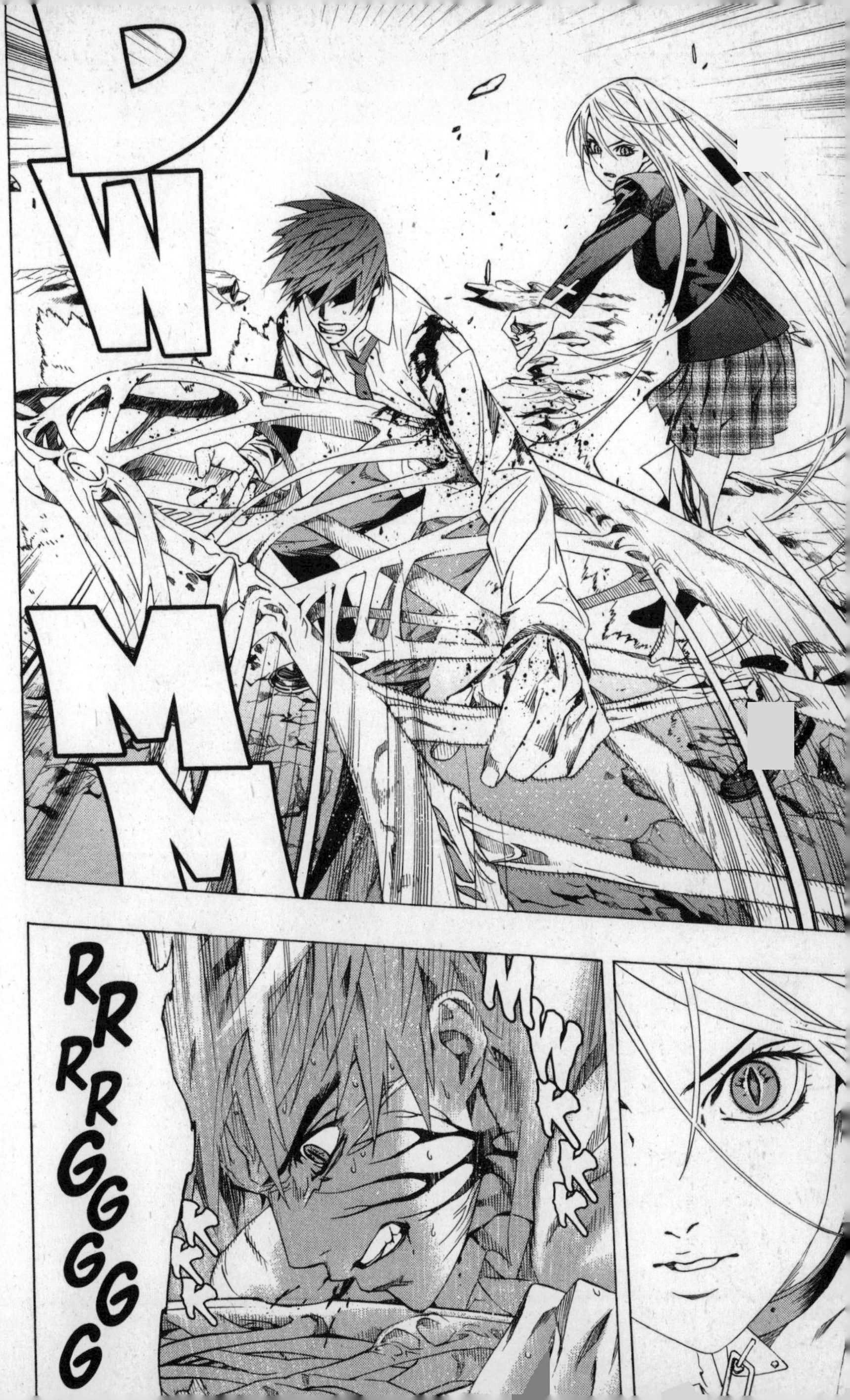
DWMM
MWKKK
KKK
RRRRGGGGG

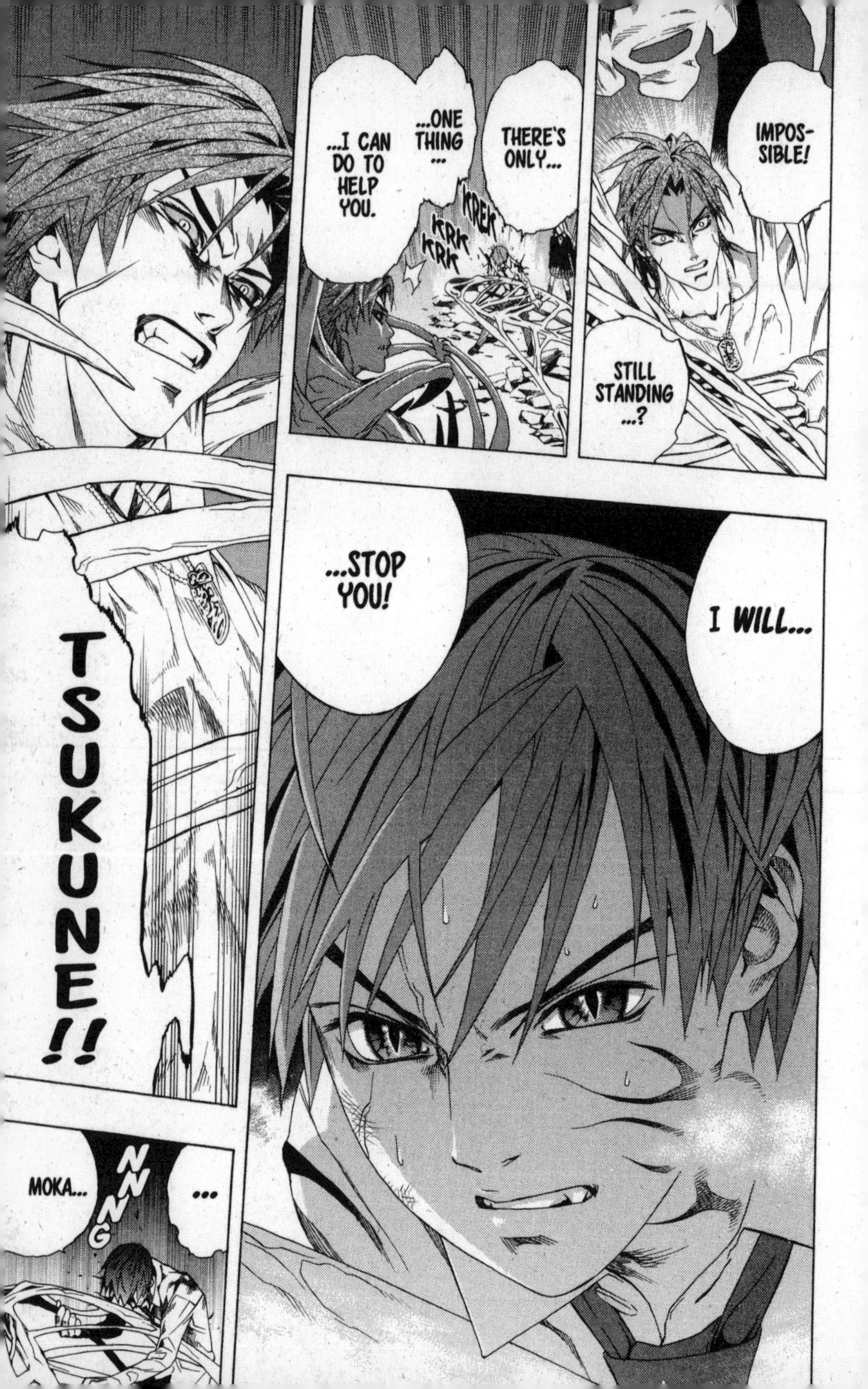
IMPOS-SIBLE!
STILL STANDING ...?
THERE'S ONLY...
...ONE THING ...
...I CAN DO TO HELP YOU.
KREK
KRK KRK
I WILL...
...STOP YOU!
TSUKUNE!!
...
MOKA...
NNNG

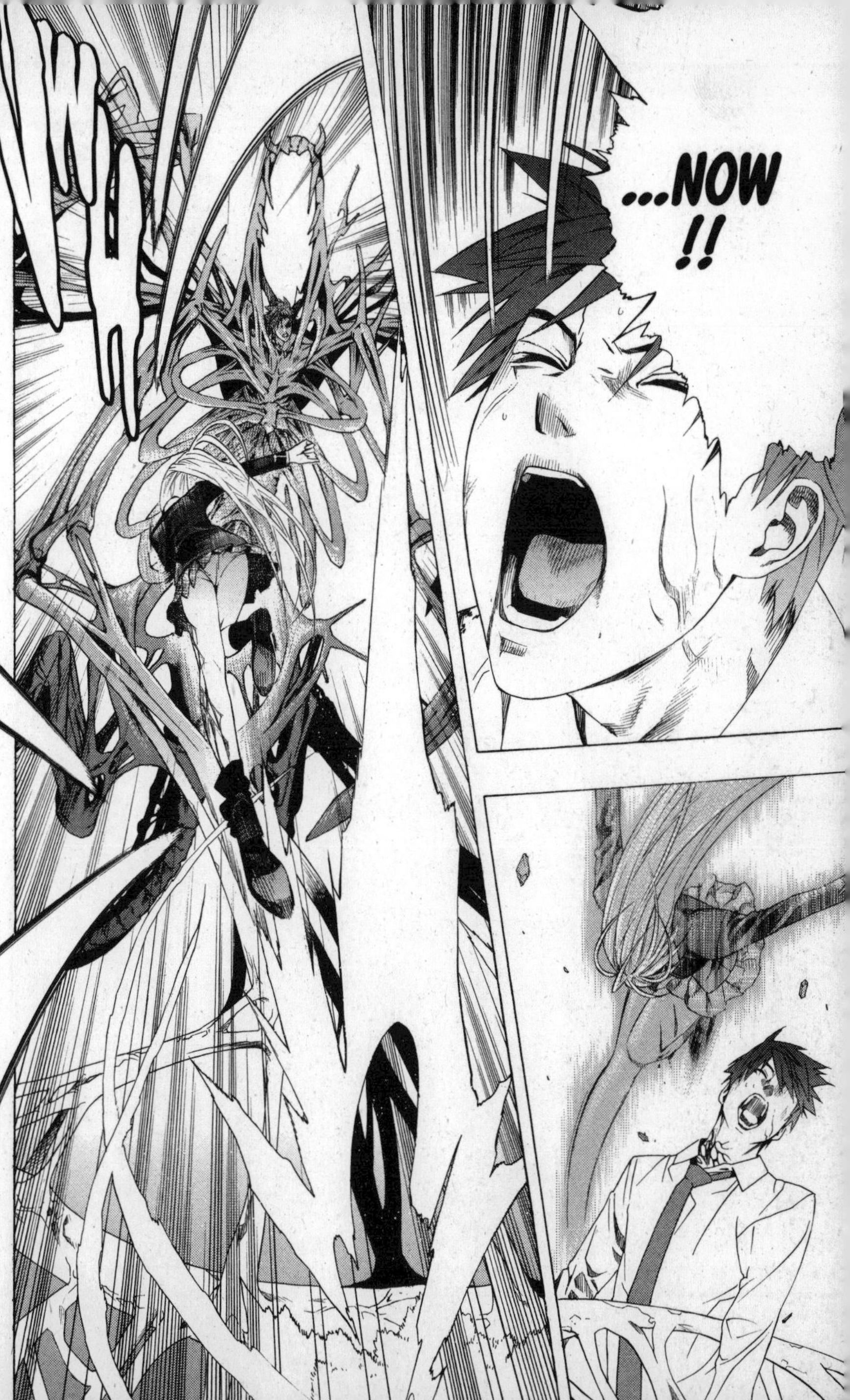
...NOW !!

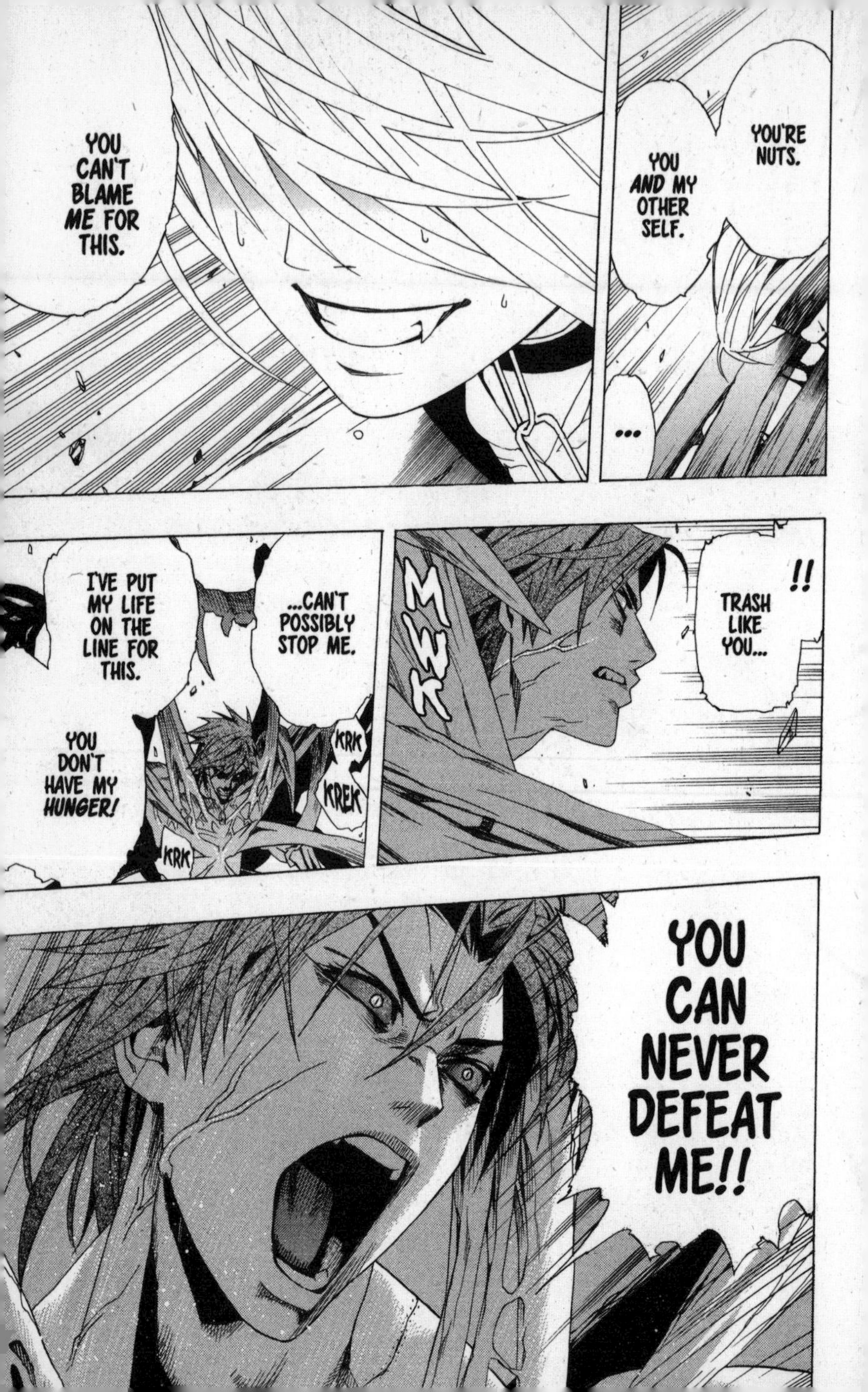
YOU'RE NUTS.
YOU AND MY OTHER SELF.
...
YOU CAN'T BLAME ME FOR THIS.
!!
TRASH LIKE YOU...
MWK
...CAN'T POSSIBLY STOP ME.
I'VE PUT MY LIFE ON THE LINE FOR THIS.
KRK
KREK
YOU DON'T HAVE MY HUNGER!
KRK
YOU CAN NEVER DEFEAT ME!!

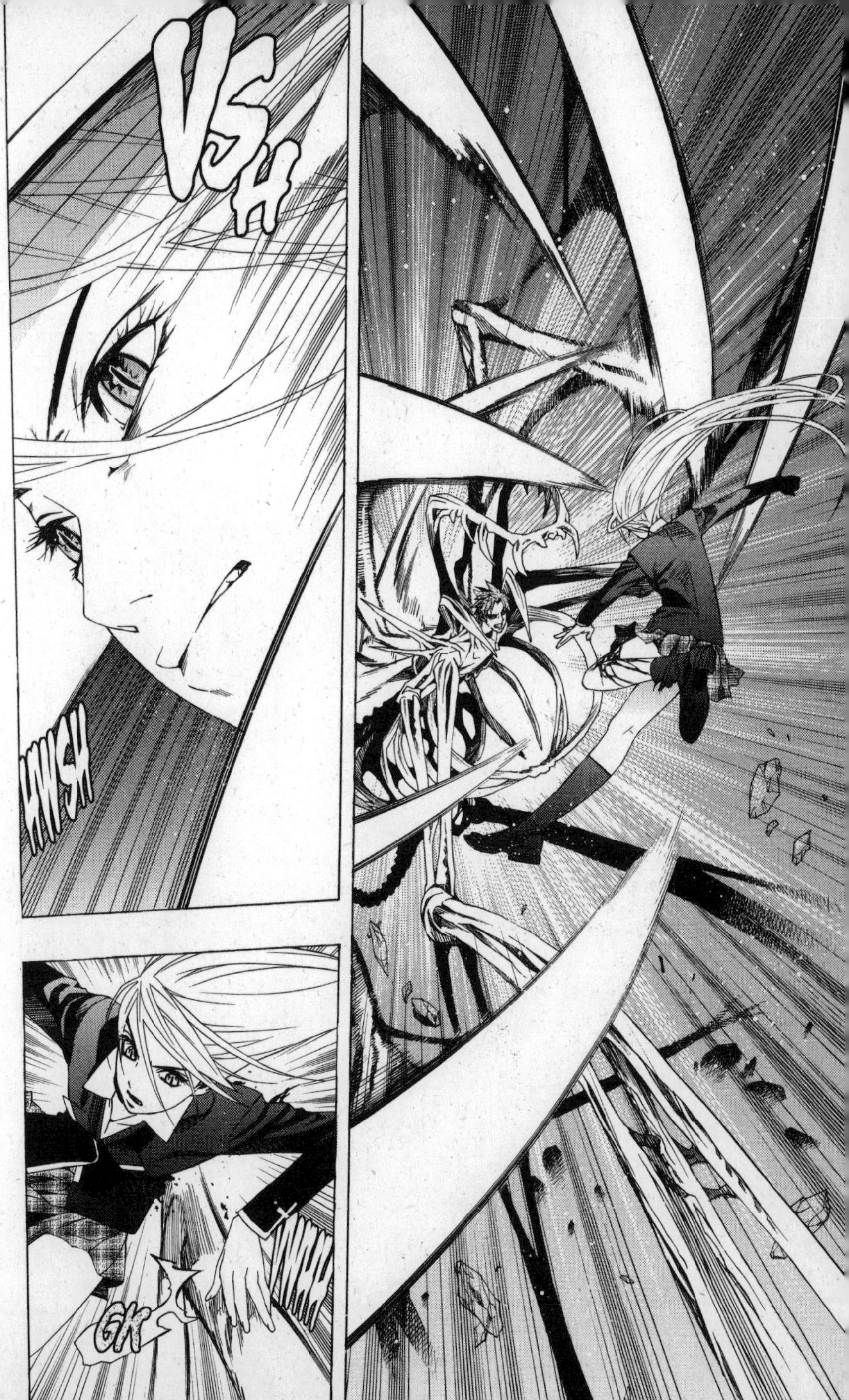
VSH
HWSH
GK

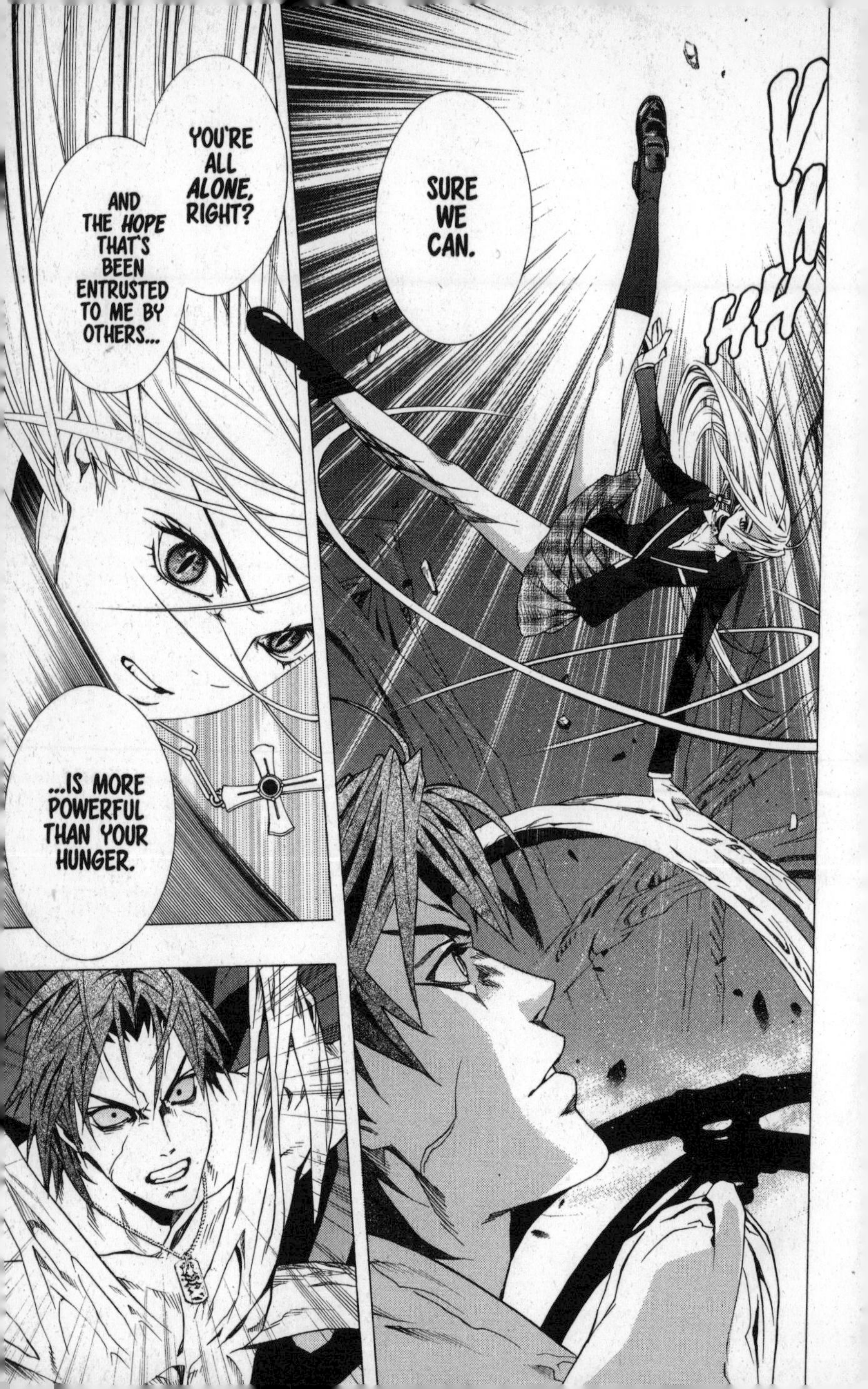
VWHH
SURE WE CAN.
YOU'RE ALL ALONE, RIGHT?
AND THE *HOPE* THAT'S BEEN ENTRUSTED TO ME BY OTHERS...
...IS MORE POWERFUL THAN YOUR HUNGER.

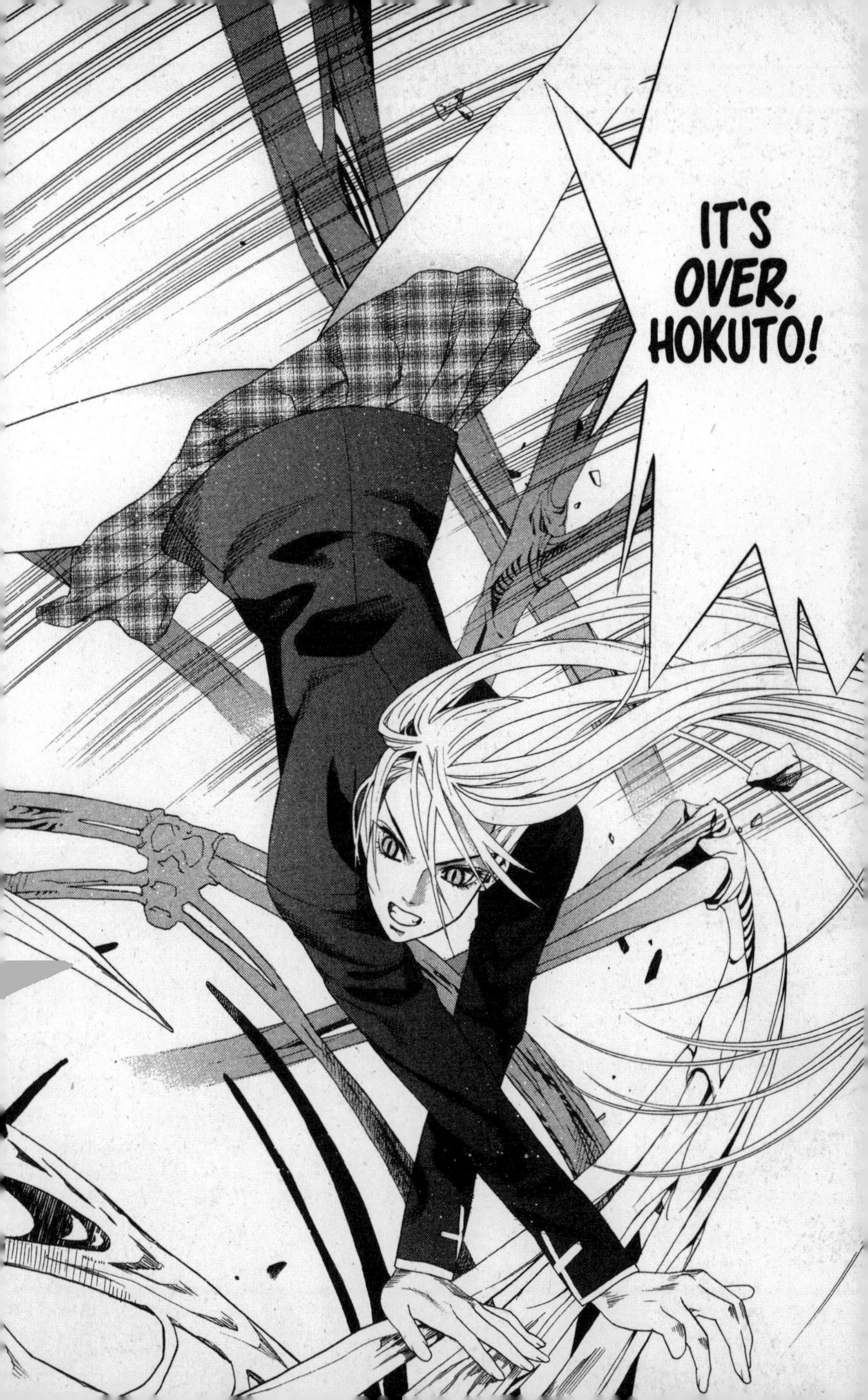
IT'S OVER, HOKUTO!

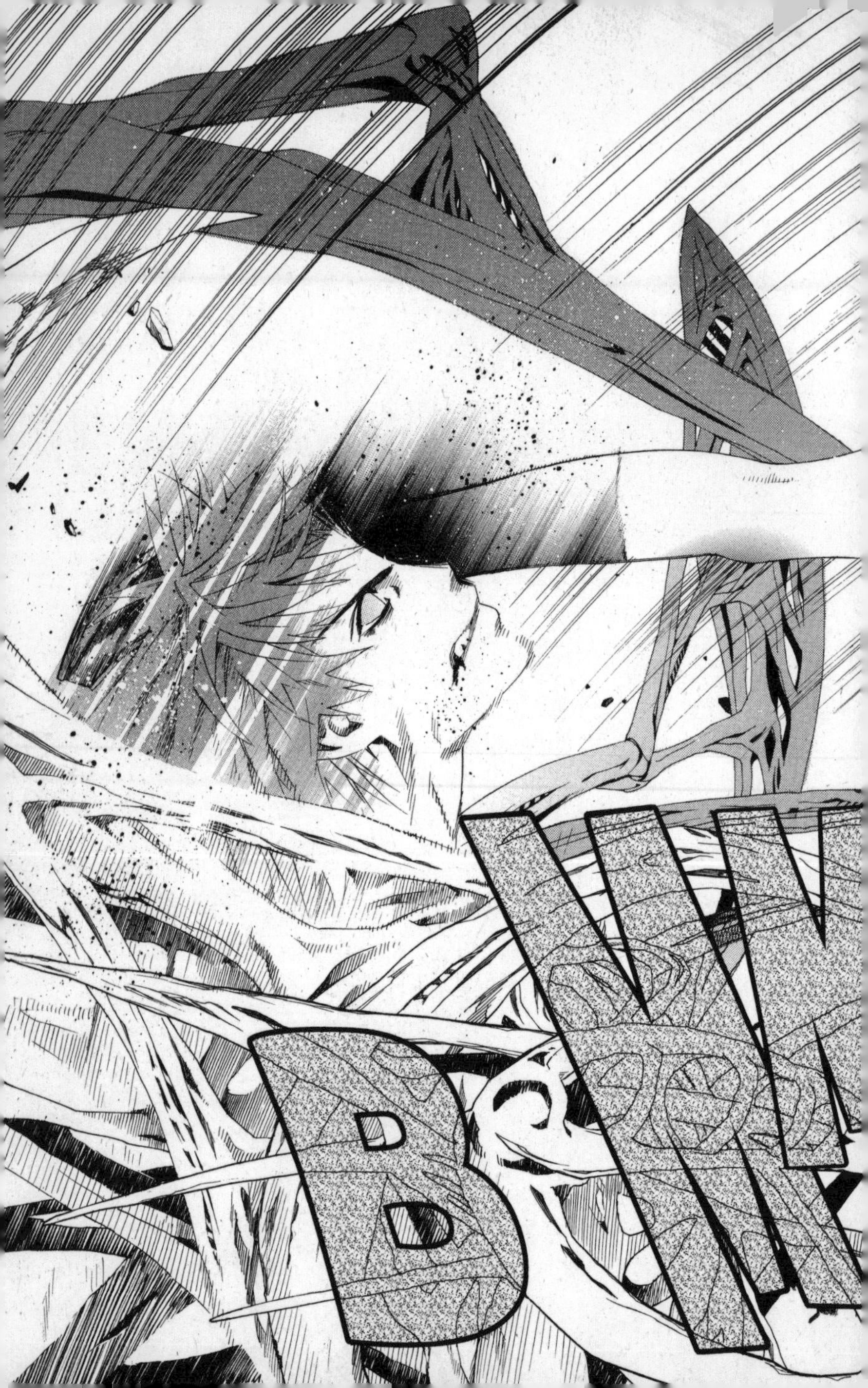

34: The Same Wish

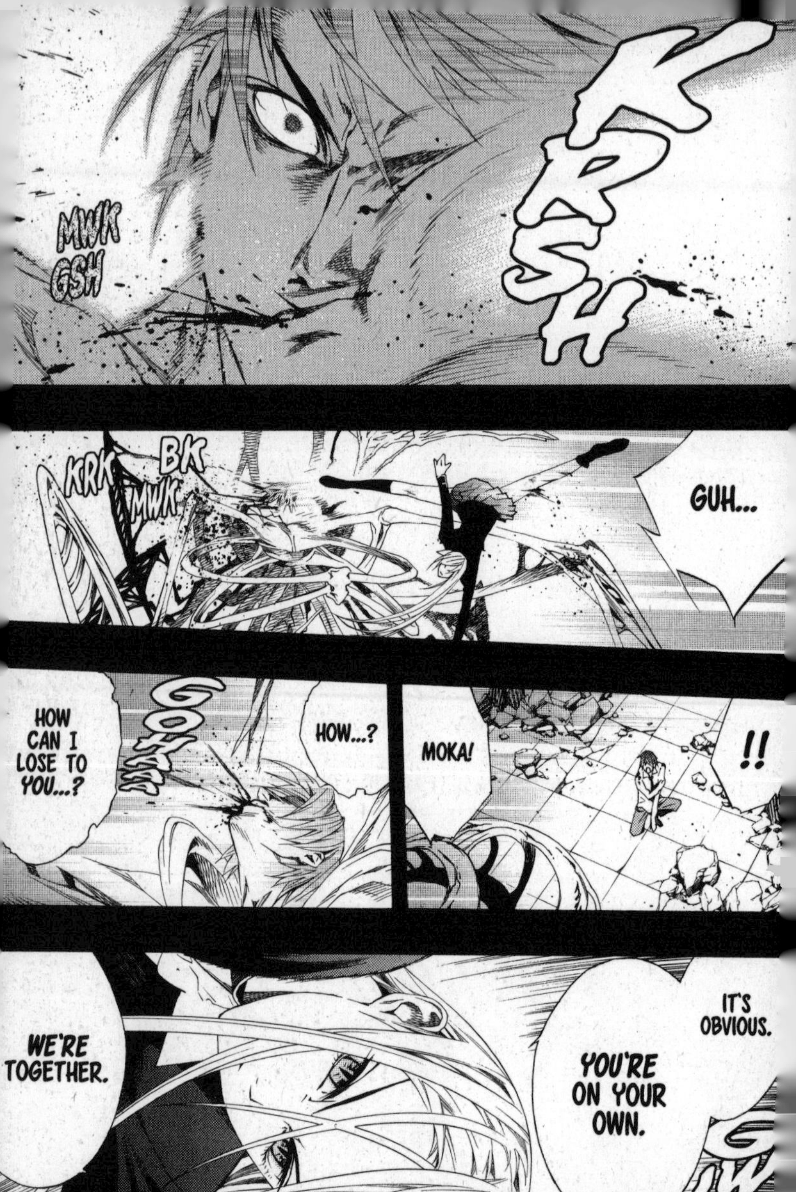
KRSH
MWK GSH
GUH...
BK
MWK
KRK
!!
MOKA!
HOW...?
HOW CAN I LOSE TO YOU...?
IT'S OBVIOUS.
YOU'RE ON YOUR OWN.
WE'RE TOGETHER.

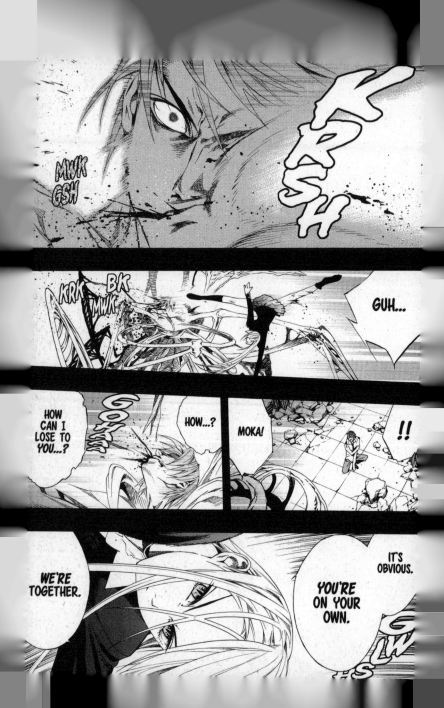

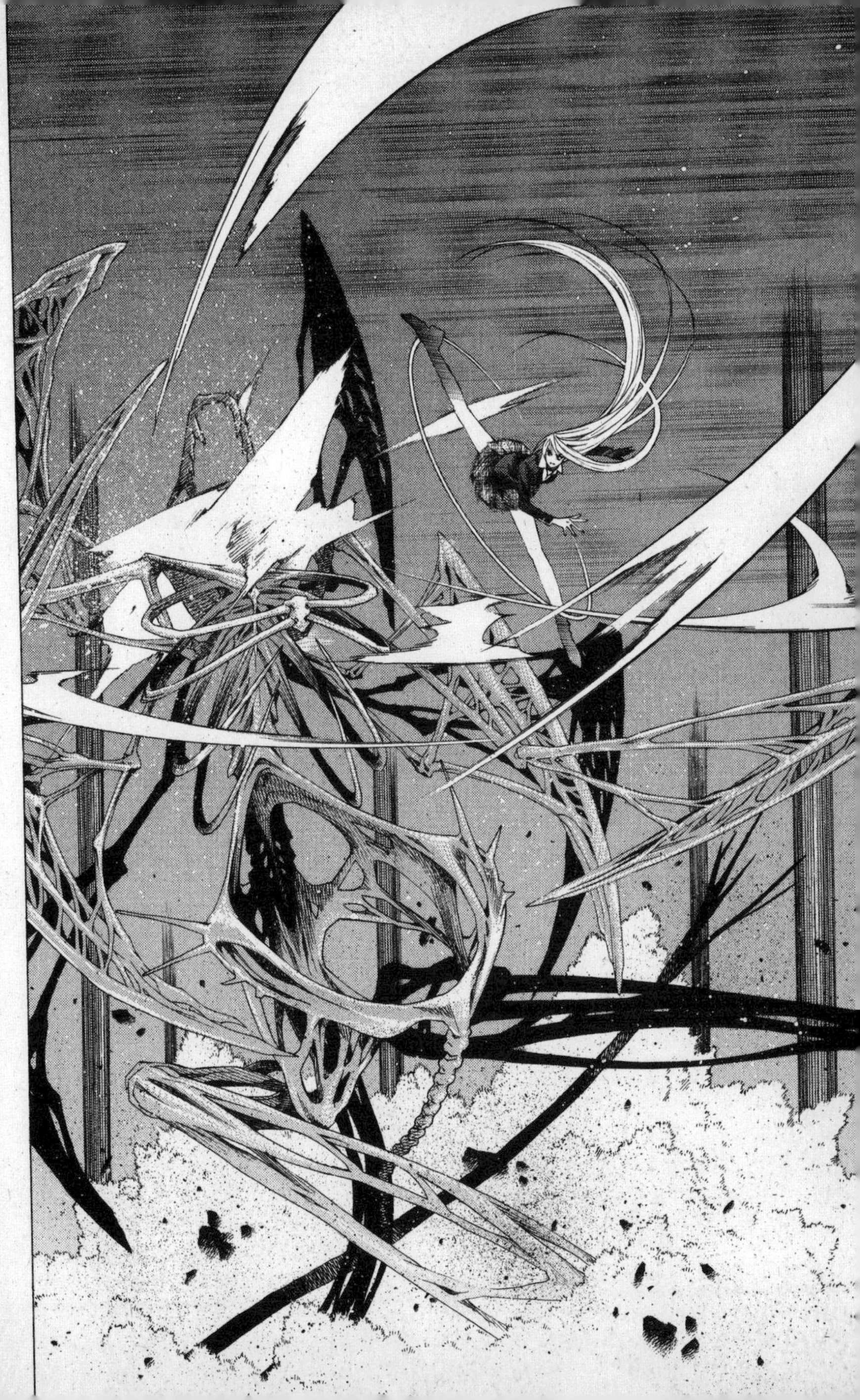

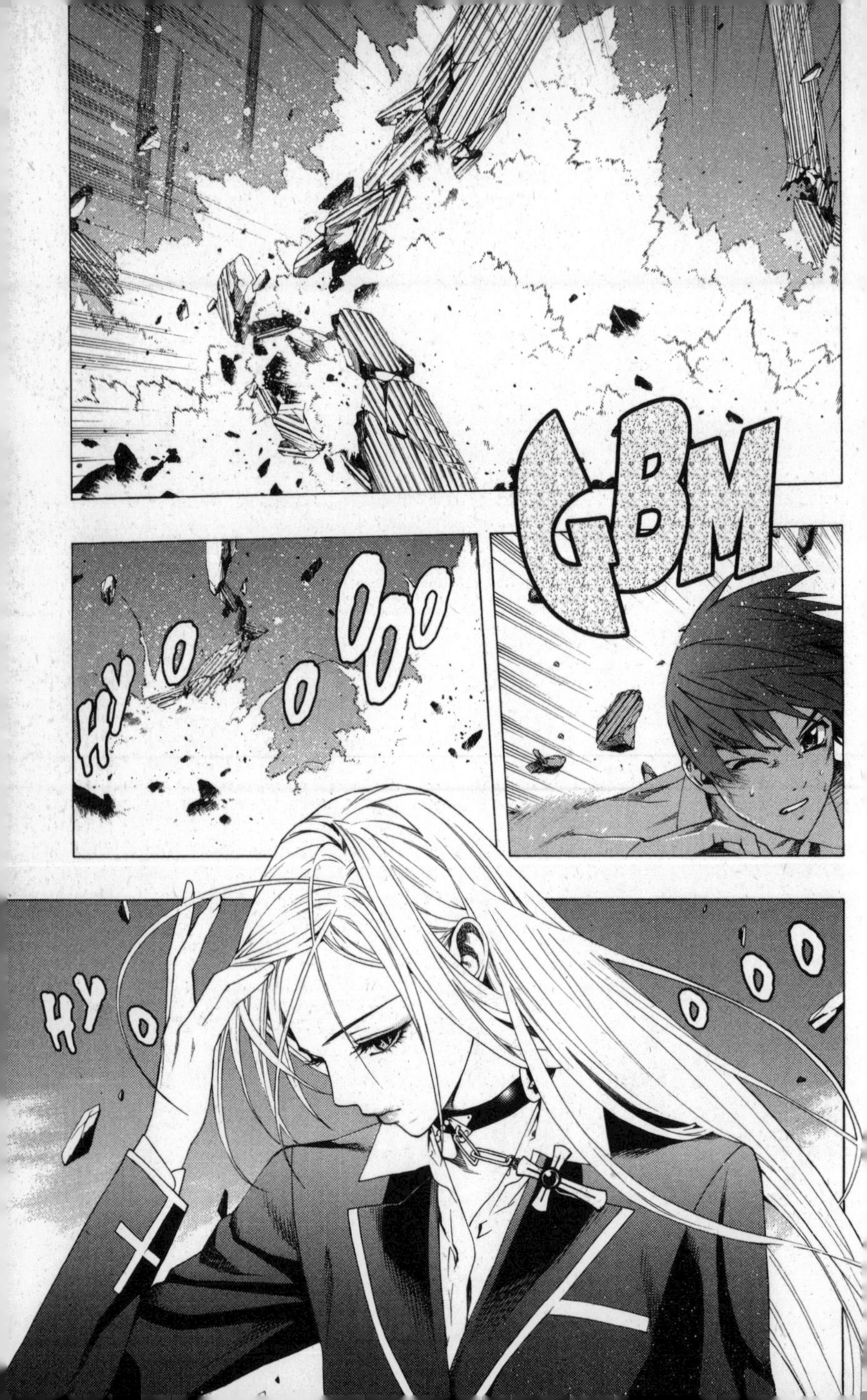
GBM
HYOOOOO
HYOOOO

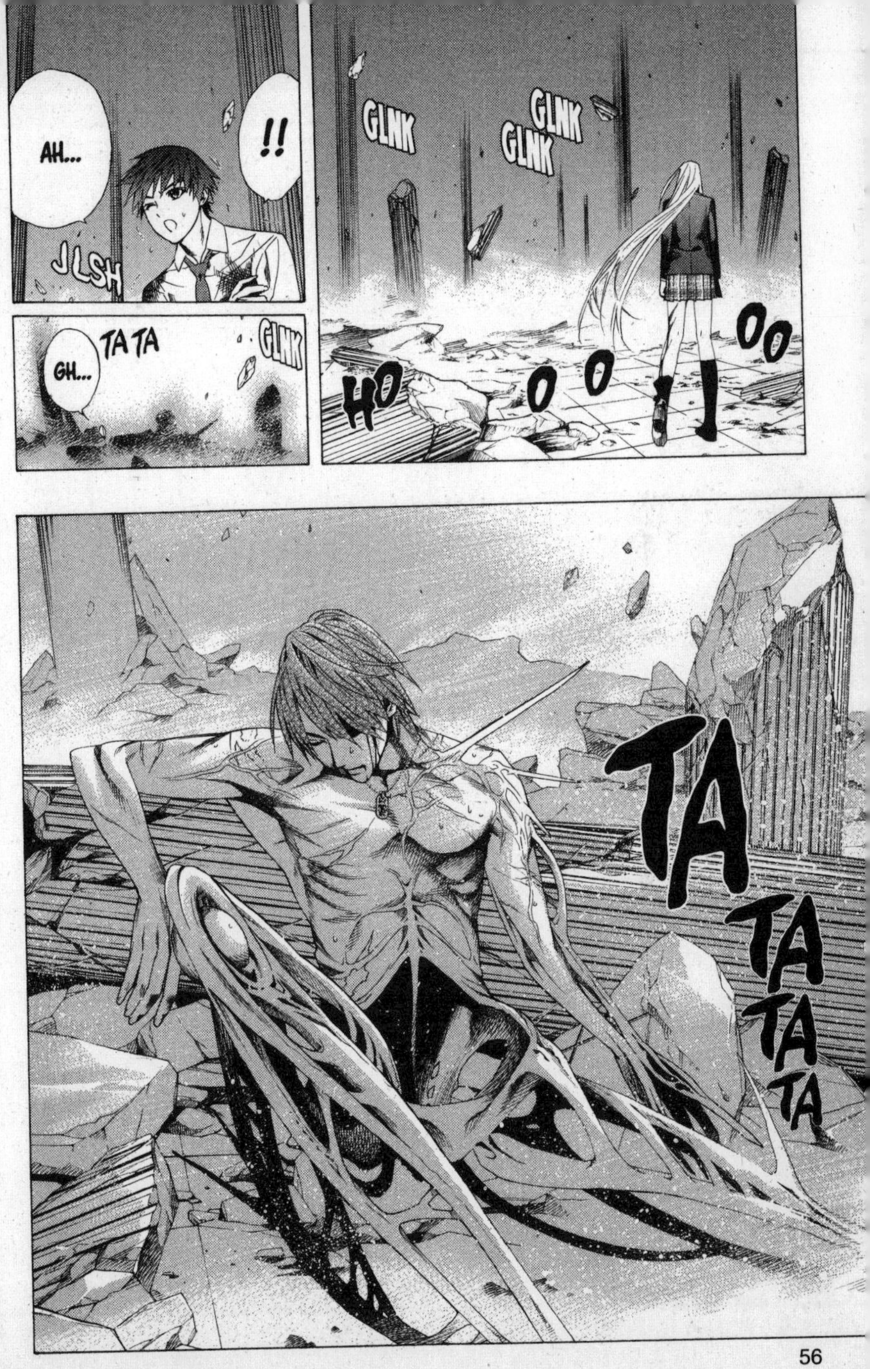
GLNK
GLNK
GLNK
HOOOOO
!!
AH...
JLSH
GLNK
TA TA
GH...
TA
TA
TA
TA
TA

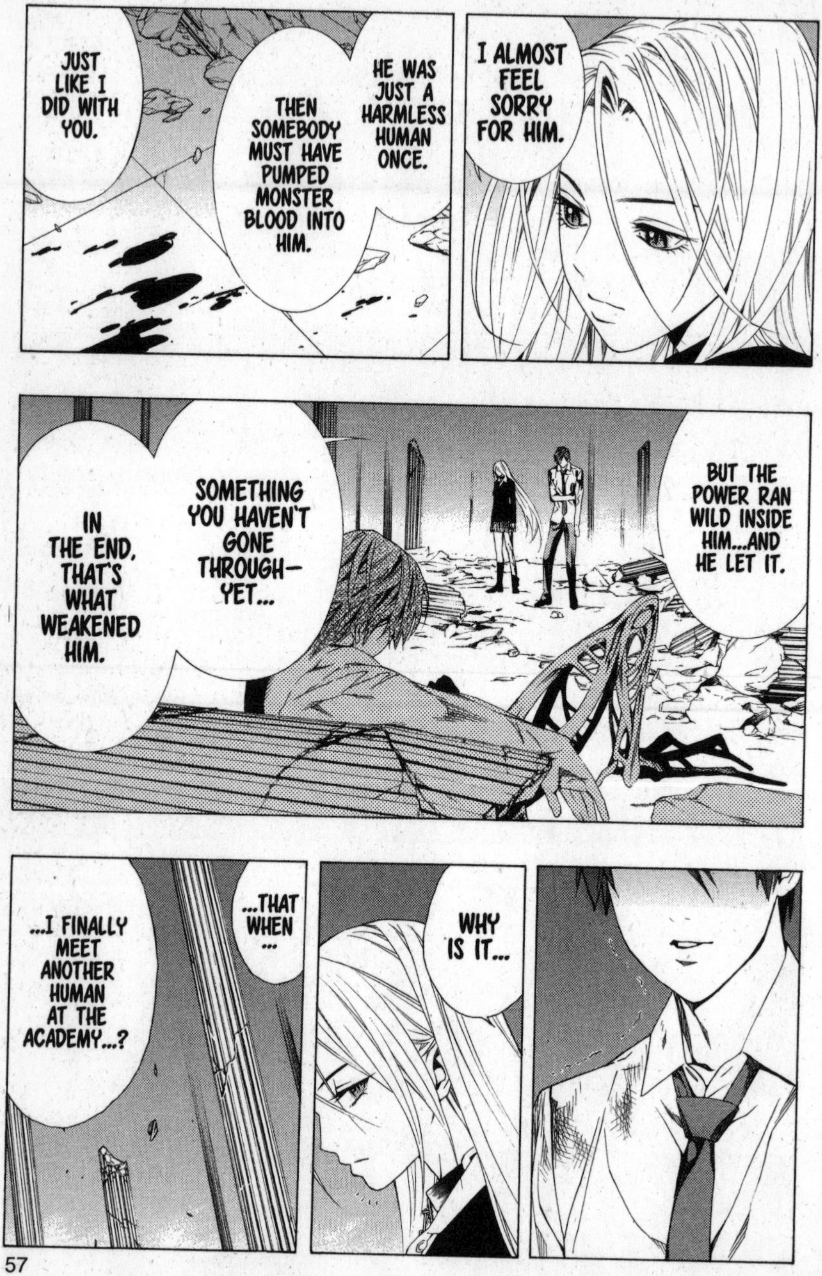
I ALMOST FEEL SORRY FOR HIM.
HE WAS JUST A HARMLESS HUMAN ONCE.
THEN SOMEBODY MUST HAVE PUMPED MONSTER BLOOD INTO HIM.
JUST LIKE I DID WITH YOU.
BUT THE POWER RAN WILD INSIDE HIM...AND HE LET IT.
SOMETHING YOU HAVEN'T GONE THROUGH—YET...
IN THE END, THAT'S WHAT WEAKENED HIM.
WHY IS IT...
...THAT WHEN...
...I FINALLY MEET ANOTHER HUMAN AT THE ACADEMY...?

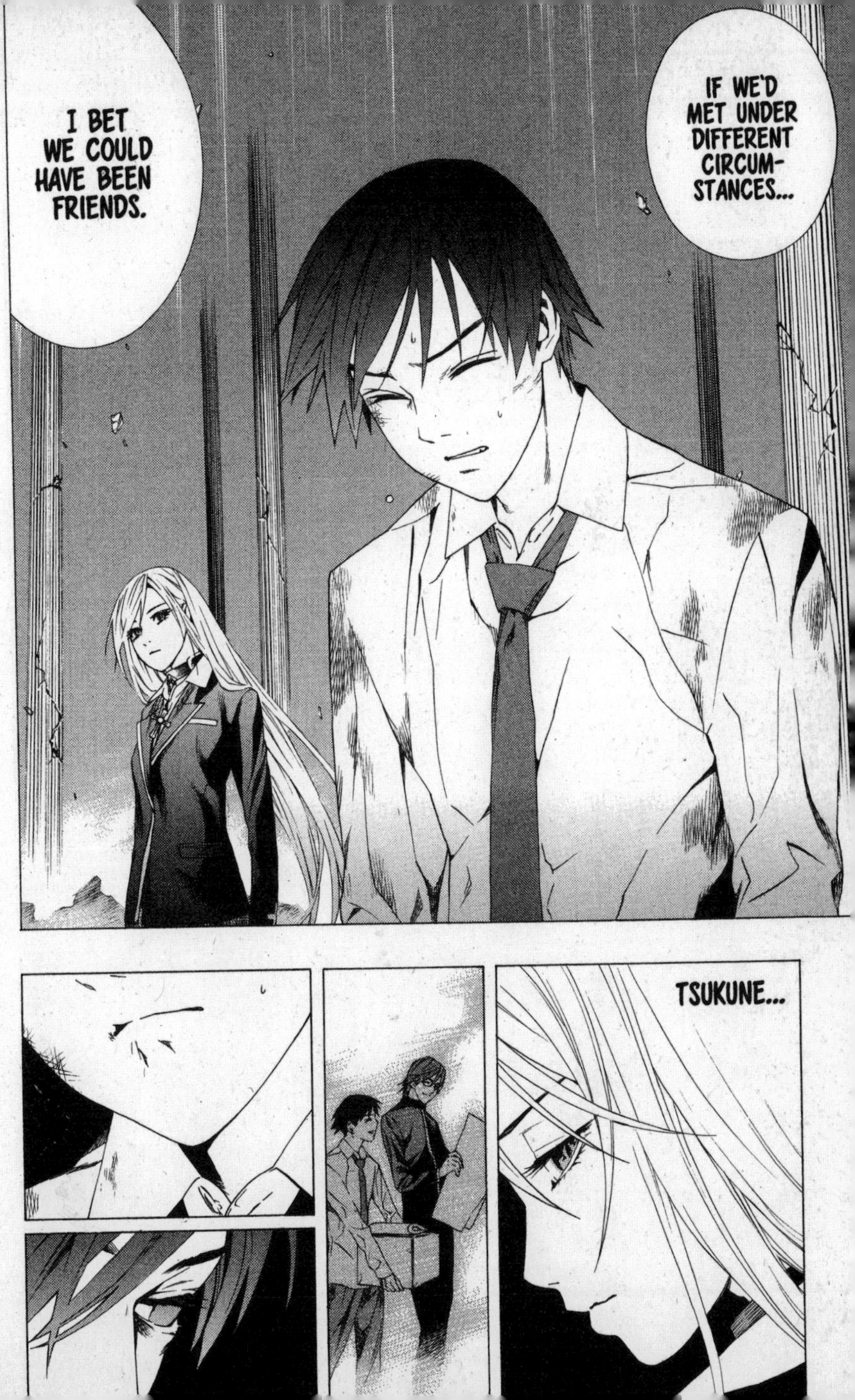
IF WE'D MET UNDER DIFFERENT CIRCUM-STANCES...
I BET WE COULD HAVE BEEN FRIENDS.
TSUKUNE...

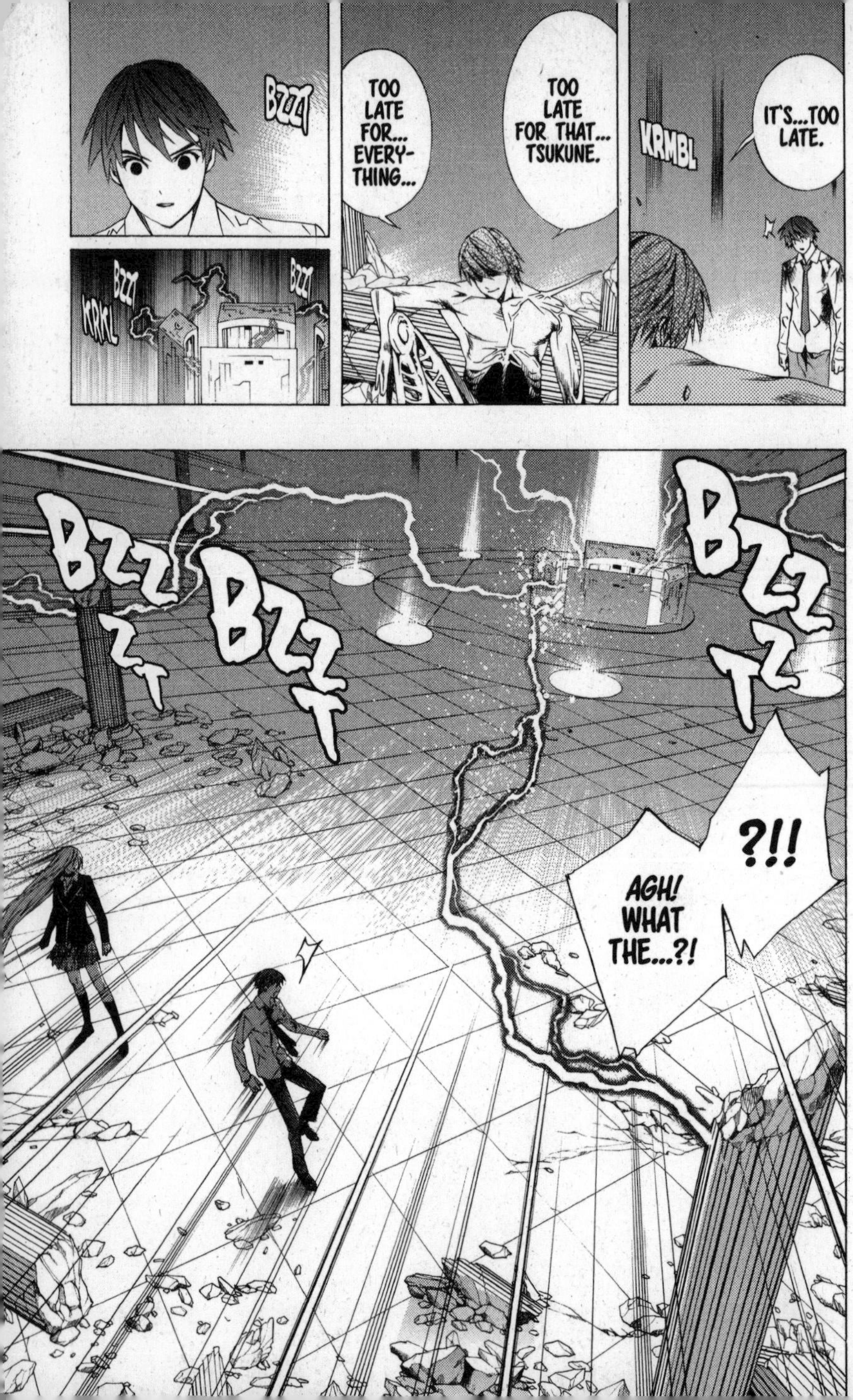
IT'S...TOO LATE.
KRMBL
TOO LATE FOR THAT... TSUKUNE.
TOO LATE FOR... EVERYTHING...
BZZT
BZZT
BZZT
KRKL
BZZZT
BZZZT
BZZZT
?!!
AGH! WHAT THE...?!

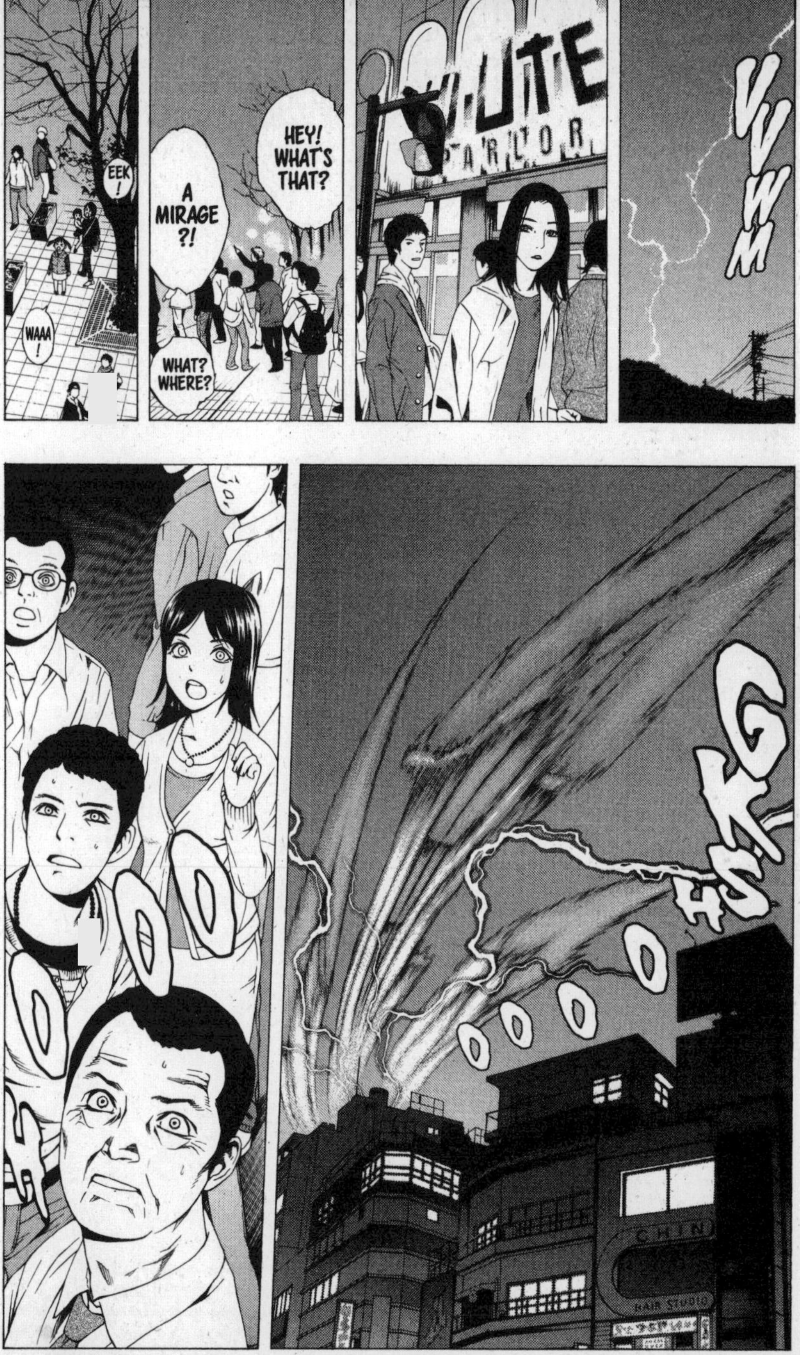
VVWM
HEY! WHAT'S THAT?
A MIRAGE?!
WHAT? WHERE?
EEK!
WAAA!
GKSH
OOOOO
OOOOO
HAIR STUDIO

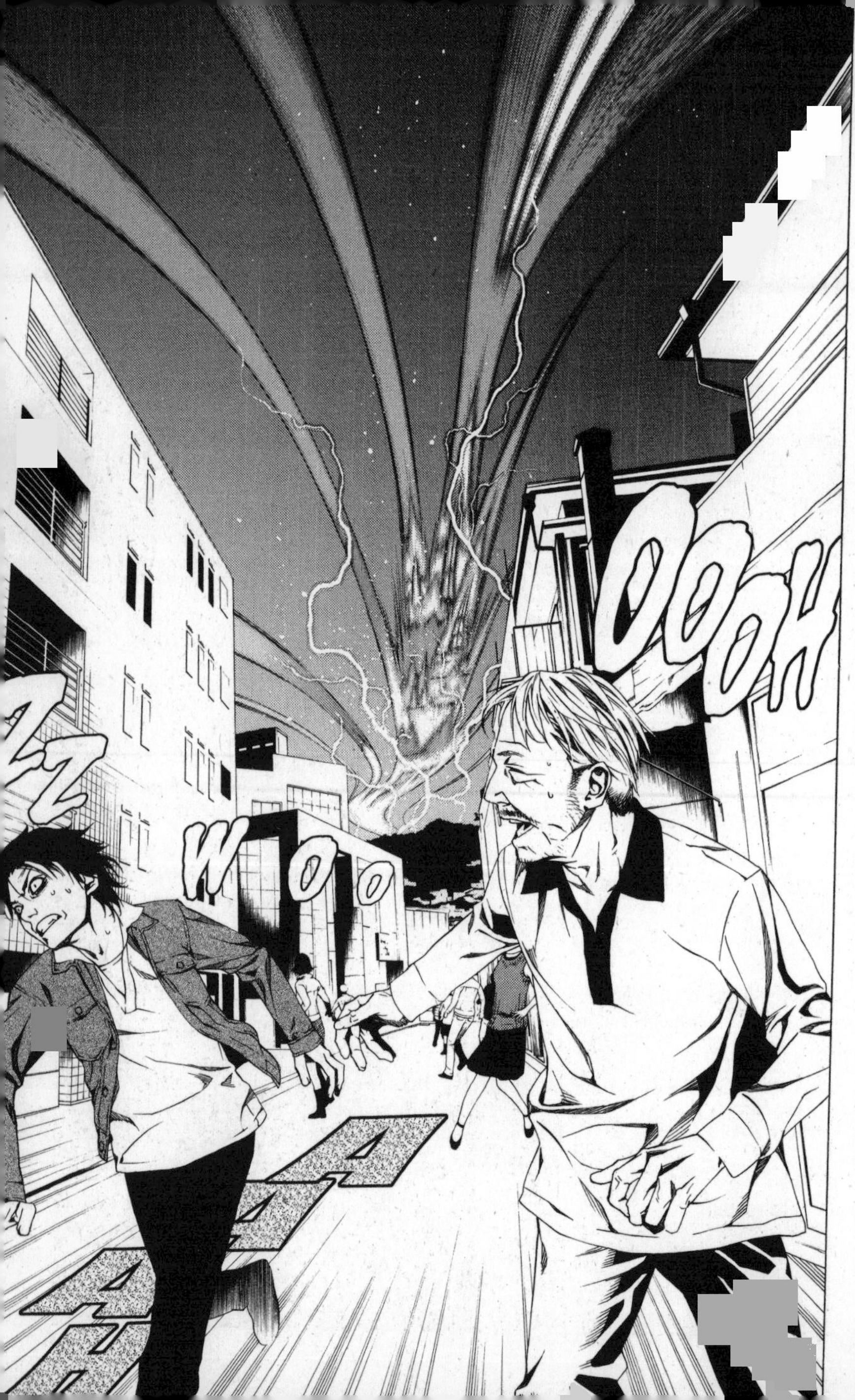
OOOH
WOOO

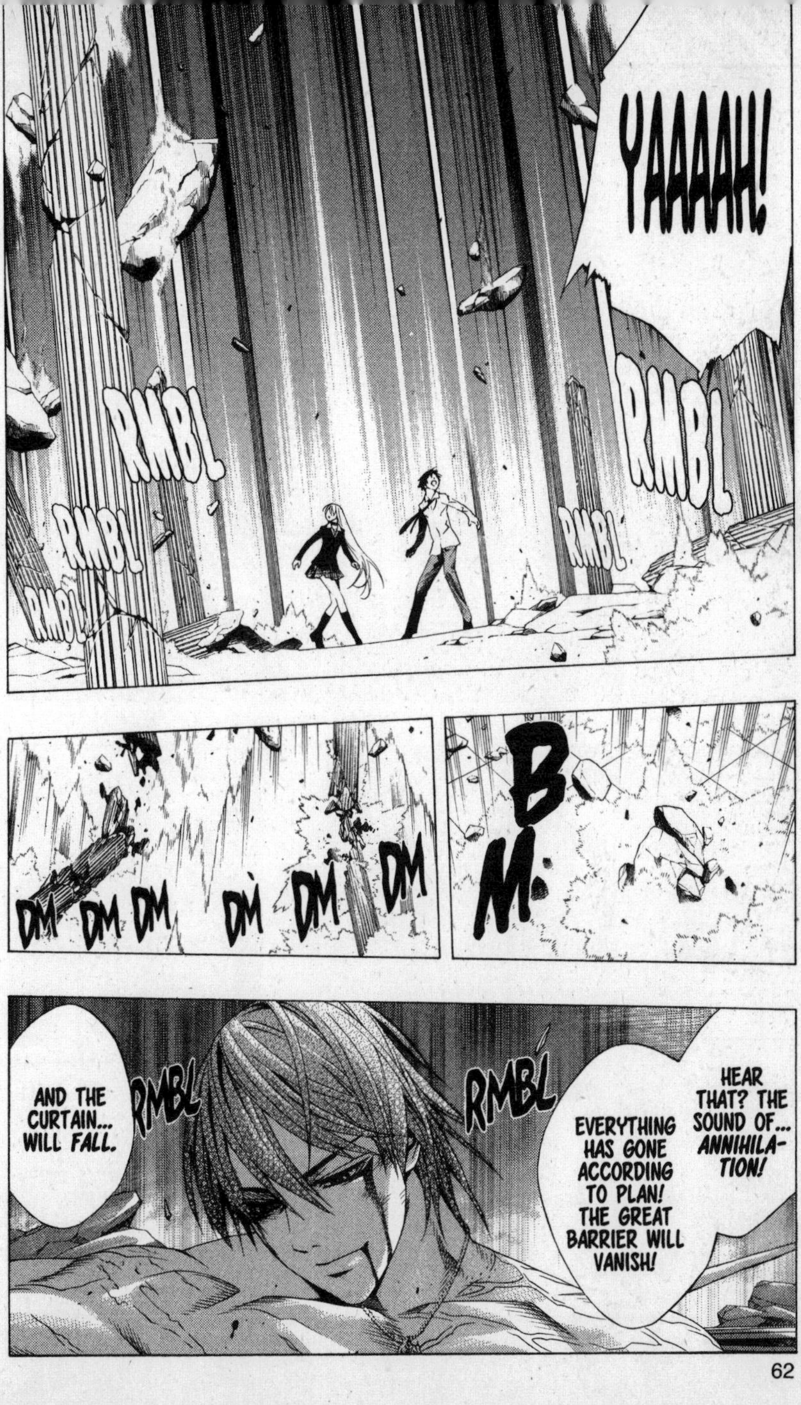
YAAAAH!
RMBL
RMBL
RMBL
RMBL
RMBL
BM
DM DM DM DM DM DM
HEAR THAT? THE SOUND OF... ANNIHILATION!
EVERYTHING HAS GONE ACCORDING TO PLAN! THE GREAT BARRIER WILL VANISH!
RMBL
RMBL
AND THE CURTAIN... WILL FALL.

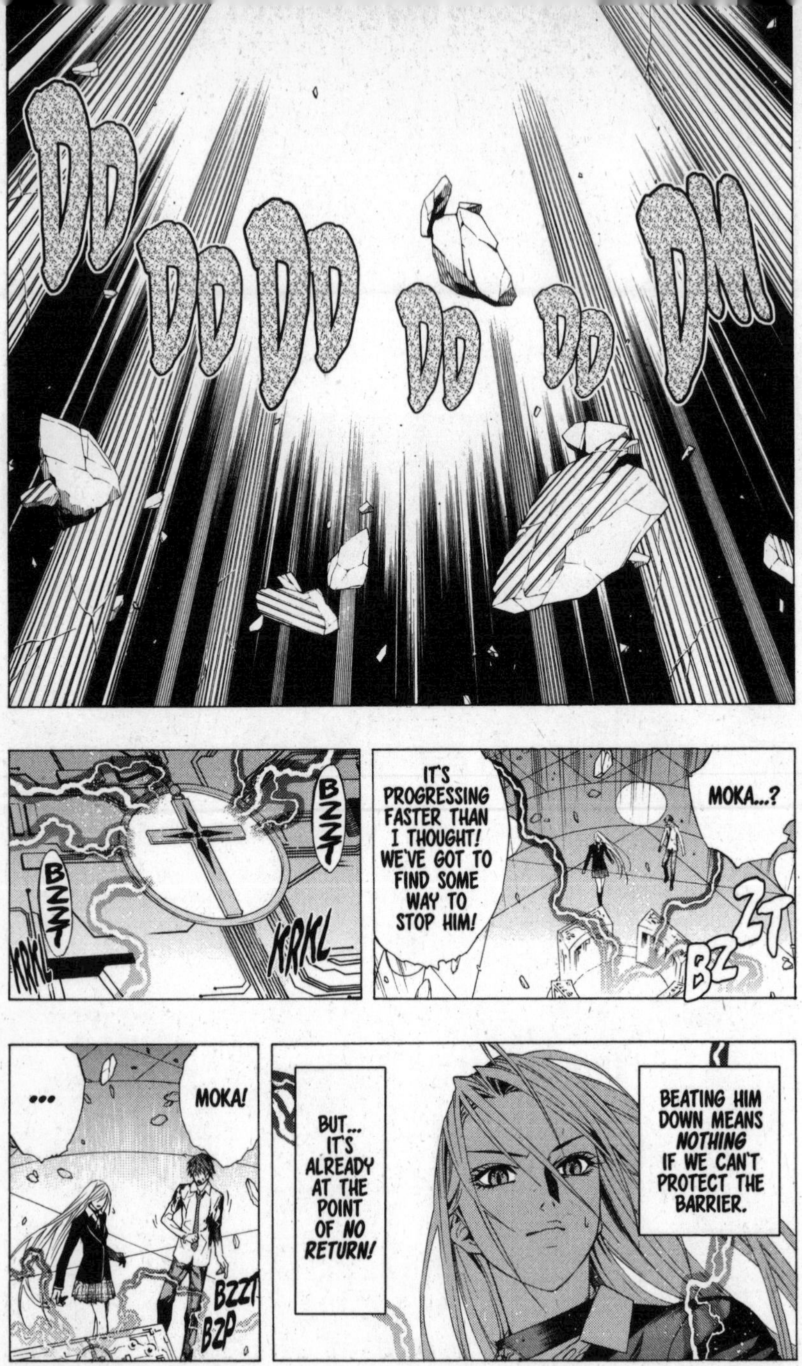
DD DD DD DD DD DD DM
MOKA...?
IT'S PROGRESSING FASTER THAN I THOUGHT! WE'VE GOT TO FIND SOME WAY TO STOP HIM!
BZZT
BZZT
KRKL
BZZT
KRKL
BEATING HIM DOWN MEANS *NOTHING* IF WE CAN'T PROTECT THE BARRIER.
BUT... IT'S ALREADY AT THE POINT OF *NO* RETURN!
MOKA!
...
BZZT
BZP

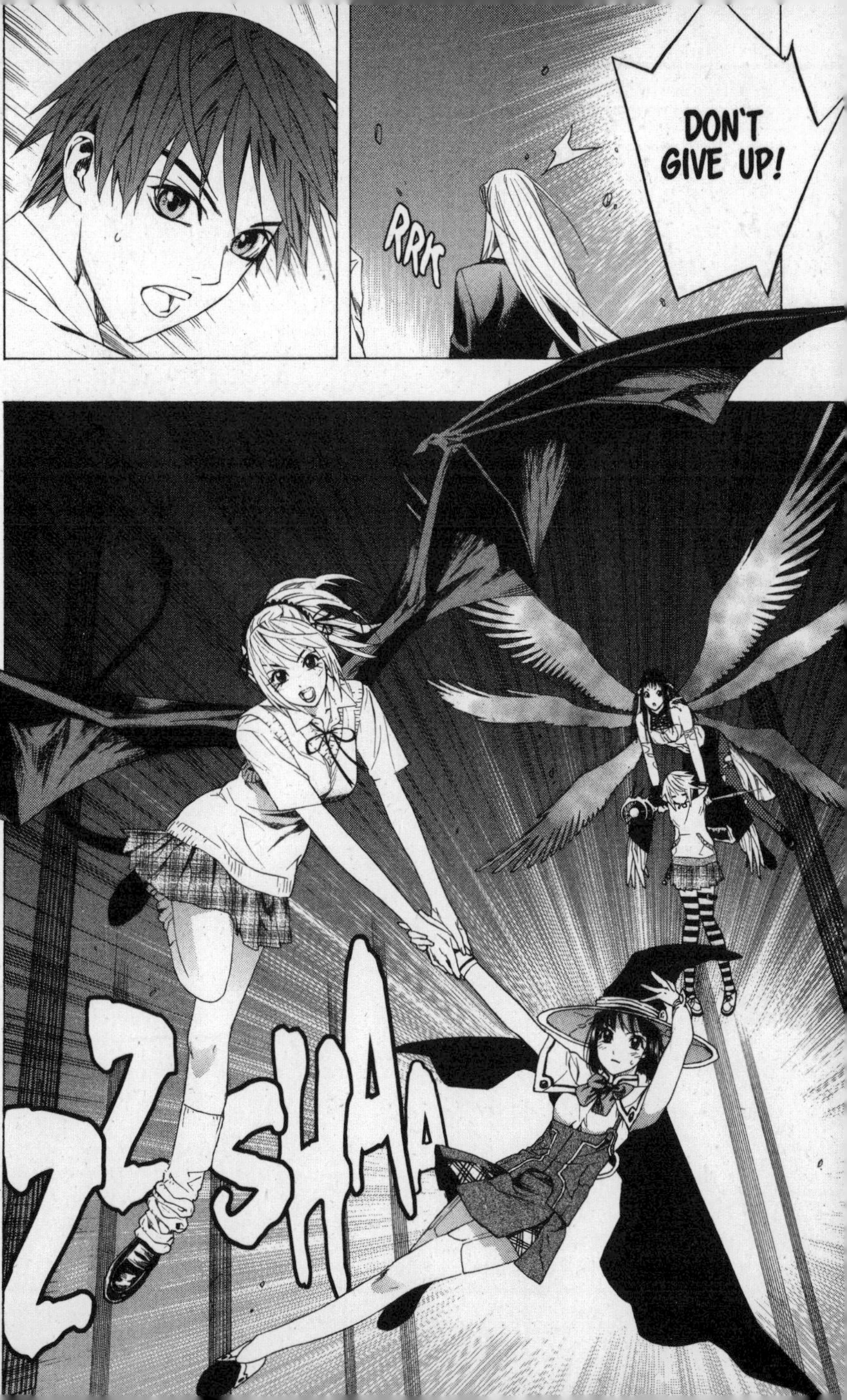
DON'T GIVE UP!
RRK
ZZSHAA

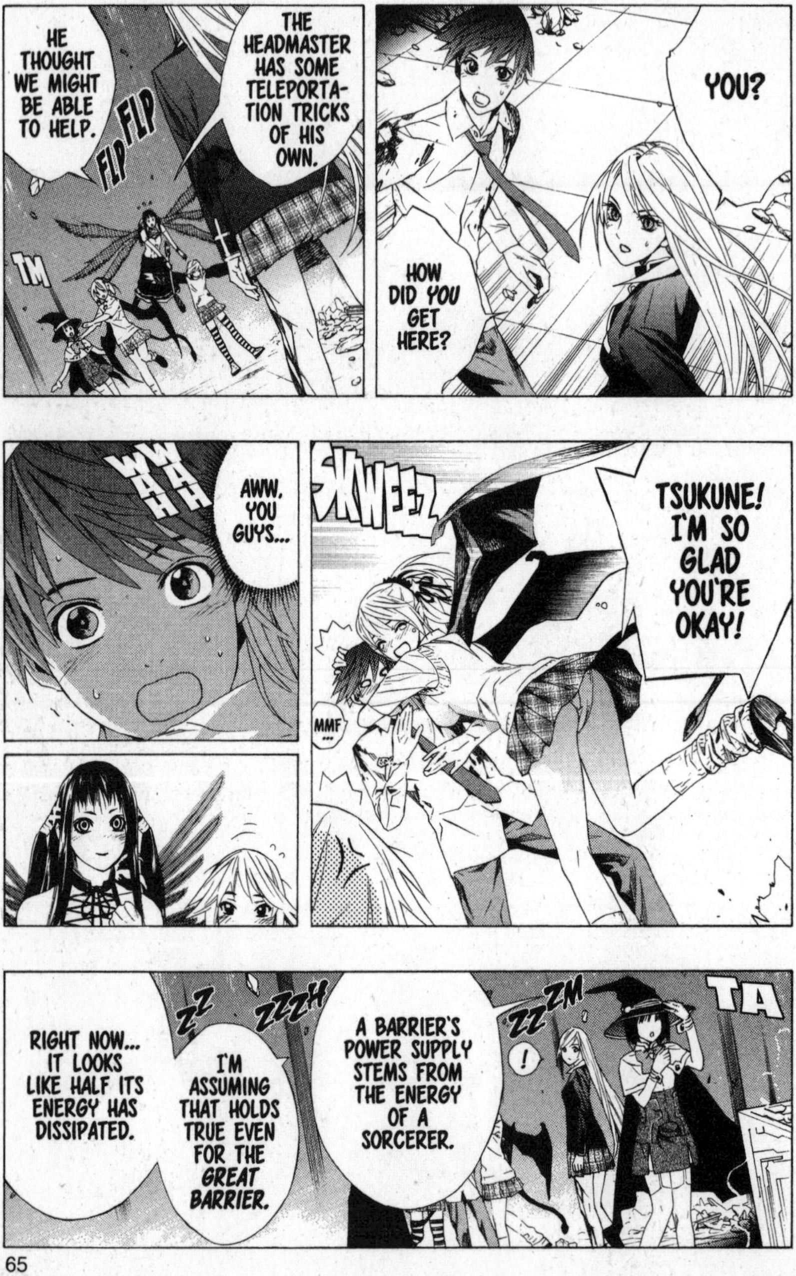
YOU?
HOW DID YOU GET HERE?
THE HEADMASTER HAS SOME TELEPORTA-TION TRICKS OF HIS OWN.
FLP FLP
HE THOUGHT WE MIGHT BE ABLE TO HELP.
TM
SKWEEZ
TSUKUNE! I'M SO GLAD YOU'RE OKAY!
MMF...
AWW, YOU GUYS...
WAH WAH
TA
ZZZM
!
A BARRIER'S POWER SUPPLY STEMS FROM THE ENERGY OF A SORCERER.
ZZZZH
ZZ
I'M ASSUMING THAT HOLDS TRUE EVEN FOR THE GREAT BARRIER.
RIGHT NOW... IT LOOKS LIKE HALF ITS ENERGY HAS DISSIPATED.

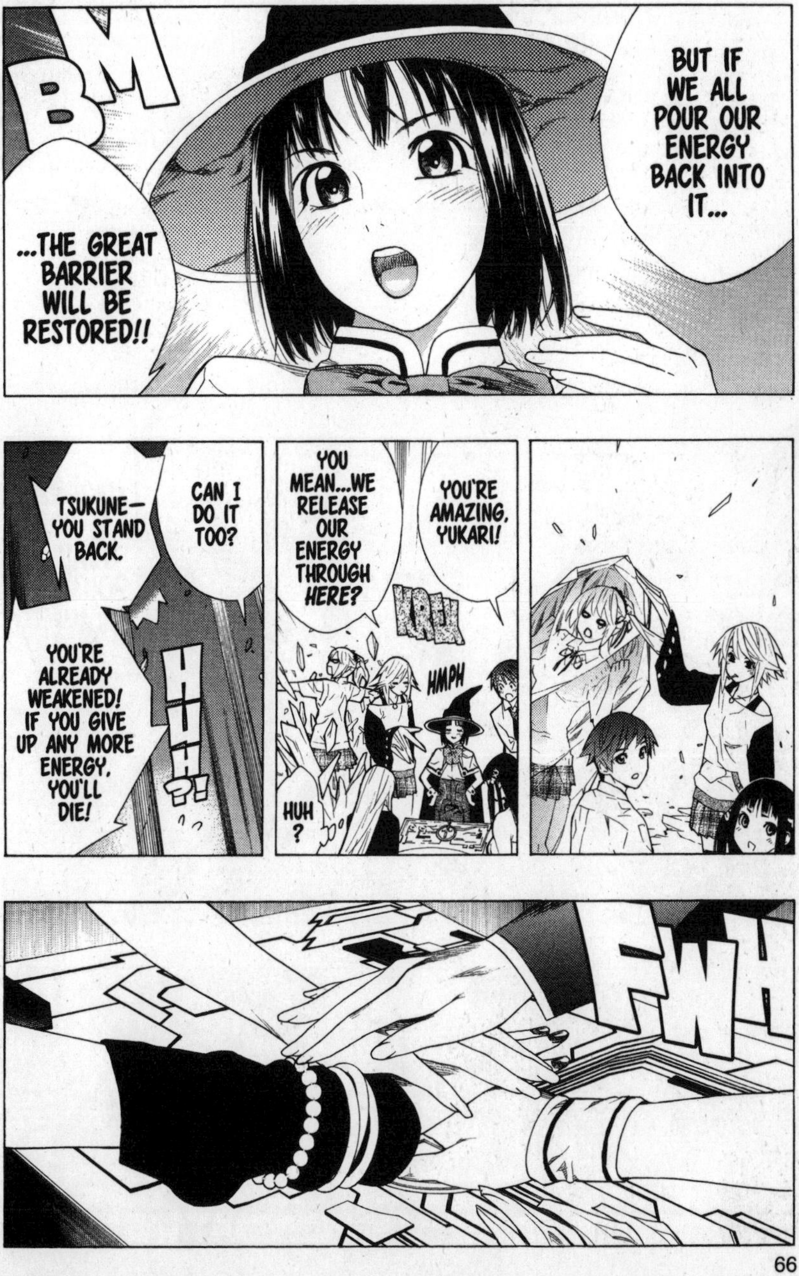
BUT IF WE ALL POUR OUR ENERGY BACK INTO IT...
BM
...THE GREAT BARRIER WILL BE RESTORED!!
YOU'RE AMAZING, YUKARI!
YOU MEAN...WE RELEASE OUR ENERGY THROUGH HERE?
HMPH
HUH?
CAN I DO IT TOO?
TSUKUNE— YOU STAND BACK.
HUH?!
YOU'RE ALREADY WEAKENED! IF YOU GIVE UP ANY MORE ENERGY, YOU'LL DIE!
FWH

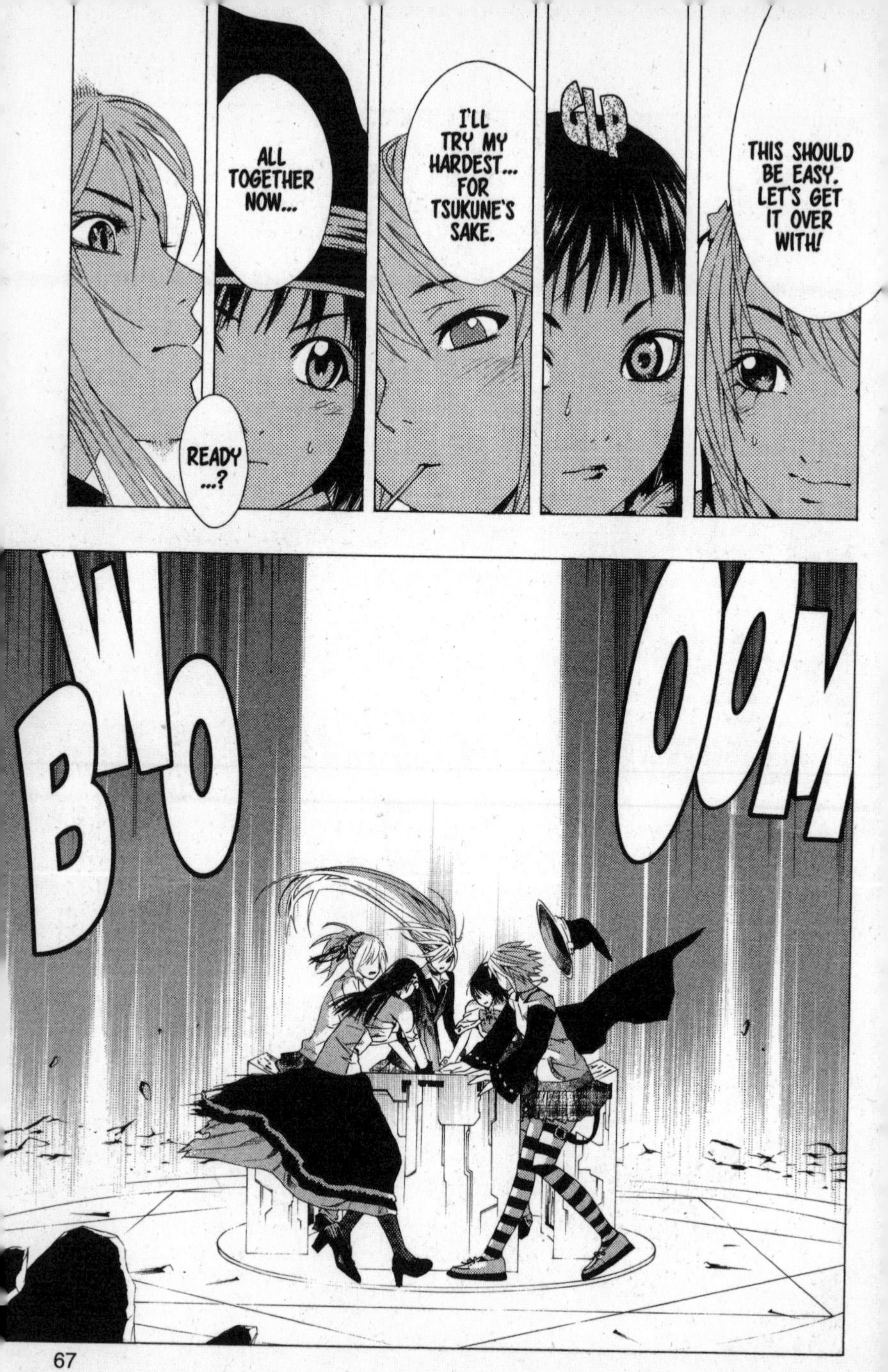
THIS SHOULD BE EASY. LET'S GET IT OVER WITH!
GLP
I'LL TRY MY HARDEST... FOR TSUKUNE'S SAKE.
ALL TOGETHER NOW...
READY ...?
BWOOOM

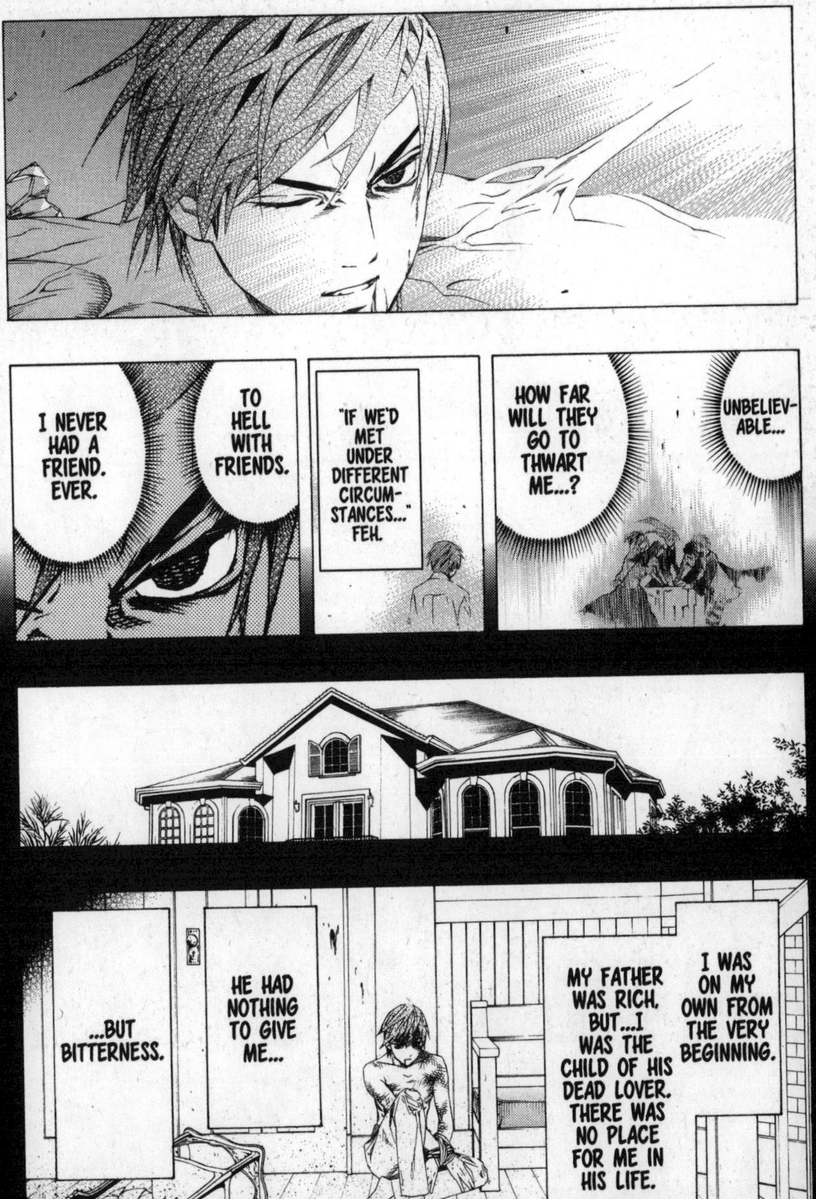
UNBELIEVABLE...
HOW FAR WILL THEY GO TO THWART ME...?
"IF WE'D MET UNDER DIFFERENT CIRCUMSTANCES..." FEH.
TO HELL WITH FRIENDS.
I NEVER HAD A FRIEND. EVER.
I WAS ON MY OWN FROM THE VERY BEGINNING.
MY FATHER WAS RICH, BUT...I WAS THE CHILD OF HIS DEAD LOVER. THERE WAS NO PLACE FOR ME IN HIS LIFE.
HE HAD NOTHING TO GIVE ME...
...BUT BITTERNESS.

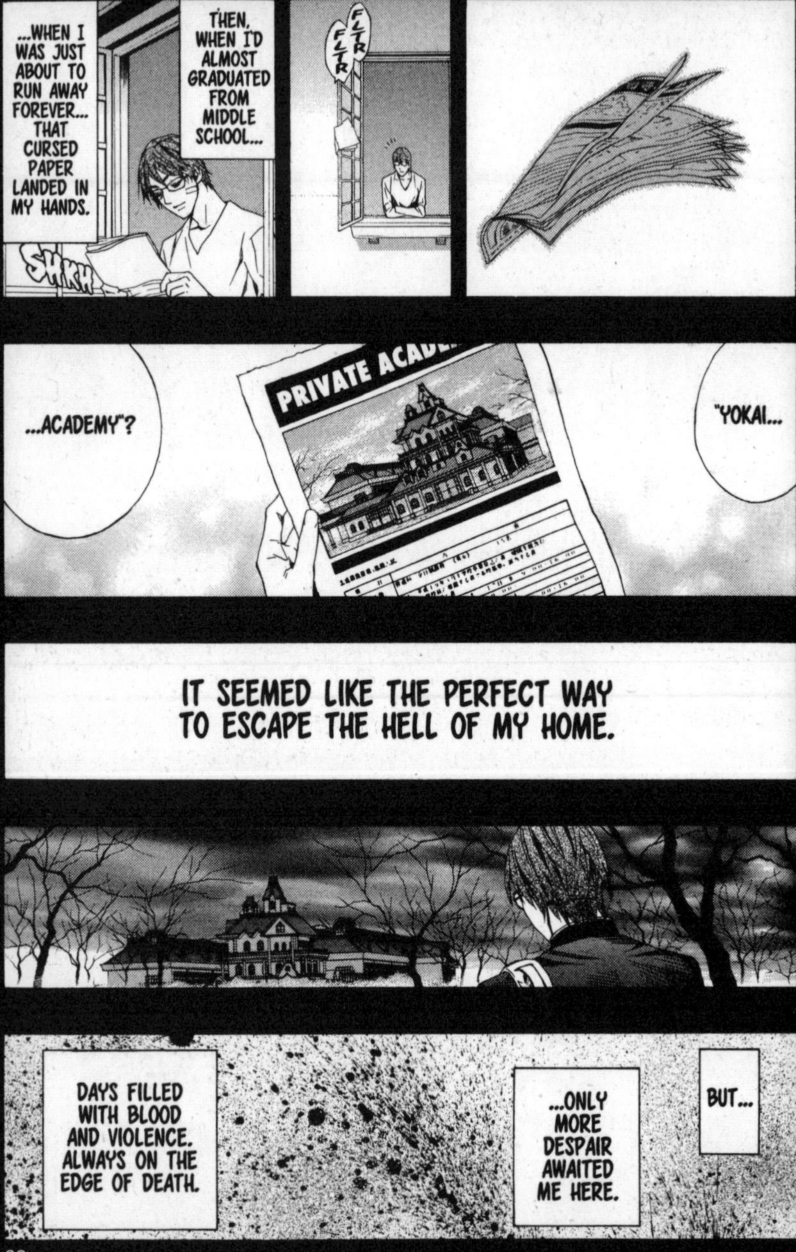
FLTR
FLTR
THEN, WHEN I'D ALMOST GRADUATED FROM MIDDLE SCHOOL...
...WHEN I WAS JUST ABOUT TO RUN AWAY FOREVER... THAT CURSED PAPER LANDED IN MY HANDS.
SHKH
"YOKAI...
PRIVATE ACADE
...ACADEMY"?
IT SEEMED LIKE THE PERFECT WAY TO ESCAPE THE HELL OF MY HOME.
BUT...
...ONLY MORE DESPAIR AWAITED ME HERE.
DAYS FILLED WITH BLOOD AND VIOLENCE. ALWAYS ON THE EDGE OF DEATH.

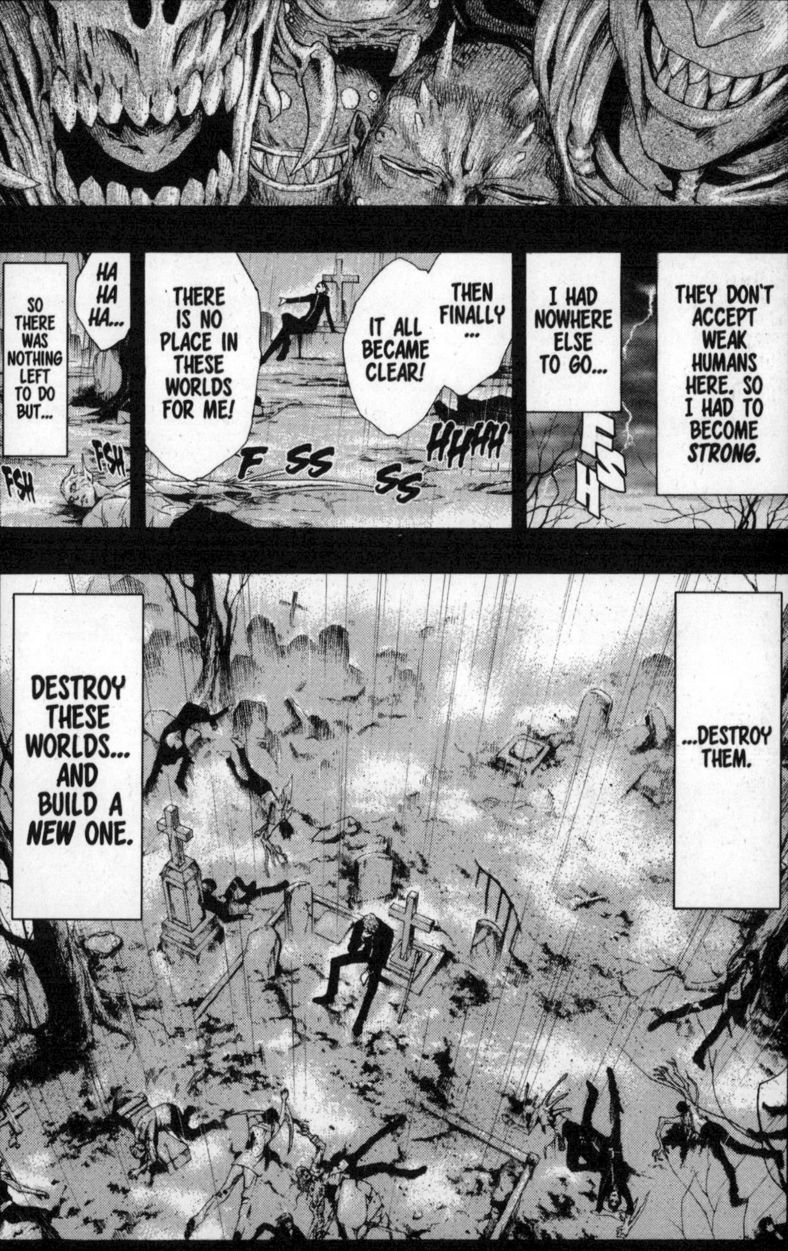
THEY DON'T ACCEPT WEAK HUMANS HERE. SO I HAD TO BECOME STRONG.
I HAD NOWHERE ELSE TO GO...
FSH H
THEN FINALLY...
IT ALL BECAME CLEAR!
HHHH
SS
F SS
THERE IS NO PLACE IN THESE WORLDS FOR ME!
HA HA HA...
SO THERE WAS NOTHING LEFT TO DO BUT...
FSH
FSH
...DESTROY THEM.
DESTROY THESE WORLDS... AND BUILD A NEW ONE.

READ THIS WAY

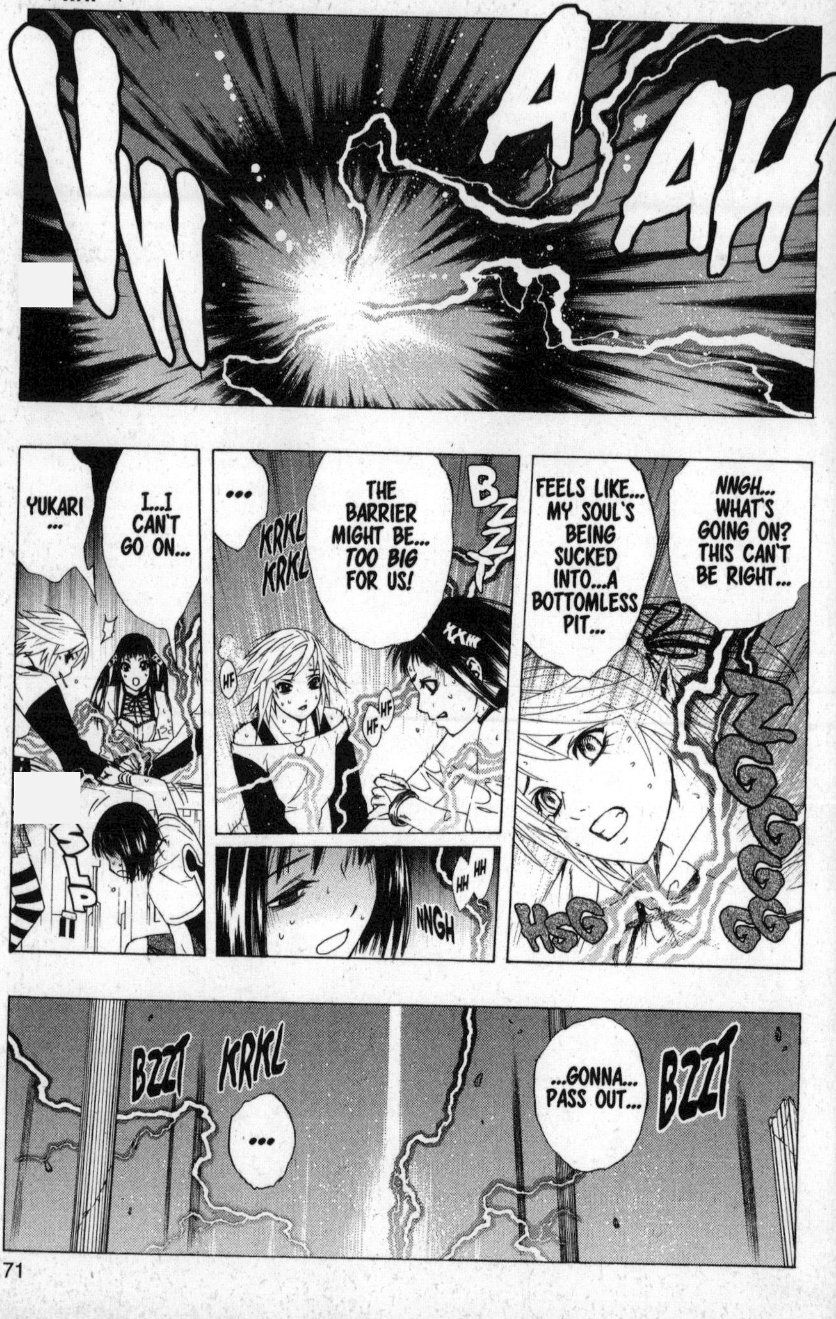
A
AH
VN
NNGH... WHAT'S GOING ON? THIS CAN'T BE RIGHT...
FEELS LIKE... MY SOUL'S BEING SUCKED INTO...A BOTTOMLESS PIT...
NNGGGGG
HSG
BZZT
THE BARRIER MIGHT BE... TOO BIG FOR US!
KRKL KRKL
...
HF
HF
HF
HH
HH
NNGH
I...I CAN'T GO ON...
YUKARI ...
SLIP
BZZT
...GONNA... PASS OUT...
...
KRKL
BZZT

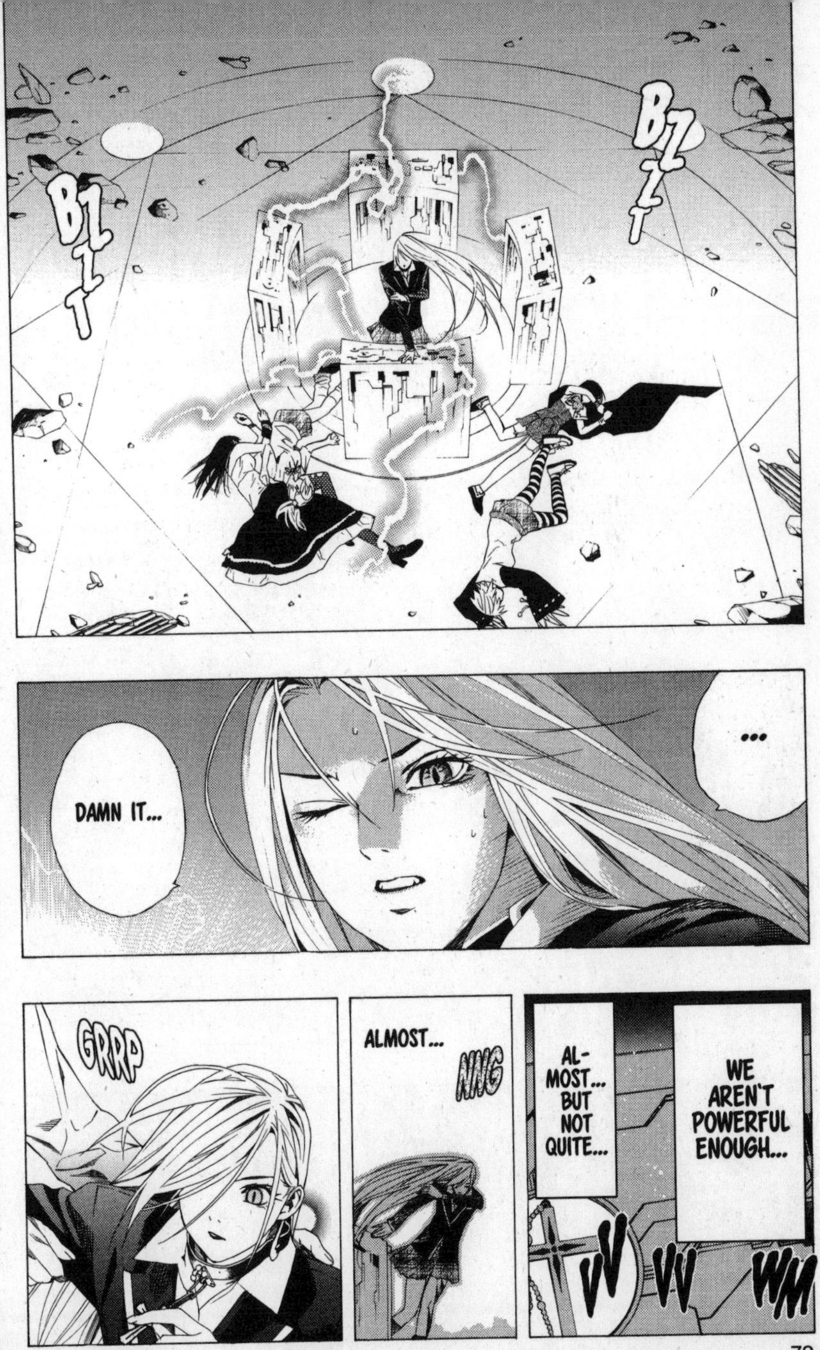
BZZZT
BZZZT
...
DAMN IT...
WE AREN'T POWERFUL ENOUGH...
AL-MOST... BUT NOT QUITE...
VV
VV
WM
ALMOST...
NNG
GRRP

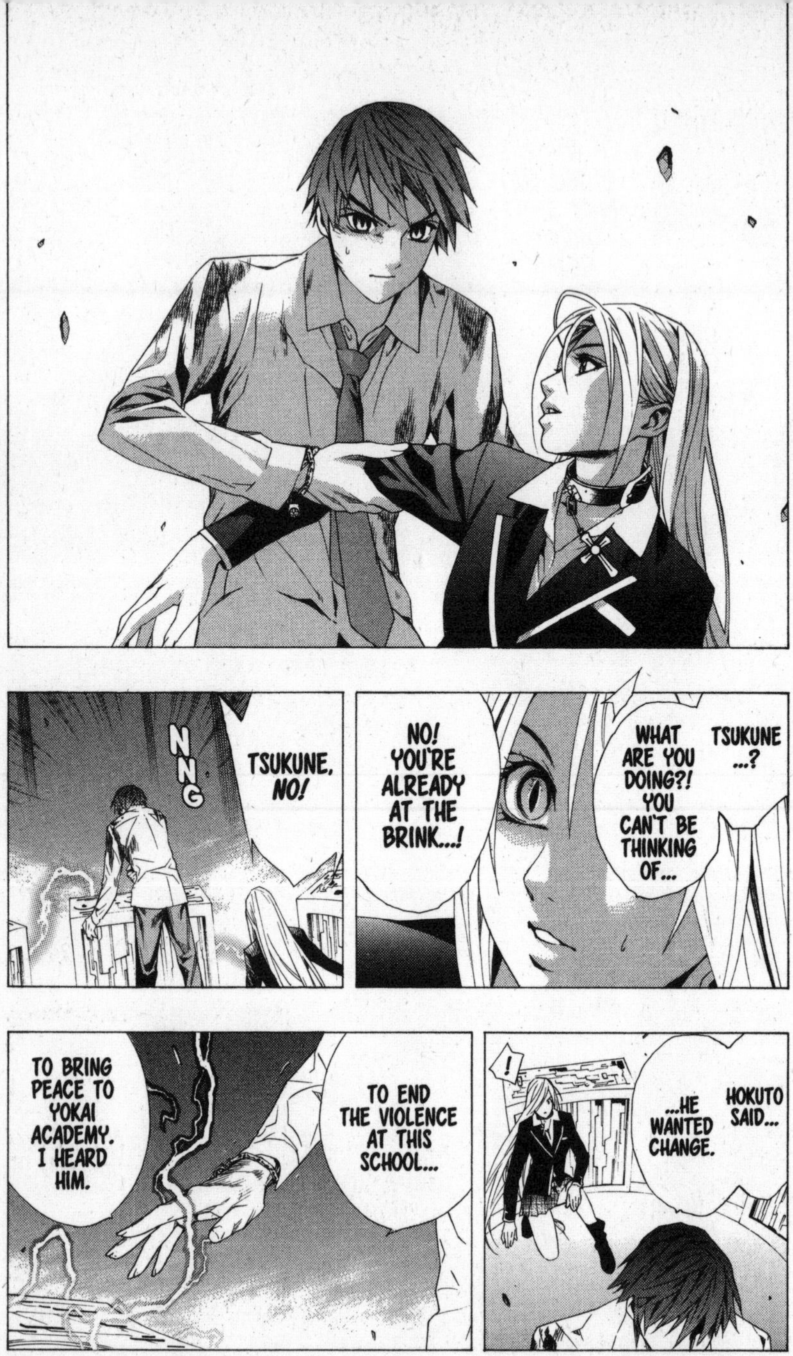
TSUKUNE ...?
WHAT ARE YOU DOING?! YOU CAN'T BE THINKING OF...
NO! YOU'RE ALREADY AT THE BRINK...!
TSUKUNE, NO!
NNG
HOKUTO SAID...
...HE WANTED CHANGE.
!
TO END THE VIOLENCE AT THIS SCHOOL...
TO BRING PEACE TO YOKAI ACADEMY. I HEARD HIM.

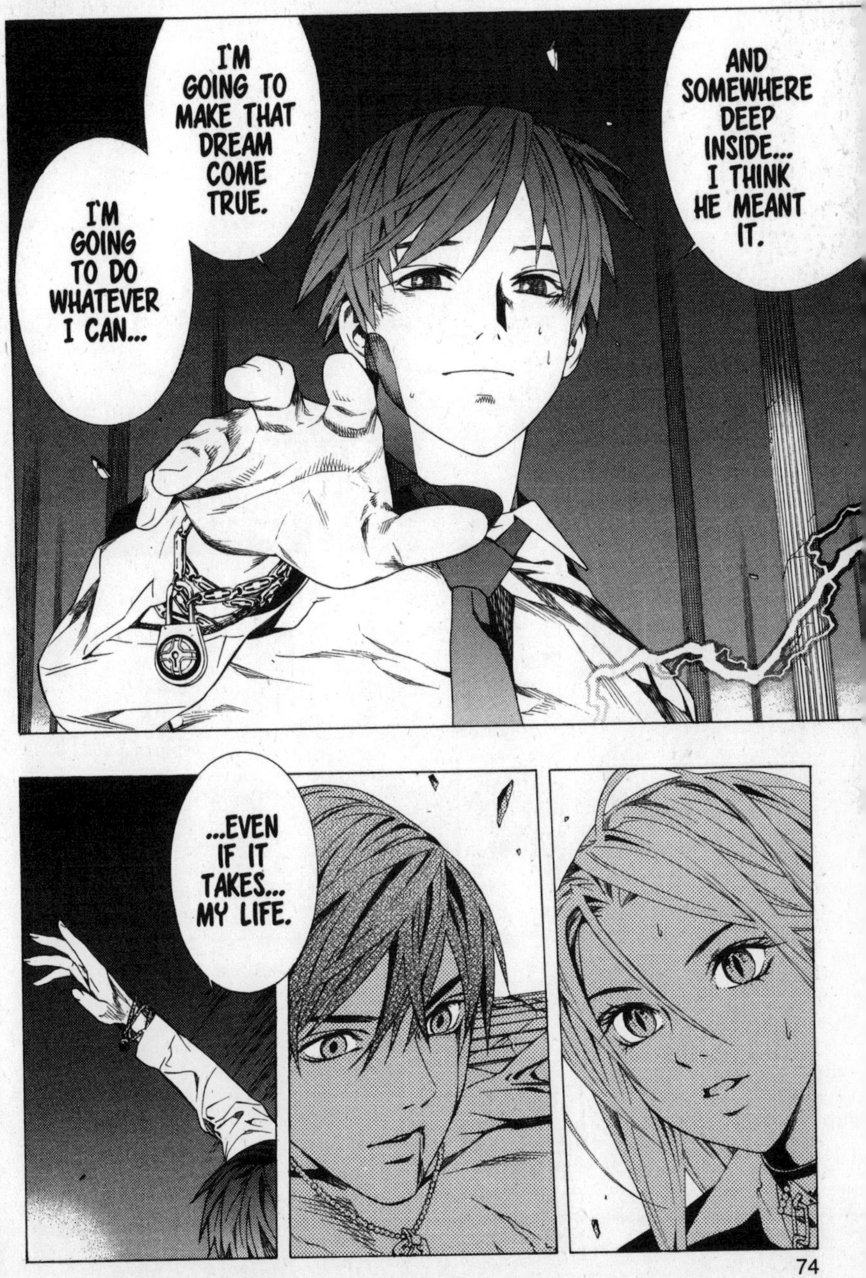
AND SOMEWHERE DEEP INSIDE... I THINK HE MEANT IT.
I'M GOING TO MAKE THAT DREAM COME TRUE.
I'M GOING TO DO WHATEVER I CAN...
...EVEN IF IT TAKES... MY LIFE.

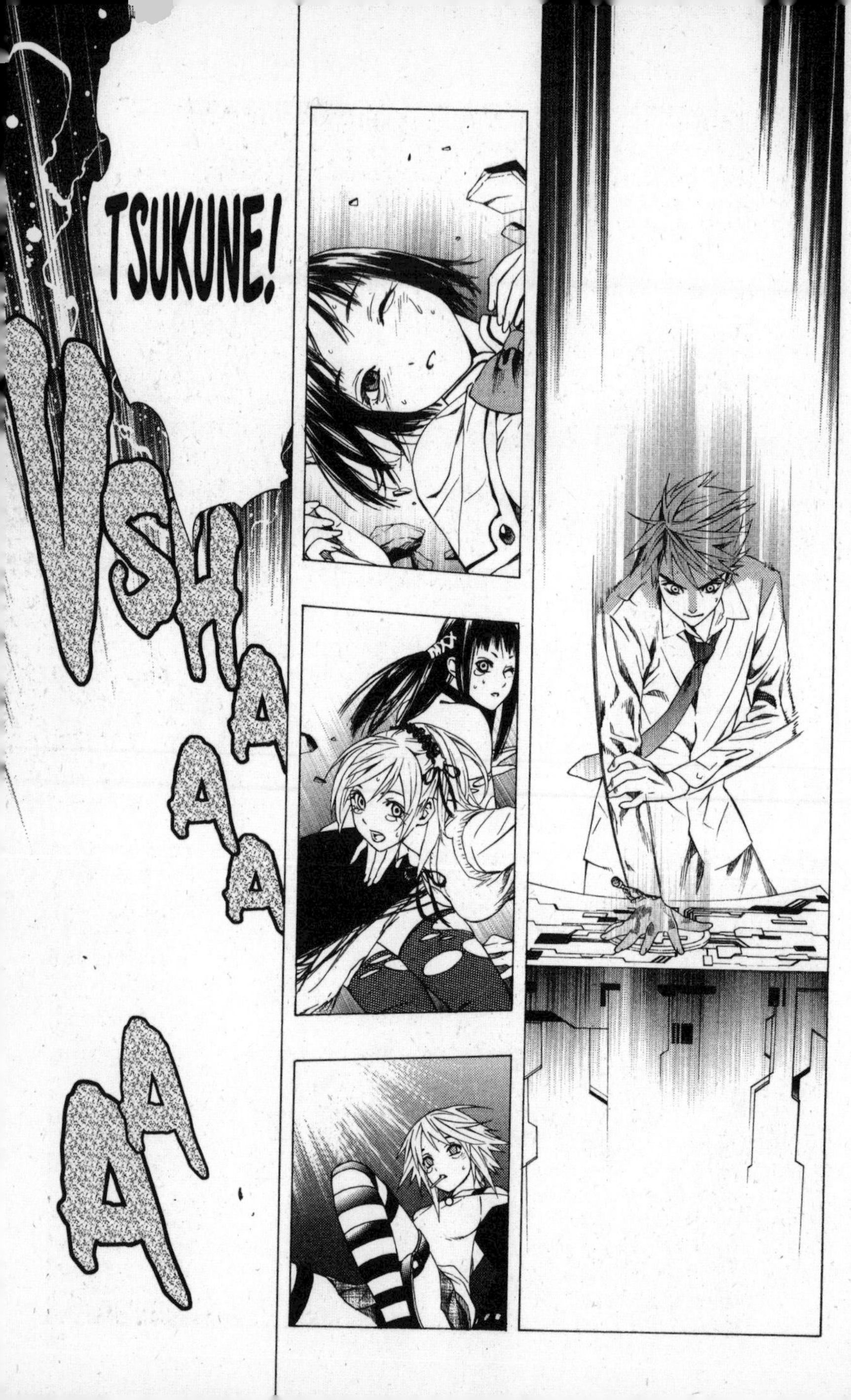
TSUKUNE!
VSHAAAAA

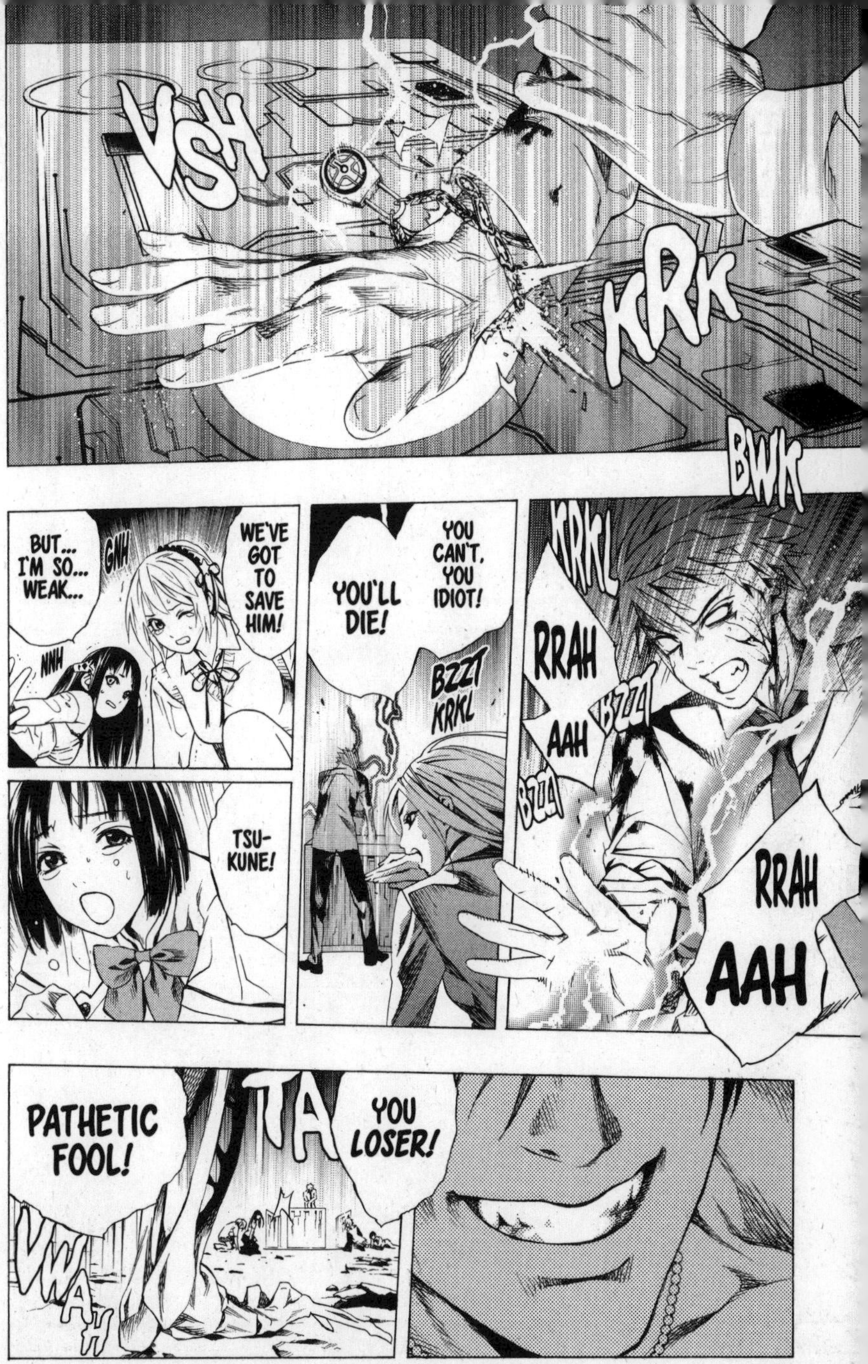
KRK
VSH
BWK
KRKL
RRAH
AAH
BZZT
BZZT
RRAH AAH
YOU CAN'T, YOU IDIOT!
YOU'LL DIE!
BZZT KRKL
WE'VE GOT TO SAVE HIM!
GNH
BUT... I'M SO... WEAK...
NNH
TSU-KUNE!
YOU LOSER!
TA
PATHETIC FOOL!
VWAH

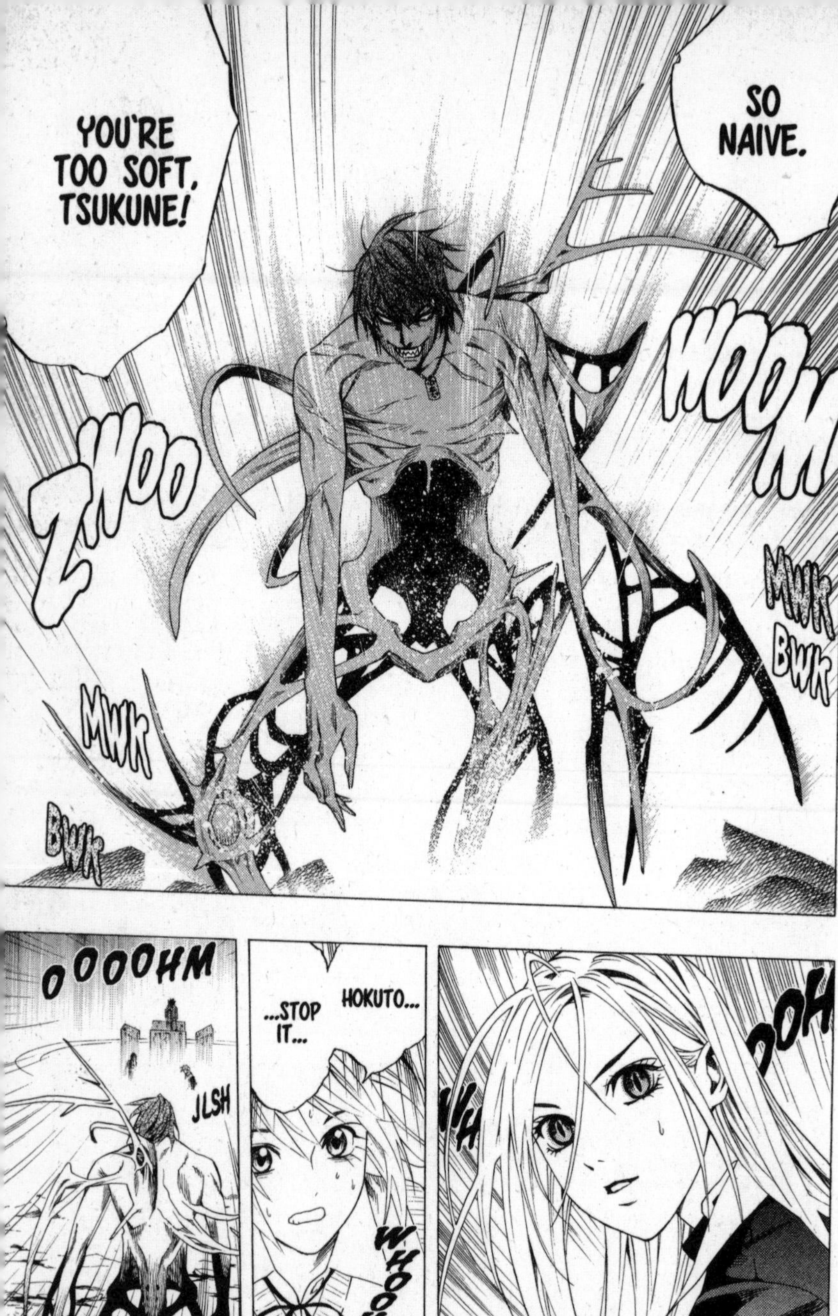
SO NAIVE.
YOU'RE TOO SOFT, TSUKUNE!
WHOOM
ZWOO
MWR BWR
MWR
BWR
DOH
HOKUTO...
...STOP IT...
WHOOOH
OOOOHM
JLSH

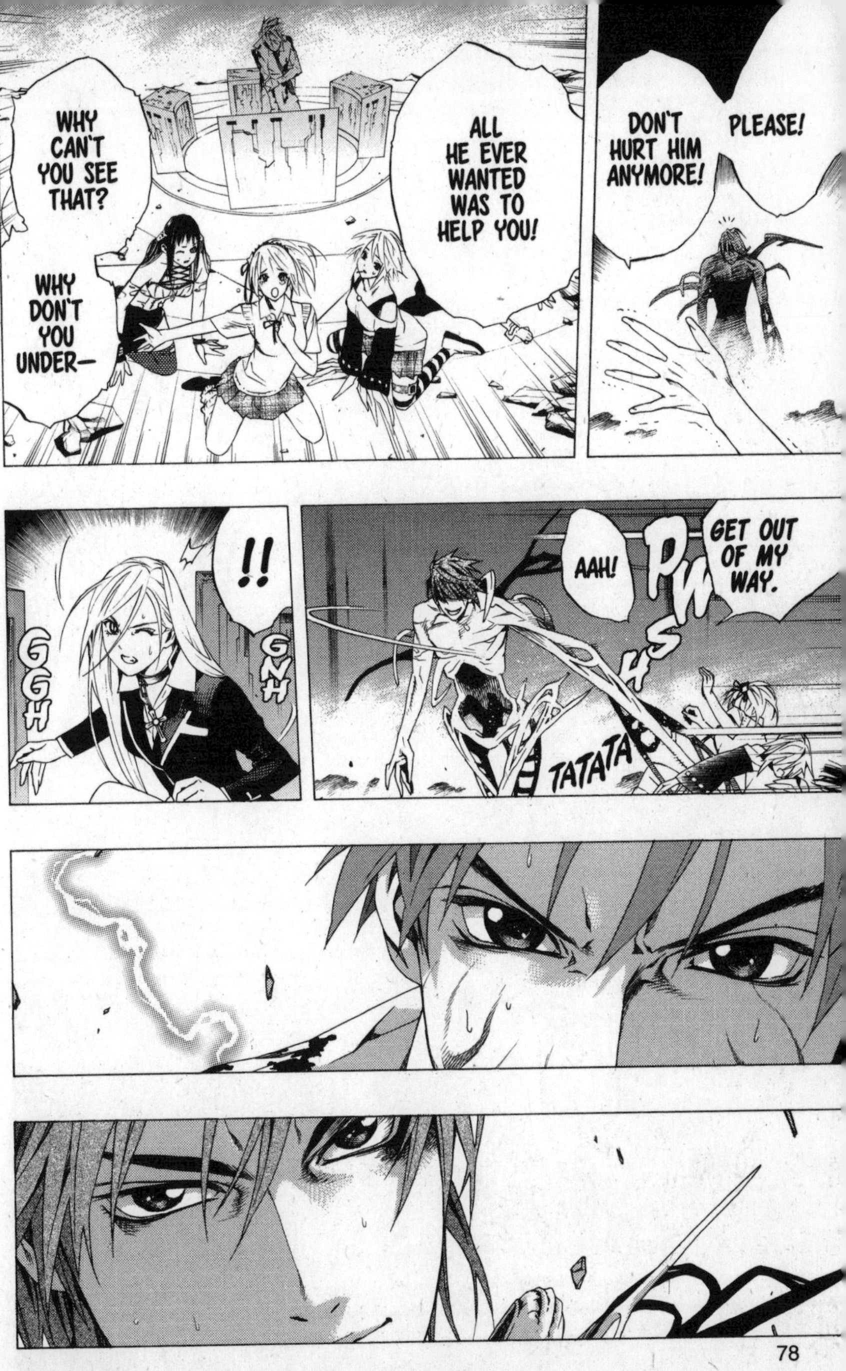
PLEASE!
DON'T HURT HIM ANYMORE!
ALL HE EVER WANTED WAS TO HELP YOU!
WHY CAN'T YOU SEE THAT?
WHY DON'T YOU UNDER—
GET OUT OF MY WAY.
PWSH
AAH!
TATATA
!!
GNH
GGH

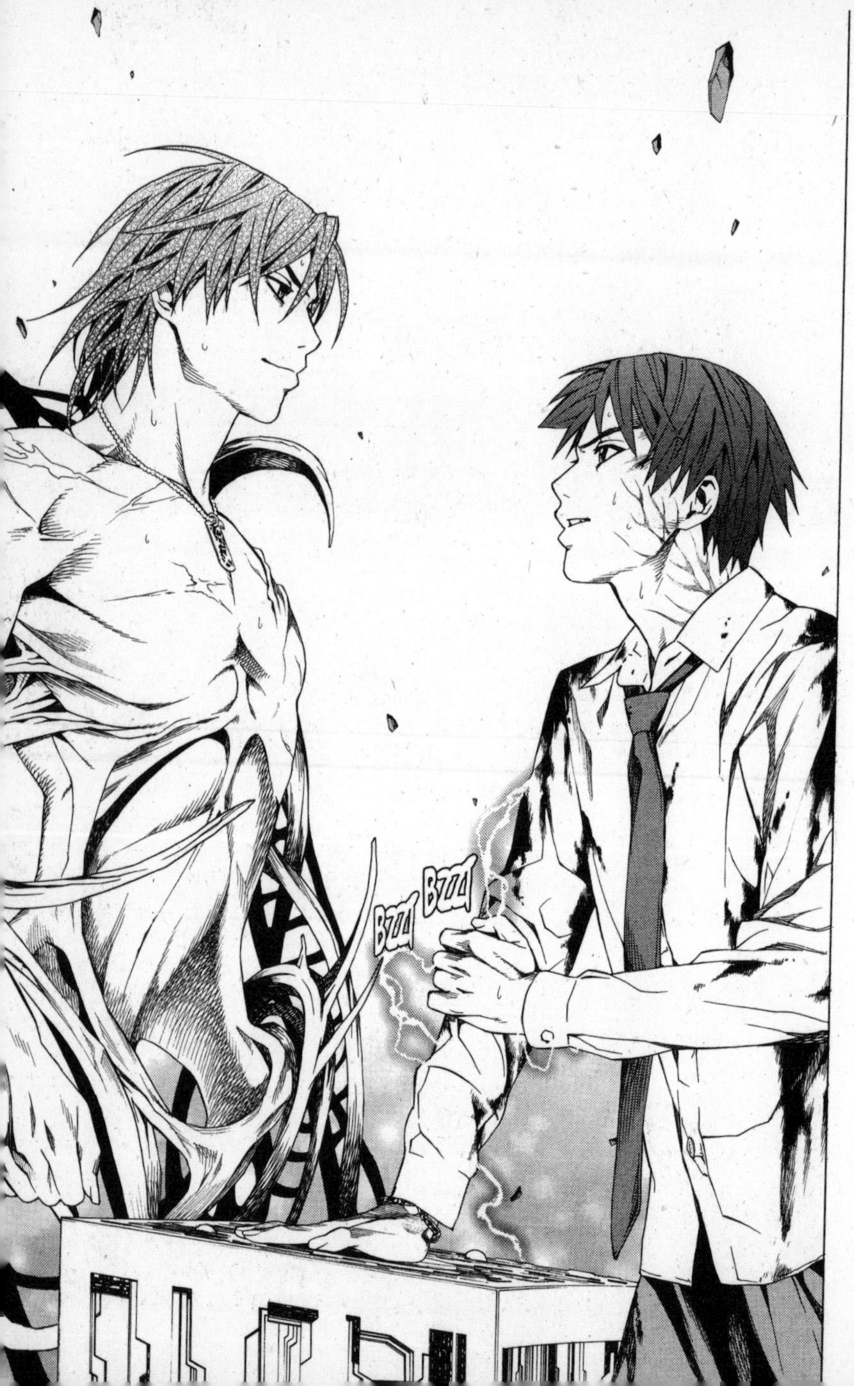
BZZT
BZZT

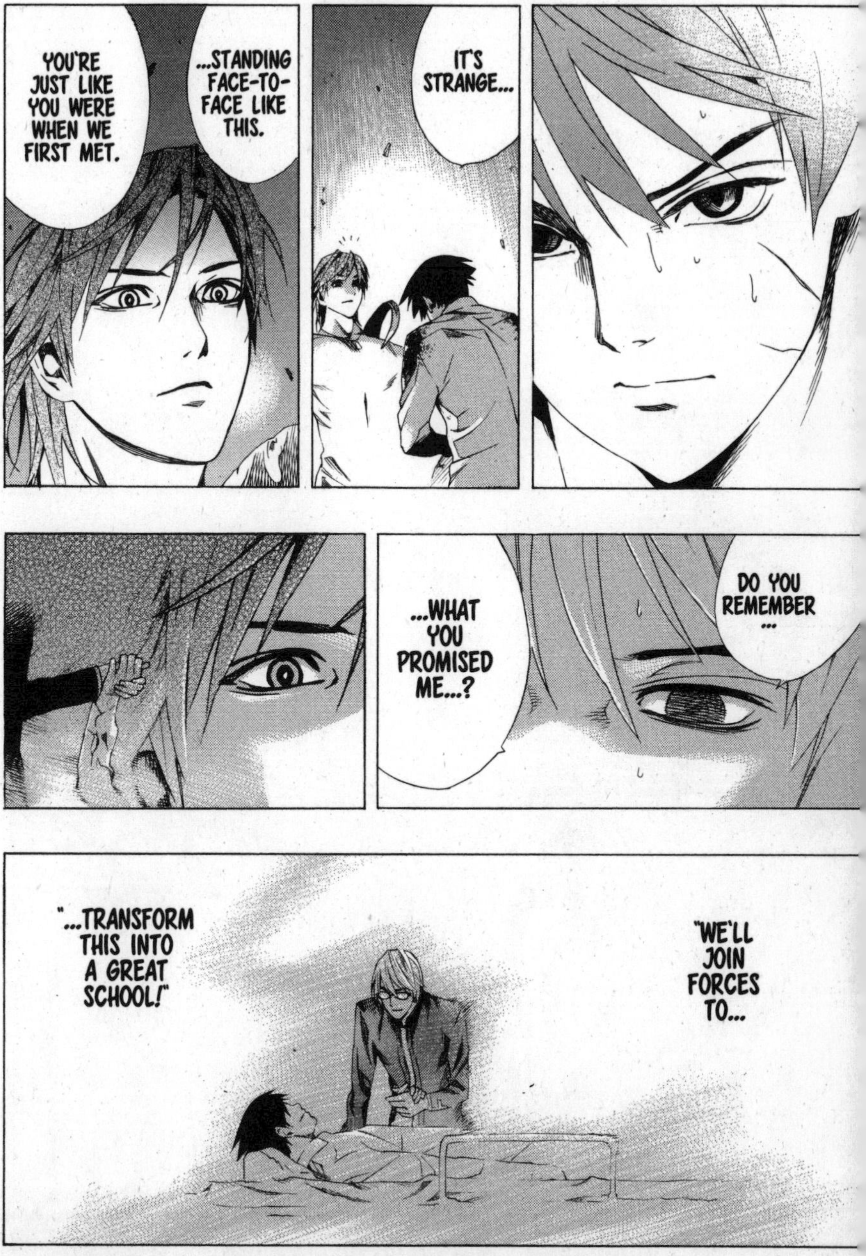
IT'S STRANGE...
...STANDING FACE-TO-FACE LIKE THIS.
YOU'RE JUST LIKE YOU WERE WHEN WE FIRST MET.
DO YOU REMEMBER...
...WHAT YOU PROMISED ME...?
"WE'LL JOIN FORCES TO...
...TRANSFORM THIS INTO A GREAT SCHOOL!"

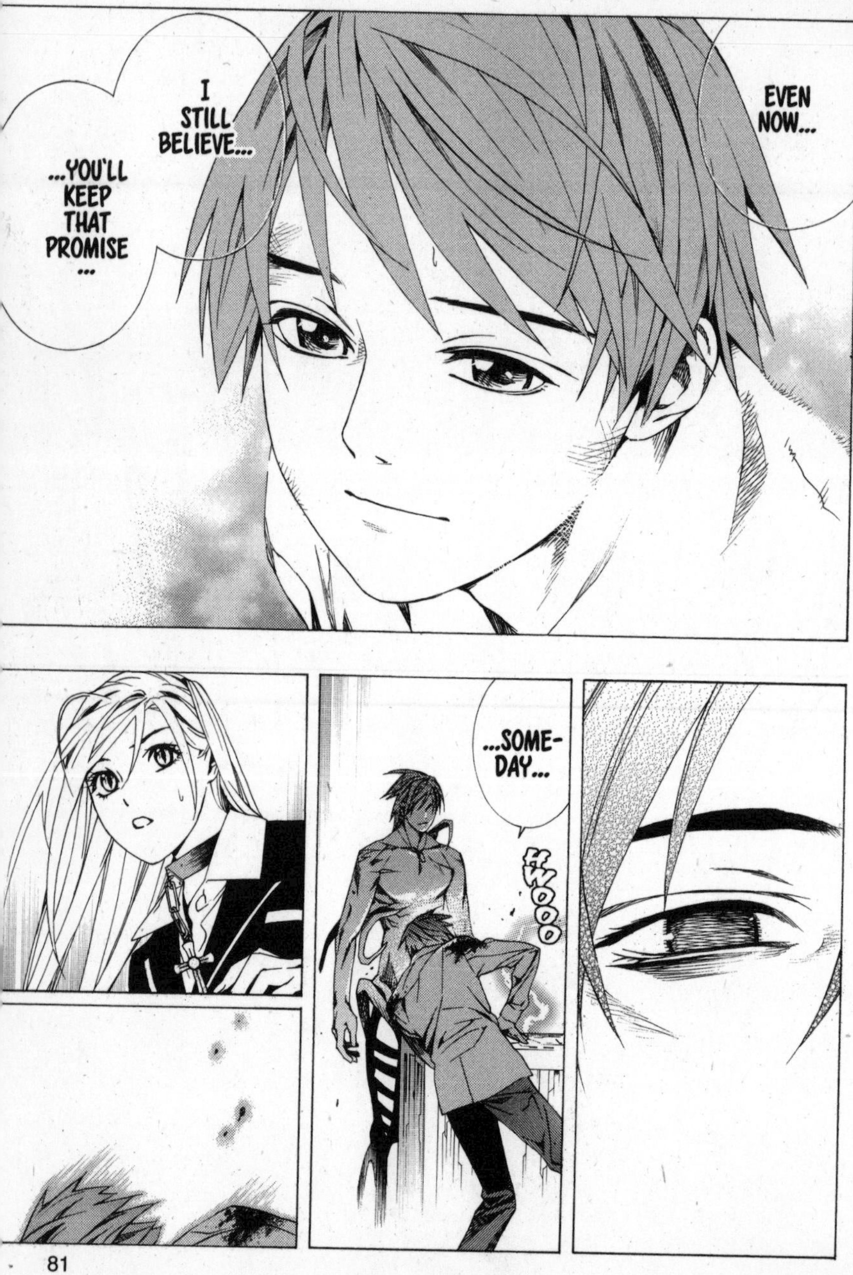
EVEN NOW...
I STILL BELIEVE...
...YOU'LL KEEP THAT PROMISE ...
...SOME-DAY...
HWOOO

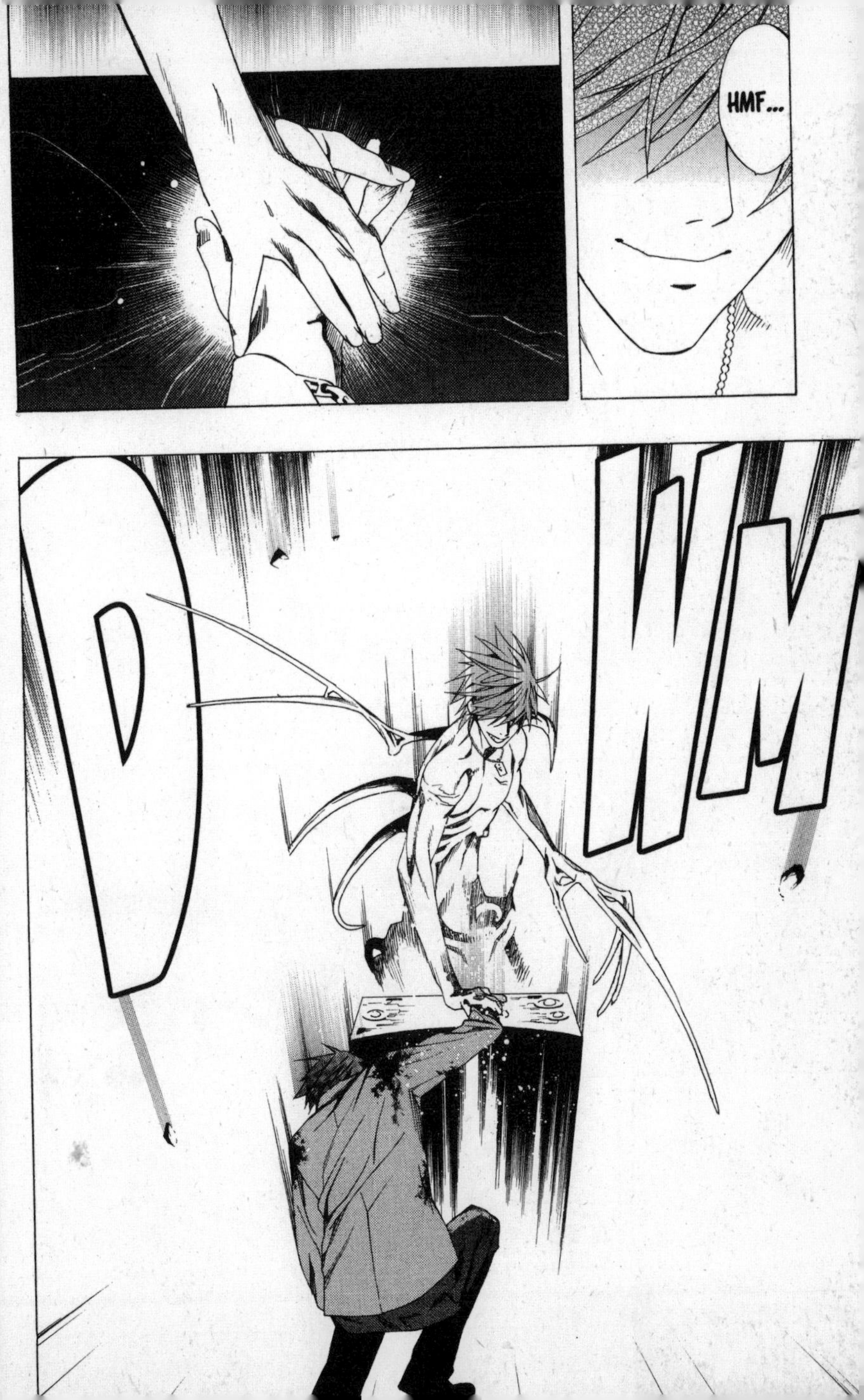
HMF...
D
WM

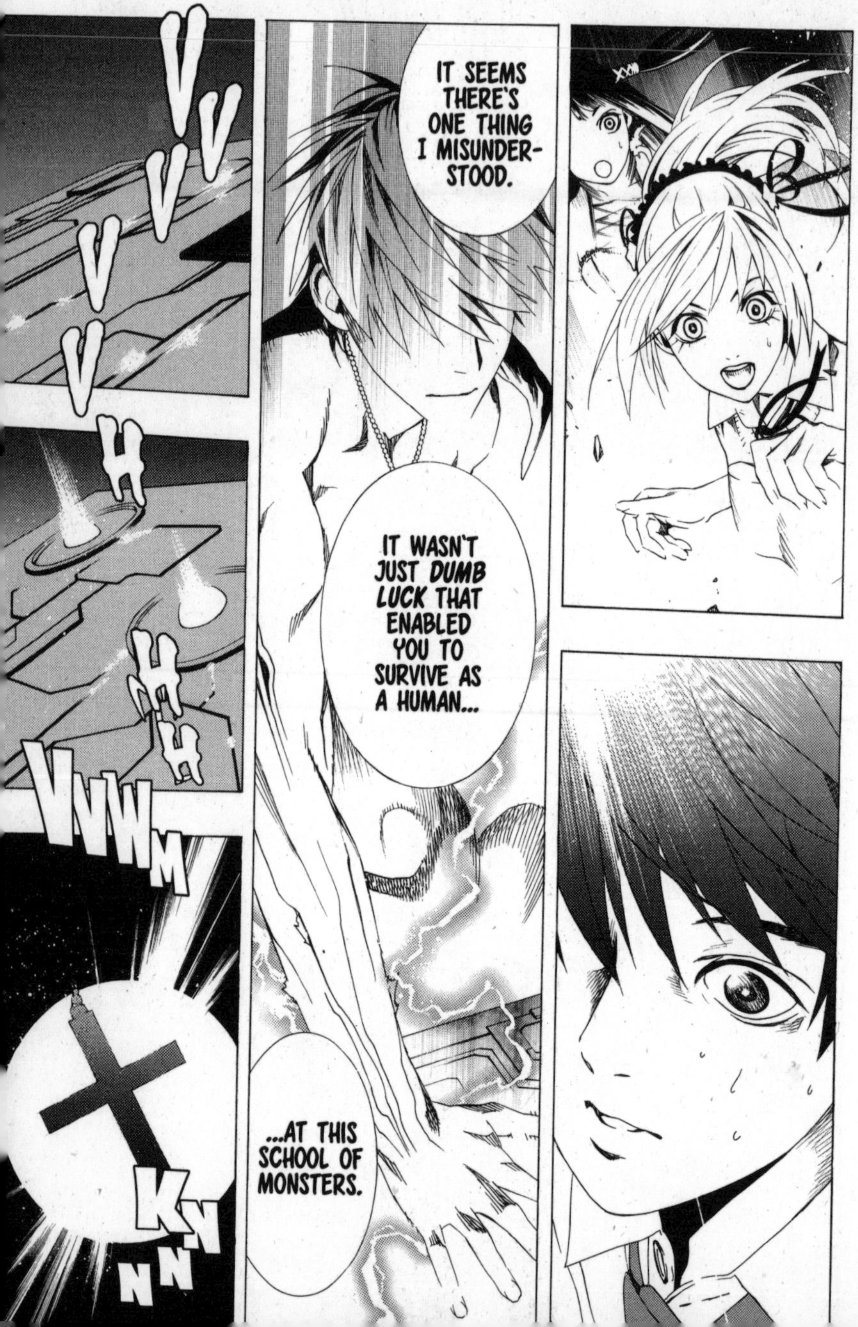
IT SEEMS THERE'S ONE THING I MISUNDER-STOOD.
IT WASN'T JUST *DUMB LUCK* THAT ENABLED YOU TO SURVIVE AS A HUMAN...
...AT THIS SCHOOL OF MONSTERS.
VVVVVHHHH
VVWM
KNNNN

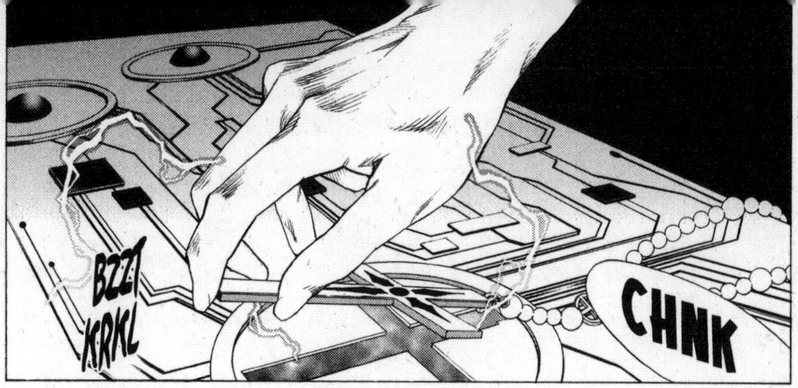
CHNK
BZZT KRKL

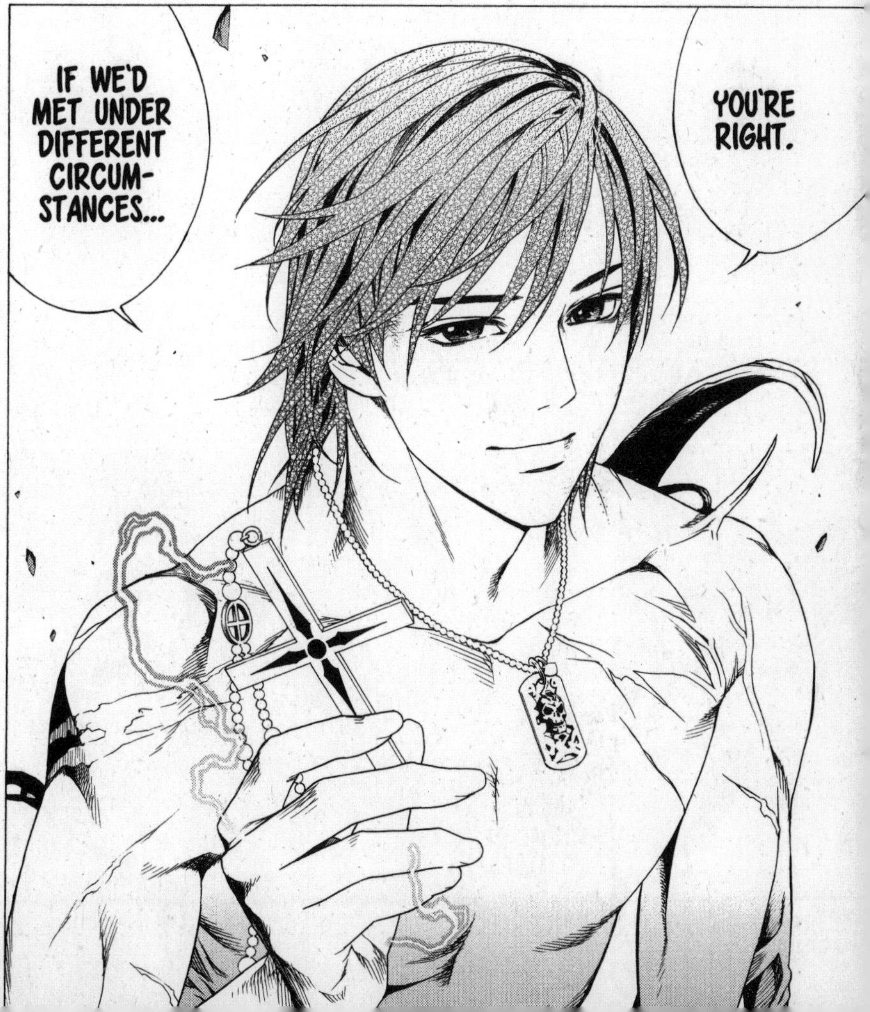
YOU'RE RIGHT.
IF WE'D MET UNDER DIFFERENT CIRCUM-STANCES...

READ THIS WAY

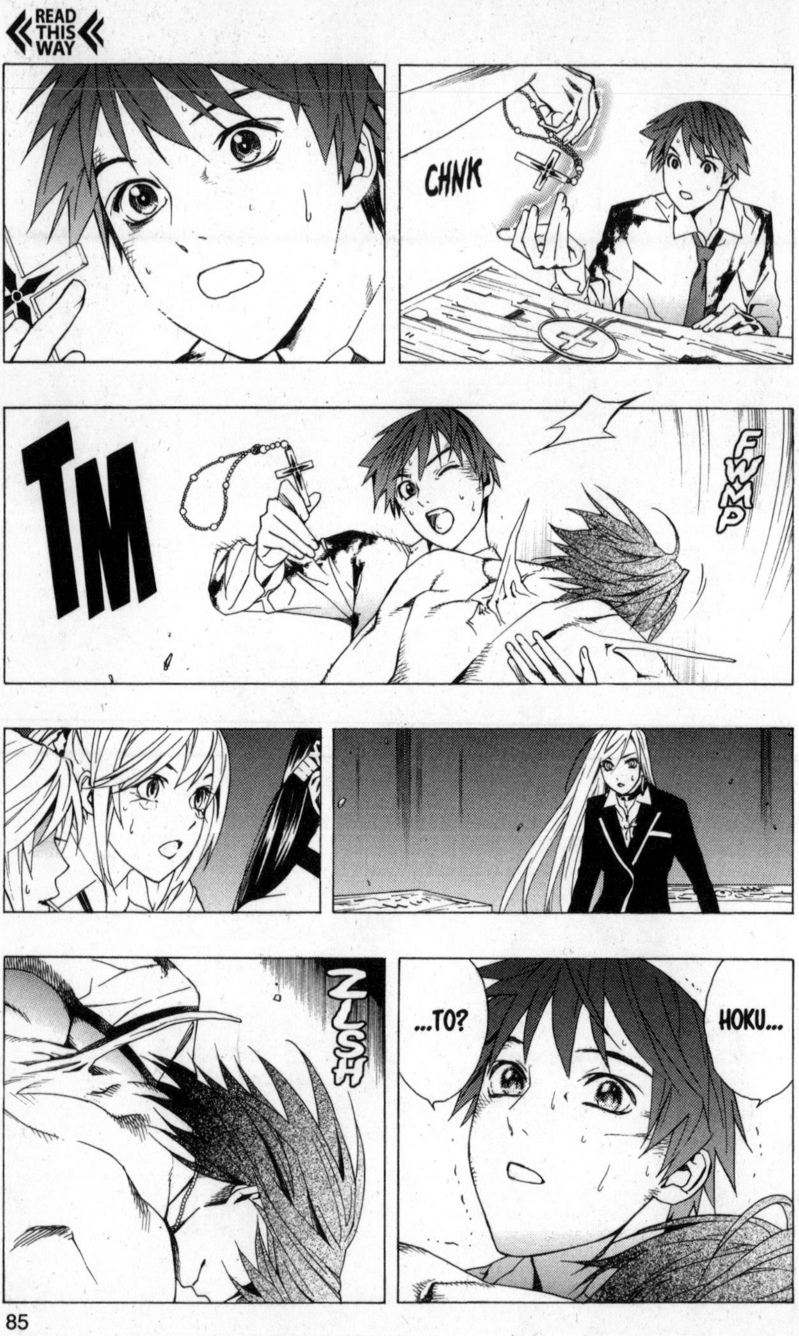
CHNK
FWMP
TM
HOKU...
...TO?
ZLSH

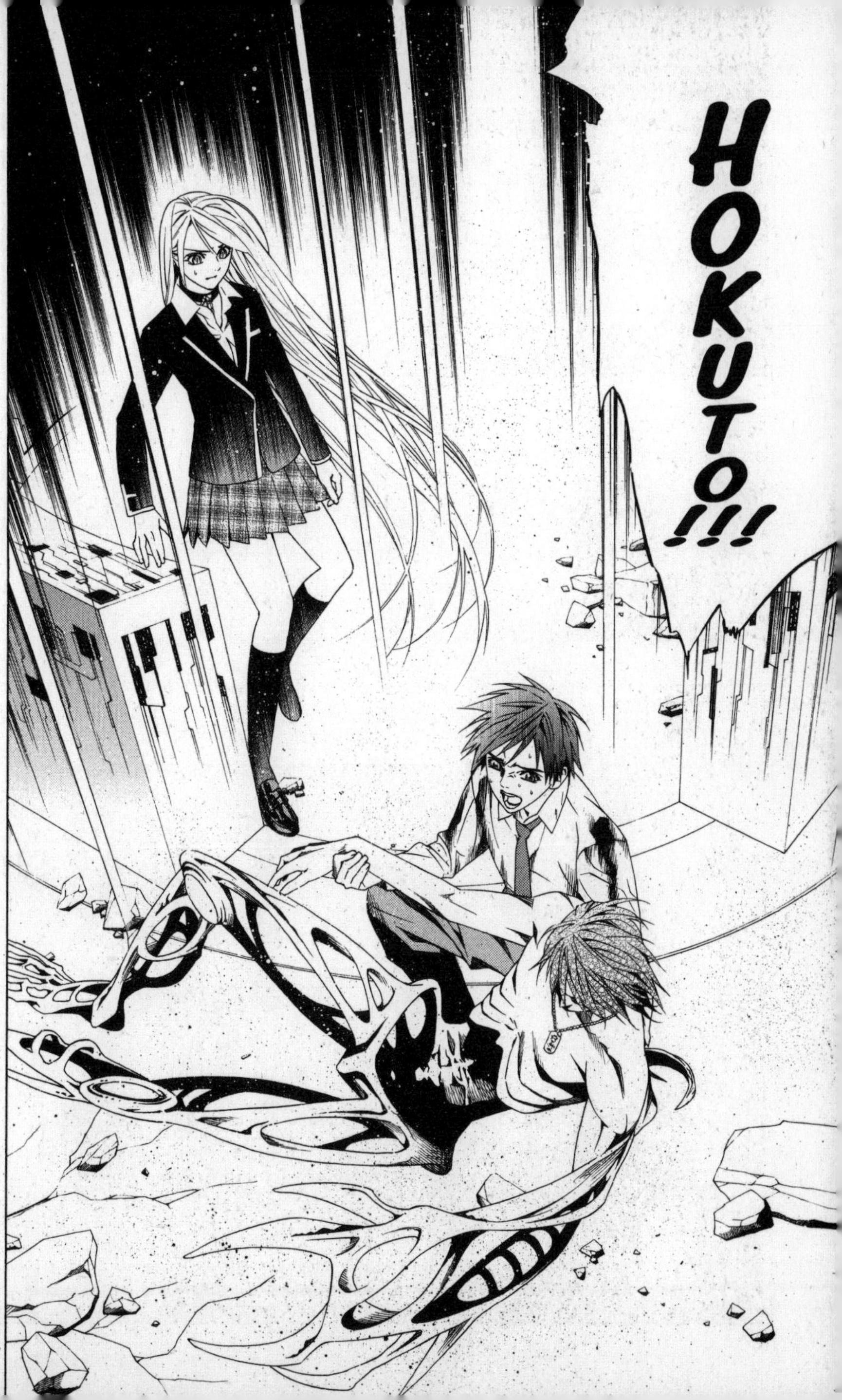
HOKUTO!!!

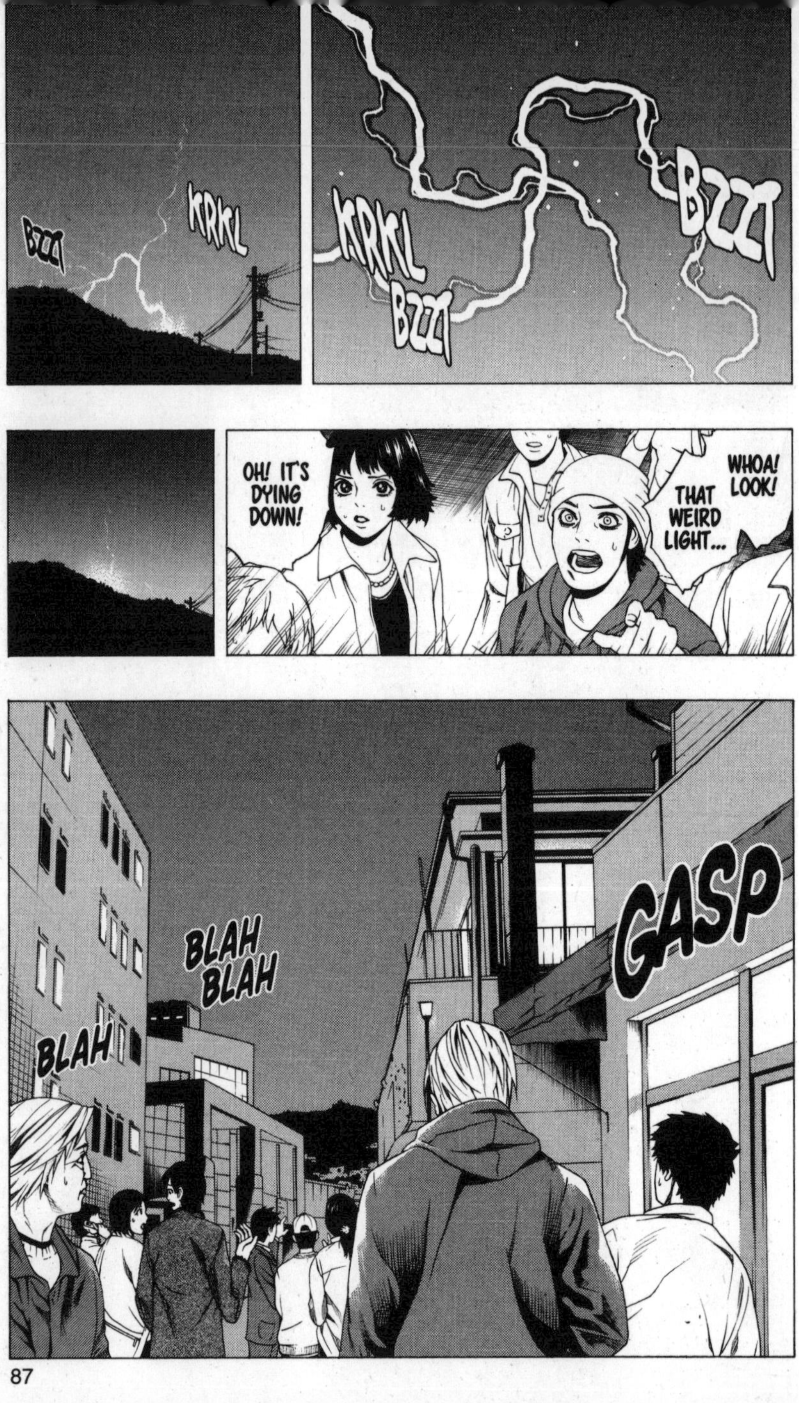
BZZT
KRKL
BZZT
KRKL
BZZT
WHOA! LOOK!
THAT WEIRD LIGHT...
OH! IT'S DYING DOWN!
GASP
BLAH BLAH
BLAH

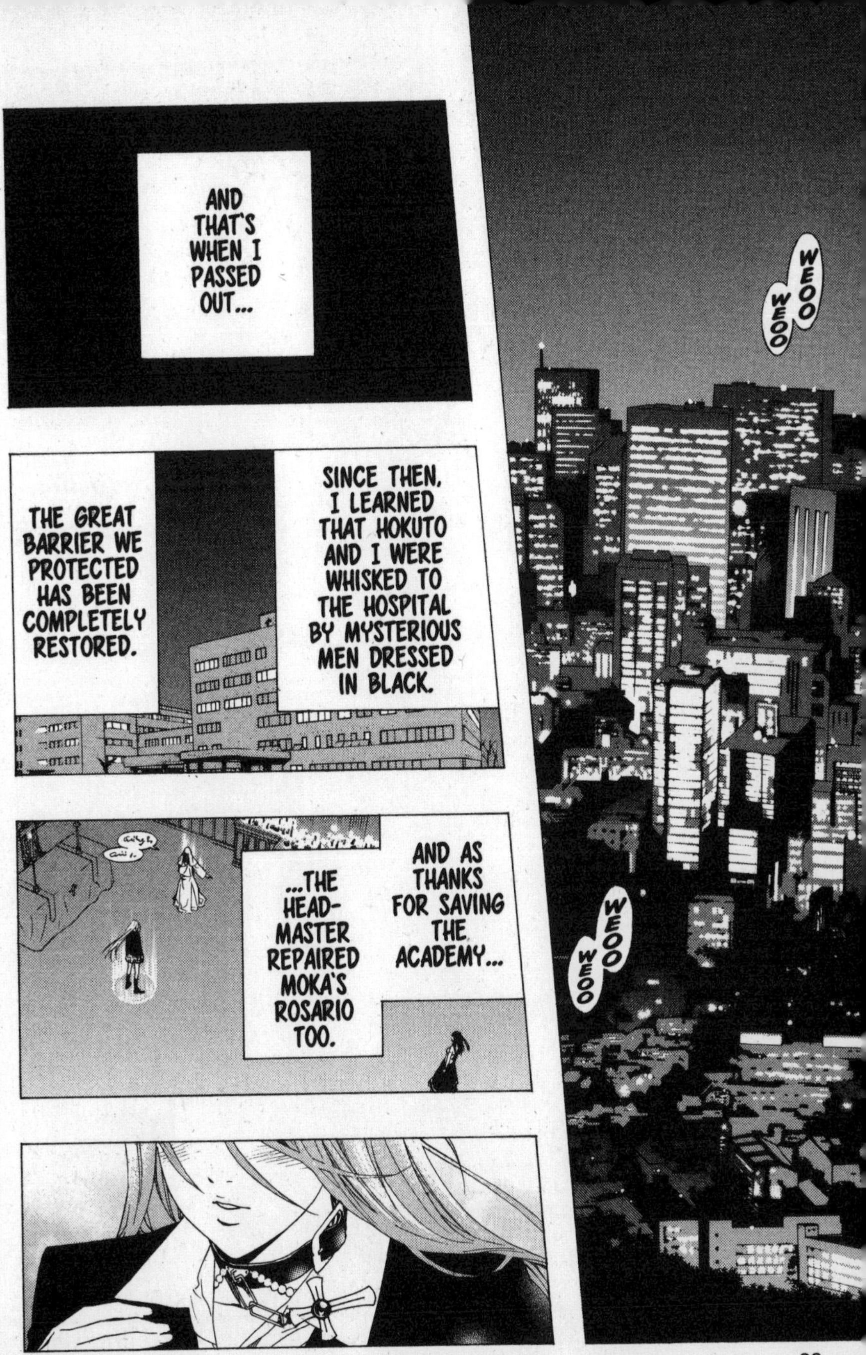
WEOO WEOO
WEOO WEOO
AND THAT'S WHEN I PASSED OUT...
SINCE THEN, I LEARNED THAT HOKUTO AND I WERE WHISKED TO THE HOSPITAL BY MYSTERIOUS MEN DRESSED IN BLACK.
THE GREAT BARRIER WE PROTECTED HAS BEEN COMPLETELY RESTORED.
AND AS THANKS FOR SAVING THE ACADEMY...
...THE HEAD-MASTER REPAIRED MOKA'S ROSARIO TOO.

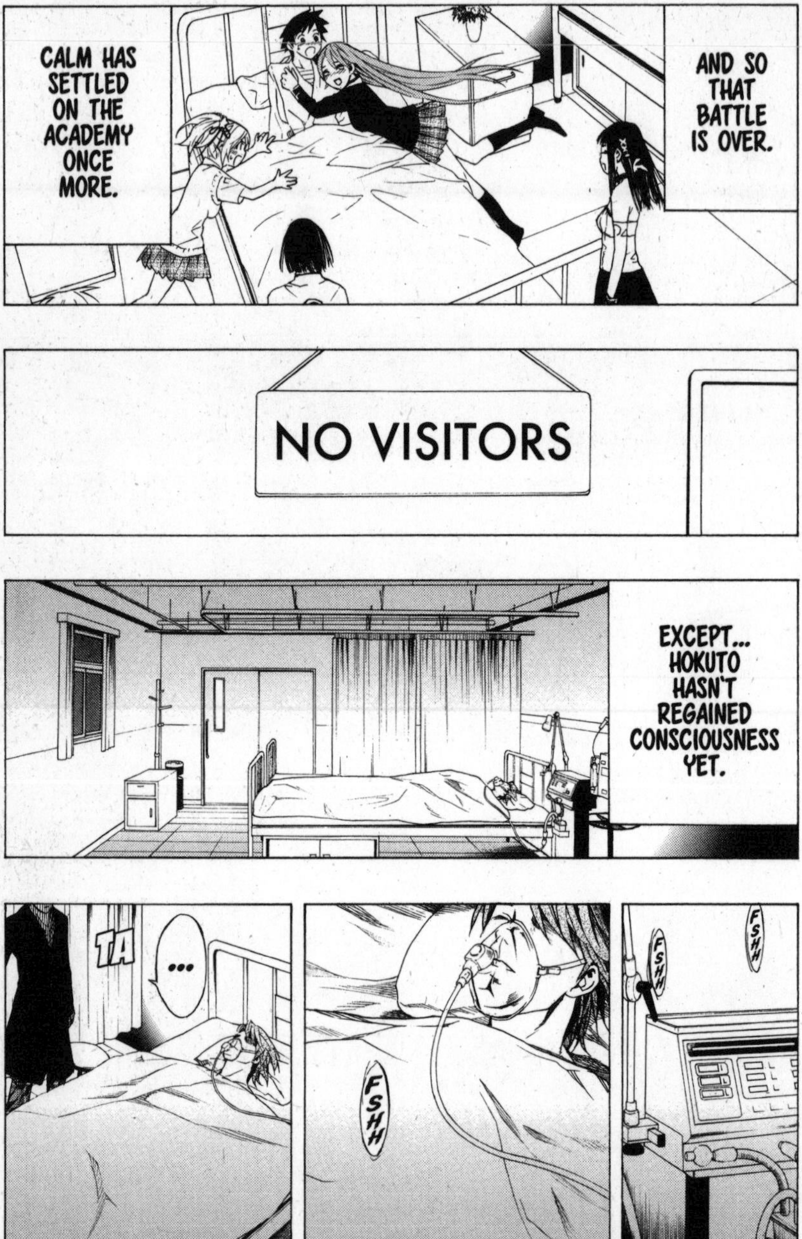
AND SO THAT BATTLE IS OVER.
CALM HAS SETTLED ON THE ACADEMY ONCE MORE.
NO VISITORS
EXCEPT... HOKUTO HASN'T REGAINED CONSCIOUSNESS YET.
FSHH
FSHH
FSHH
TA
...

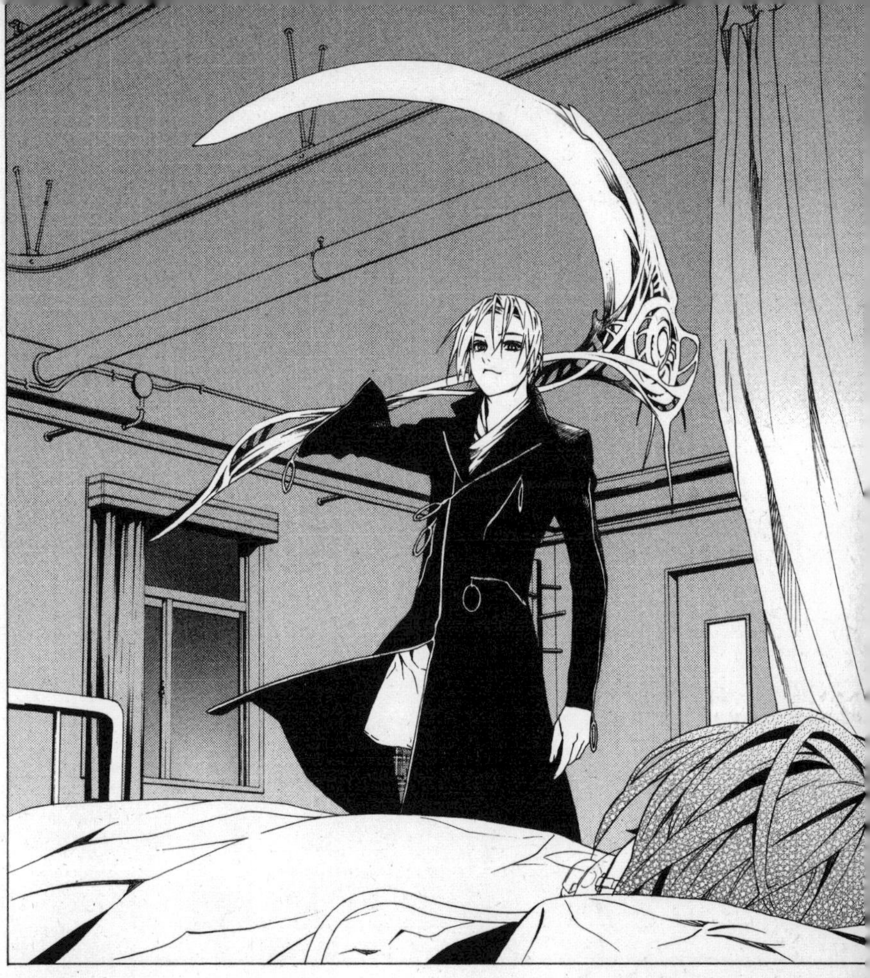

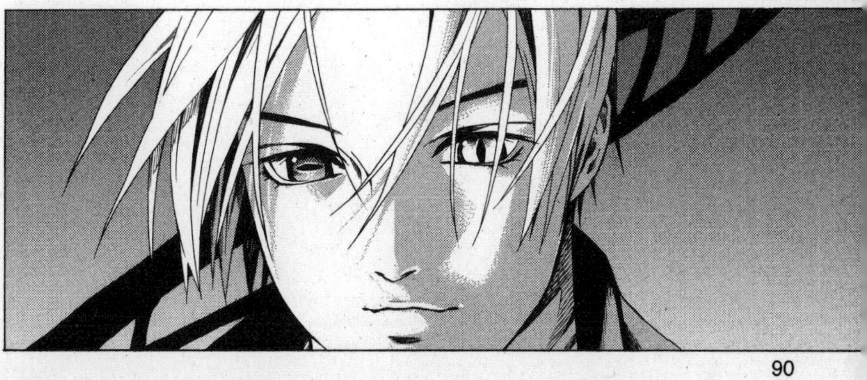

READ THIS WAY

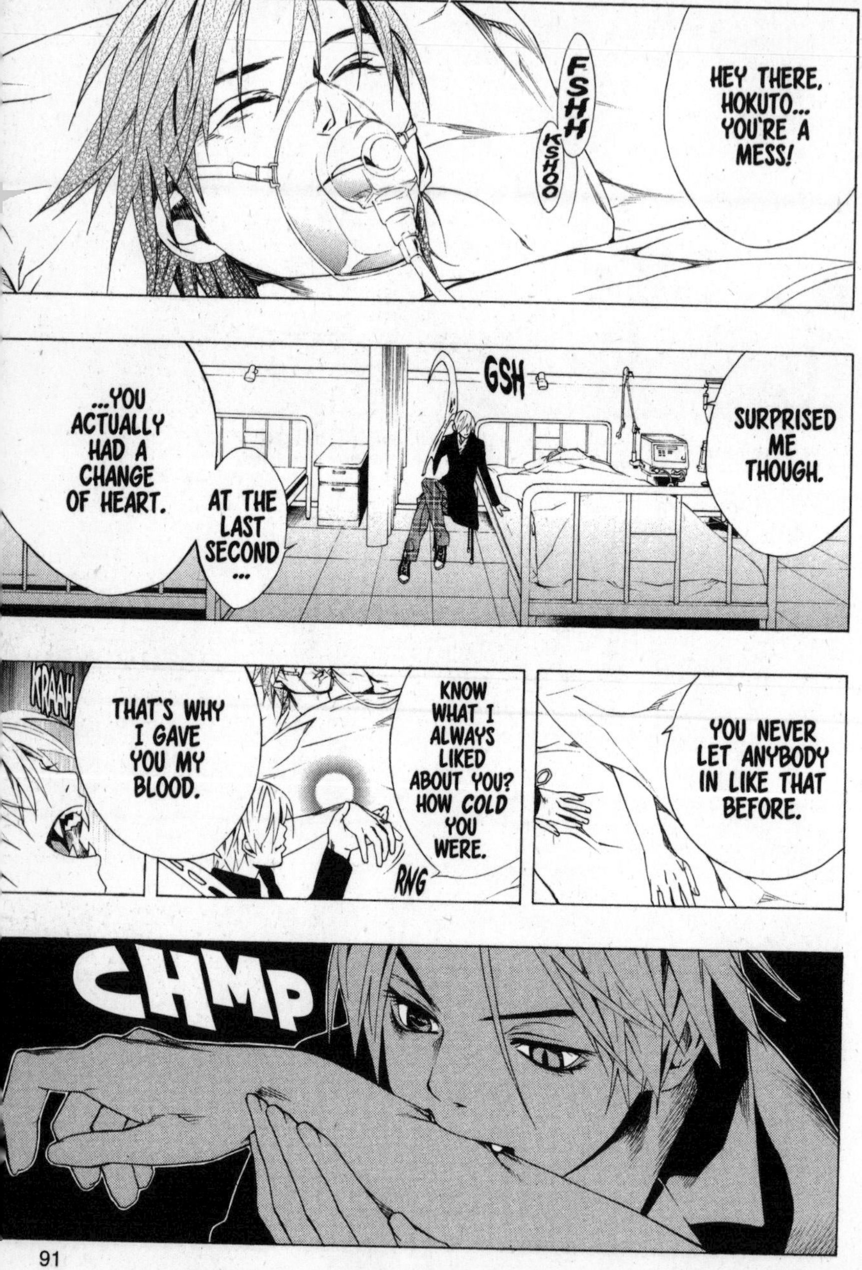

HEY THERE, HOKUTO... YOU'RE A MESS!
FSHH
KSHOO
SURPRISED ME THOUGH.
GSH
AT THE LAST SECOND...
...YOU ACTUALLY HAD A CHANGE OF HEART.
YOU NEVER LET ANYBODY IN LIKE THAT BEFORE.
KNOW WHAT I ALWAYS LIKED ABOUT YOU? HOW COLD YOU WERE.
RNG
THAT'S WHY I GAVE YOU MY BLOOD.
KRAAH
CHMP

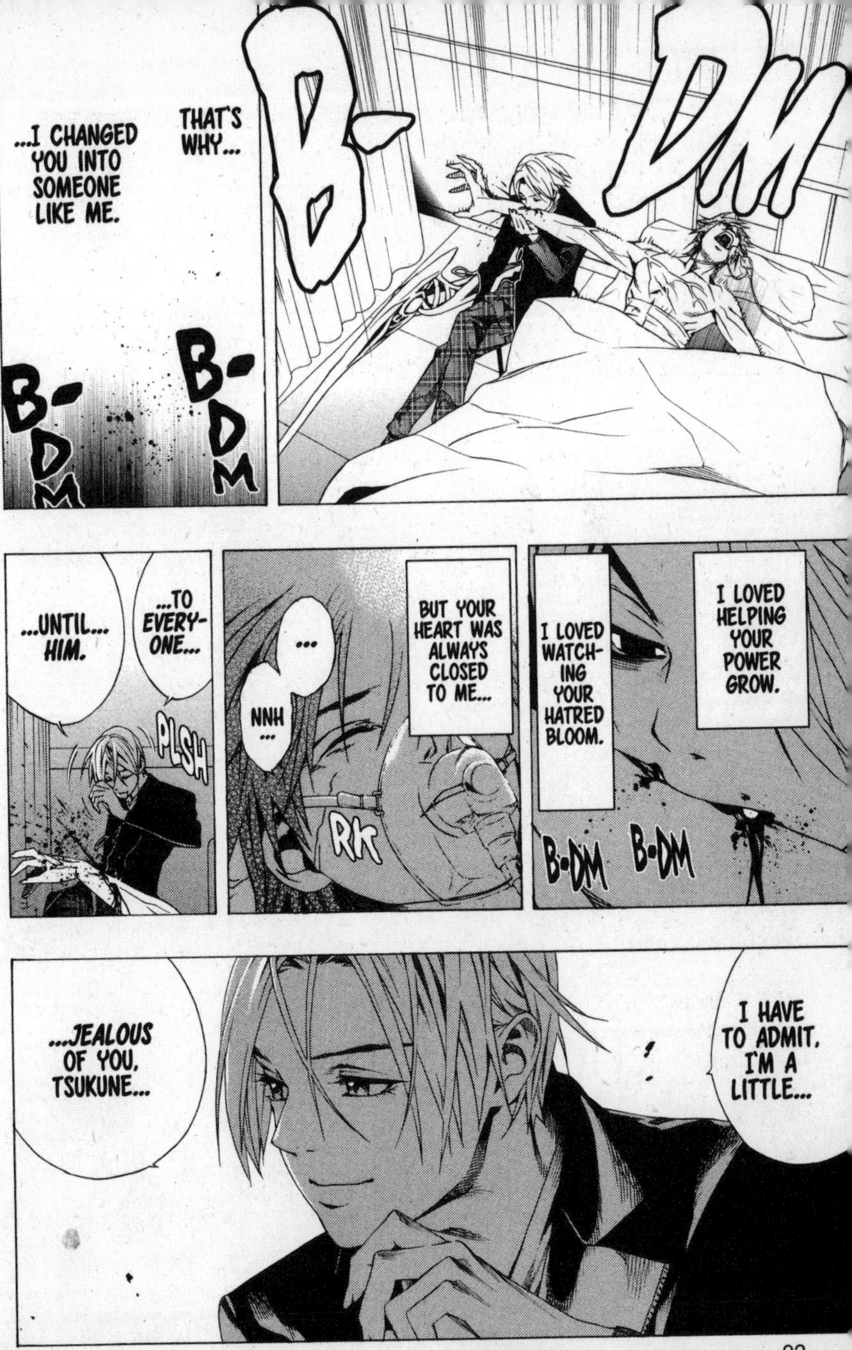
B-DM
THAT'S WHY...
...I CHANGED YOU INTO SOMEONE LIKE ME.
B-DM
B-DM
I LOVED HELPING YOUR POWER GROW.
I LOVED WATCHING YOUR HATRED BLOOM.
B-DM B-DM
BUT YOUR HEART WAS ALWAYS CLOSED TO ME...
...
NNH...
RK
...TO EVERYONE...
...UNTIL... HIM.
PLSH
I HAVE TO ADMIT, I'M A LITTLE...
...JEALOUS OF YOU, TSUKUNE...

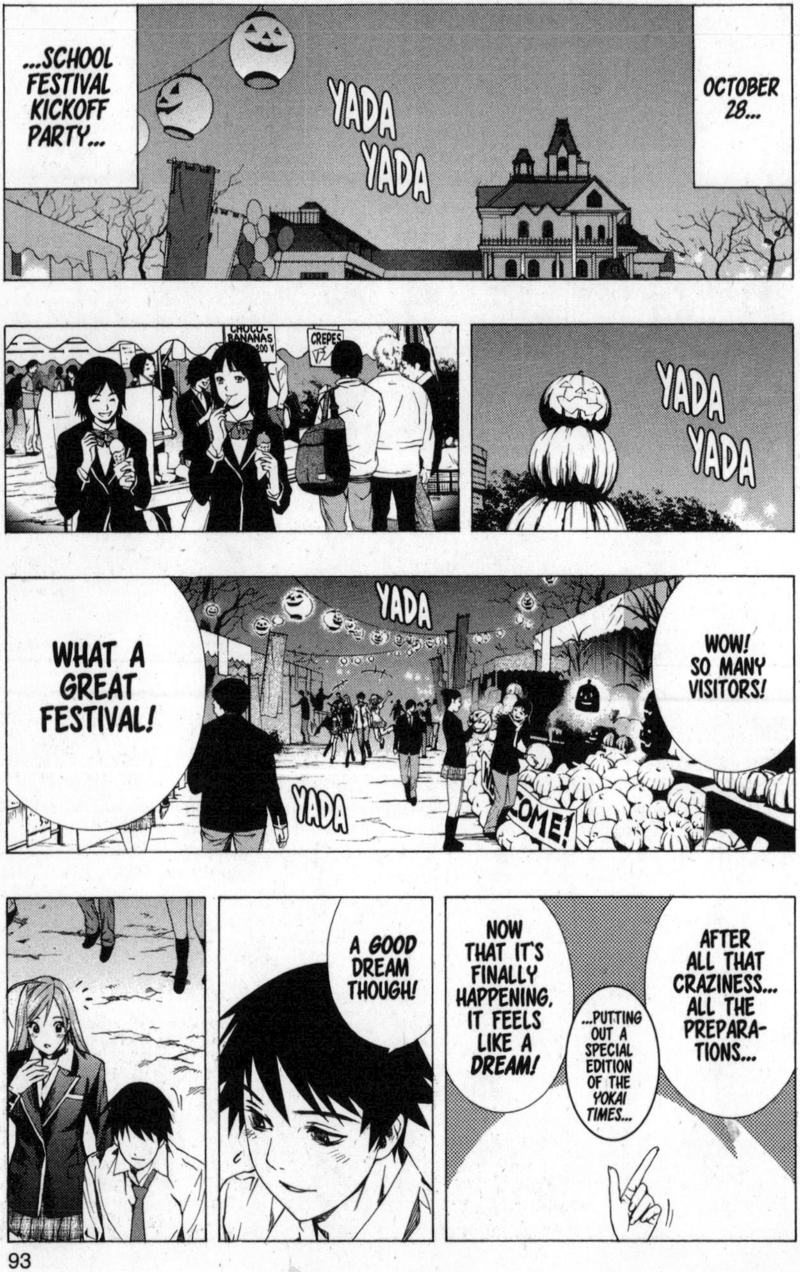
OCTOBER 28...
YADA YADA
...SCHOOL FESTIVAL KICKOFF PARTY...
YADA YADA
CREPES
CHOCO-BANANAS 200 ¥
WOW! SO MANY VISITORS!
YADA
WHAT A GREAT FESTIVAL!
YADA
AFTER ALL THAT CRAZINESS... ALL THE PREPARA-TIONS...
...PUTTING OUT A SPECIAL EDITION OF THE YOKAI TIMES...
NOW THAT IT'S FINALLY HAPPENING, IT FEELS LIKE A DREAM!
A GOOD DREAM THOUGH!

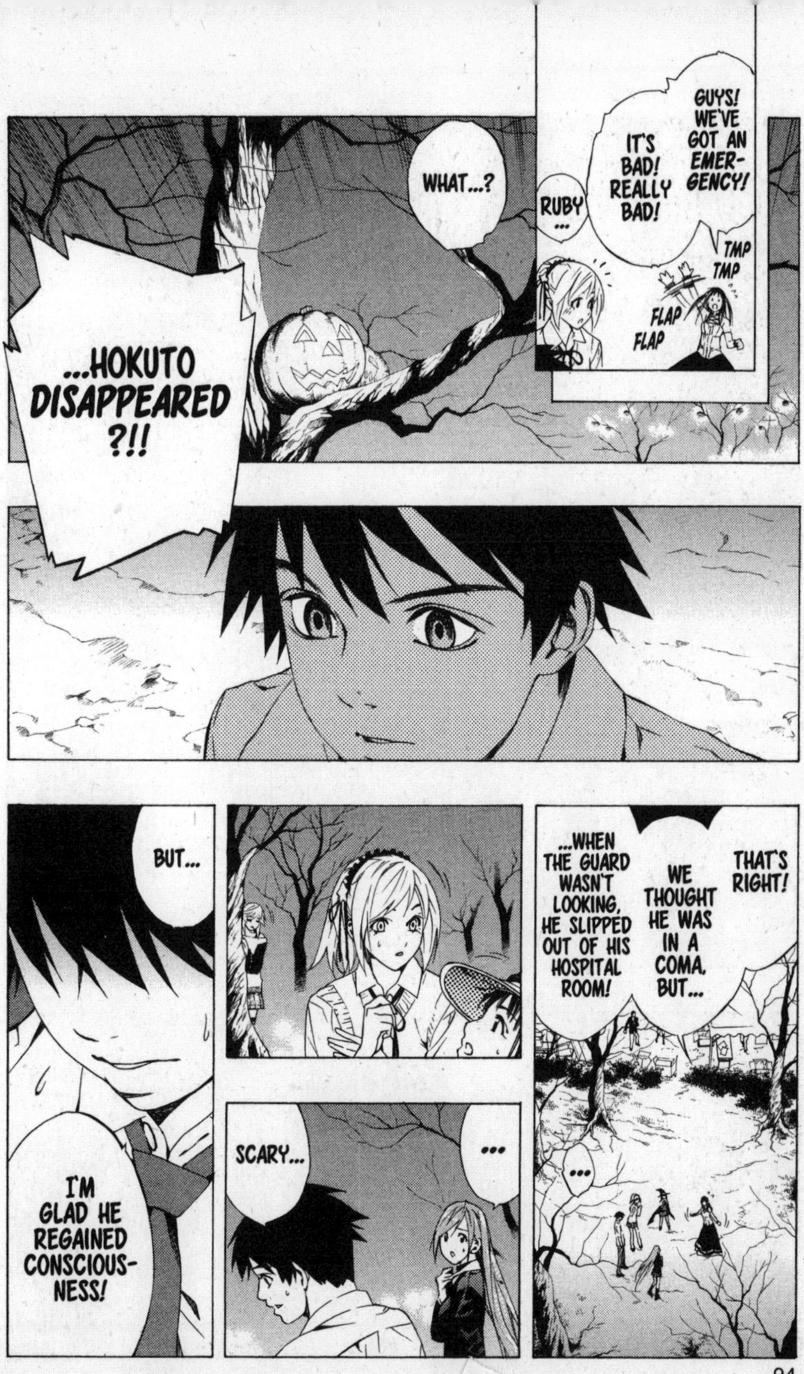
GUYS! WE'VE GOT AN EMERGENCY!
IT'S BAD! REALLY BAD!
RUBY...
TMP TMP
FLAP FLAP
WHAT...?
...HOKUTO DISAPPEARED?!!
THAT'S RIGHT!
WE THOUGHT HE WAS IN A COMA, BUT...
...WHEN THE GUARD WASN'T LOOKING, HE SLIPPED OUT OF HIS HOSPITAL ROOM!
...
...
SCARY...
BUT...
I'M GLAD HE REGAINED CONSCIOUSNESS!

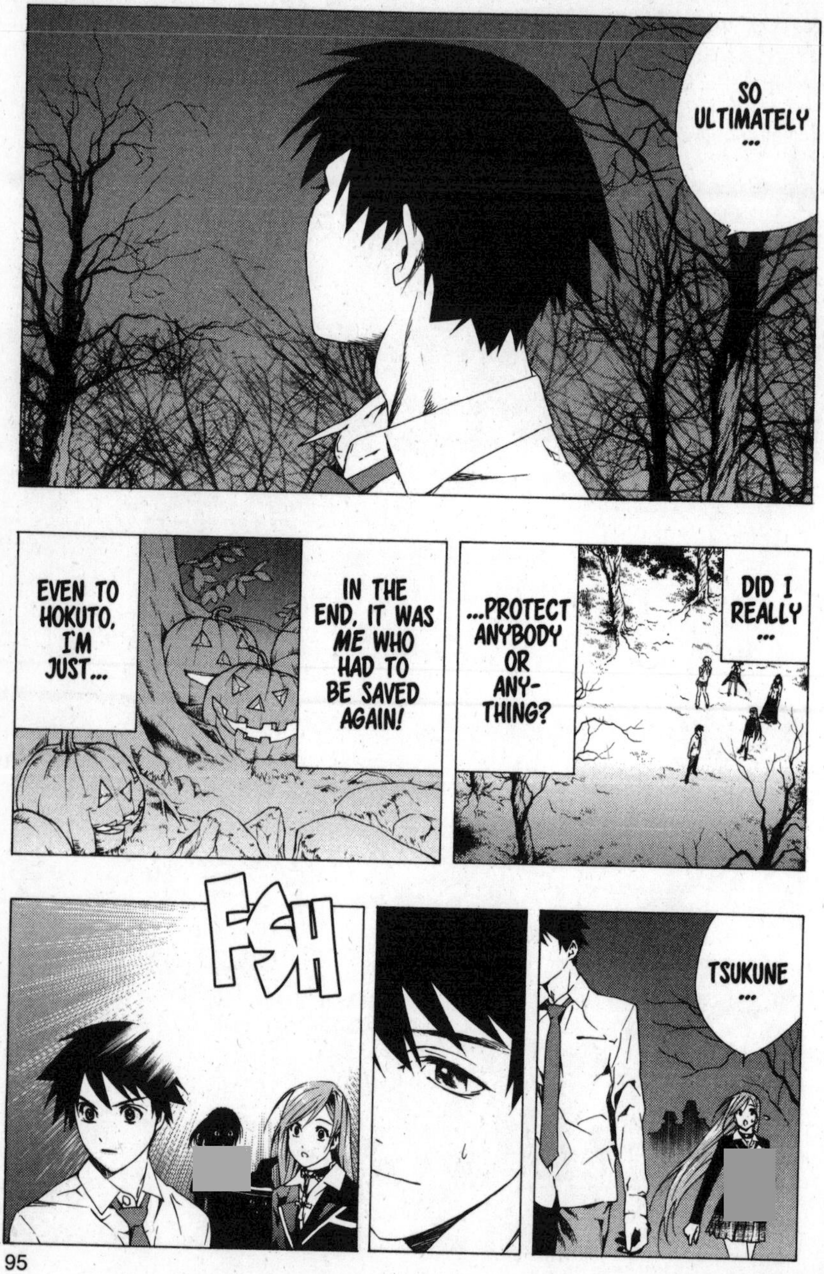
SO ULTIMATELY...
DID I REALLY...
...PROTECT ANYBODY OR ANYTHING?
IN THE END, IT WAS *ME* WHO HAD TO BE SAVED AGAIN!
EVEN TO HOKUTO, I'M JUST...
TSUKUNE...
FSH

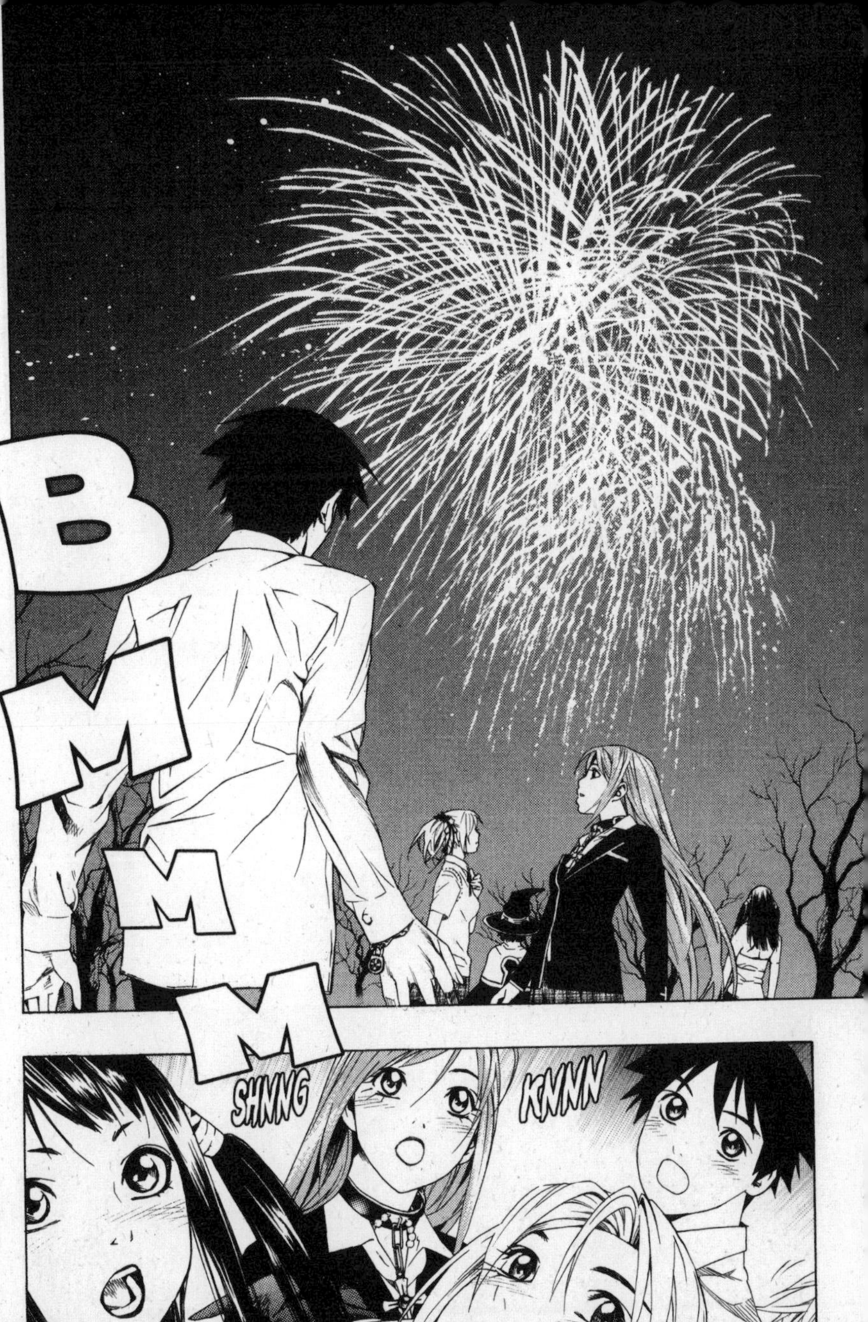
BMMM
KNNN
SHNNG

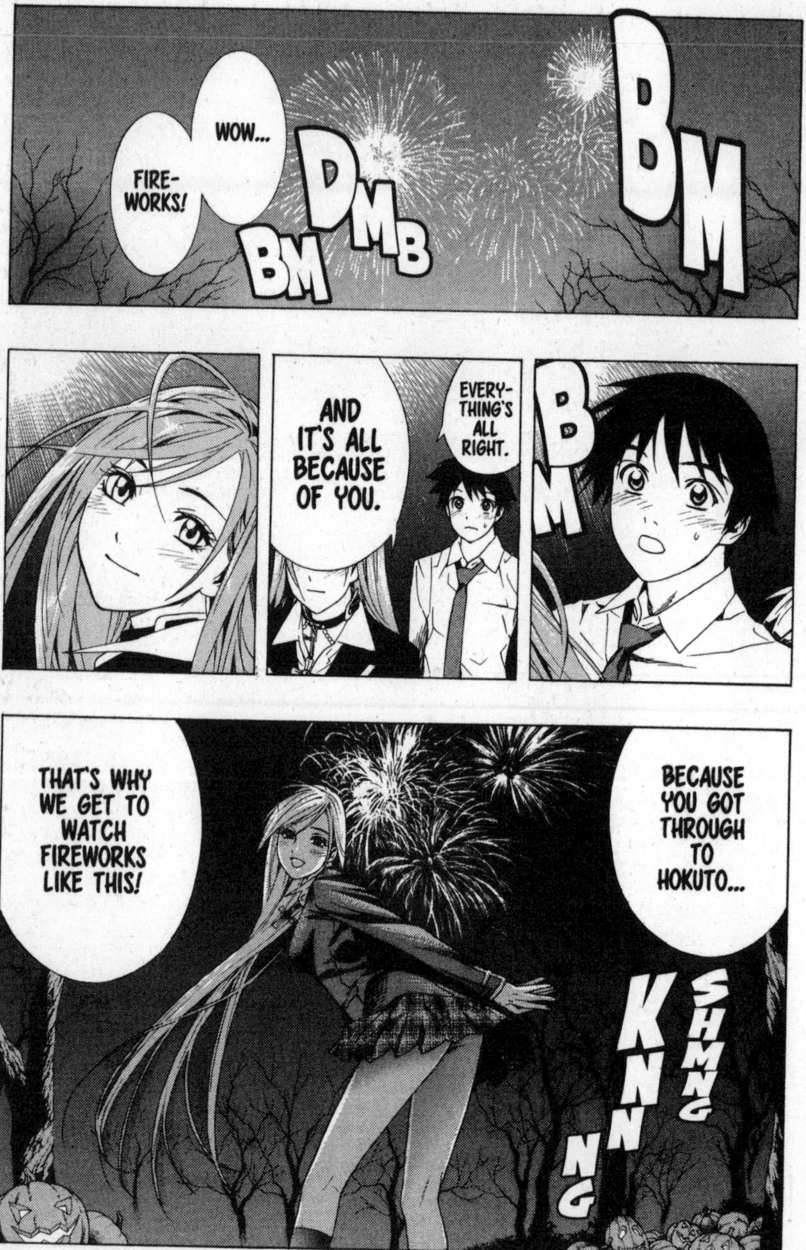

WOW...
FIRE-WORKS!
BM
DMB
BM
BM
EVERYTHING'S ALL RIGHT.
AND IT'S ALL BECAUSE OF YOU.
BECAUSE YOU GOT THROUGH TO HOKUTO...
THAT'S WHY WE GET TO WATCH FIREWORKS LIKE THIS!
SHMNG
KNNNG

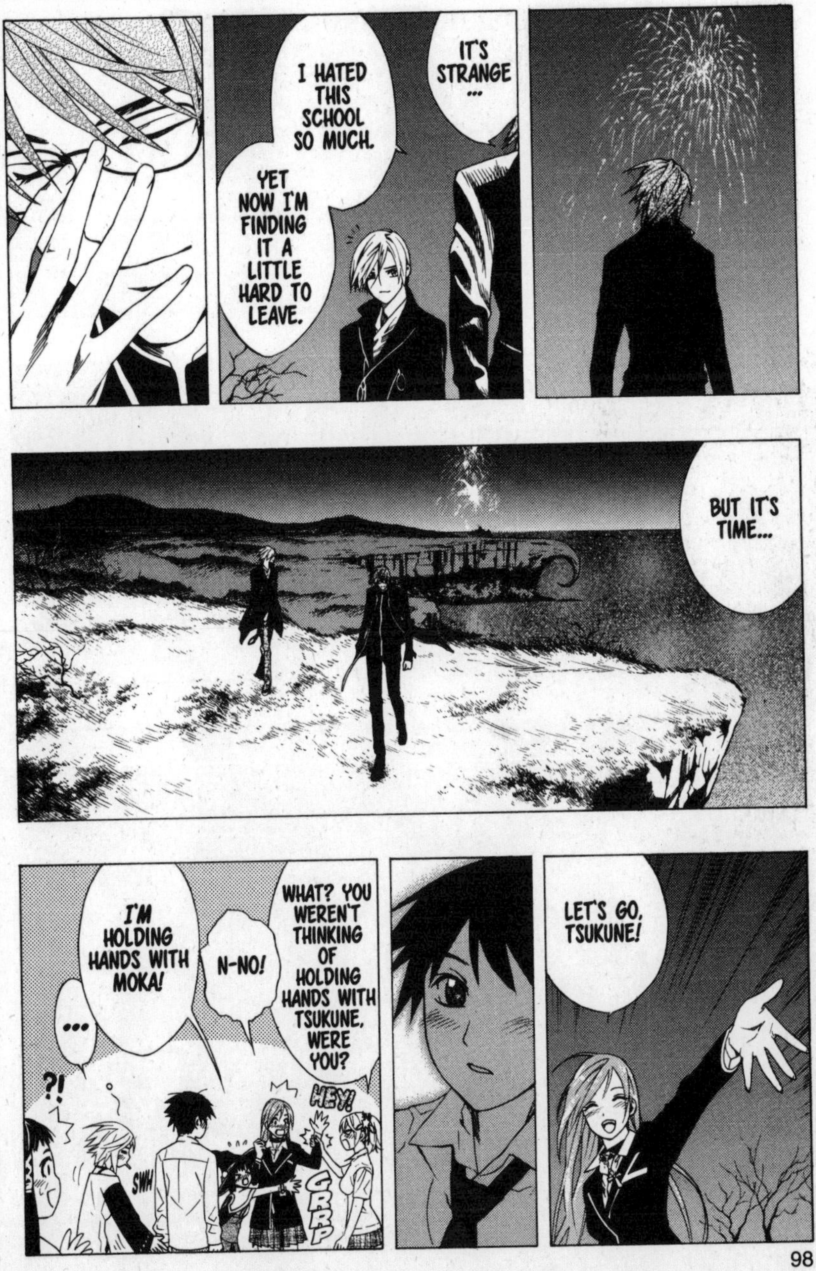
IT'S STRANGE ...
I HATED THIS SCHOOL SO MUCH.
YET NOW I'M FINDING IT A LITTLE HARD TO LEAVE.
BUT IT'S TIME...
LET'S GO, TSUKUNE!
WHAT? YOU WEREN'T THINKING OF HOLDING HANDS WITH TSUKUNE, WERE YOU?
N-NO!
I'M HOLDING HANDS WITH MOKA!
...
HEY!
GRRP
SWH
?!

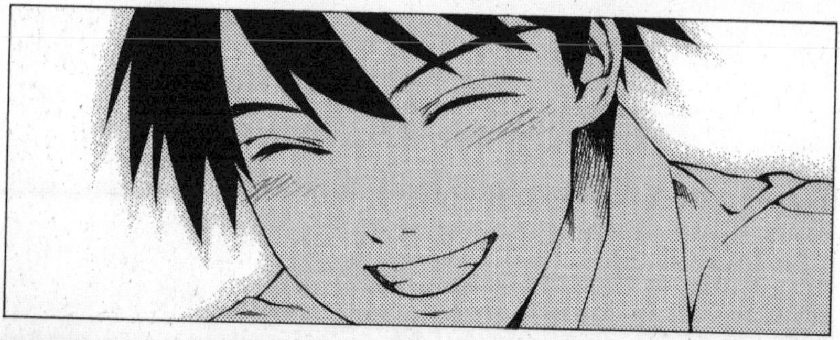

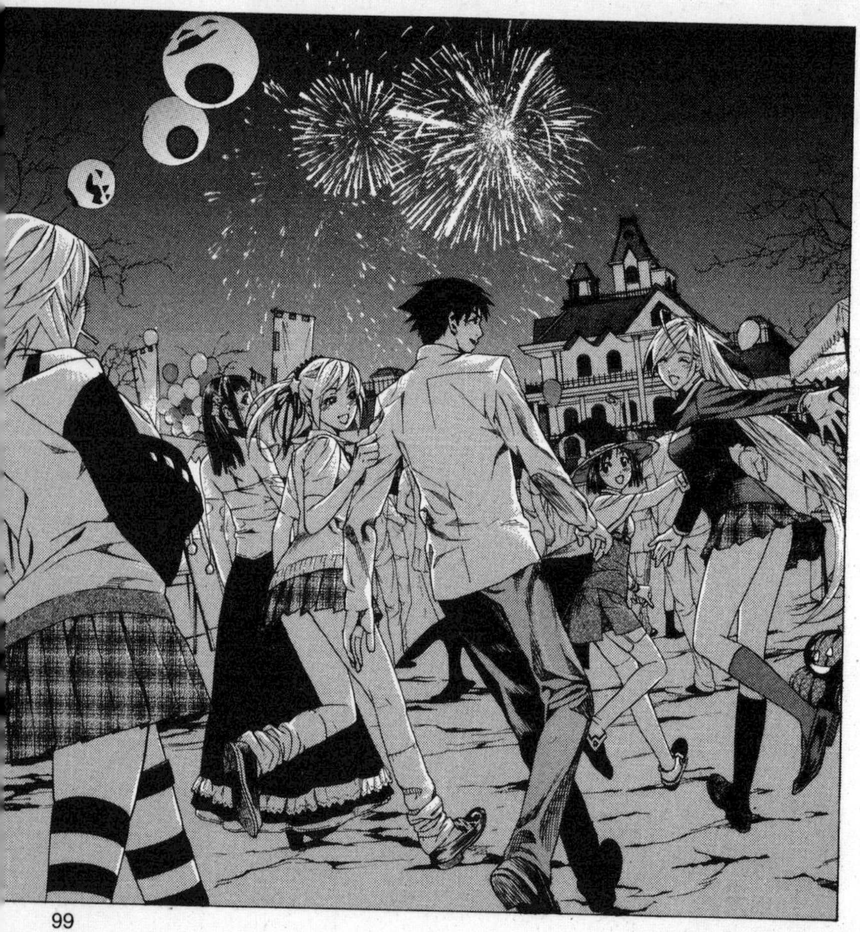

35: School Festival

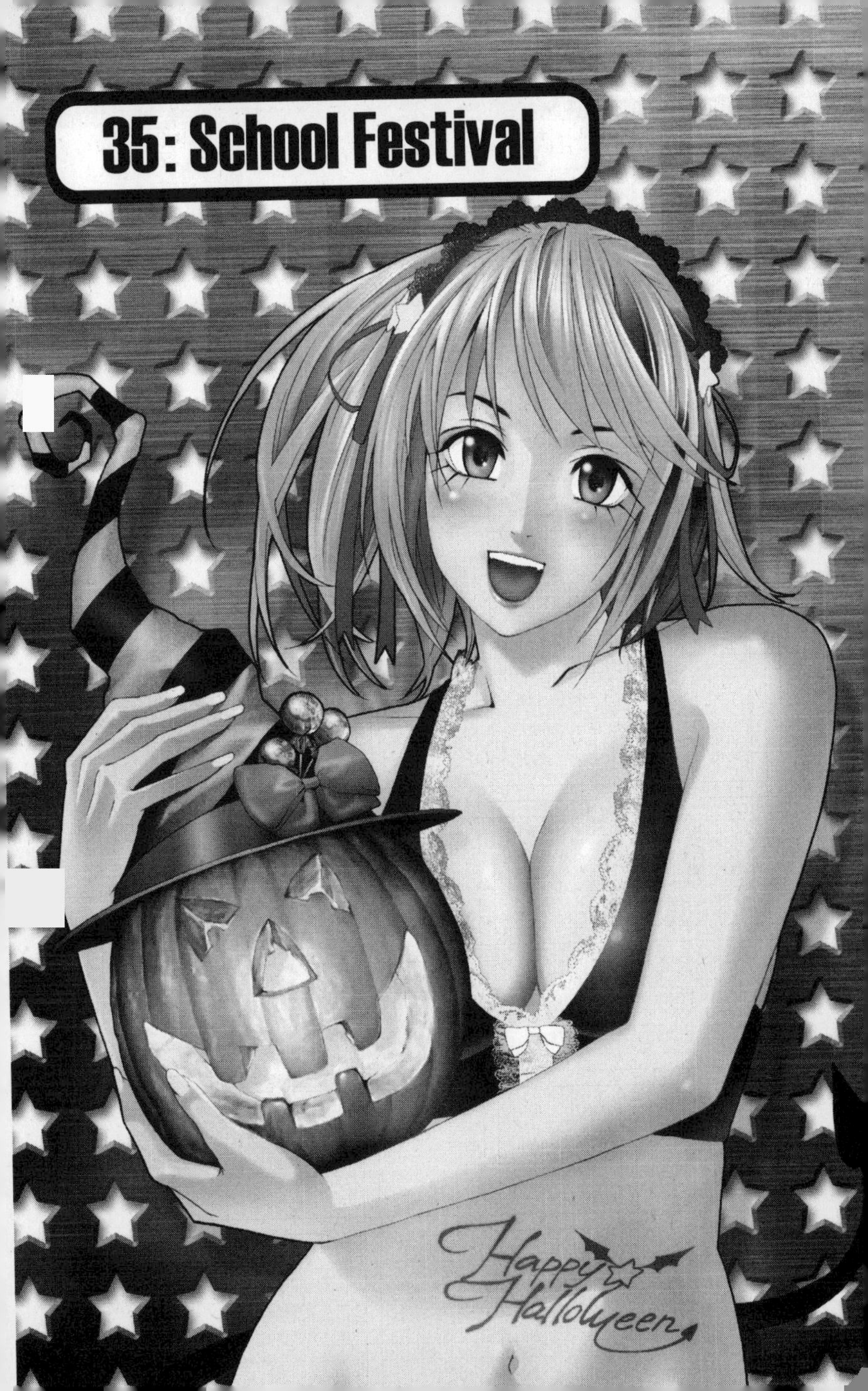
Happy Halloween

READ THIS WAY

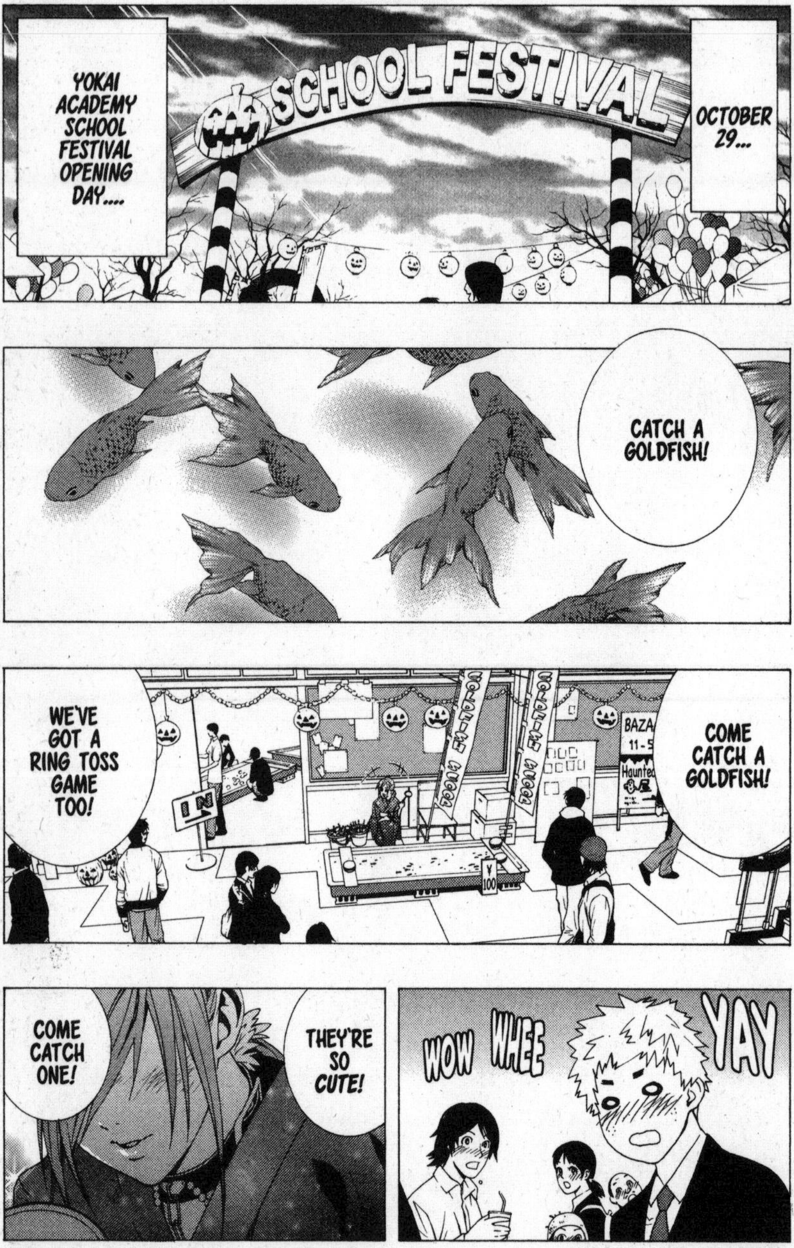
SCHOOL FESTIVAL
OCTOBER 29...
YOKAI ACADEMY SCHOOL FESTIVAL OPENING DAY....
CATCH A GOLDFISH!
COME CATCH A GOLDFISH!
WE'VE GOT A RING TOSS GAME TOO!
YAY
WHEE
WOW
THEY'RE SO CUTE!
COME CATCH ONE!

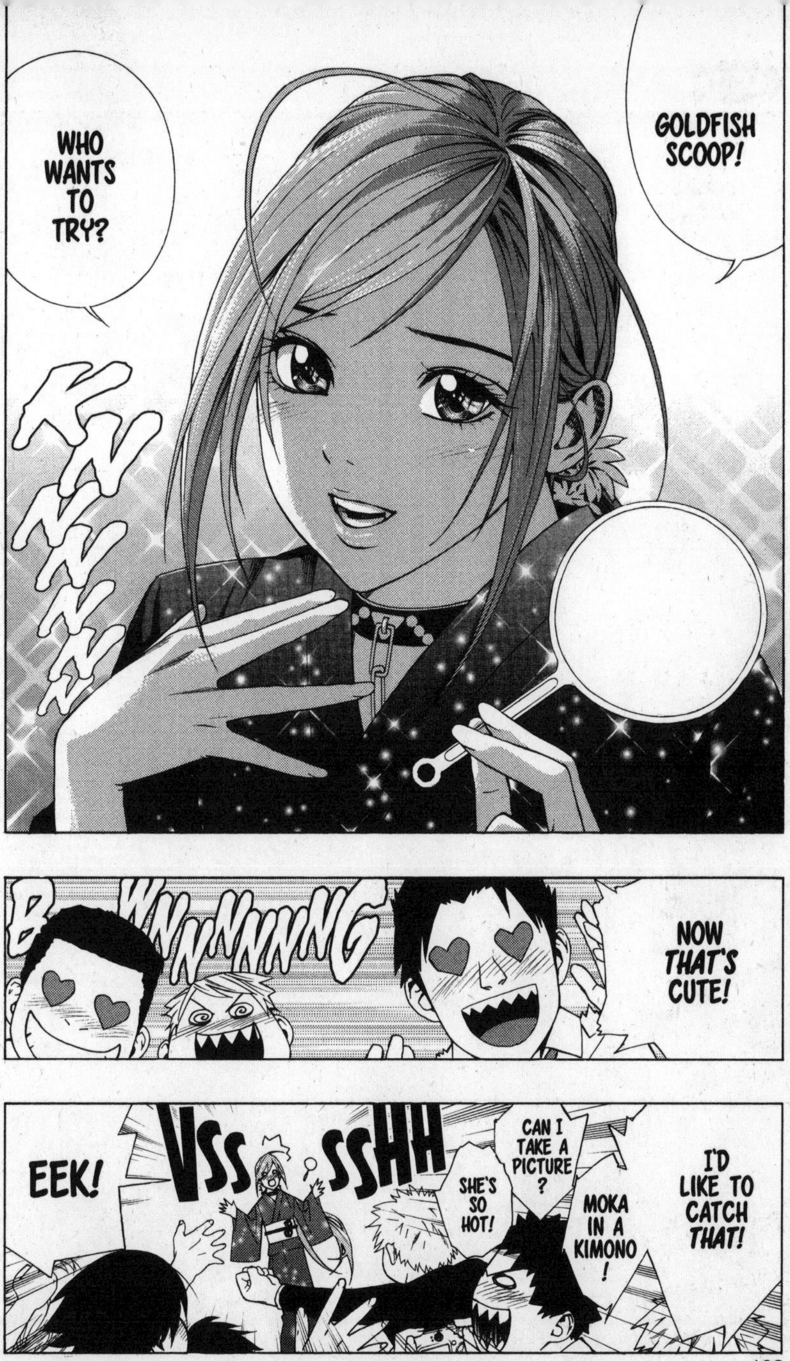
GOLDFISH SCOOP!
WHO WANTS TO TRY?
NOW THAT'S CUTE!
I'D LIKE TO CATCH THAT!
CAN I TAKE A PICTURE?
MOKA IN A KIMONO!
SHE'S SO HOT!
VSS SSHH
EEK!

READ THIS WAY

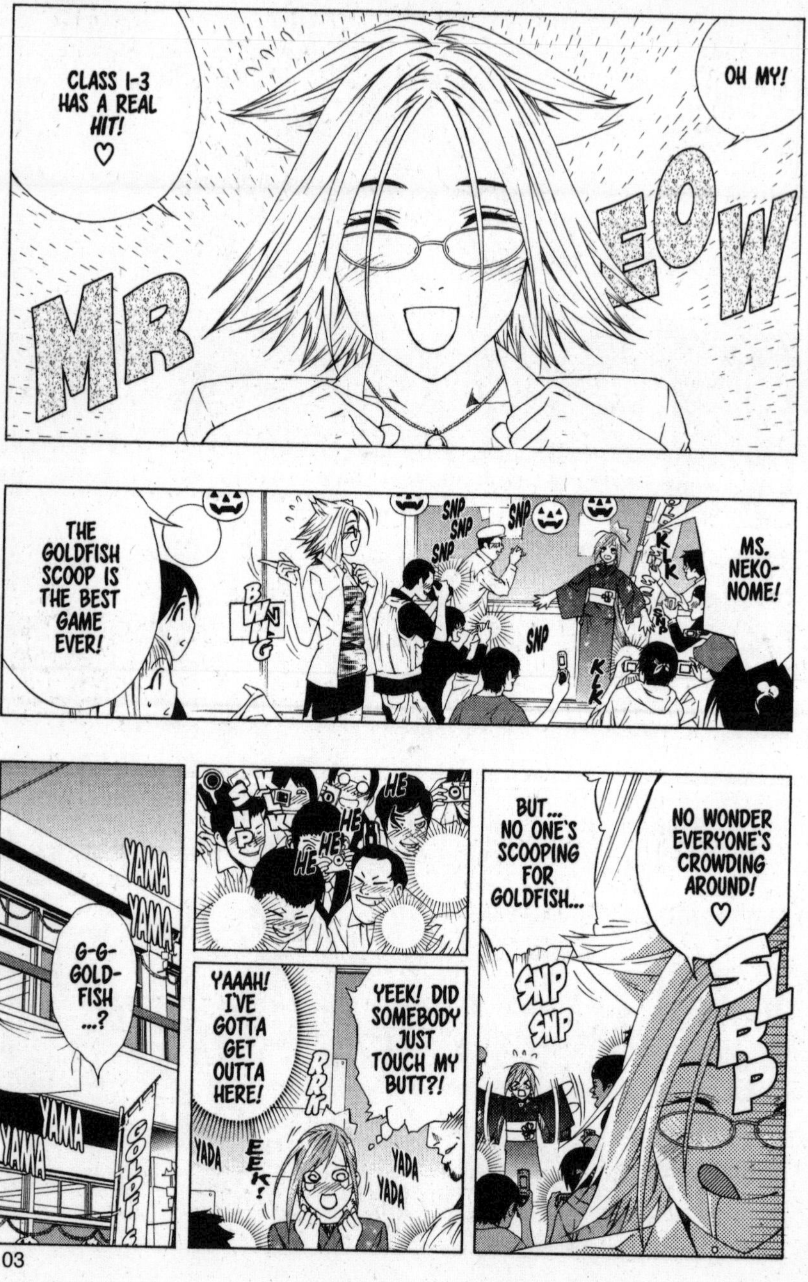
OH MY!
CLASS 1-3 HAS A REAL HIT! ♡
MREOW
MS. NEKO-NOME!
KLIK
SNP
SNP SNP
SNP
BWING
THE GOLDFISH SCOOP IS THE BEST GAME EVER!
NO WONDER EVERYONE'S CROWDING AROUND! ♡
SLRP
BUT... NO ONE'S SCOOPING FOR GOLDFISH...
SNP SNP
HE HE HE HE
YEEK! DID SOMEBODY JUST TOUCH MY BUTT?!
YAAAH! I'VE GOTTA GET OUTTA HERE!
RRK
YADA YADA
EEEK!
YADA
YAMA YAMA
G-G-GOLDFISH ...?
YAMA YAMA

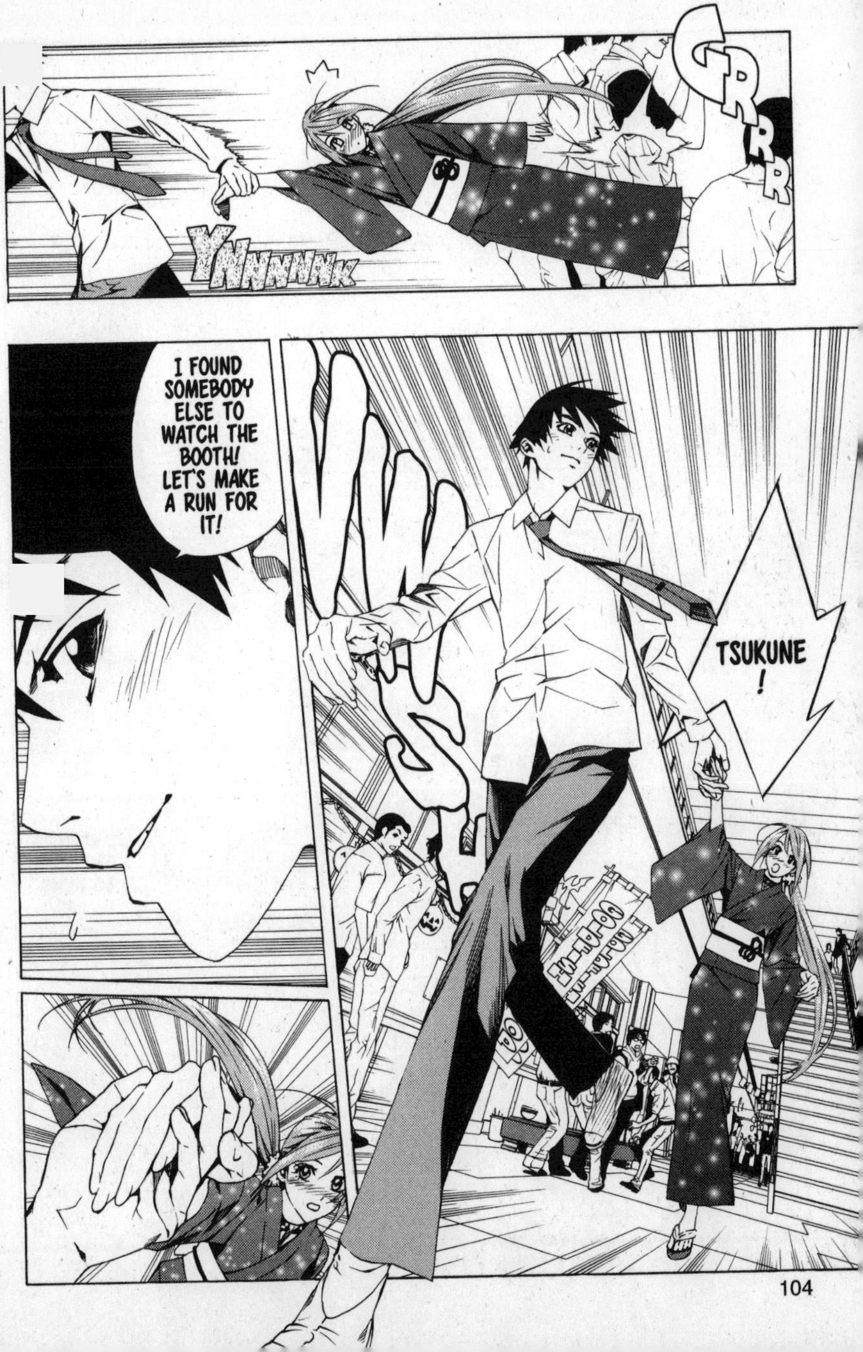
GRRR
YNNNNNK
TSUKUNE!
I FOUND SOMEBODY ELSE TO WATCH THE BOOTH! LET'S MAKE A RUN FOR IT!

READ THIS WAY

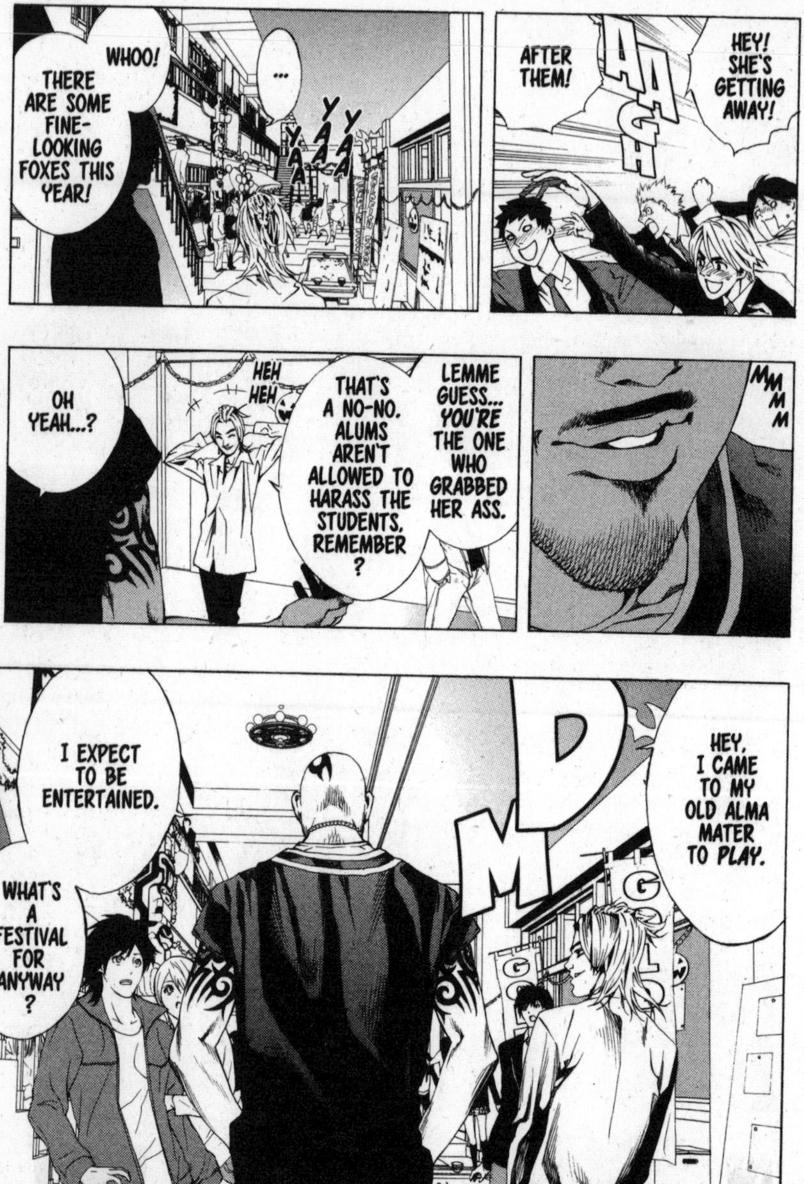
HEY! SHE'S GETTING AWAY!
AAGH
AFTER THEM!
WHOO! THERE ARE SOME FINE-LOOKING FOXES THIS YEAR!
...
YAAA
YAAA
YAAA
MMMM
LEMME GUESS... YOU'RE THE ONE WHO GRABBED HER ASS.
THAT'S A NO-NO. ALUMS AREN'T ALLOWED TO HARASS THE STUDENTS, REMEMBER?
HEH HEH
OH YEAH...?
HEY, I CAME TO MY OLD ALMA MATER TO PLAY.
DM
I EXPECT TO BE ENTERTAINED.
WHAT'S A FESTIVAL FOR ANYWAY?

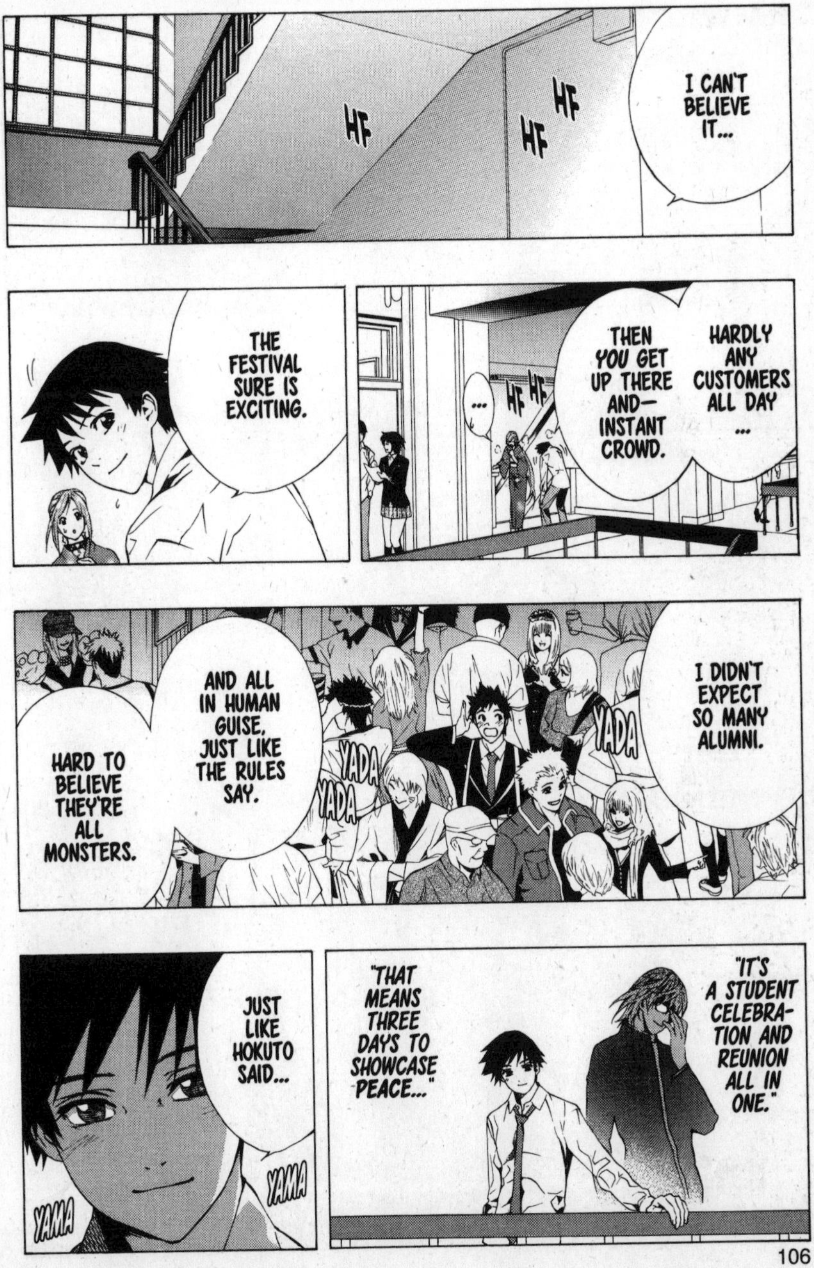
I CAN'T BELIEVE IT...
HF
HF
HF
HARDLY ANY CUSTOMERS ALL DAY ...
THEN YOU GET UP THERE AND—INSTANT CROWD.
HF HF
...
THE FESTIVAL SURE IS EXCITING.
I DIDN'T EXPECT SO MANY ALUMNI.
YADA
AND ALL IN HUMAN GUISE, JUST LIKE THE RULES SAY.
YADA
YADA
HARD TO BELIEVE THEY'RE ALL MONSTERS.
"IT'S A STUDENT CELEBRATION AND REUNION ALL IN ONE."
"THAT MEANS THREE DAYS TO SHOWCASE PEACE..."
JUST LIKE HOKUTO SAID...
YAMA
YAMA

READ THIS WAY

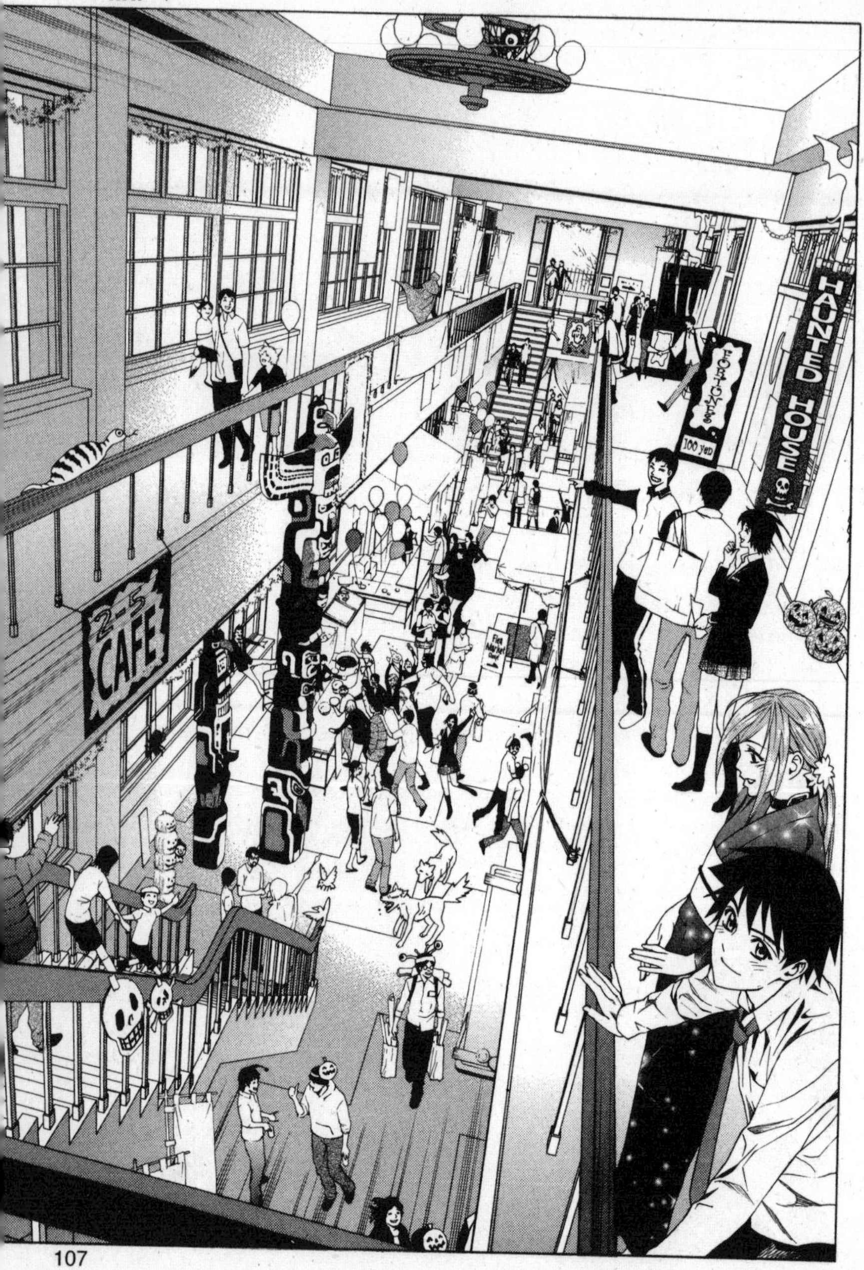
2-5 CAFE
FORTUNES
100 yen
HAUNTED HOUSE
Flea Market

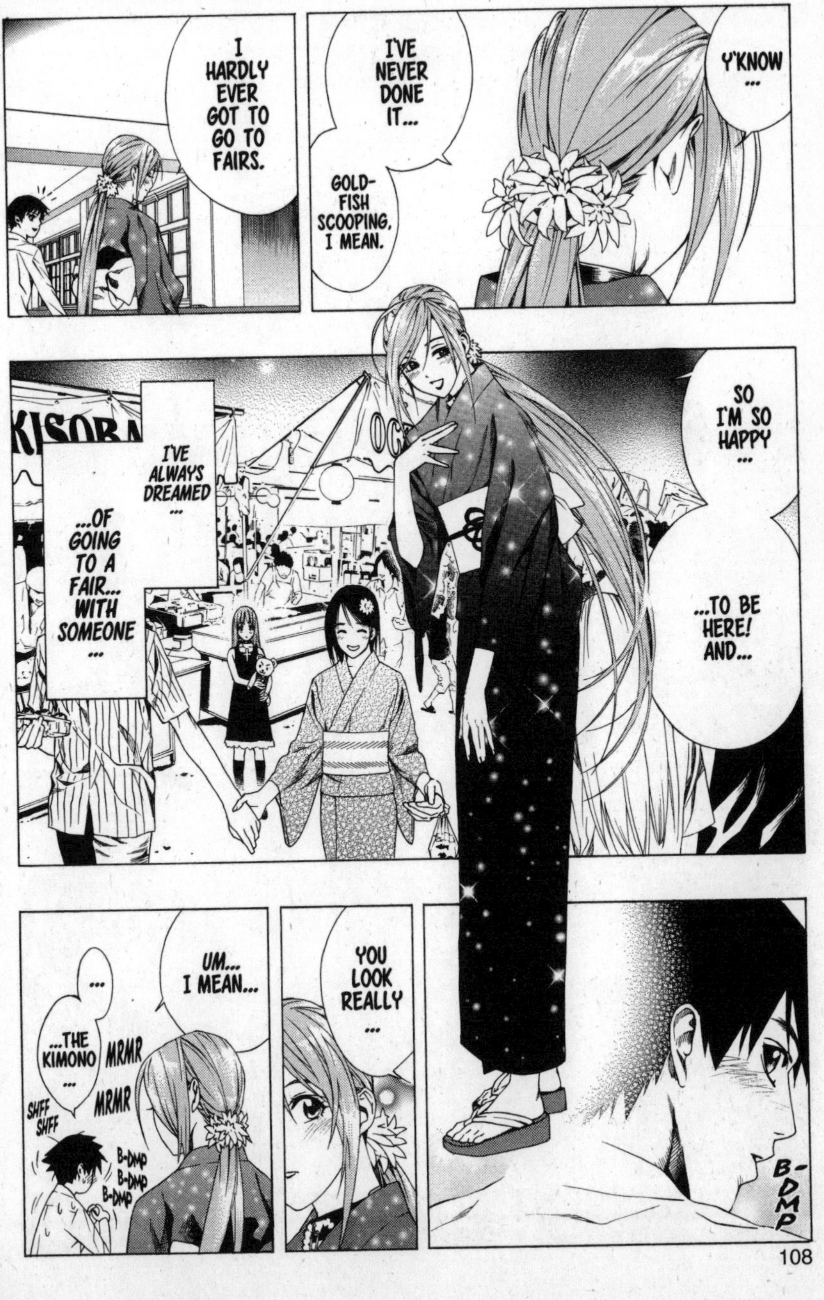
Y'KNOW ...
I'VE NEVER DONE IT...
GOLD-FISH SCOOPING, I MEAN.
I HARDLY EVER GOT TO GO TO FAIRS.
SO I'M SO HAPPY ...
...TO BE HERE! AND...
I'VE ALWAYS DREAMED ...
...OF GOING TO A FAIR... WITH SOMEONE ...
B-DMP
YOU LOOK REALLY ...
UM... I MEAN...
...
...THE KIMONO ...
MRMR
MRMR
SHFF SHFF
B-DMP B-DMP B-DMP

READ THIS WAY

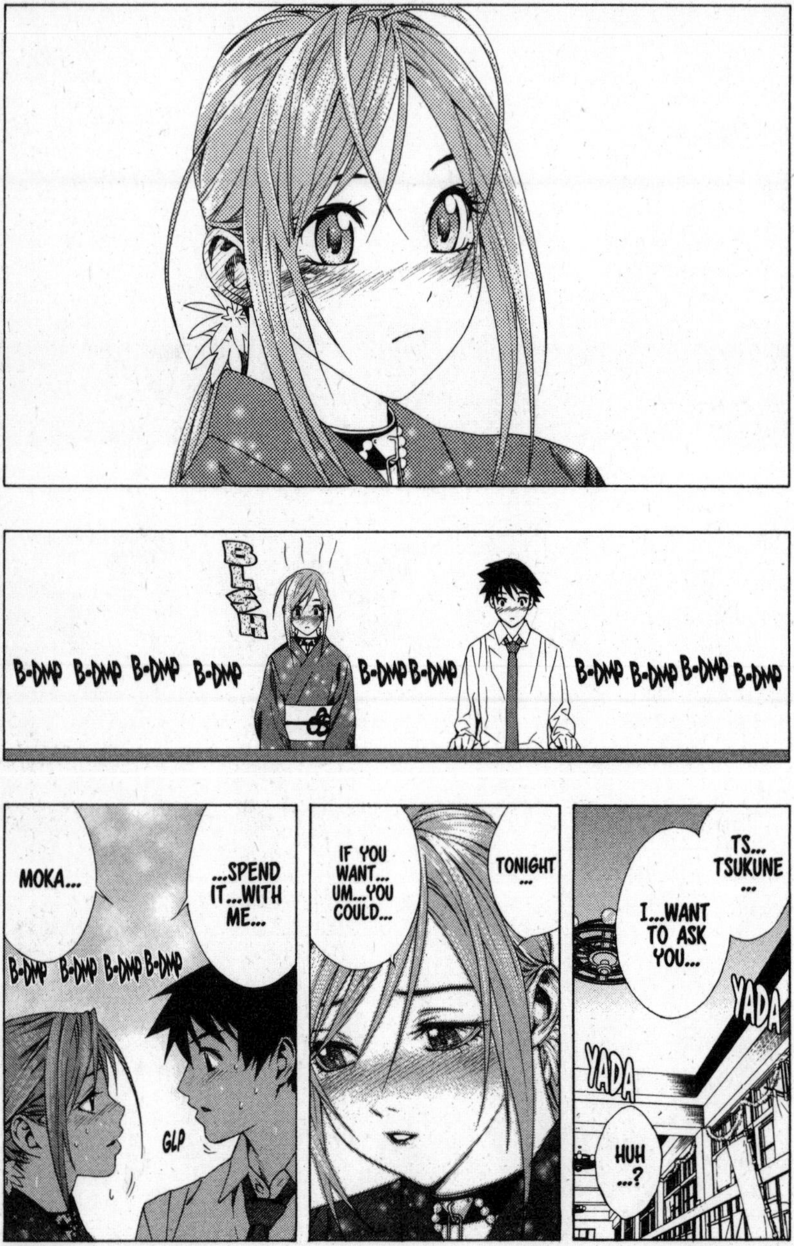
BLSH
B-DMP B-DMP B-DMP B-DMP
B-DMP B-DMP
B-DMP B-DMP B-DMP B-DMP
TS... TSUKUNE ...
I...WANT TO ASK YOU...
YADA
YADA
HUH ...?
TONIGHT ...
IF YOU WANT... UM...YOU COULD...
...SPEND IT...WITH ME...
MOKA...
B-DMP B-DMP B-DMP B-DMP
GLP

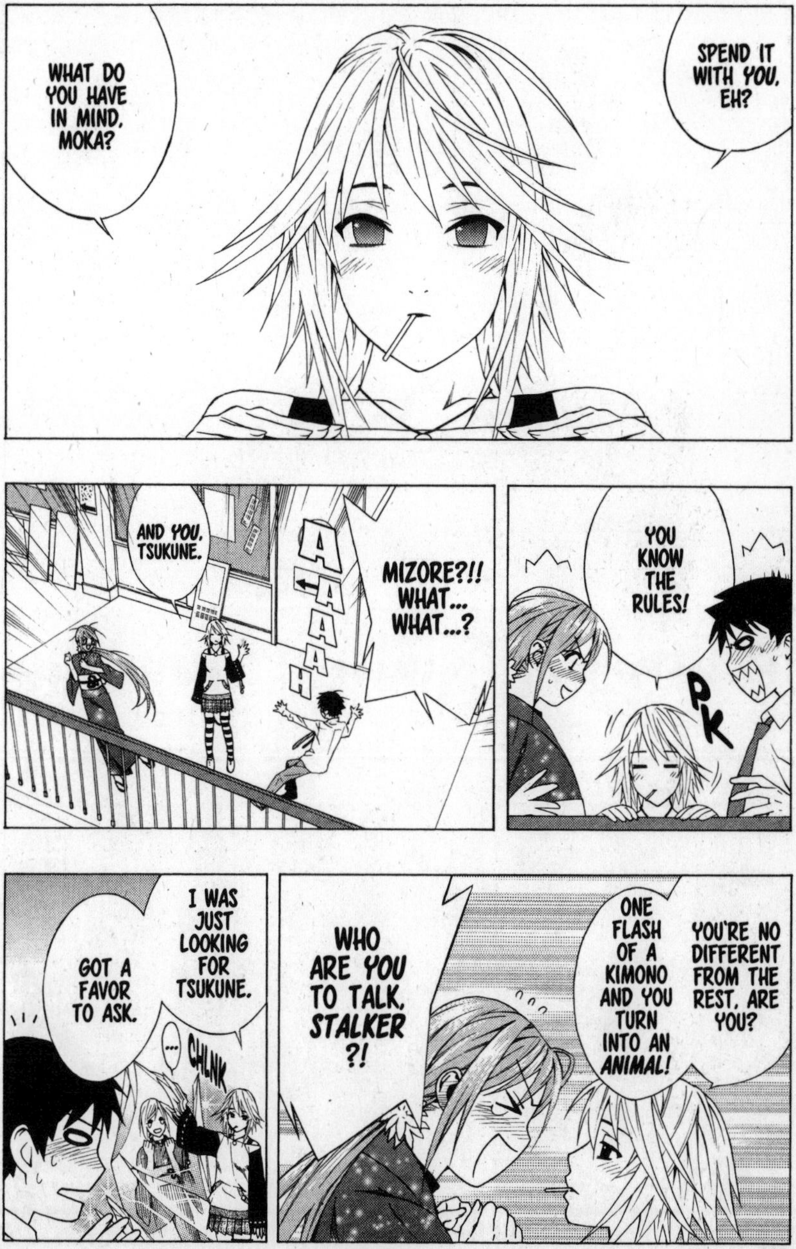
SPEND IT WITH YOU, EH?
WHAT DO YOU HAVE IN MIND, MOKA?
YOU KNOW THE RULES!
PK
MIZORE?!! WHAT... WHAT...?
AAAAAH
AND YOU, TSUKUNE.
YOU'RE NO DIFFERENT FROM THE REST, ARE YOU?
ONE FLASH OF A KIMONO AND YOU TURN INTO AN ANIMAL!
WHO ARE YOU TO TALK, STALKER?!
I WAS JUST LOOKING FOR TSUKUNE.
GOT A FAVOR TO ASK.
...
CHLNK

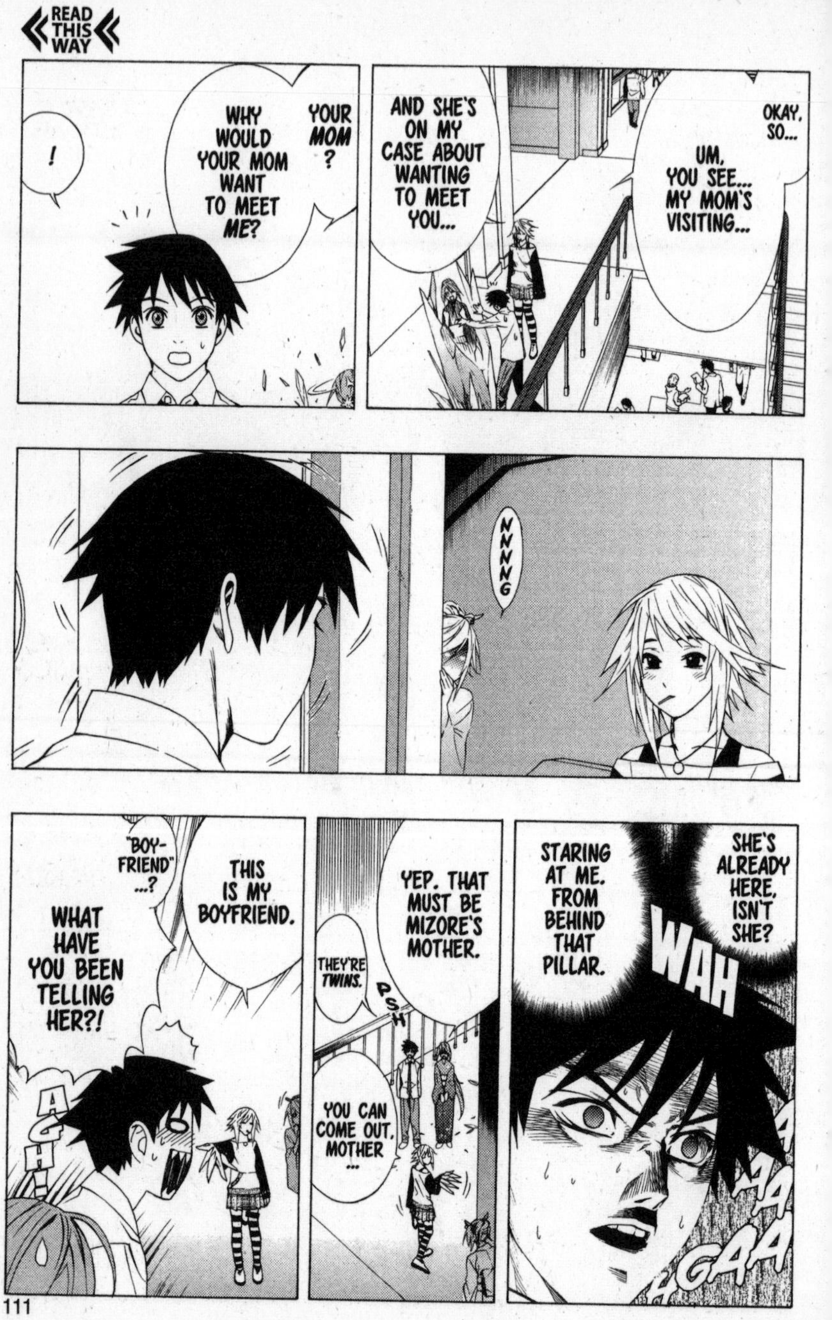
OKAY, SO...
UM, YOU SEE... MY MOM'S VISITING...
AND SHE'S ON MY CASE ABOUT WANTING TO MEET YOU...
YOUR MOM?
WHY WOULD YOUR MOM WANT TO MEET ME?
!
NNNNG
SHE'S ALREADY HERE, ISN'T SHE?
STARING AT ME. FROM BEHIND THAT PILLAR.
WAH
YEP. THAT MUST BE MIZORE'S MOTHER.
THEY'RE TWINS.
PSH
YOU CAN COME OUT, MOTHER...
THIS IS MY BOYFRIEND.
"BOY-FRIEND"...?
WHAT HAVE YOU BEEN TELLING HER?!
AGH

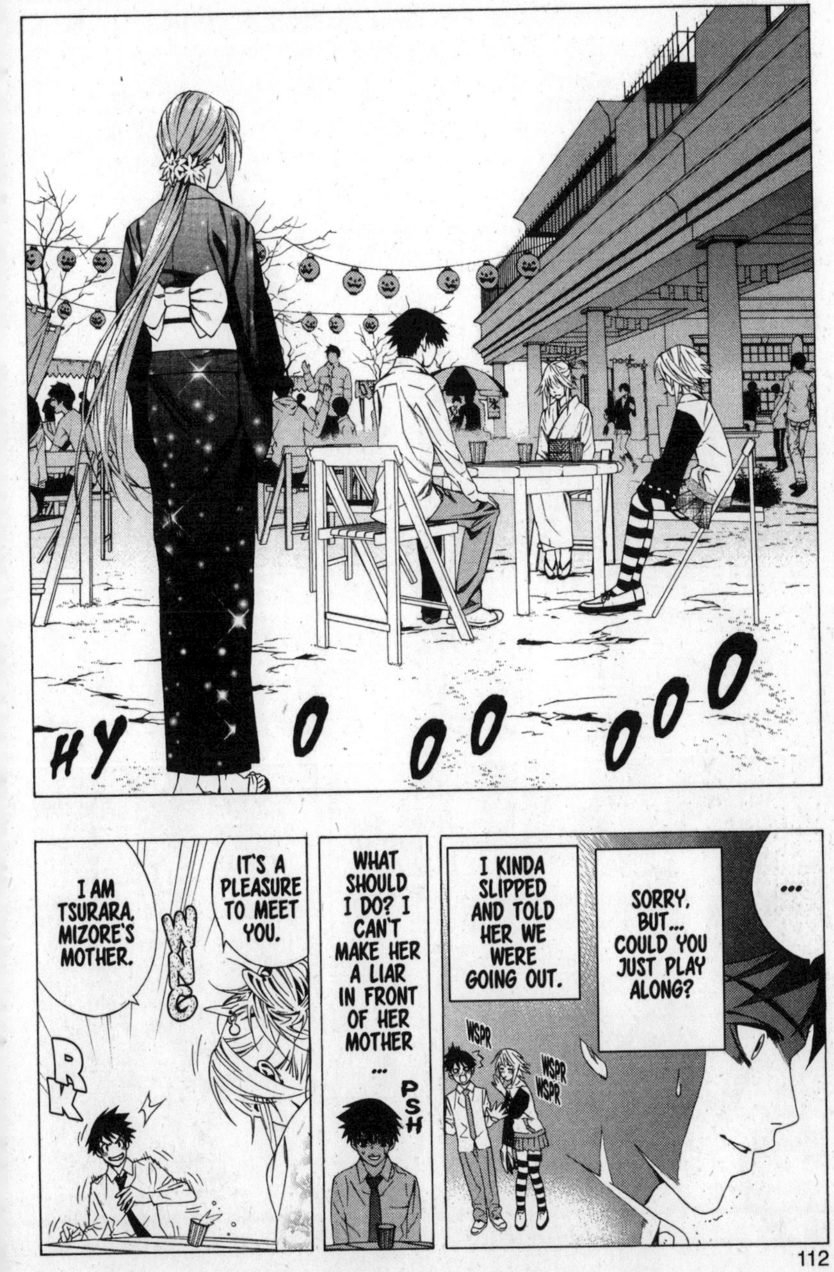
HYOOOOOO
...
SORRY, BUT... COULD YOU JUST PLAY ALONG?
I KINDA SLIPPED AND TOLD HER WE WERE GOING OUT.
WSPR
WSPR WSPR
WHAT SHOULD I DO? I CAN'T MAKE HER A LIAR IN FRONT OF HER MOTHER ...
PSH
IT'S A PLEASURE TO MEET YOU.
I AM TSURARA, MIZORE'S MOTHER.
RK

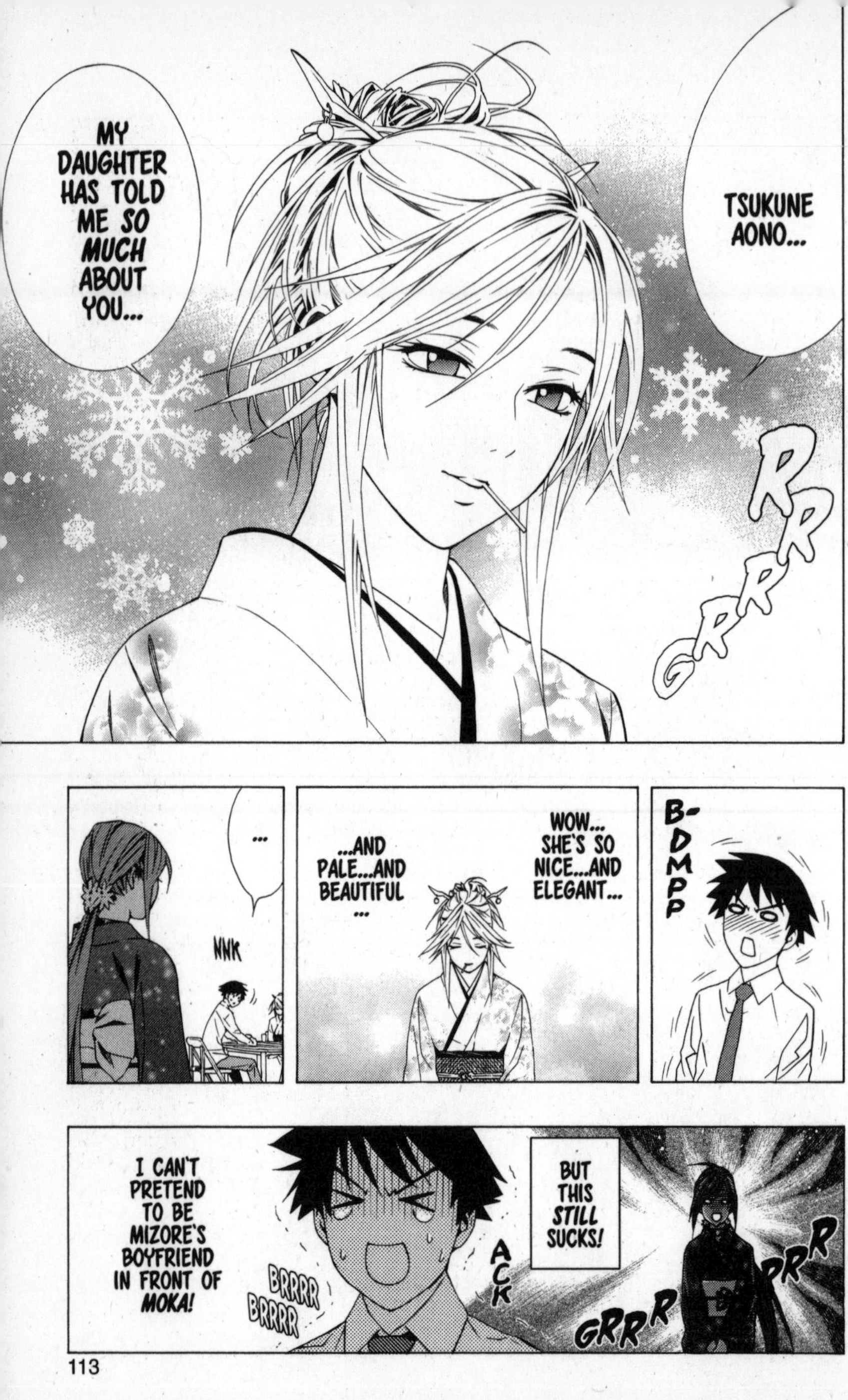
TSUKUNE AONO...
MY DAUGHTER HAS TOLD ME SO *MUCH* ABOUT YOU...
GRRRR
B-DMPP
WOW... SHE'S SO NICE...AND ELEGANT...
...AND PALE...AND BEAUTIFUL ...
...
NNK
GRRRR
BUT THIS *STILL* SUCKS!
ACK
BRRRR BRRRR
I CAN'T PRETEND TO BE MIZORE'S BOYFRIEND IN FRONT OF *MOKA!*

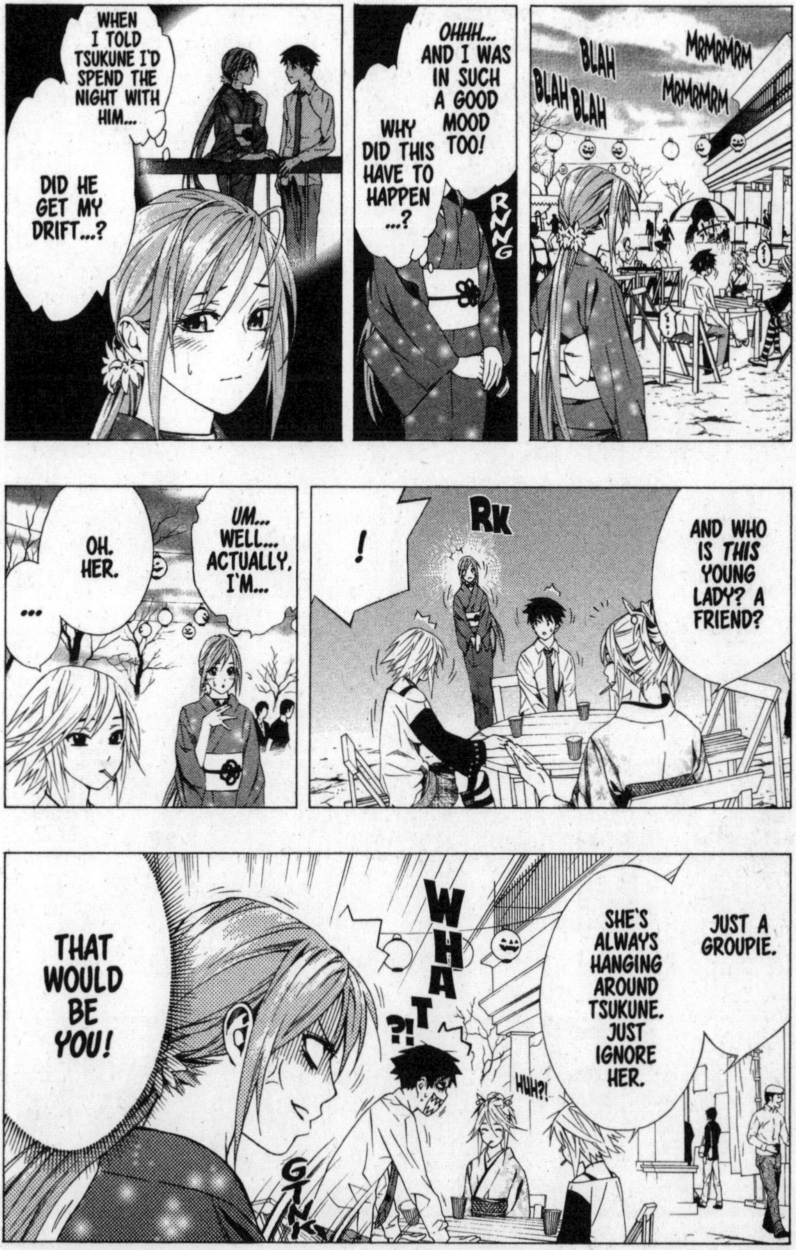
BLAH
BLAH BLAH
MRMRMRM
MRMRMRM
OHHH... AND I WAS IN SUCH A GOOD MOOD TOO!
WHY DID THIS HAVE TO HAPPEN ...?
RNNG
WHEN I TOLD TSUKUNE I'D SPEND THE NIGHT WITH HIM...
DID HE GET MY DRIFT...?
AND WHO IS THIS YOUNG LADY? A FRIEND?
RK
!
UM... WELL... ACTUALLY, I'M...
OH. HER.
...
JUST A GROUPIE.
SHE'S ALWAYS HANGING AROUND TSUKUNE. JUST IGNORE HER.
HUH?!
WHAT
?!
THAT WOULD BE YOU!
GTINK

READ THIS WAY

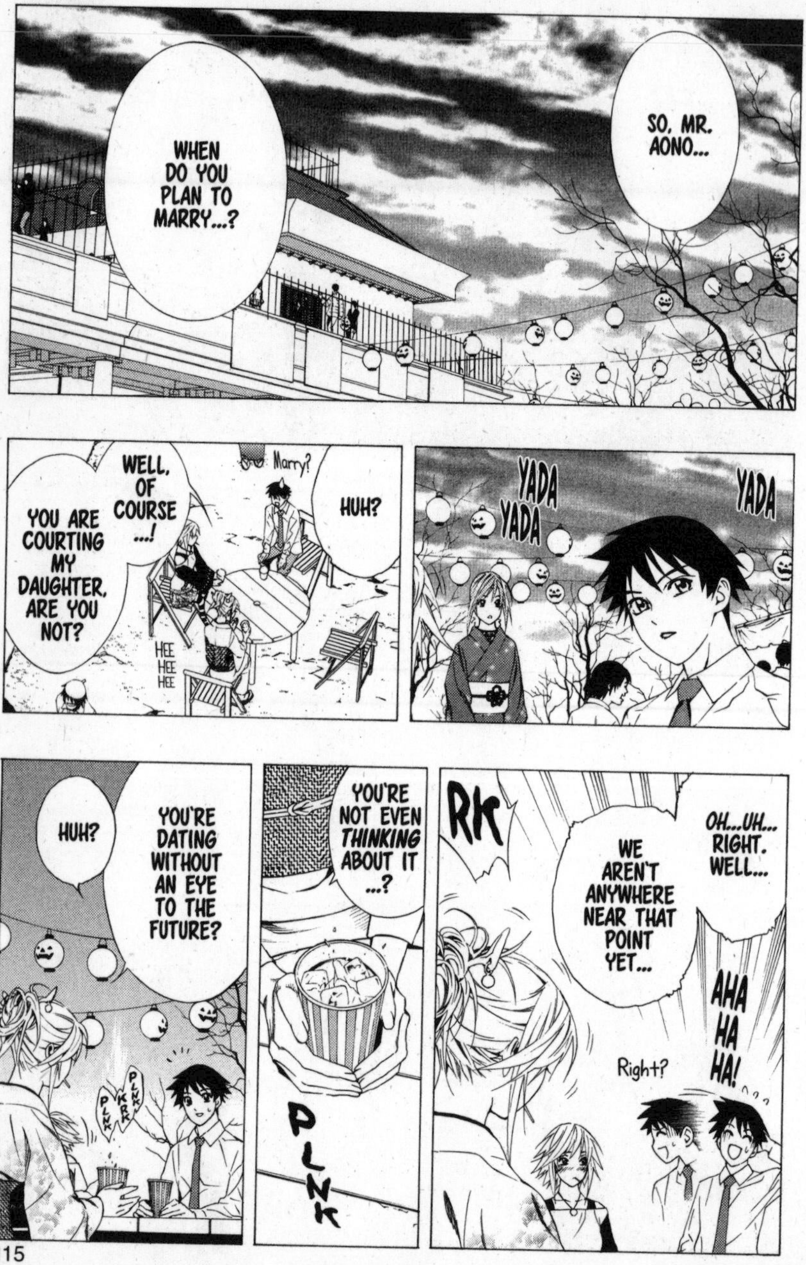

SO, MR. AONO...
WHEN DO YOU PLAN TO MARRY...?
YADA
YADA YADA
YADA
HUH?
Marry?
WELL, OF COURSE...!
YOU ARE COURTING MY DAUGHTER, ARE YOU NOT?
HEE HEE HEE
OH...UH... RIGHT. WELL...
WE AREN'T ANYWHERE NEAR THAT POINT YET...
RK
AHA HA HA!
Right?
YOU'RE NOT EVEN THINKING ABOUT IT ...?
PLNK
YOU'RE DATING WITHOUT AN EYE TO THE FUTURE?
HUH?
PLNK KRK PLNK

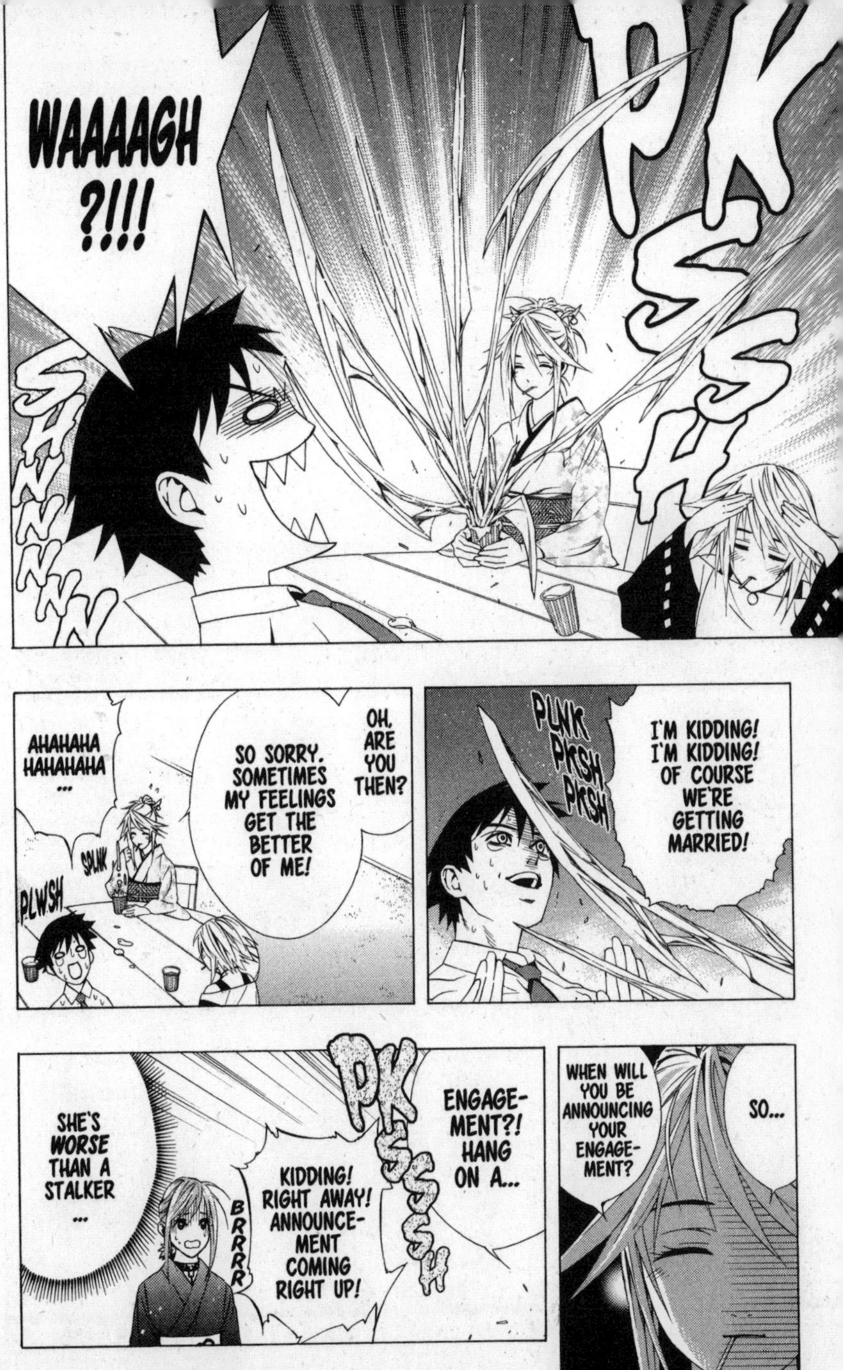
PKSSH
WAAAAGH ?!!!
SHNNNNN
PLNK PKSH PKSH
I'M KIDDING! I'M KIDDING! OF COURSE WE'RE GETTING MARRIED!
OH, ARE YOU THEN?
SO SORRY. SOMETIMES MY FEELINGS GET THE BETTER OF ME!
AHAHAHA HAHAHAHA ...
SPLNK
PLWSH
SO...
WHEN WILL YOU BE ANNOUNCING YOUR ENGAGE-MENT?
PKSSSH
ENGAGE-MENT?! HANG ON A...
KIDDING! RIGHT AWAY! ANNOUNCE-MENT COMING RIGHT UP!
BRRRR
SHE'S WORSE THAN A STALKER ...

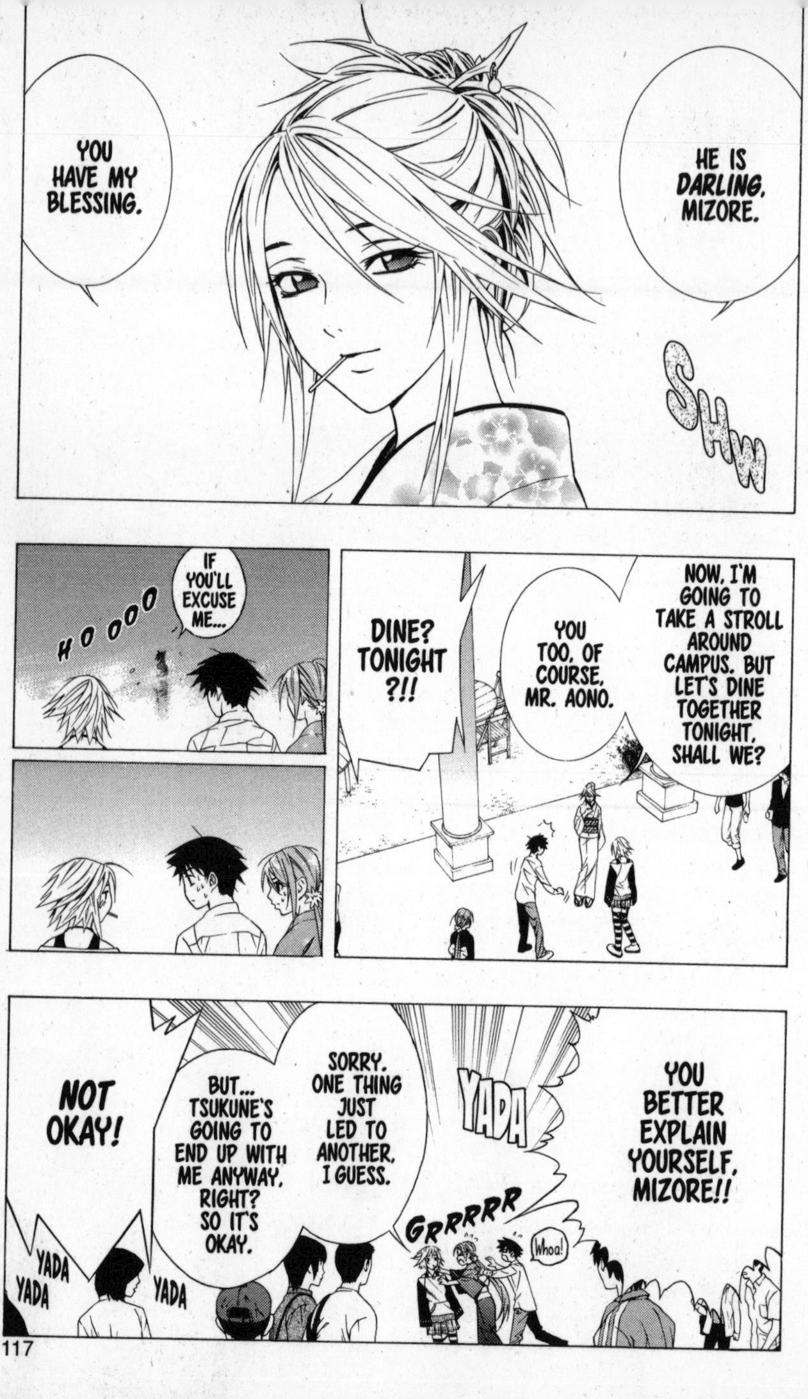
HE IS DARLING, MIZORE.
SHW
YOU HAVE MY BLESSING.
NOW, I'M GOING TO TAKE A STROLL AROUND CAMPUS. BUT LET'S DINE TOGETHER TONIGHT, SHALL WE?
YOU TOO, OF COURSE, MR. AONO.
DINE? TONIGHT?!!
IF YOU'LL EXCUSE ME...
HOOOO
YOU BETTER EXPLAIN YOURSELF, MIZORE!!
YADA
Whoa!
GRRRRR
SORRY. ONE THING JUST LED TO ANOTHER, I GUESS.
BUT... TSUKUNE'S GOING TO END UP WITH ME ANYWAY, RIGHT? SO IT'S OKAY.
YADA
NOT OKAY!
YADA
YADA

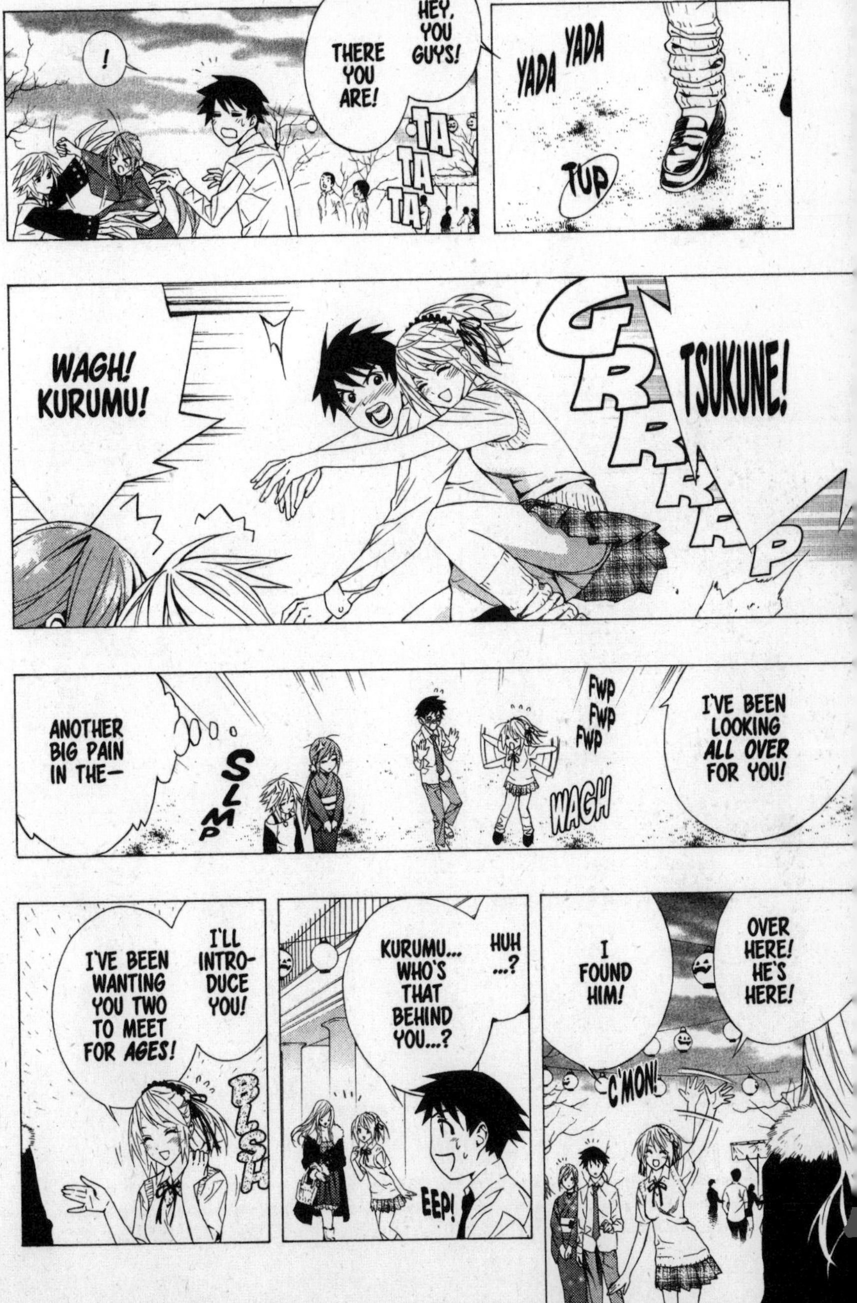
YADA YADA
TUP
HEY, YOU GUYS!
THERE YOU ARE!
TA TA TA
!
TSUKUNE!
GRRRAP
WAGH! KURUMU!
I'VE BEEN LOOKING ALL OVER FOR YOU!
FWP FWP FWP
WAGH
SLMP
ANOTHER BIG PAIN IN THE—
OVER HERE! HE'S HERE!
I FOUND HIM!
C'MON!
HUH...?
KURUMU... WHO'S THAT BEHIND YOU...?
EEP!
I'LL INTRODUCE YOU!
I'VE BEEN WANTING YOU TWO TO MEET FOR AGES!
BLSH

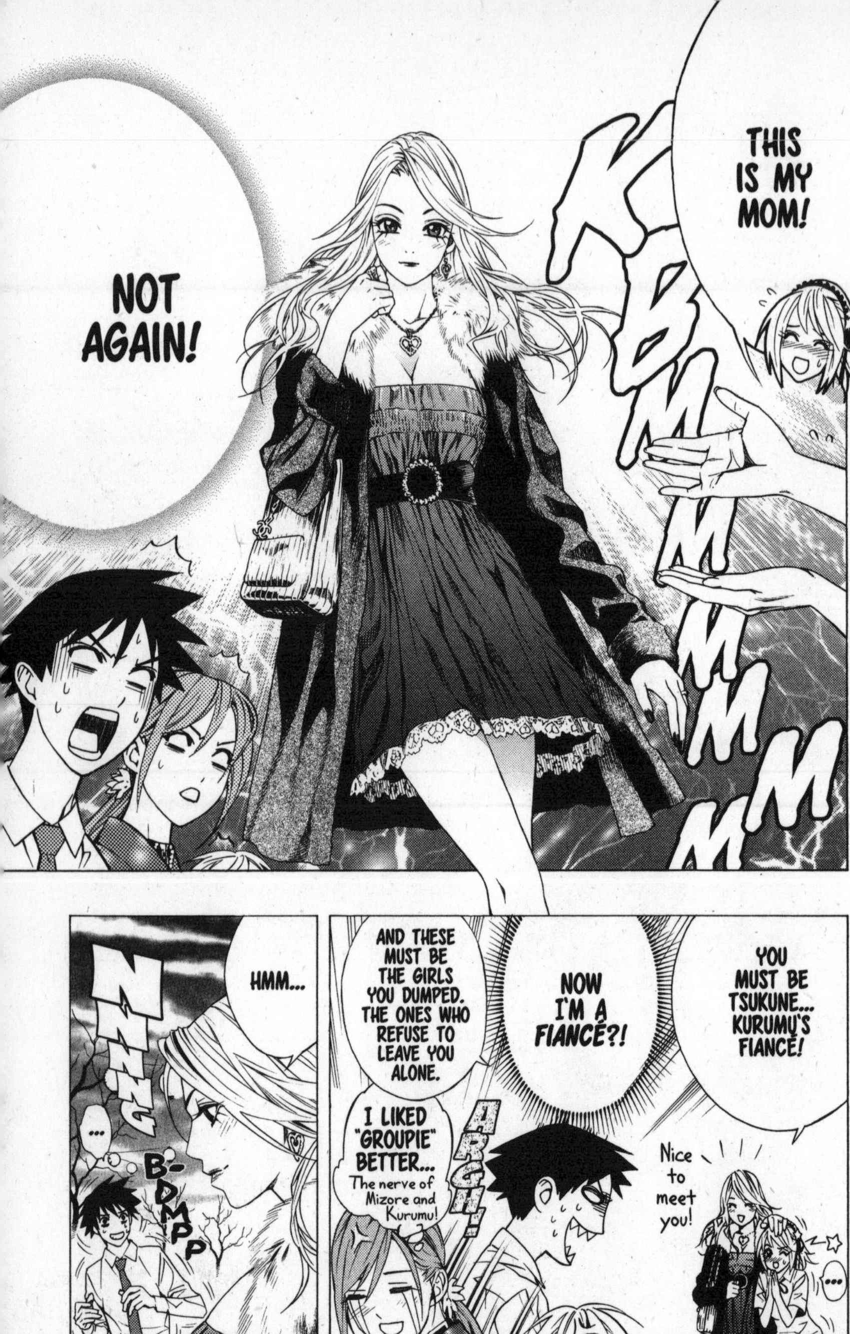
THIS IS MY MOM!
NOT AGAIN!
YOU MUST BE TSUKUNE... KURUMU'S FIANCÉ!
Nice to meet you!
...
NOW I'M A FIANCÉ?!
ARGH!
AND THESE MUST BE THE GIRLS YOU DUMPED. THE ONES WHO REFUSE TO LEAVE YOU ALONE.
I LIKED "GROUPIE" BETTER...
The nerve of Mizore and Kurumu!
HMM...
NNNNG
...
B-DMPP

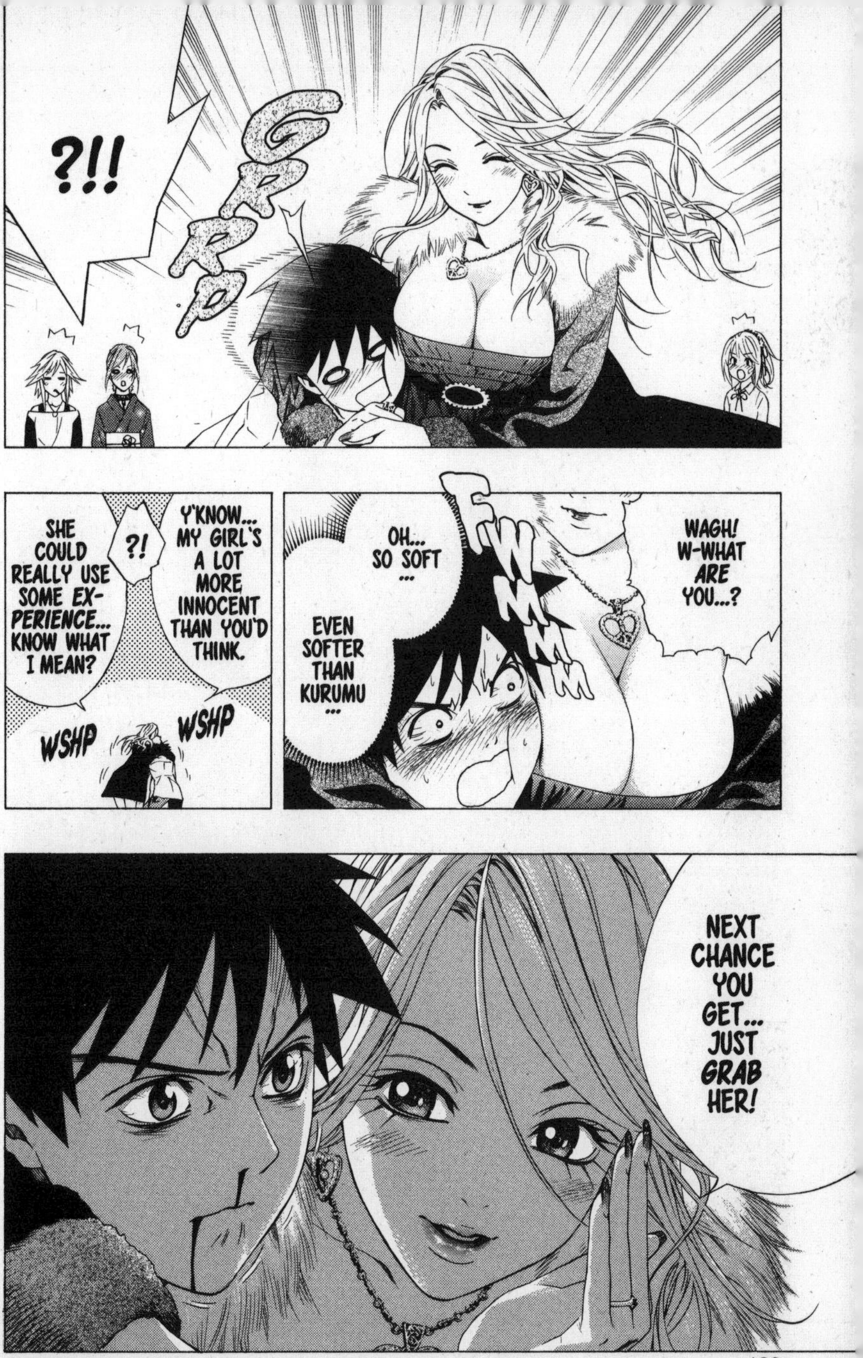
GRRP
?!!
WAGH! W-WHAT ARE YOU...?
FWMMM
OH... SO SOFT ...
EVEN SOFTER THAN KURUMU ...
Y'KNOW... MY GIRL'S A LOT MORE INNOCENT THAN YOU'D THINK.
?!
SHE COULD REALLY USE SOME EX-PERIENCE... KNOW WHAT I MEAN?
WSHP
WSHP
NEXT CHANCE YOU GET... JUST GRAB HER!

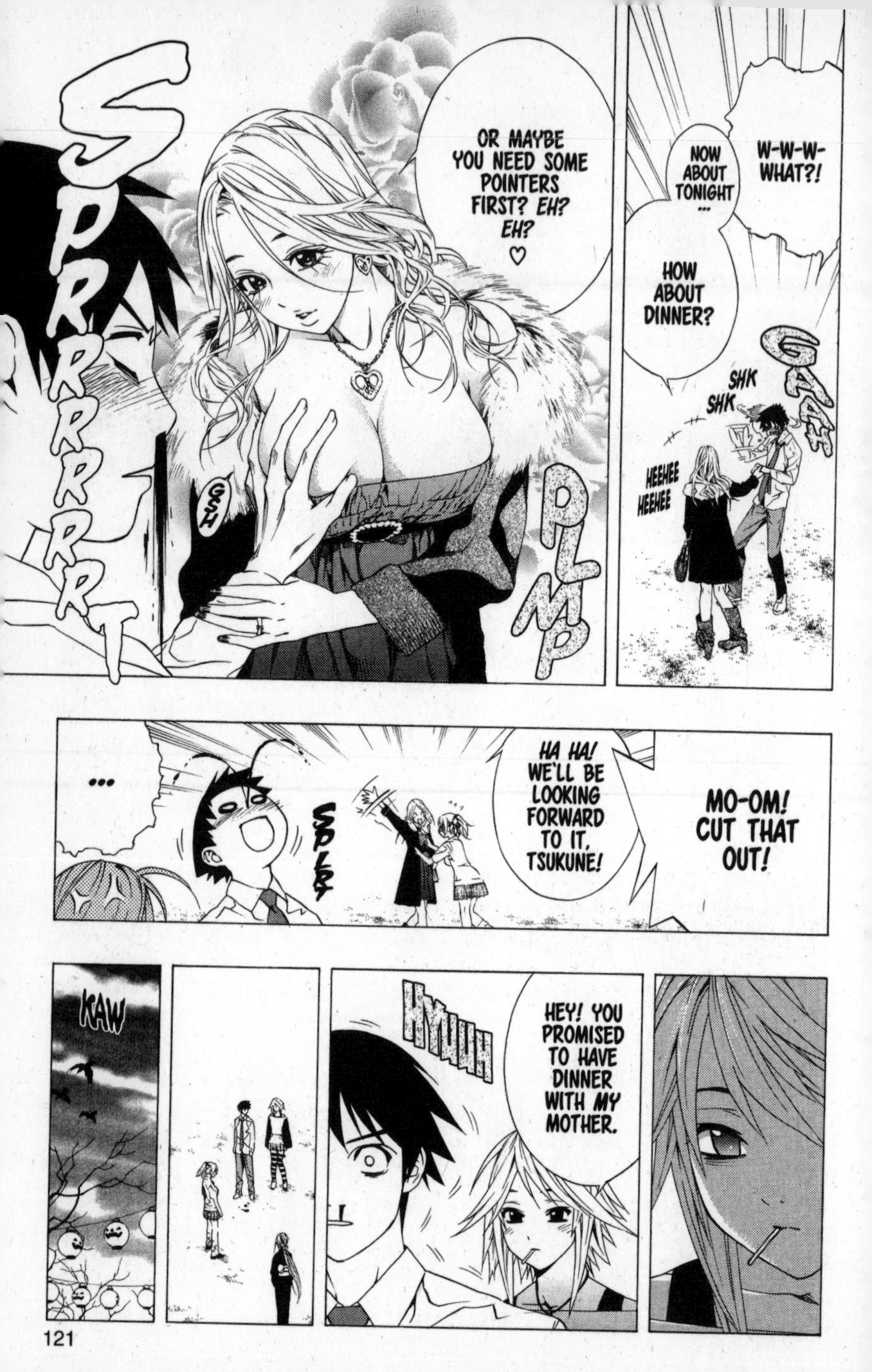
W-W-W-WHAT?!
NOW ABOUT TONIGHT...
HOW ABOUT DINNER?
GAAAH
SHK SHK
HEEHEE HEEHEE
OR MAYBE YOU NEED SOME POINTERS FIRST? EH? EH? ♡
SPRRRRRRT
PLMP
GSH
MO-OM! CUT THAT OUT!
HA HA! WE'LL BE LOOKING FORWARD TO IT, TSUKUNE!
...
HEY! YOU PROMISED TO HAVE DINNER WITH MY MOTHER.
HYUUH
KAW

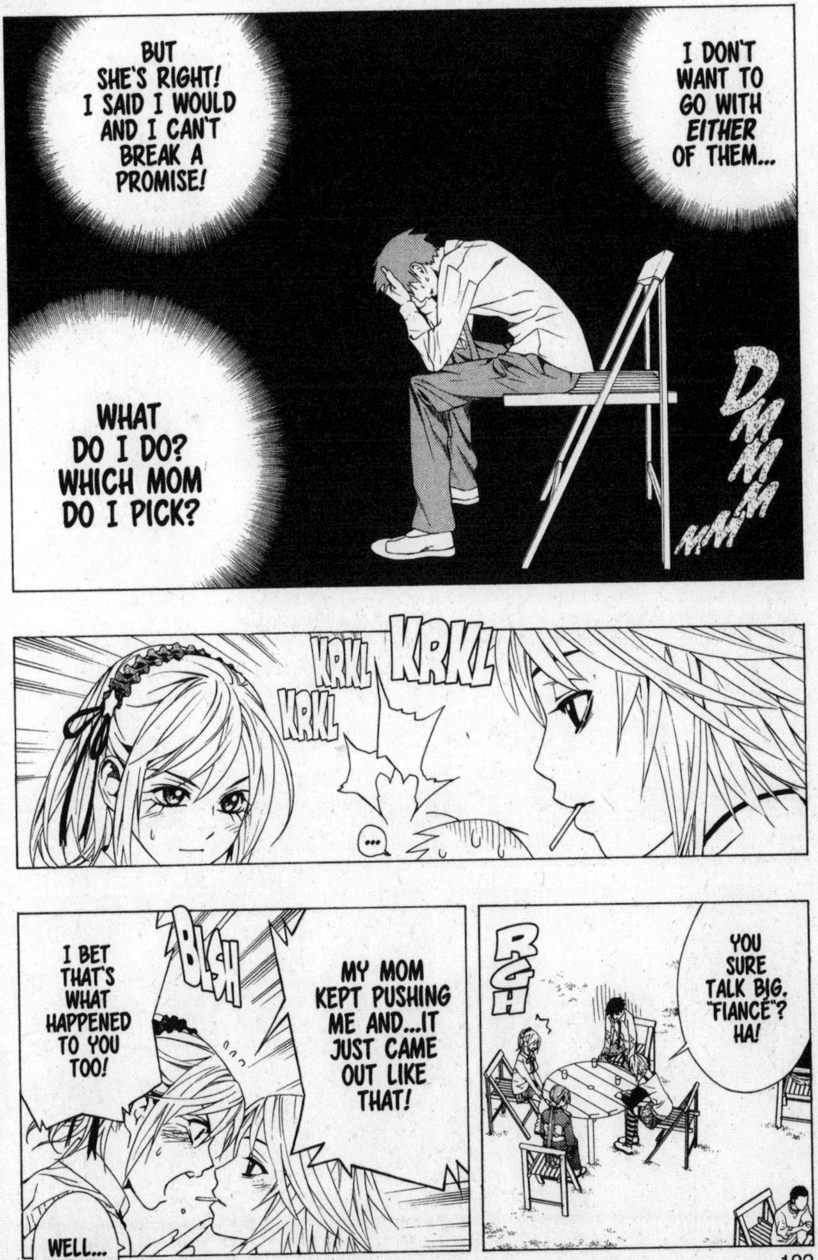
I DON'T WANT TO GO WITH *EITHER* OF THEM...
BUT SHE'S RIGHT! I SAID I WOULD AND I CAN'T BREAK A PROMISE!
WHAT DO I DO? WHICH MOM DO I PICK?
DMMMMM
KRKL KRKL
KRKL
...
RGH
YOU SURE TALK BIG. "FIANCÉ"? HA!
BLSH
MY MOM KEPT PUSHING ME AND...IT JUST CAME OUT LIKE THAT!
I BET THAT'S WHAT HAPPENED TO YOU TOO!
WELL... YEAH.

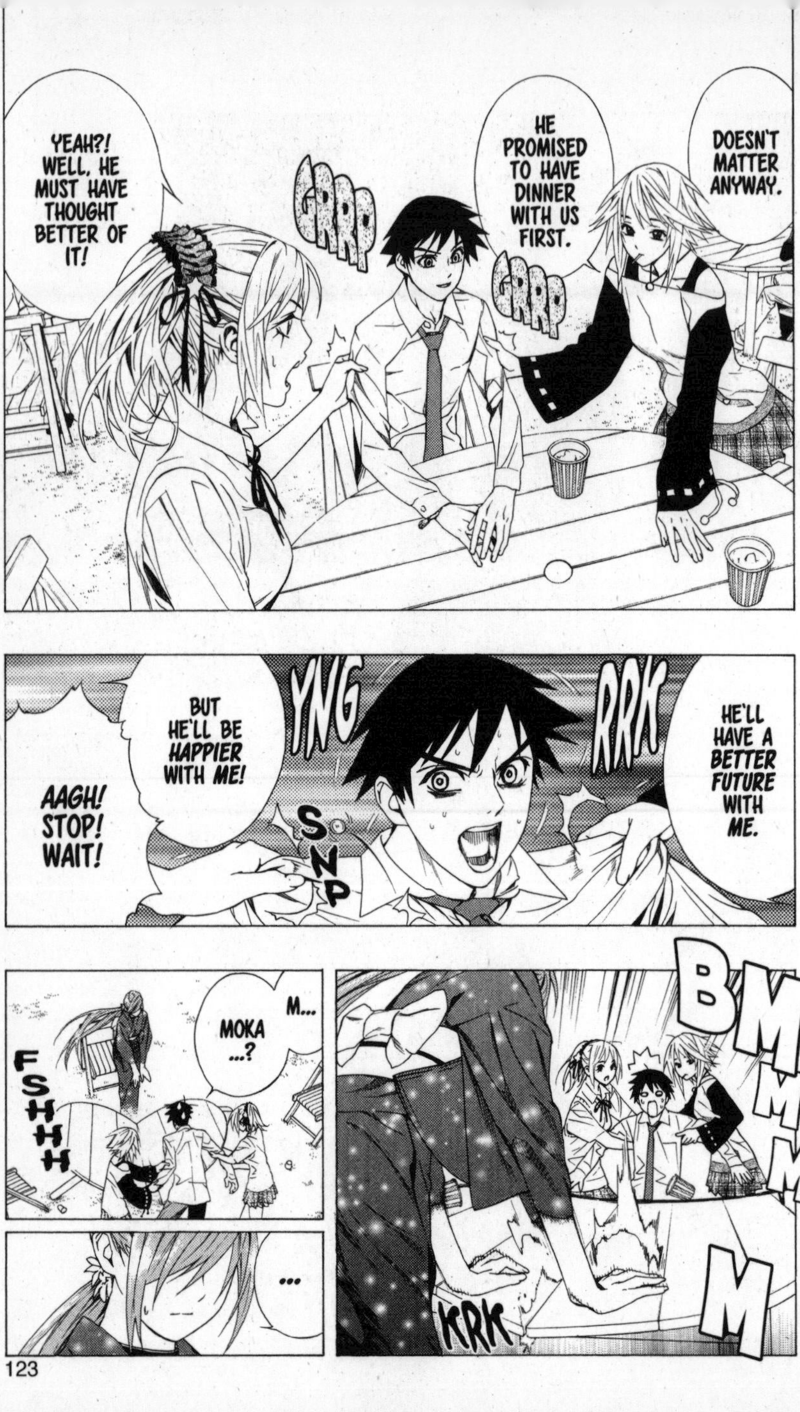
DOESN'T MATTER ANYWAY.
HE PROMISED TO HAVE DINNER WITH US FIRST.
GRRP
GRRP
YEAH?! WELL, HE MUST HAVE THOUGHT BETTER OF IT!
HE'LL HAVE A BETTER FUTURE WITH ME.
RRK
YNG
BUT HE'LL BE HAPPIER WITH ME!
SNP
AAGH! STOP! WAIT!
BMMMMM
KRK
M... MOKA ...?
FSHHH
...

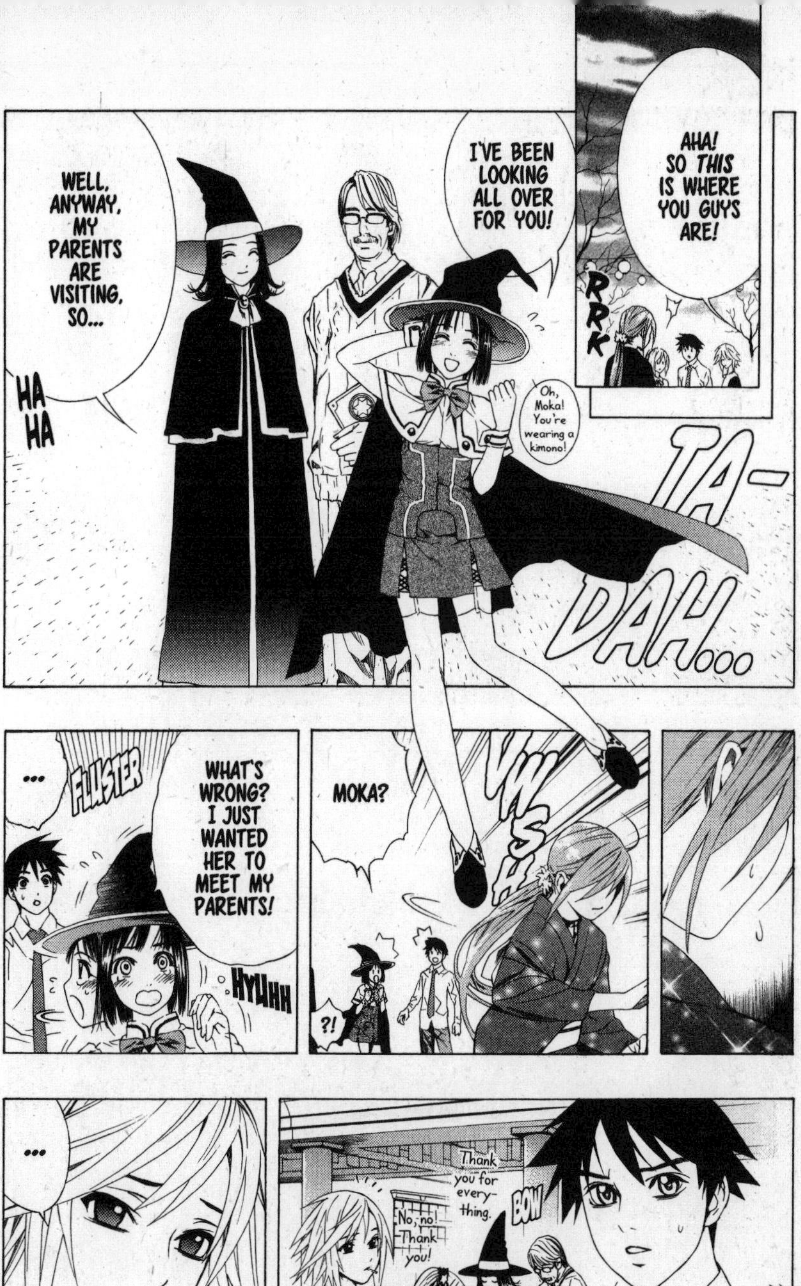
AHA! SO THIS IS WHERE YOU GUYS ARE!
RRK
I'VE BEEN LOOKING ALL OVER FOR YOU!
Oh, Moka! You're wearing a kimono!
TA-DAH...
WELL, ANYWAY, MY PARENTS ARE VISITING, SO...
HA HA
VWSH
MOKA?
?!
WHAT'S WRONG? I JUST WANTED HER TO MEET MY PARENTS!
FLUSTER
...
HYUHH
Thank you for everything.
BOW
No, no! Thank you!
BOW
BOW
...

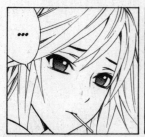

READ THIS WAY

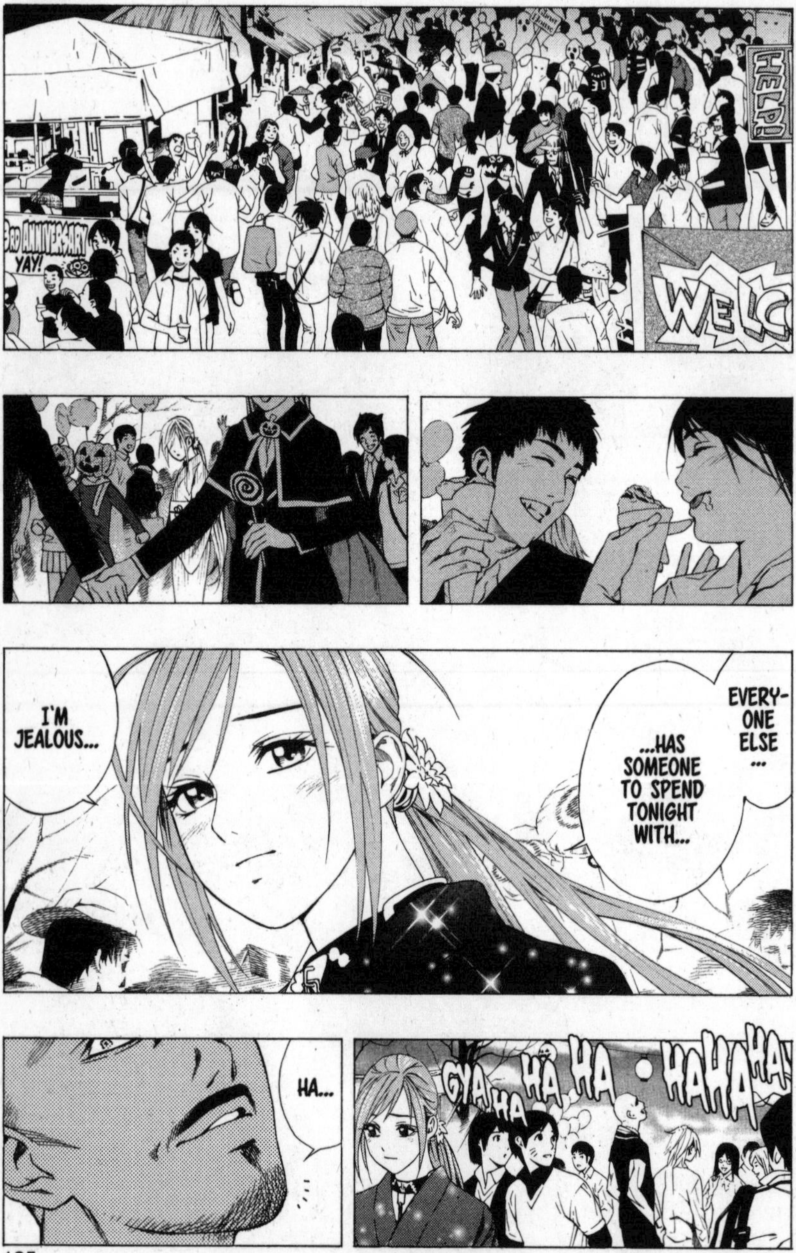
HELP!
3RD ANNIVERSARY
YAY!
WELC
EVERY-ONE ELSE...
...HAS SOMEONE TO SPEND TONIGHT WITH...
I'M JEALOUS...
GYA HA HA HA HA HA HAHAHA HA
HA...
...

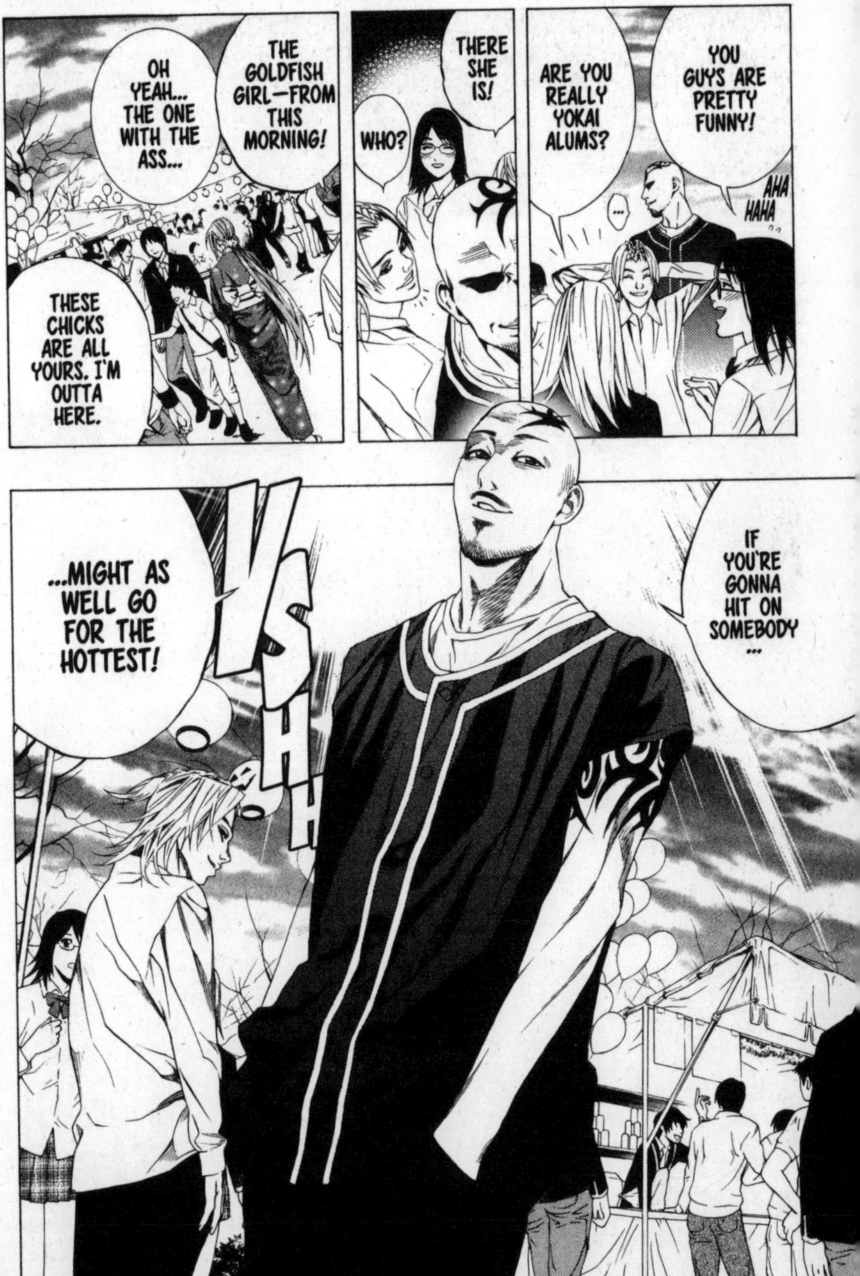
YOU GUYS ARE PRETTY FUNNY!
AHA HAHA
ARE YOU REALLY YOKAI ALUMS?
...
THERE SHE IS!
WHO?
THE GOLDFISH GIRL—FROM THIS MORNING!
OH YEAH... THE ONE WITH THE ASS...
THESE CHICKS ARE ALL YOURS. I'M OUTTA HERE.
IF YOU'RE GONNA HIT ON SOMEBODY...
VSHH
...MIGHT AS WELL GO FOR THE HOTTEST!

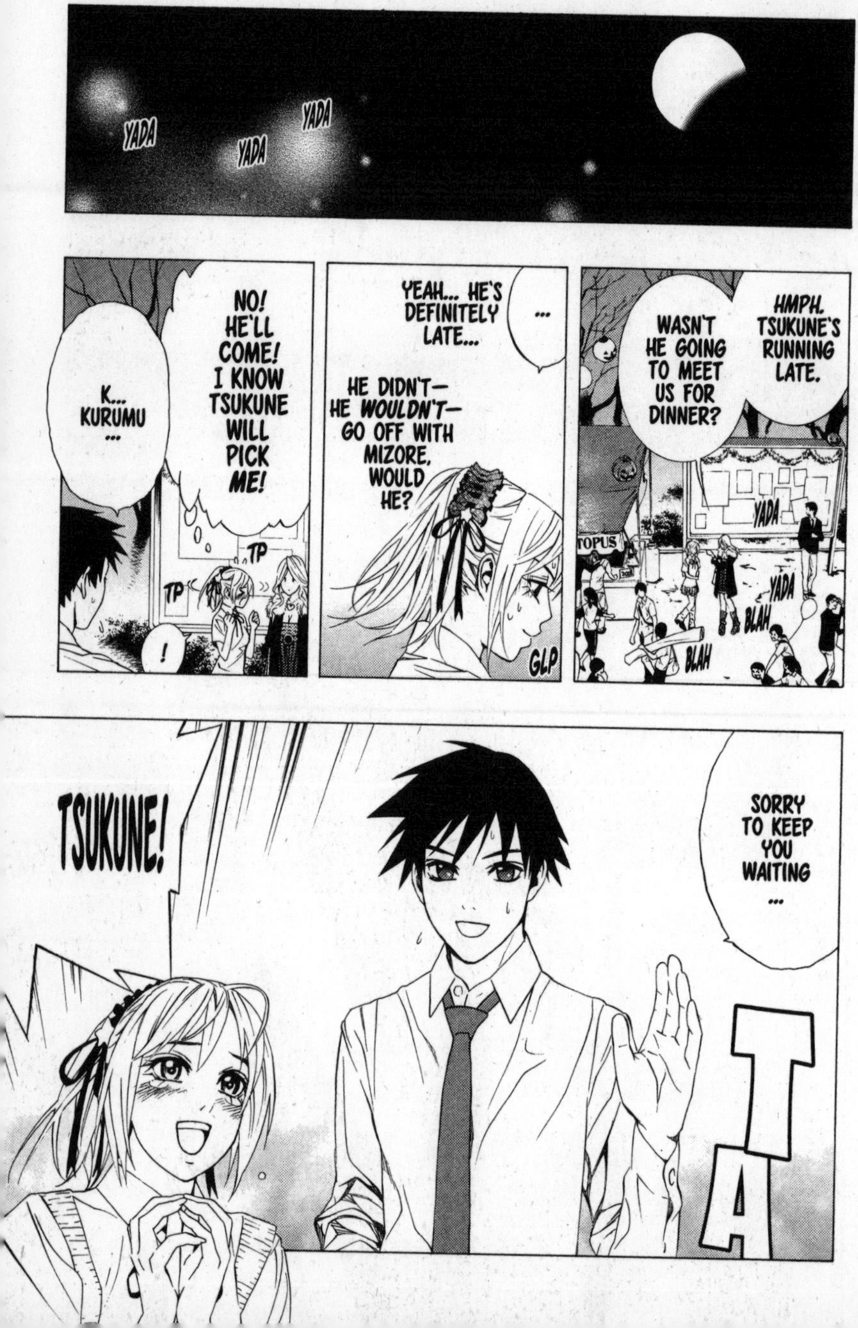
YADA
YADA
YADA
HMPH. TSUKUNE'S RUNNING LATE.
WASN'T HE GOING TO MEET US FOR DINNER?
YADA
YADA
BLAH
BLAH
...
YEAH... HE'S DEFINITELY LATE...
HE DIDN'T—HE *WOULDN'T*—GO OFF WITH MIZORE, WOULD HE?
GLP
NO! HE'LL COME! I KNOW TSUKUNE WILL PICK *ME!*
K... KURUMU ...
TP
TP
!
SORRY TO KEEP YOU WAITING ...
TA
TSUKUNE!

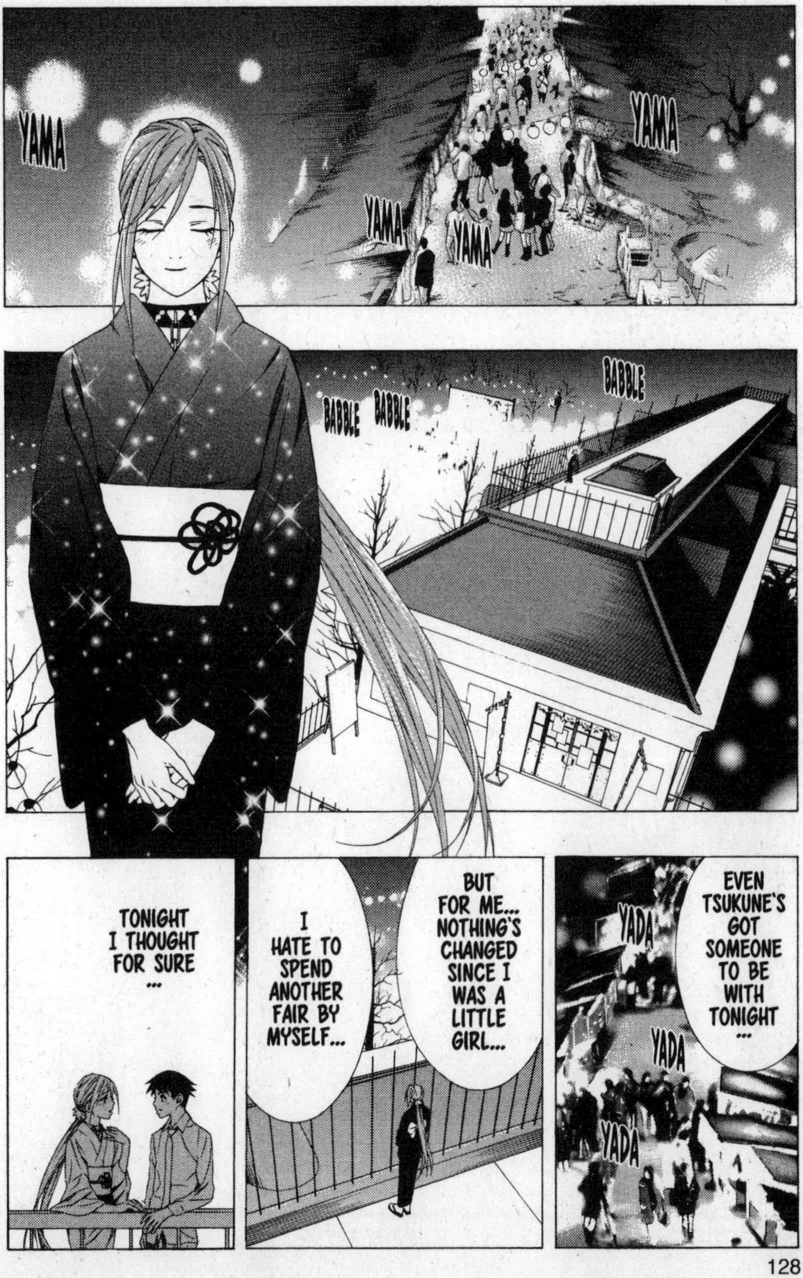
YAMA
YAMA
YAMA
YAMA
BABBLE
BABBLE
BABBLE
EVEN TSUKUNE'S GOT SOMEONE TO BE WITH TONIGHT...
YADA
YADA
YADA
BUT FOR ME... NOTHING'S CHANGED SINCE I WAS A LITTLE GIRL...
I HATE TO SPEND ANOTHER FAIR BY MYSELF...
TONIGHT I THOUGHT FOR SURE...

READ THIS WAY

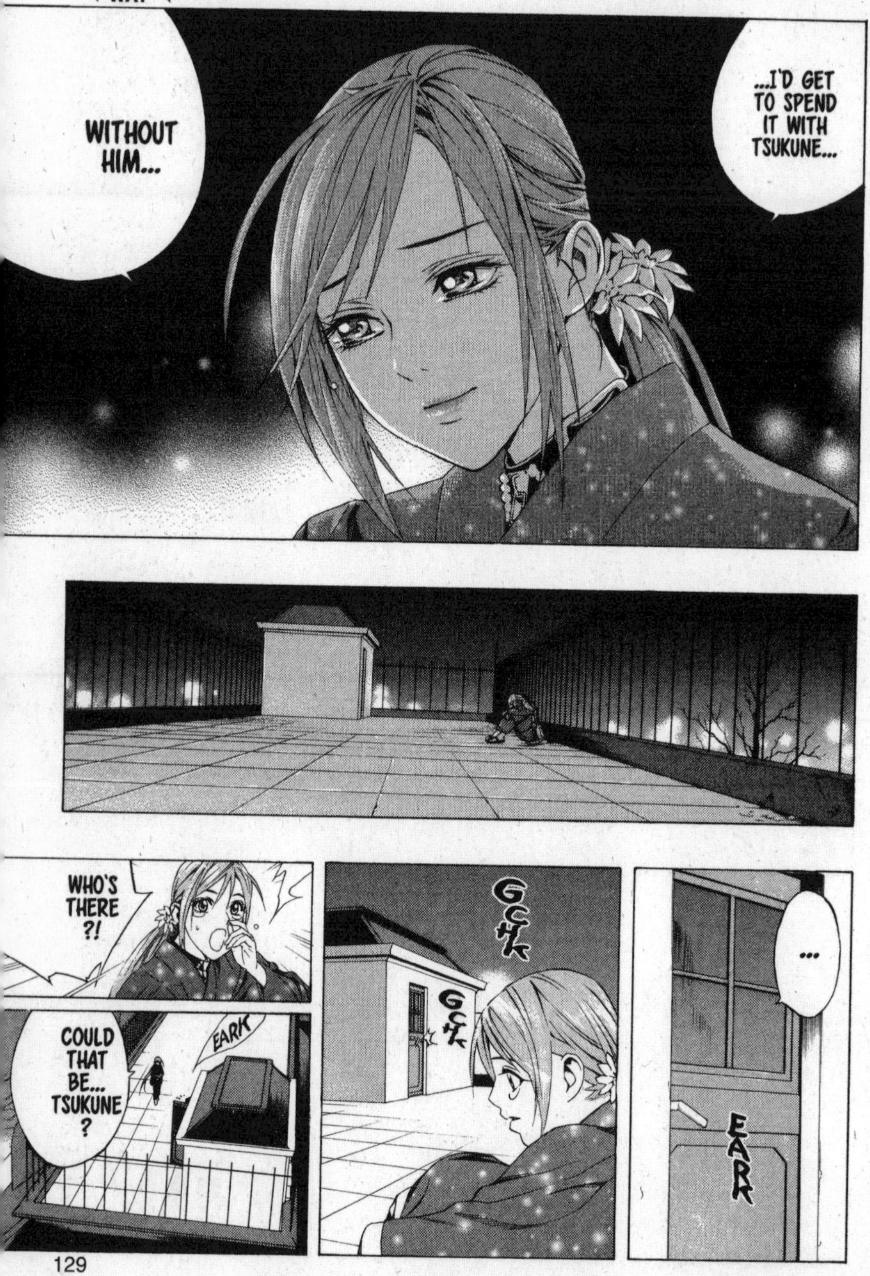

...I'D GET TO SPEND IT WITH TSUKUNE...
WITHOUT HIM...
...
EARK
GCHK
GCHK
WHO'S THERE?!
COULD THAT BE... TSUKUNE?
EARK

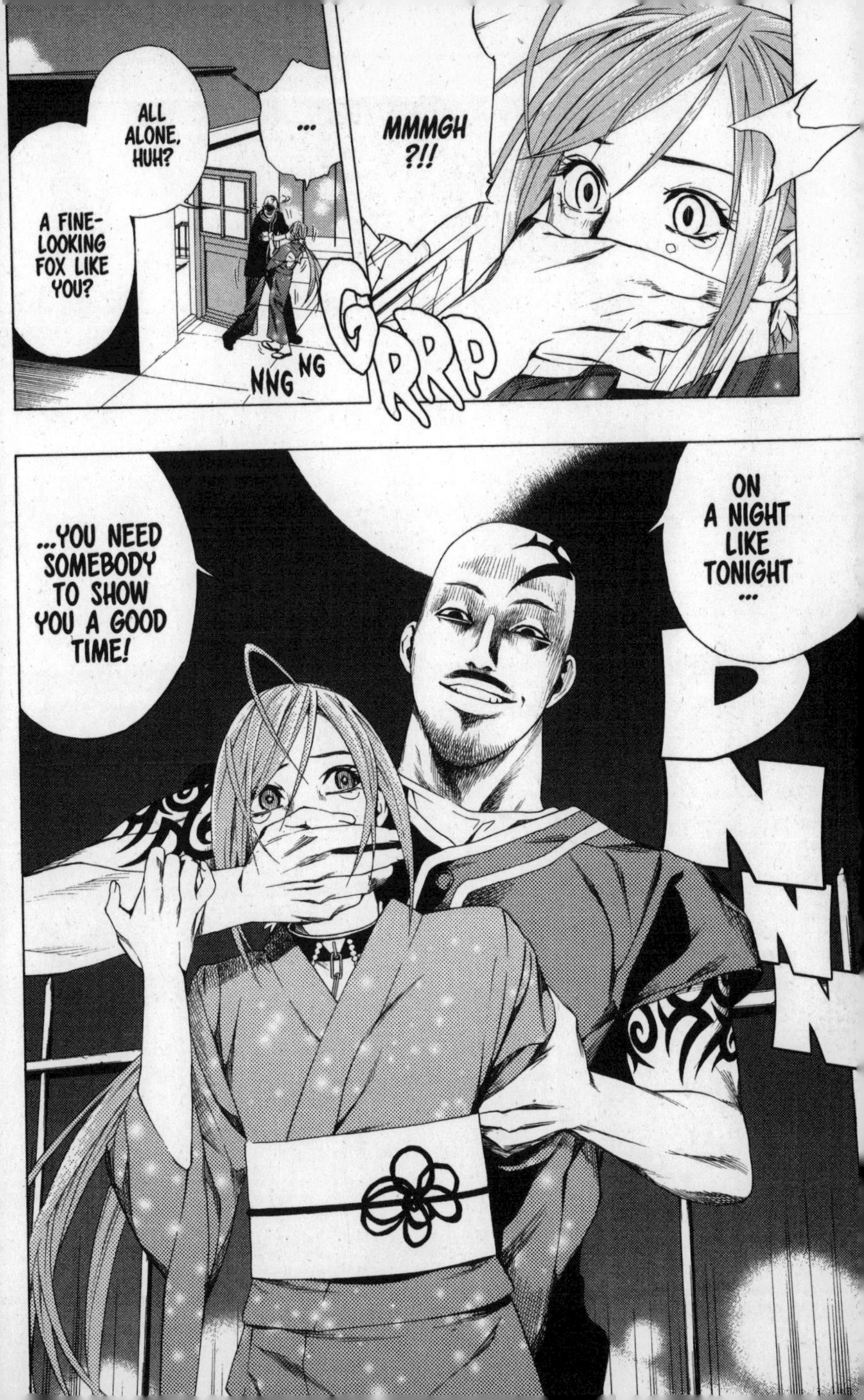
MMMGH ?!!
GRRP
...
ALL ALONE, HUH?
A FINE-LOOKING FOX LIKE YOU?
NNG NG
ON A NIGHT LIKE TONIGHT ...
...YOU NEED SOMEBODY TO SHOW YOU A GOOD TIME!
DNN

READ THIS WAY

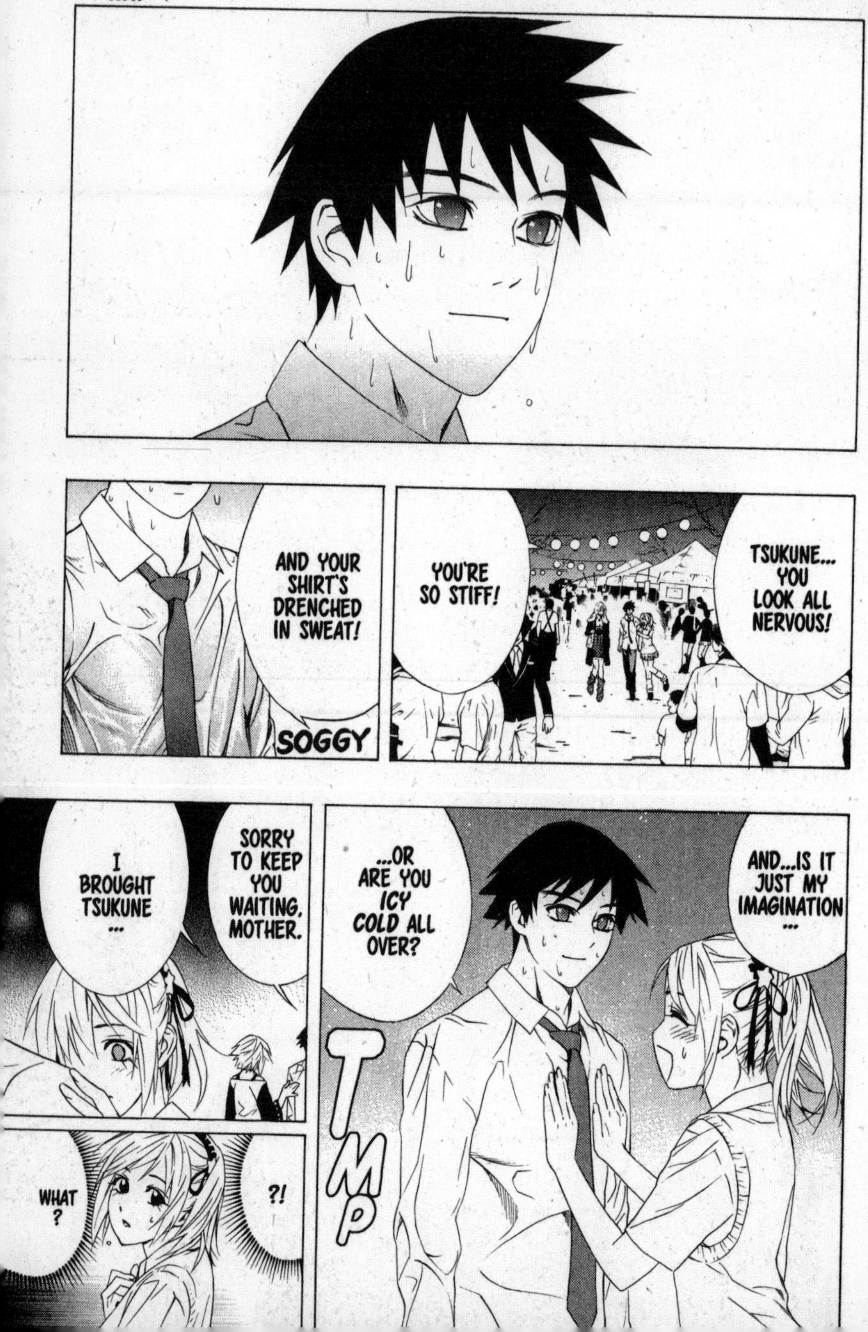
TSUKUNE... YOU LOOK ALL NERVOUS!
YOU'RE SO STIFF!
AND YOUR SHIRT'S DRENCHED IN SWEAT!
SOGGY
AND...IS IT JUST MY IMAGINATION...
...OR ARE YOU ICY COLD ALL OVER?
TMP
SORRY TO KEEP YOU WAITING, MOTHER.
I BROUGHT TSUKUNE...
?!
WHAT?

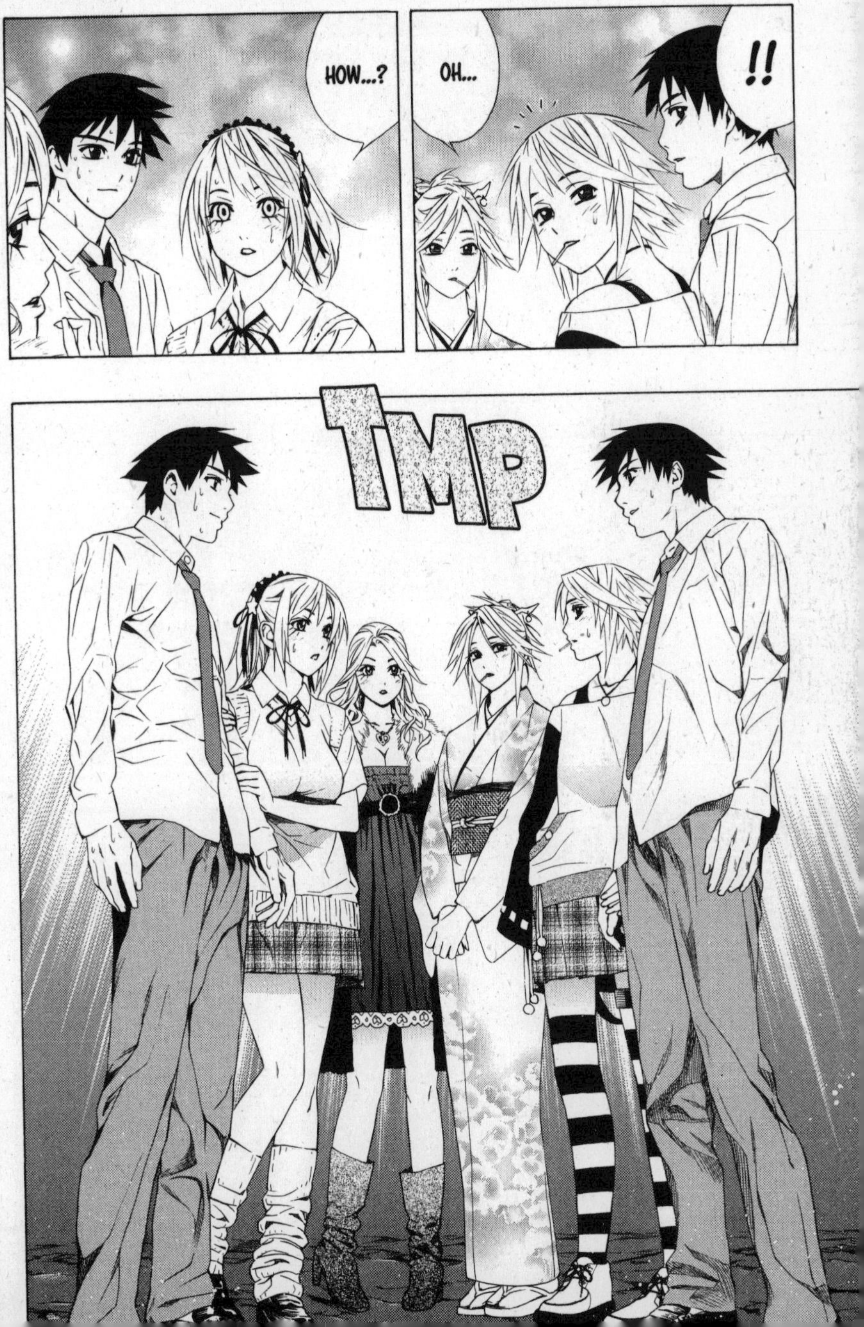
!!
OH...
HOW...?
TMP

READ THIS WAY

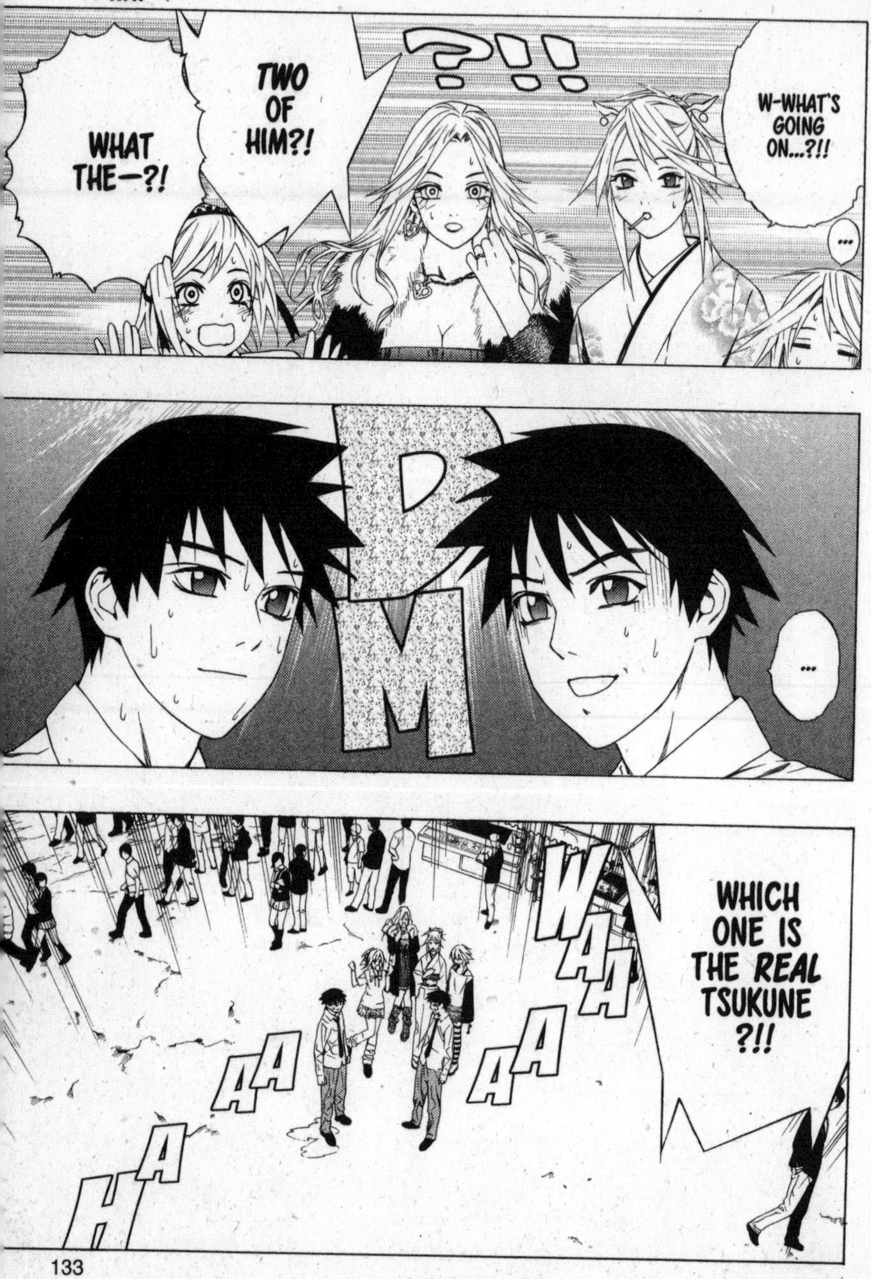
W-WHAT'S GOING ON...?!!
...
?!!
TWO OF HIM?!
WHAT THE—?!
...
DM
WHICH ONE IS THE REAL TSUKUNE?!!
WAAAAA
HAAA

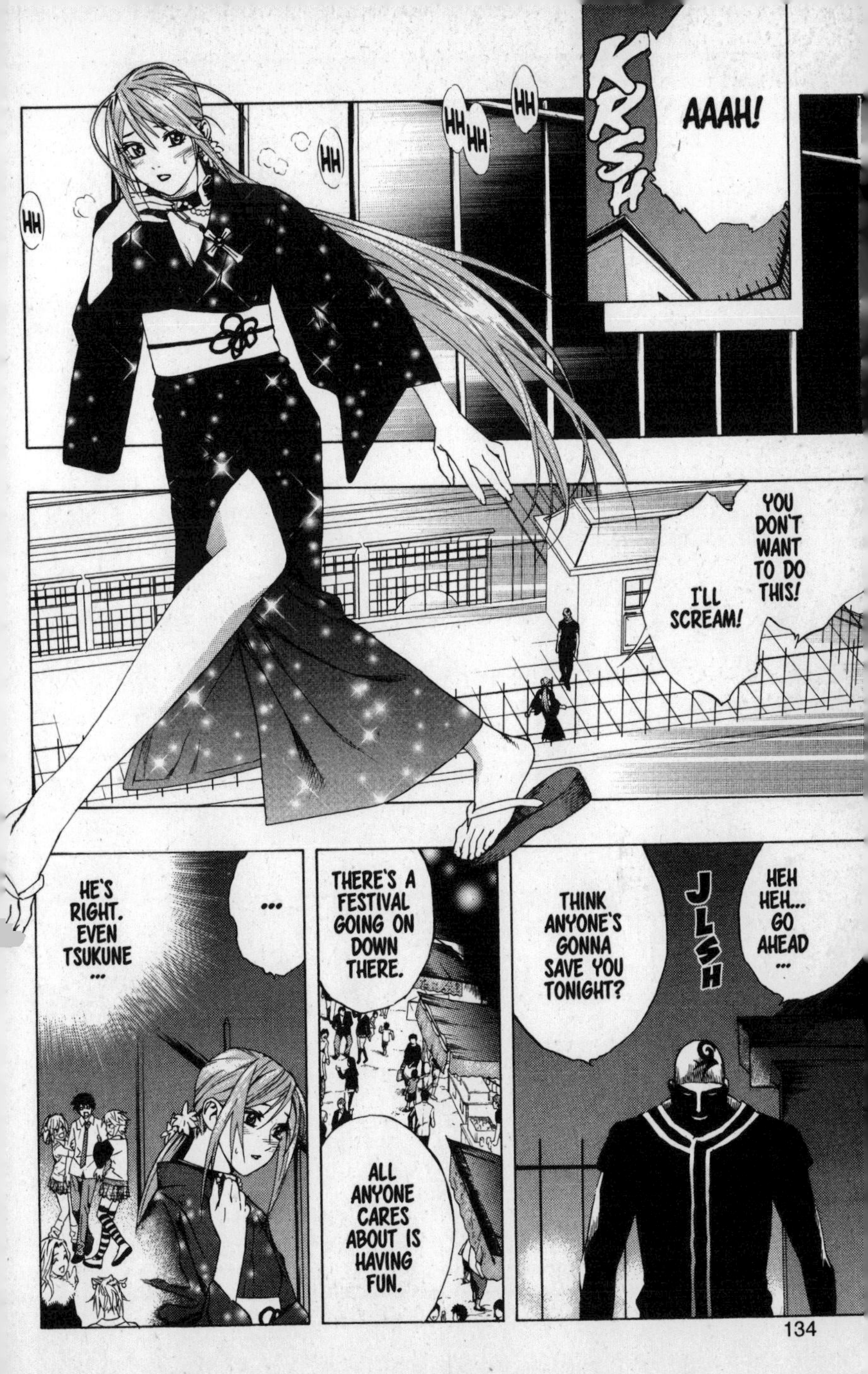
KRSH
AAAH!
HH
HH
HH
HH
HH
YOU DON'T WANT TO DO THIS!
I'LL SCREAM!
HEH HEH... GO AHEAD...
JLSH
THINK ANYONE'S GONNA SAVE YOU TONIGHT?
THERE'S A FESTIVAL GOING ON DOWN THERE.
ALL ANYONE CARES ABOUT IS HAVING FUN.
...
HE'S RIGHT. EVEN TSUKUNE...

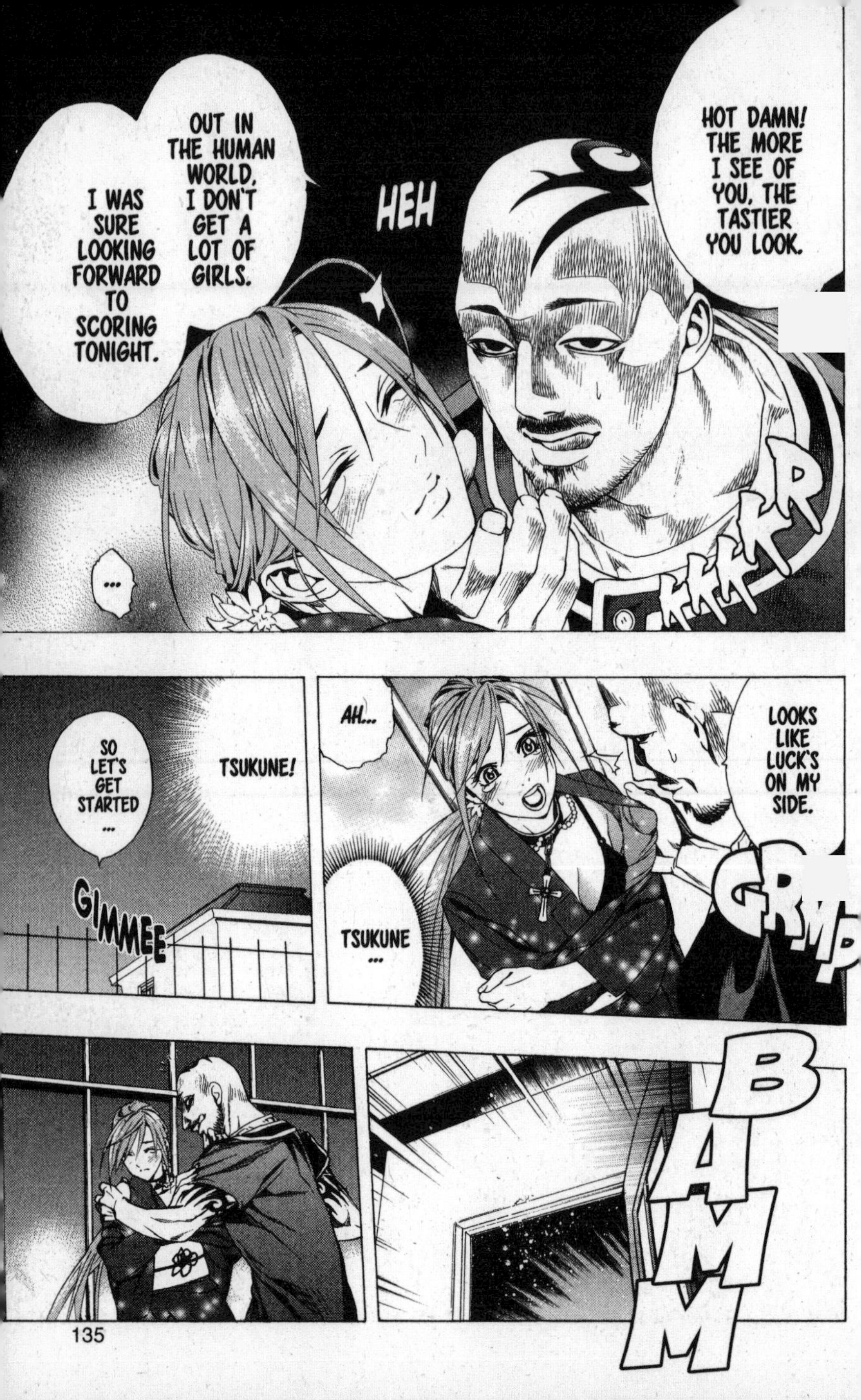
HOT DAMN! THE MORE I SEE OF YOU, THE TASTIER YOU LOOK.
HEH
OUT IN THE HUMAN WORLD, I DON'T GET A LOT OF GIRLS.
I WAS SURE LOOKING FORWARD TO SCORING TONIGHT.
KKKKR
...
LOOKS LIKE LUCK'S ON MY SIDE.
GRMP
AH...
TSUKUNE ...
TSUKUNE!
SO LET'S GET STARTED ...
GIMMEE
BAMM

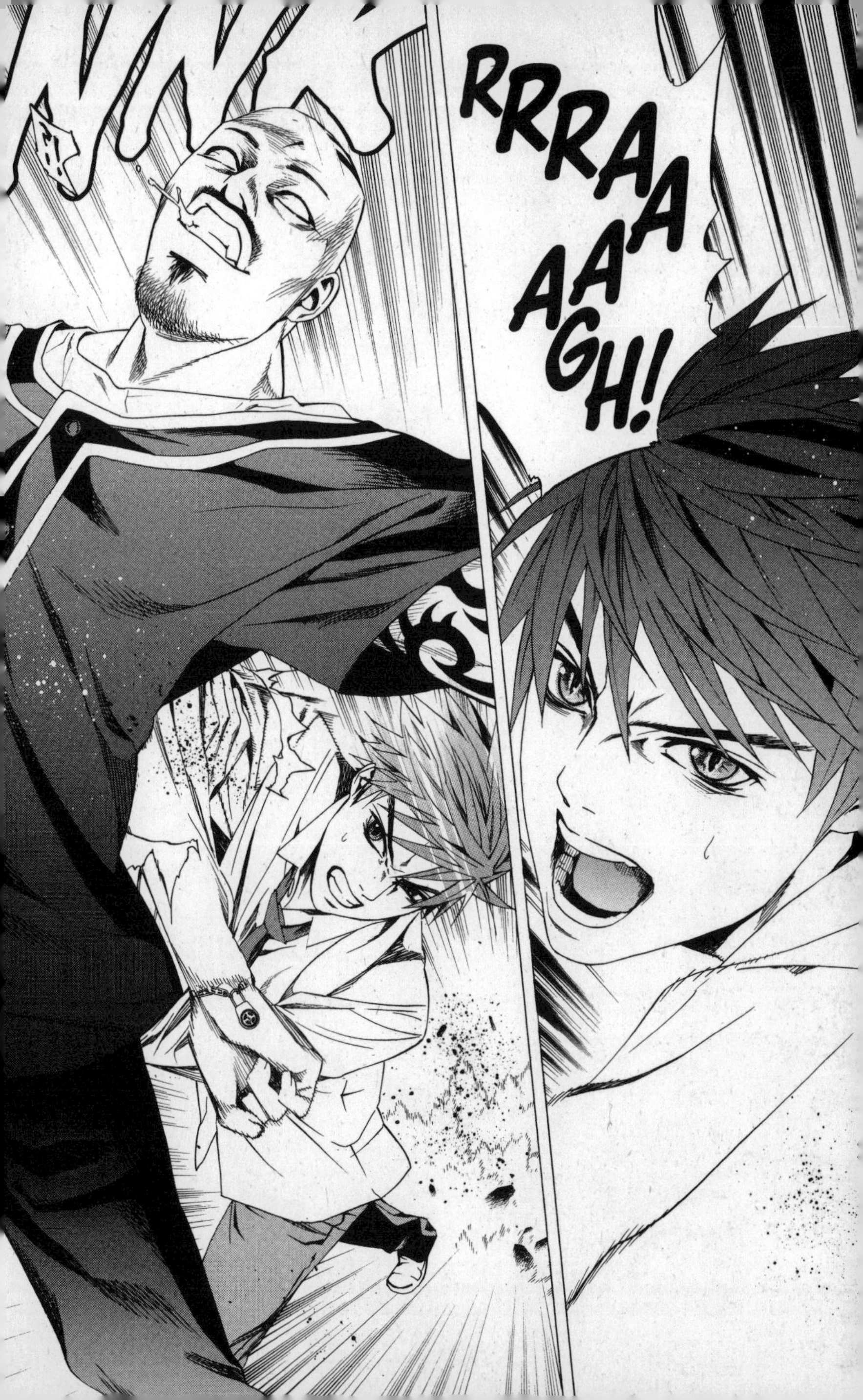
RRRAAAAGH!
?!

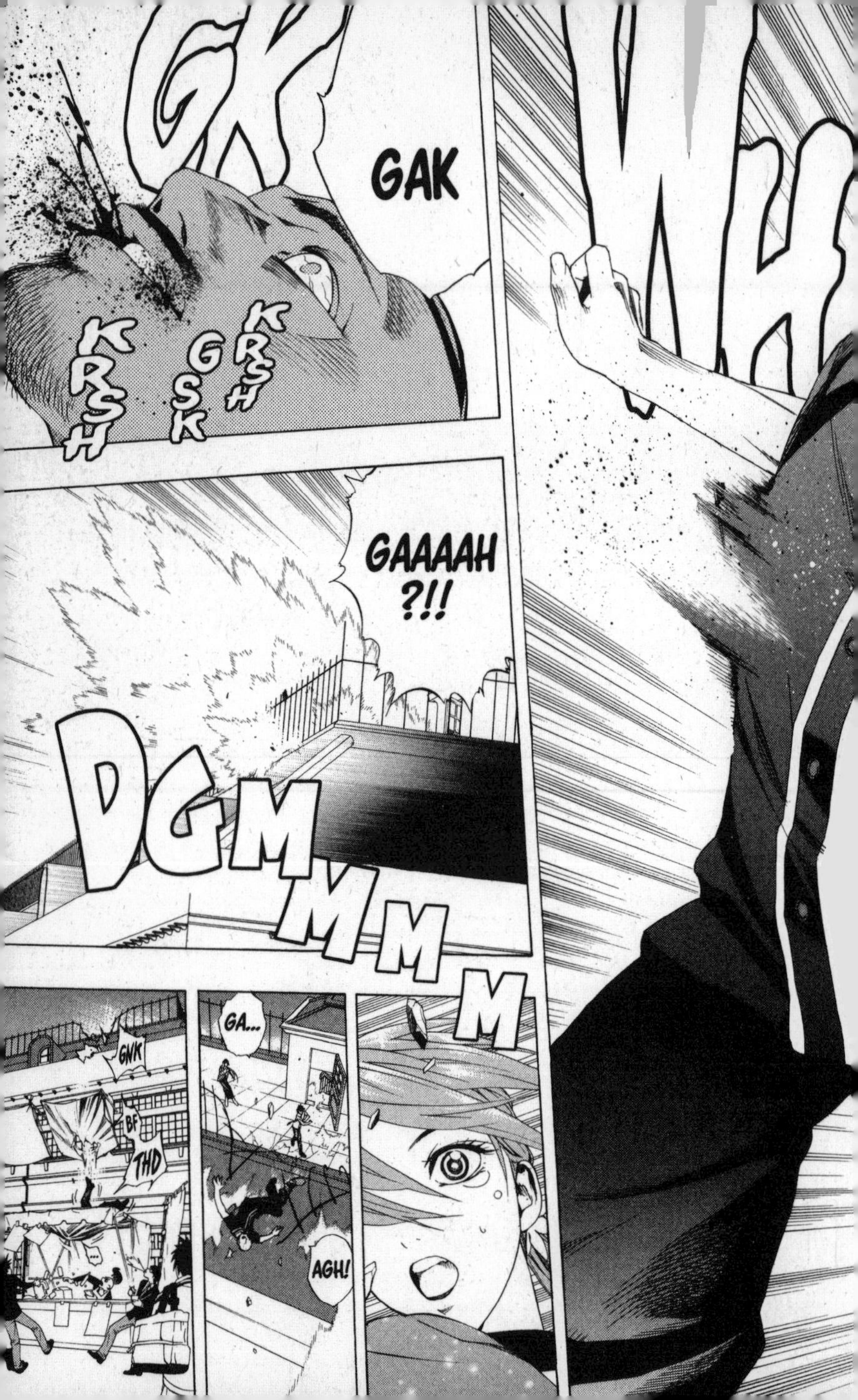
WH
GK
GAK
KRSH
GSK
KRSH
GAAAAH ?!!
DGMMMMM
AGH!
GA...
GNK
BF
THD
...

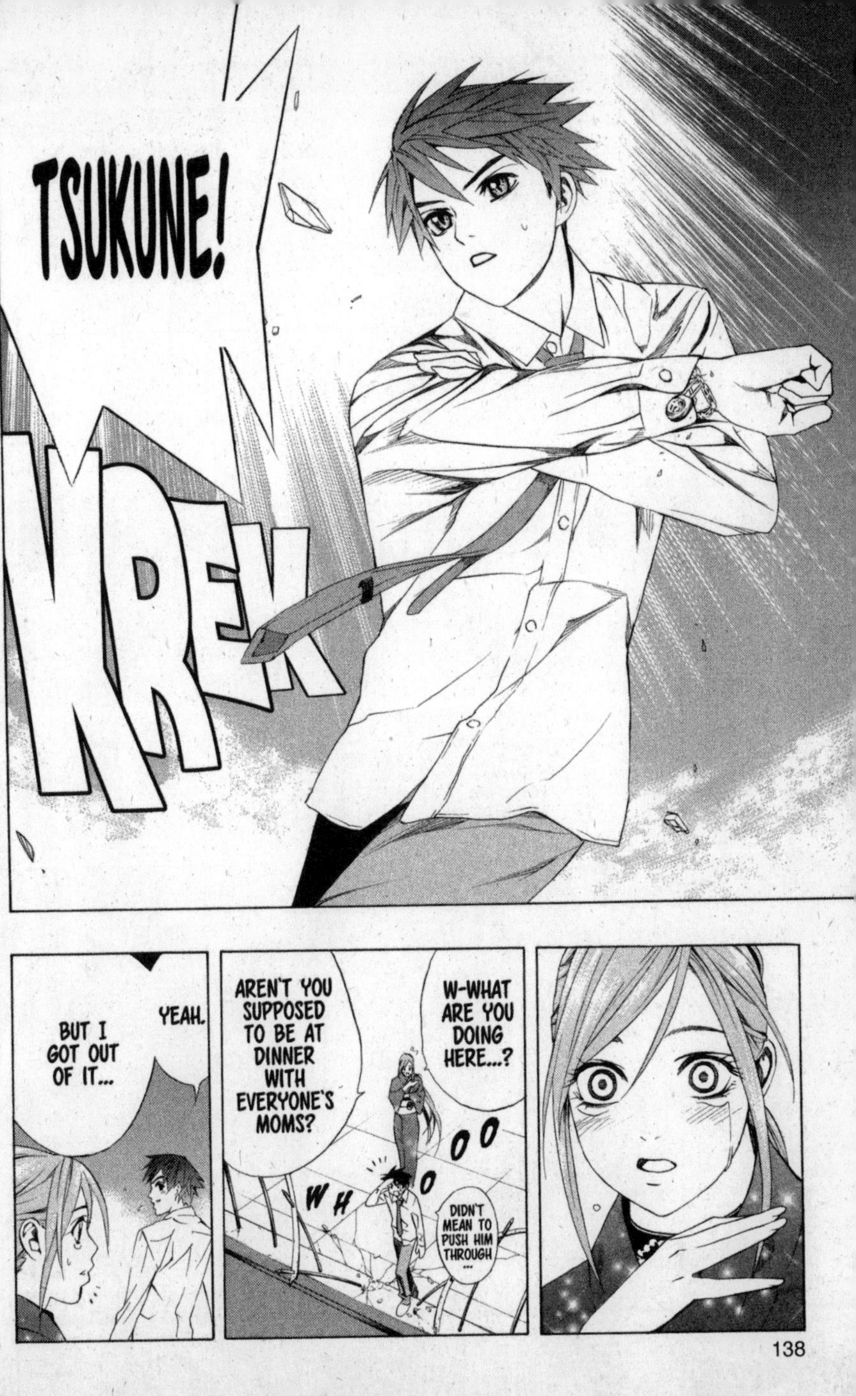
TSUKUNE!
KREK
W-WHAT ARE YOU DOING HERE...?
AREN'T YOU SUPPOSED TO BE AT DINNER WITH EVERYONE'S MOMS?
WHOOO
DIDN'T MEAN TO PUSH HIM THROUGH ...
YEAH.
BUT I GOT OUT OF IT...

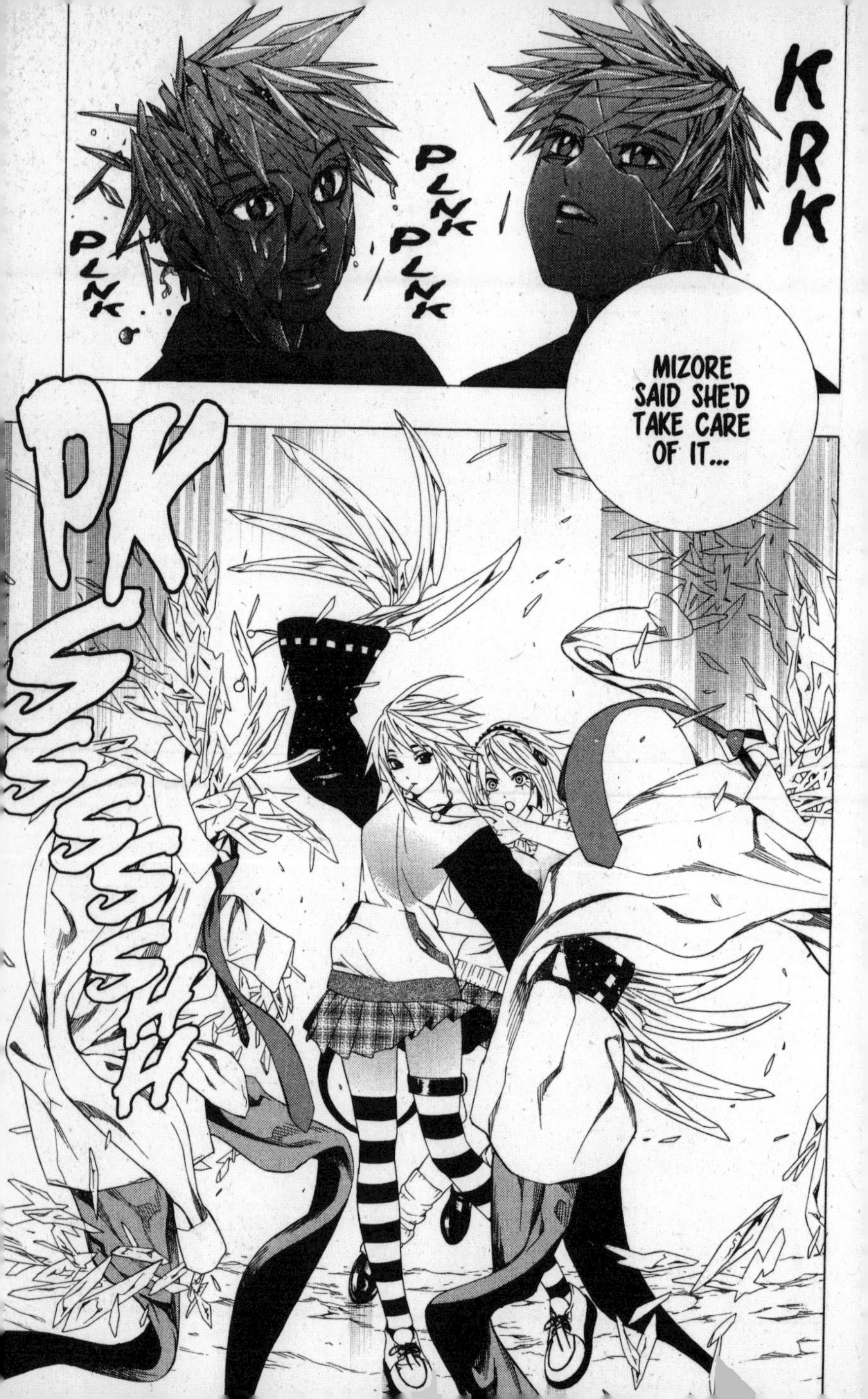
KRK
PLNK PLNK
PLNK
MIZORE SAID SHE'D TAKE CARE OF IT...
PK
SSSSSH

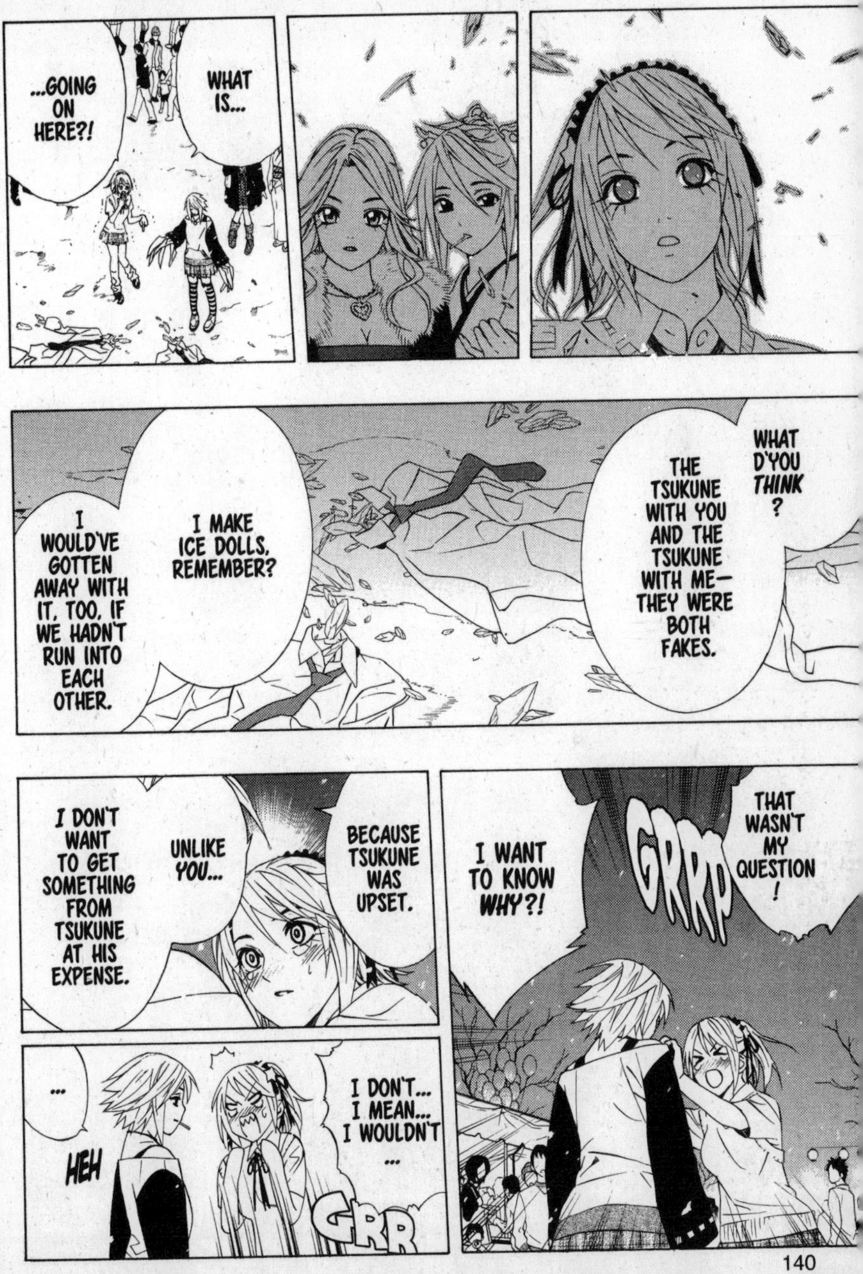
WHAT IS...
...GOING ON HERE?!
WHAT D'YOU *THINK*?
THE TSUKUNE WITH YOU AND THE TSUKUNE WITH ME—THEY WERE BOTH FAKES.
I MAKE ICE DOLLS, REMEMBER?
I WOULD'VE GOTTEN AWAY WITH IT, TOO, IF WE HADN'T RUN INTO EACH OTHER.
THAT WASN'T MY QUESTION!
GRRR
I WANT TO KNOW *WHY*?!
BECAUSE TSUKUNE WAS UPSET.
UNLIKE *YOU*...
I DON'T WANT TO GET SOMETHING FROM TSUKUNE AT HIS EXPENSE.
I DON'T... I MEAN... I WOULDN'T ...
GRR
...
HEH

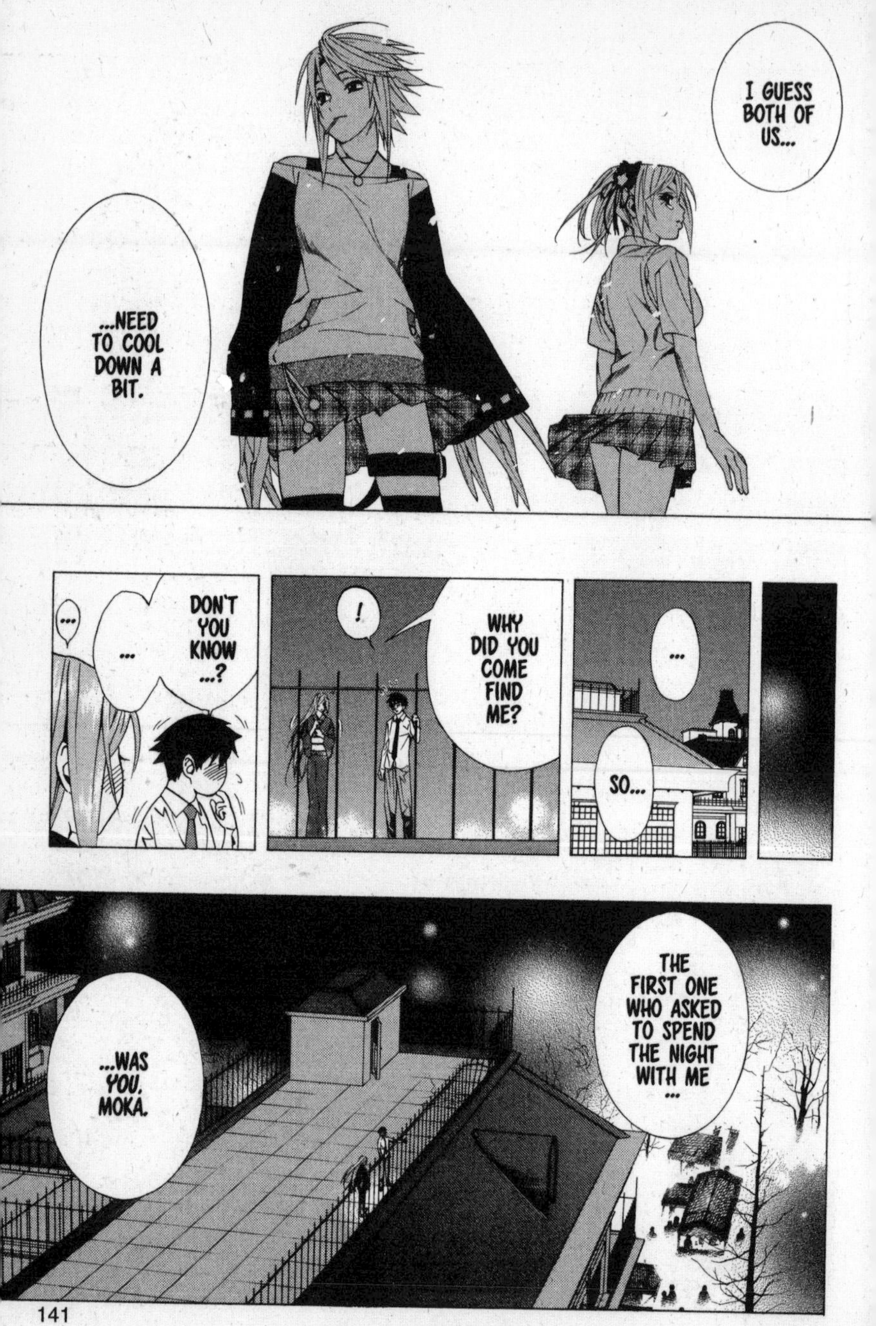
I GUESS BOTH OF US...
...NEED TO COOL DOWN A BIT.
...
SO...
WHY DID YOU COME FIND ME?
!
DON'T YOU KNOW ...?
...
...
THE FIRST ONE WHO ASKED TO SPEND THE NIGHT WITH ME ...
...WAS YOU, MOKA.

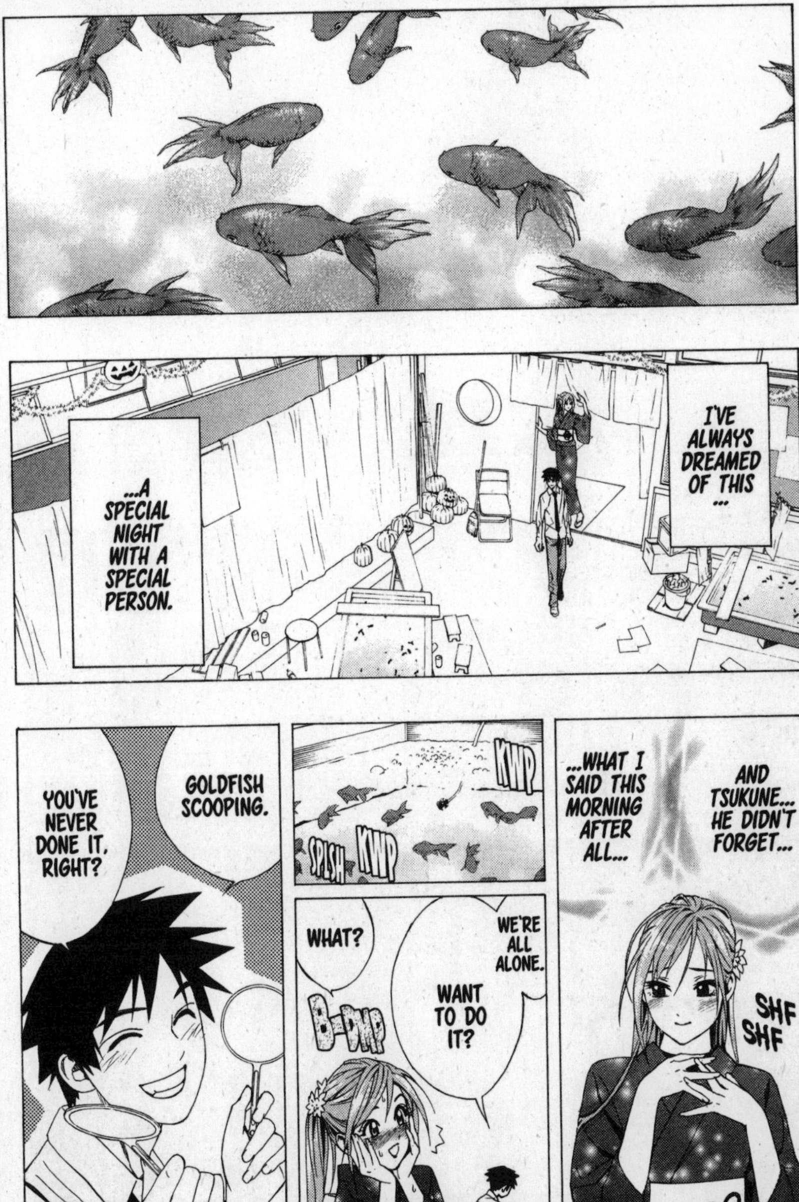
I'VE ALWAYS DREAMED OF THIS...
...A SPECIAL NIGHT WITH A SPECIAL PERSON.
AND TSUKUNE... HE DIDN'T FORGET...
...WHAT I SAID THIS MORNING AFTER ALL...
SHF SHF
KWP
KWP
SPLISH
WE'RE ALL ALONE.
WANT TO DO IT?
WHAT?
B-DMP
GOLDFISH SCOOPING.
YOU'VE NEVER DONE IT, RIGHT?

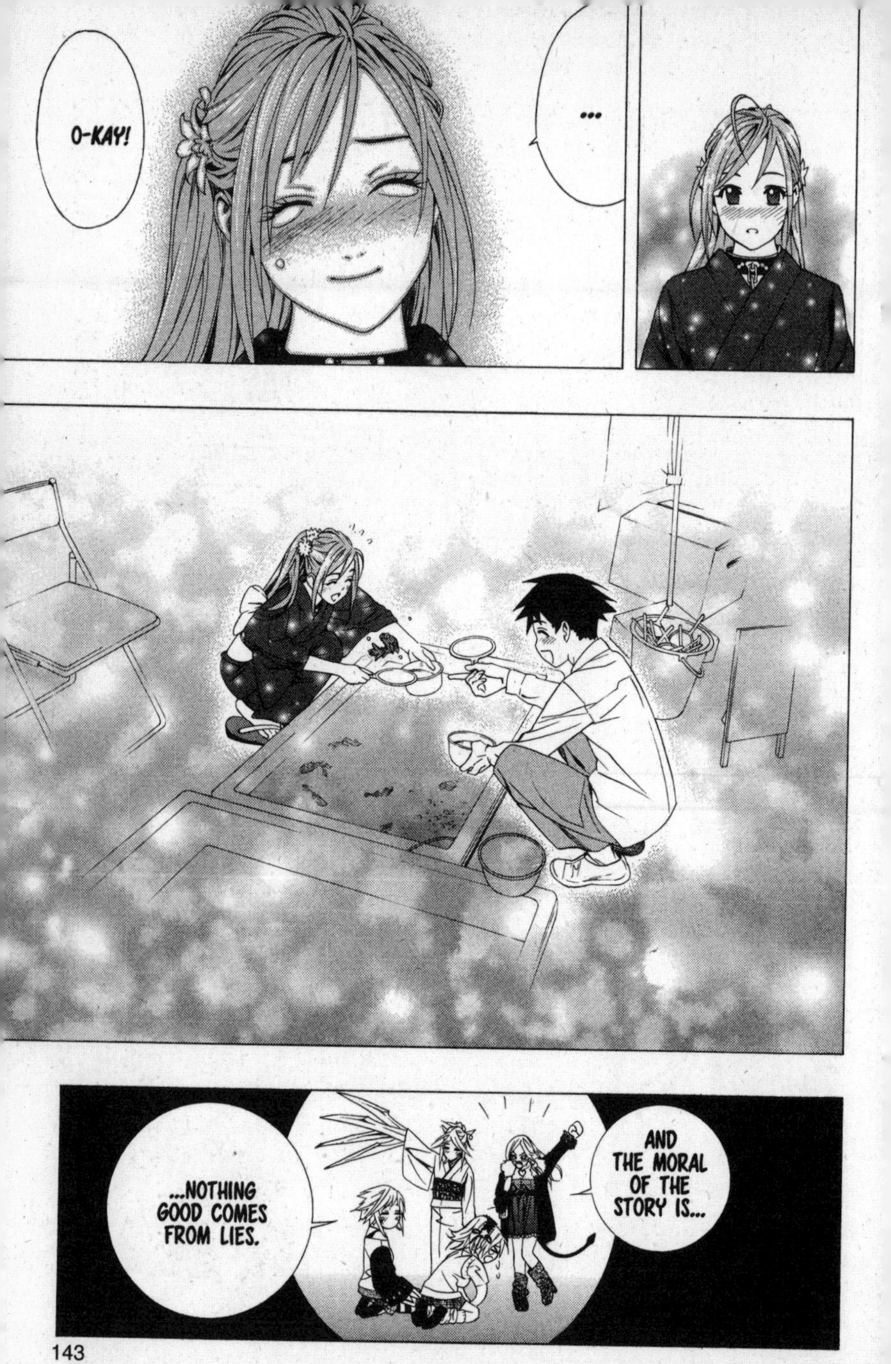
...
O-KAY!
AND THE MORAL OF THE STORY IS...
...NOTHING GOOD COMES FROM LIES.

36: The Visitor

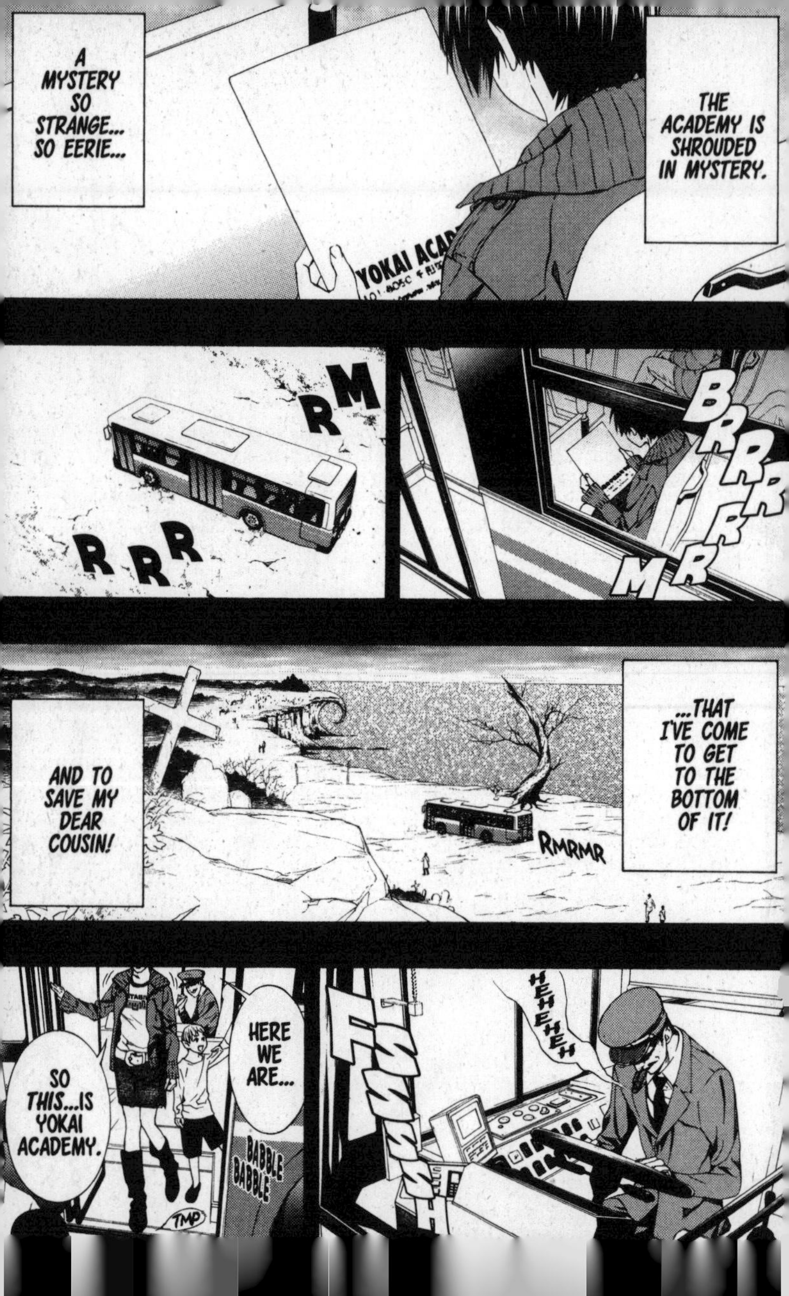
THE ACADEMY IS SHROUDED IN MYSTERY.
A MYSTERY SO STRANGE... SO EERIE...
BRRRRRRMR
RRRRM
...THAT I'VE COME TO GET TO THE BOTTOM OF IT!
RMRMR
AND TO SAVE MY DEAR COUSIN!
HEHEHEH
FSSSSH
HERE WE ARE...
BABBLE BABBLE
SO THIS...IS YOKAI ACADEMY.
TMP

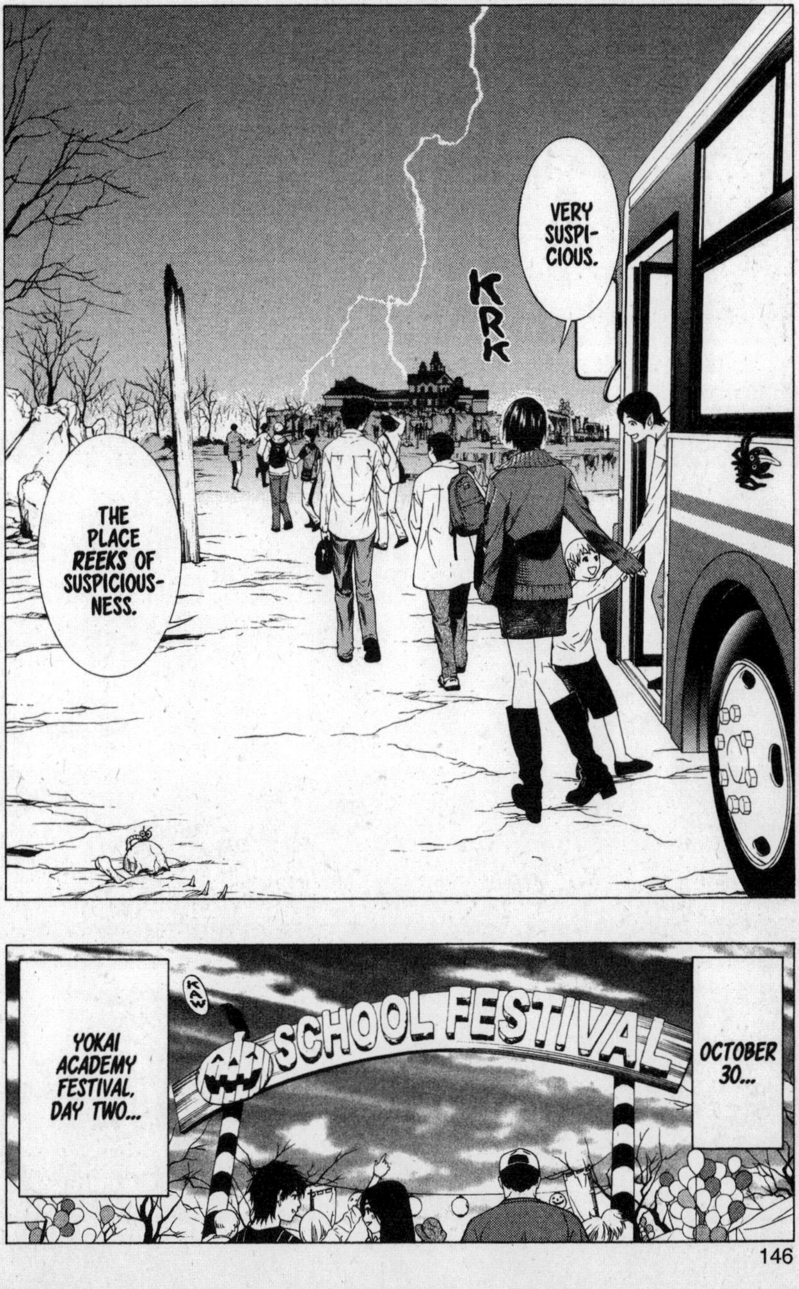
VERY SUSPICIOUS.
KRK
THE PLACE REEKS OF SUSPICIOUSNESS.
OCTOBER 30...
SCHOOL FESTIVAL
KAW
YOKAI ACADEMY FESTIVAL, DAY TWO...

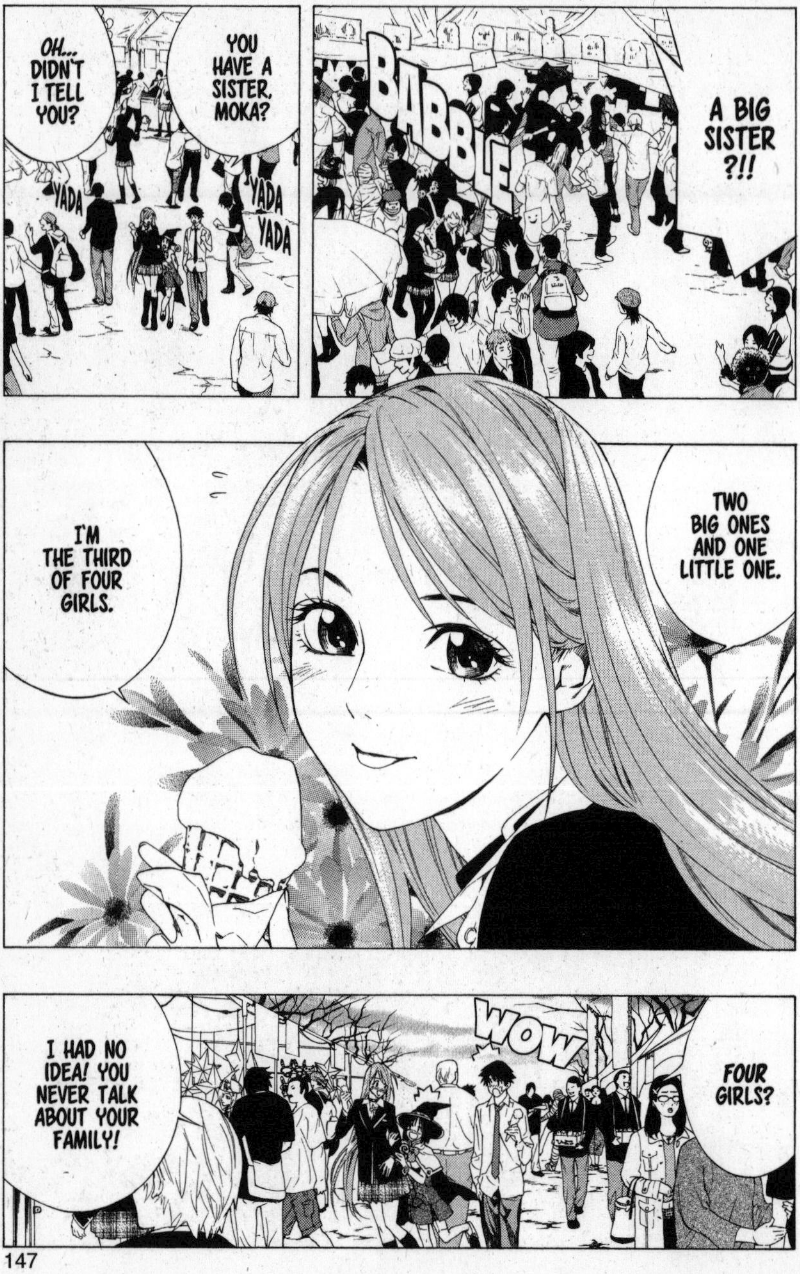
A BIG SISTER ?!!
BABBLE
YOU HAVE A SISTER, MOKA?
OH... DIDN'T I TELL YOU?
YADA
YADA
YADA
TWO BIG ONES AND ONE LITTLE ONE.
I'M THE THIRD OF FOUR GIRLS.
FOUR GIRLS?
WOW
I HAD NO IDEA! YOU NEVER TALK ABOUT YOUR FAMILY!

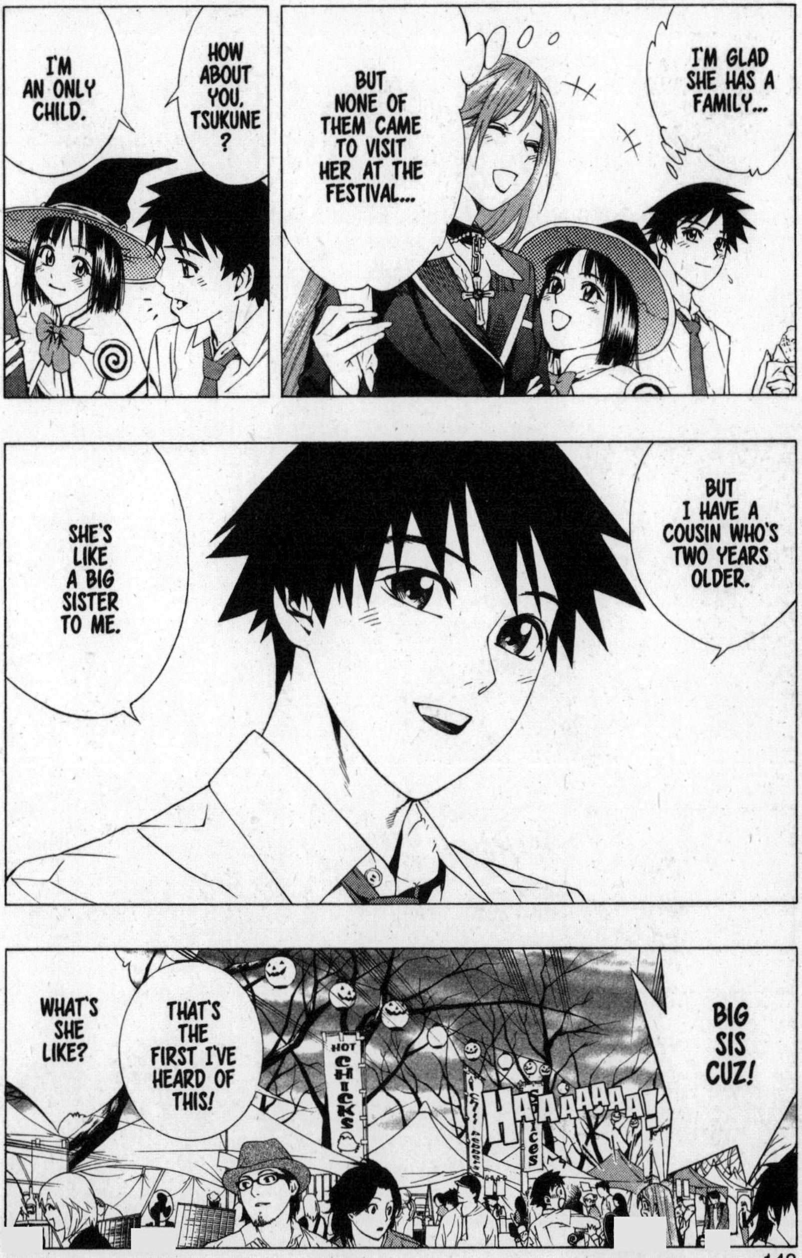
I'M GLAD SHE HAS A FAMILY...
BUT NONE OF THEM CAME TO VISIT HER AT THE FESTIVAL...
HOW ABOUT YOU, TSUKUNE?
I'M AN ONLY CHILD.
BUT I HAVE A COUSIN WHO'S TWO YEARS OLDER.
SHE'S LIKE A BIG SISTER TO ME.
BIG SIS CUZ!
HAAAAAAA!
HOT CHICKS
THAT'S THE FIRST I'VE HEARD OF THIS!
WHAT'S SHE LIKE?

READ THIS WAY

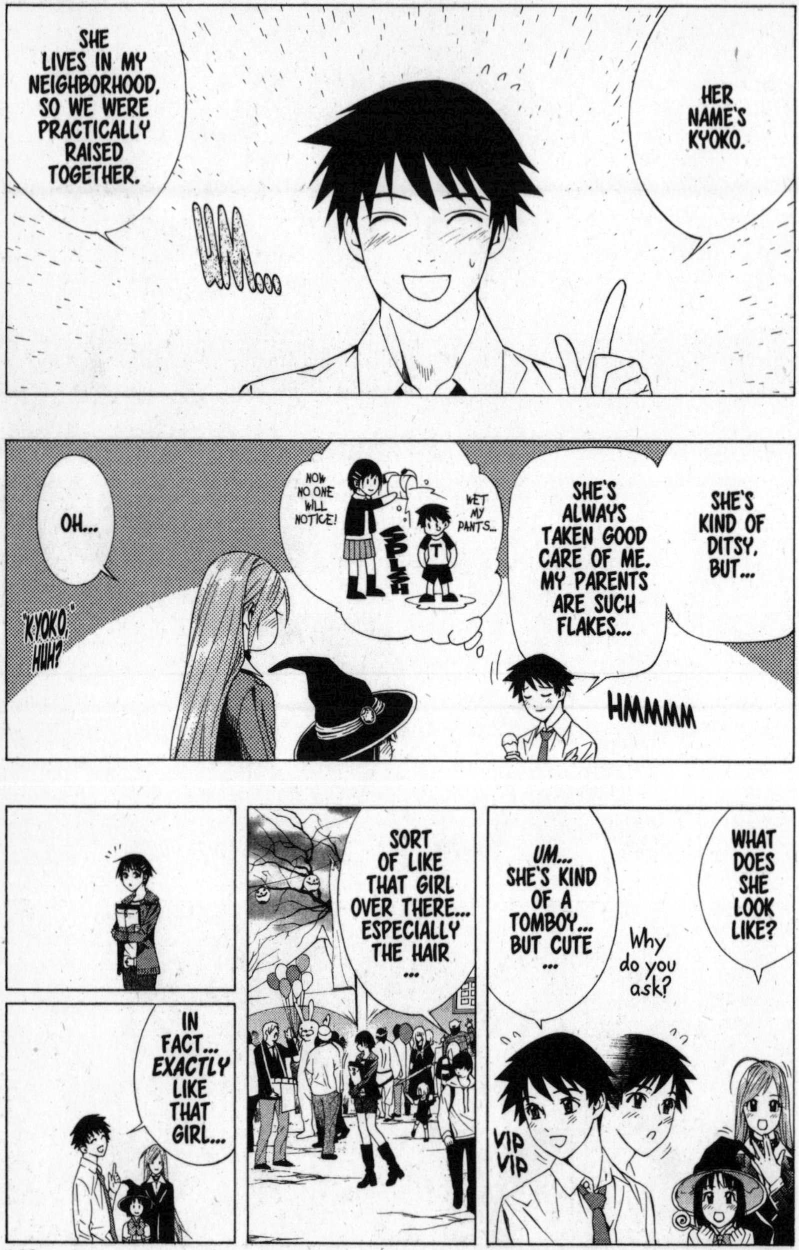

HER NAME'S KYOKO.
SHE LIVES IN MY NEIGHBORHOOD, SO WE WERE PRACTICALLY RAISED TOGETHER.
UM...
SHE'S KIND OF DITSY, BUT...
SHE'S ALWAYS TAKEN GOOD CARE OF ME. MY PARENTS ARE SUCH FLAKES...
HMMMM
WET MY PANTS...
NOW NO ONE WILL NOTICE!
SPLSH
OH...
"KYOKO," HUH?
WHAT DOES SHE LOOK LIKE?
UM... SHE'S KIND OF A TOMBOY... BUT CUTE ...
Why do you ask?
VIP VIP
SORT OF LIKE THAT GIRL OVER THERE... ESPECIALLY THE HAIR ...
IN FACT... EXACTLY LIKE THAT GIRL...

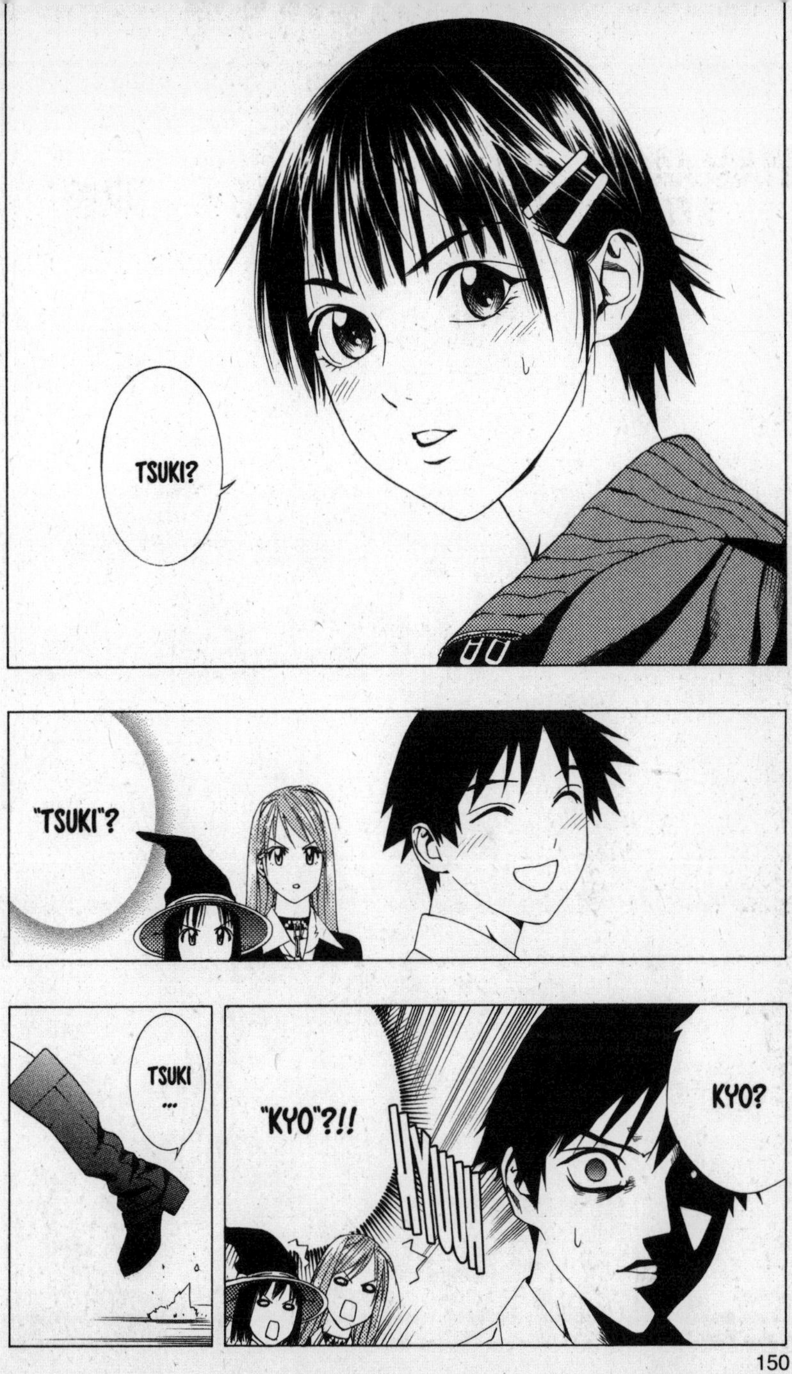
TSUKI?
"TSUKI"?
KYO?
"KYO"?!!
TSUKI ...

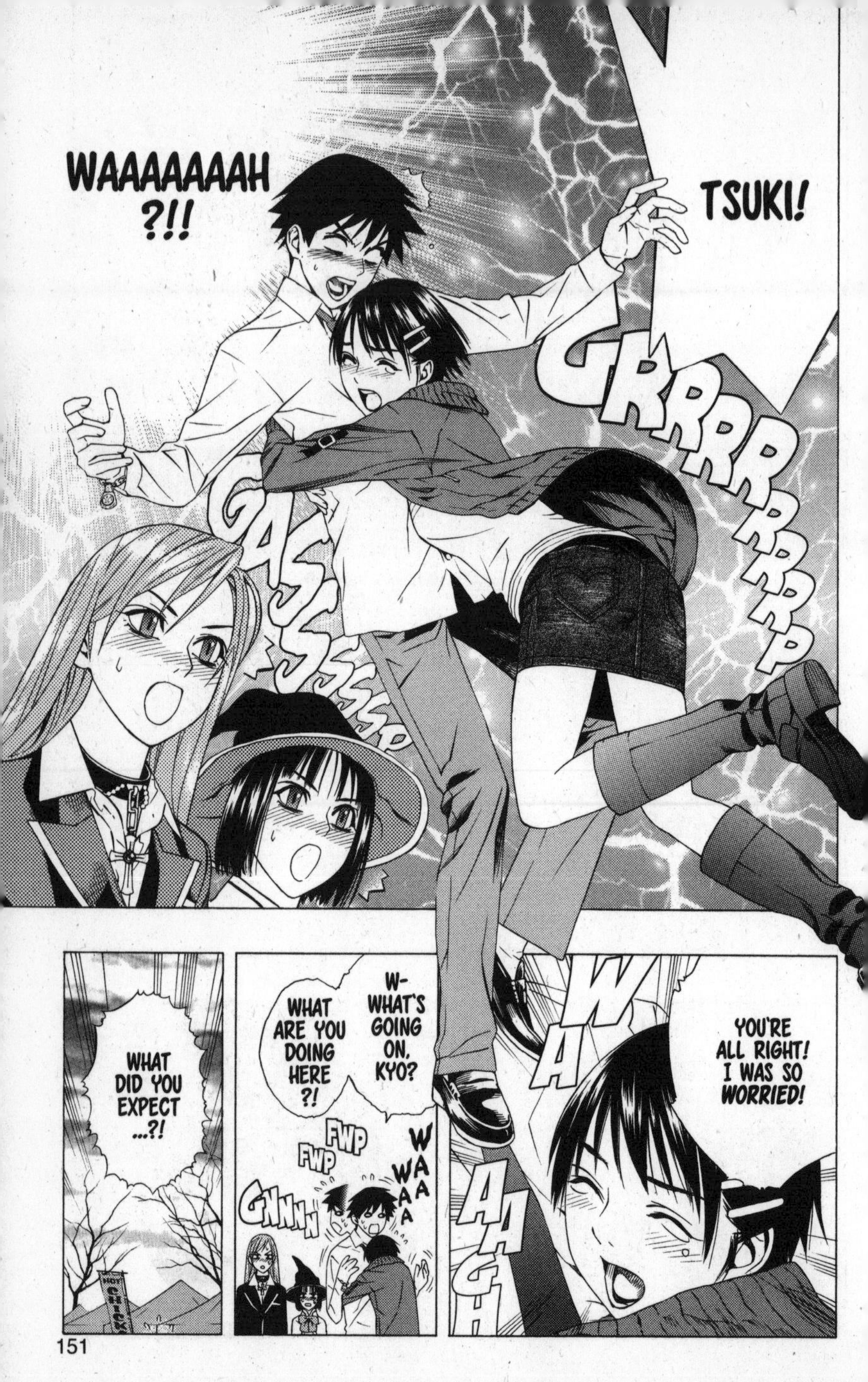
TSUKI!
WAAAAAAAH ?!!
GRRRRRRRRP
GASSSSSP
YOU'RE ALL RIGHT! I WAS SO WORRIED!
WA
AAAGH
W- WHAT'S GOING ON, KYO?
WHAT ARE YOU DOING HERE ?!
WAAAA
FWP
FWP
GNNNN
WHAT DID YOU EXPECT ...?!

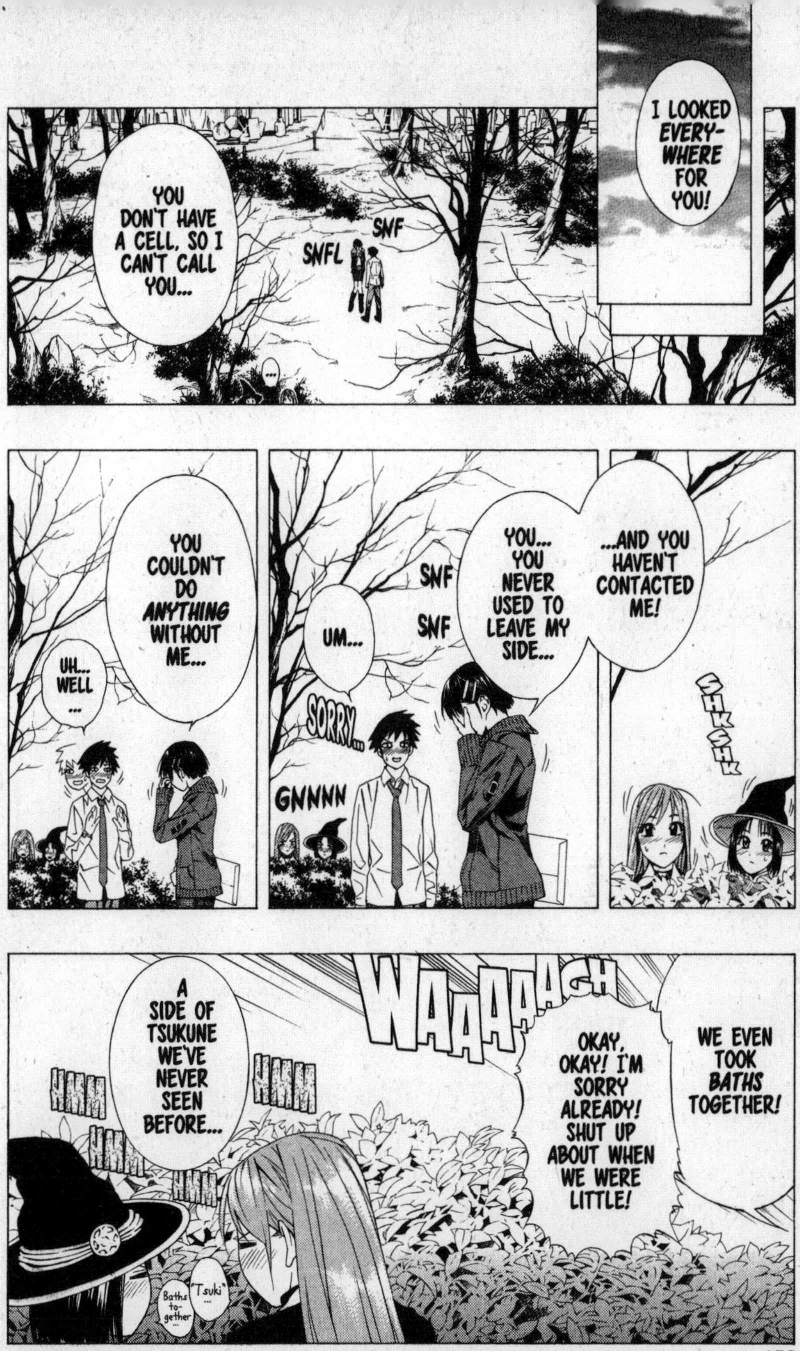
I LOOKED EVERY-WHERE FOR YOU!
YOU DON'T HAVE A CELL, SO I CAN'T CALL YOU...
SNF
SNFL
...
...AND YOU HAVEN'T CONTACTED ME!
SHKSHK
YOU... YOU NEVER USED TO LEAVE MY SIDE...
SNF
SNF
UM...
SORRY...
GNNNN
YOU COULDN'T DO *ANYTHING* WITHOUT ME...
UH... WELL ...
WE EVEN TOOK *BATHS* TOGETHER!
WAAAAACH
OKAY, OKAY! I'M SORRY ALREADY! SHUT UP ABOUT WHEN WE WERE LITTLE!
A SIDE OF TSUKUNE WE'VE NEVER SEEN BEFORE...
HMM
HMM
HMM
HMM
"Tsuki" ...
Baths to-gether ...

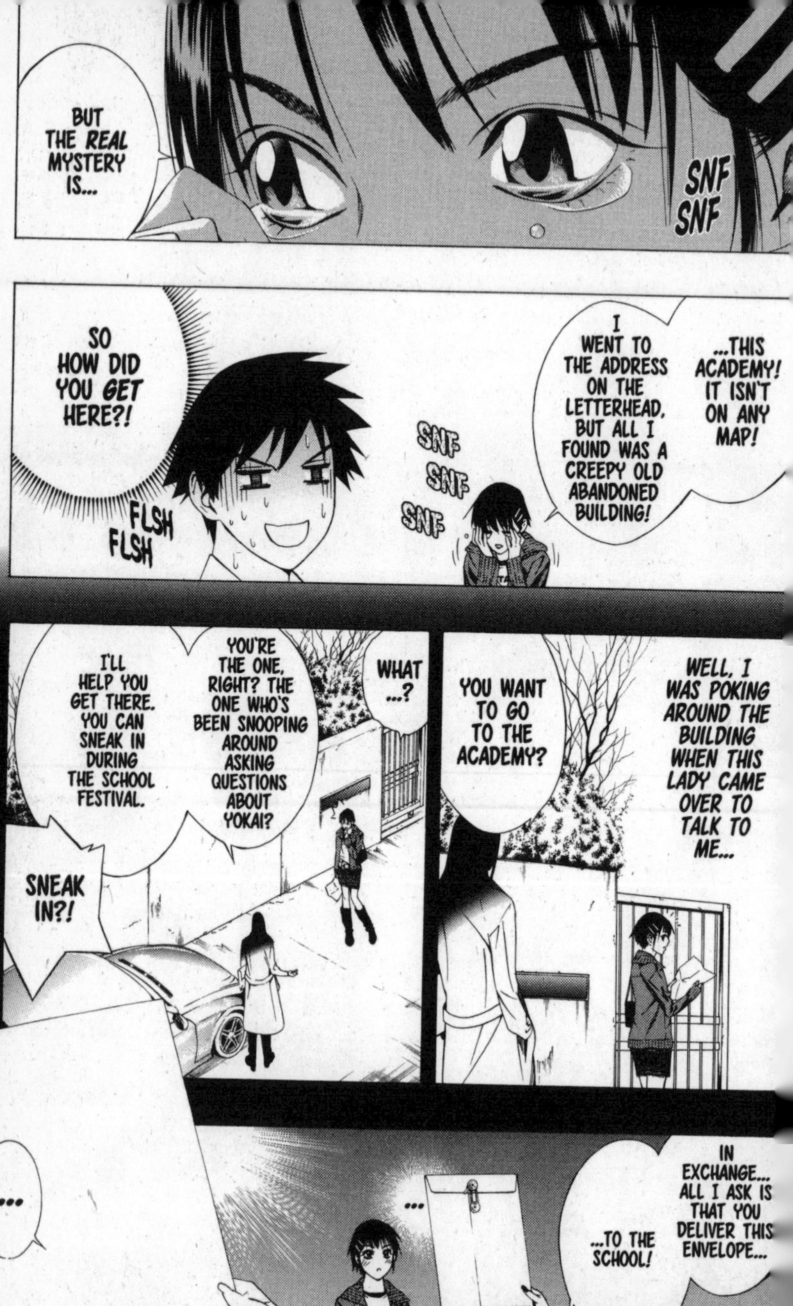
BUT THE REAL MYSTERY IS...
SNF SNF
...THIS ACADEMY! IT ISN'T ON ANY MAP!
I WENT TO THE ADDRESS ON THE LETTERHEAD, BUT ALL I FOUND WAS A CREEPY OLD ABANDONED BUILDING!
SNF SNF SNF
SO HOW DID YOU GET HERE?!
FLSH FLSH
WELL, I WAS POKING AROUND THE BUILDING WHEN THIS LADY CAME OVER TO TALK TO ME...
YOU WANT TO GO TO THE ACADEMY?
WHAT ...?
YOU'RE THE ONE, RIGHT? THE ONE WHO'S BEEN SNOOPING AROUND ASKING QUESTIONS ABOUT YOKAI?
I'LL HELP YOU GET THERE. YOU CAN SNEAK IN DURING THE SCHOOL FESTIVAL.
SNEAK IN?!
IN EXCHANGE... ALL I ASK IS THAT YOU DELIVER THIS ENVELOPE...
...TO THE SCHOOL!
...
...

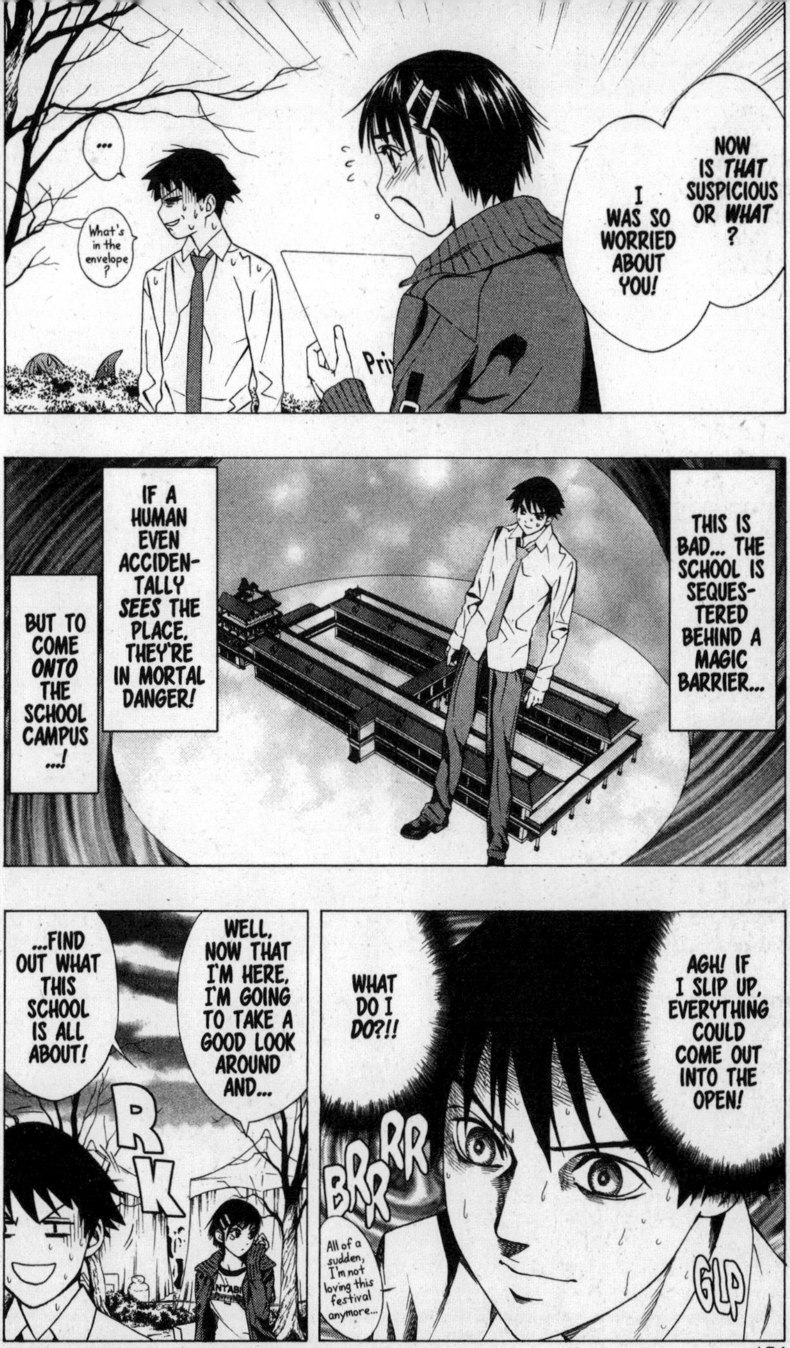
NOW IS *THAT* SUSPICIOUS OR *WHAT*?
I WAS SO WORRIED ABOUT YOU!
...
What's in the envelope?
THIS IS BAD... THE SCHOOL IS SEQUESTERED BEHIND A MAGIC BARRIER...
IF A HUMAN EVEN ACCIDENTALLY *SEES* THE PLACE, THEY'RE IN MORTAL DANGER!
BUT TO COME *ONTO* THE SCHOOL CAMPUS ...!
AGH! IF I SLIP UP, EVERYTHING COULD COME OUT INTO THE OPEN!
WHAT DO I *DO*?!!
BRRRRR
GLP
All of a sudden, I'm not loving this festival anymore...
WELL, NOW THAT I'M HERE, I'M GOING TO TAKE A GOOD LOOK AROUND AND...
...FIND OUT WHAT THIS SCHOOL IS ALL ABOUT!
RK

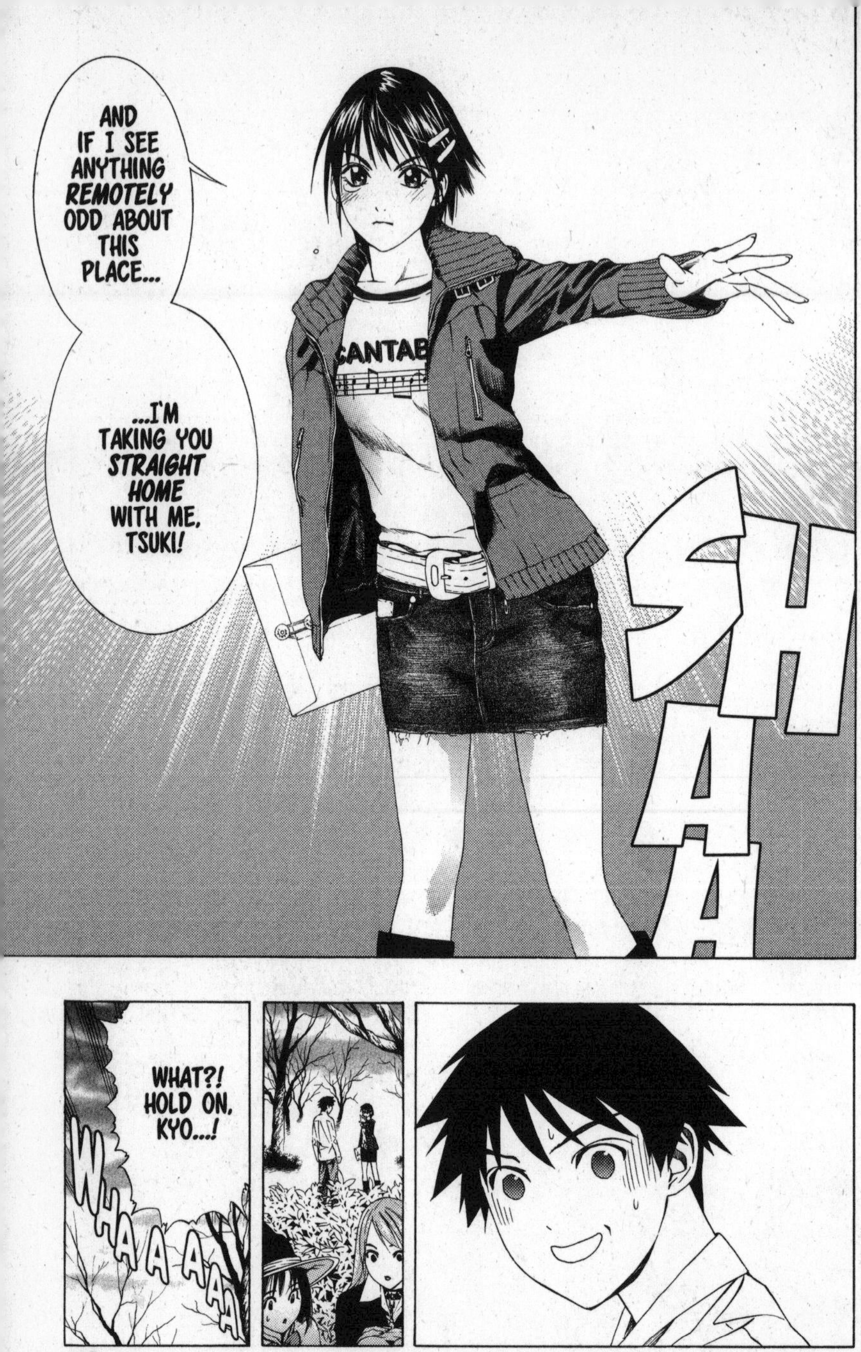
AND IF I SEE ANYTHING REMOTELY ODD ABOUT THIS PLACE...
...I'M TAKING YOU STRAIGHT HOME WITH ME, TSUKI!
CANTAB
SHAAA
WHAT?! HOLD ON, KYO...!
WHAAAAAA

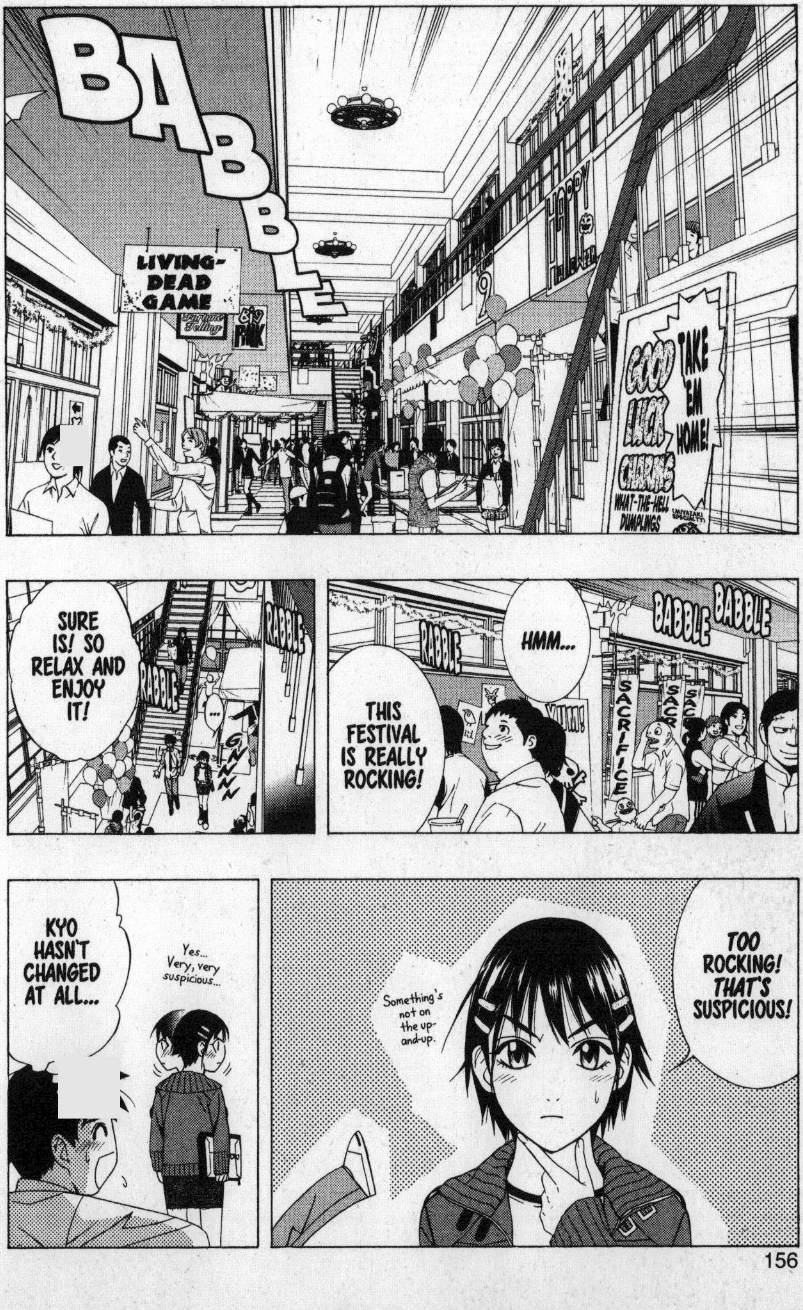
BABBLE
LIVING-DEAD GAME
Fortune Telling
GOOD LUCK CHARMS
TAKE 'EM HOME!
WHAT-THE-HELL DUMPLINGS
HMM...
THIS FESTIVAL IS REALLY ROCKING!
BABBLE
BABBLE
RABBLE
SACRIFICE
YUM!
SURE IS! SO RELAX AND ENJOY IT!
RABBLE
RABBLE
...
GNNNN
TOO ROCKING! THAT'S SUSPICIOUS!
Something's not on the up-and-up.
KYO HASN'T CHANGED AT ALL...
Yes... Very, very suspicious...

READ THIS WAY

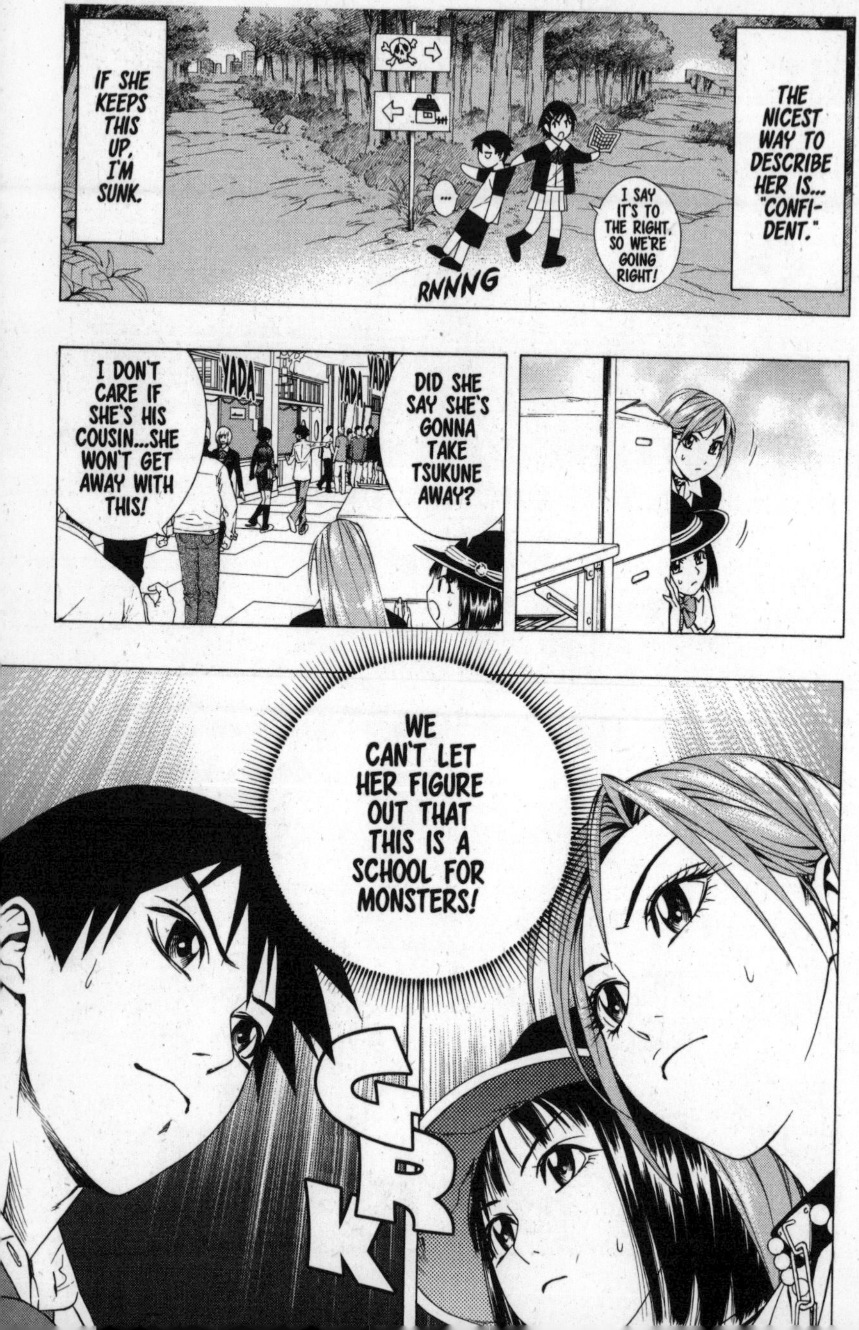
THE NICEST WAY TO DESCRIBE HER IS... "CONFI-DENT."
I SAY IT'S TO THE RIGHT, SO WE'RE GOING RIGHT!
...
RNNNG
IF SHE KEEPS THIS UP, I'M SUNK.
DID SHE SAY SHE'S GONNA TAKE TSUKUNE AWAY?
YADA
YADA
YADA
I DON'T CARE IF SHE'S HIS COUSIN...SHE WON'T GET AWAY WITH THIS!
WE CAN'T LET HER FIGURE OUT THAT THIS IS A SCHOOL FOR MONSTERS!
GRRK

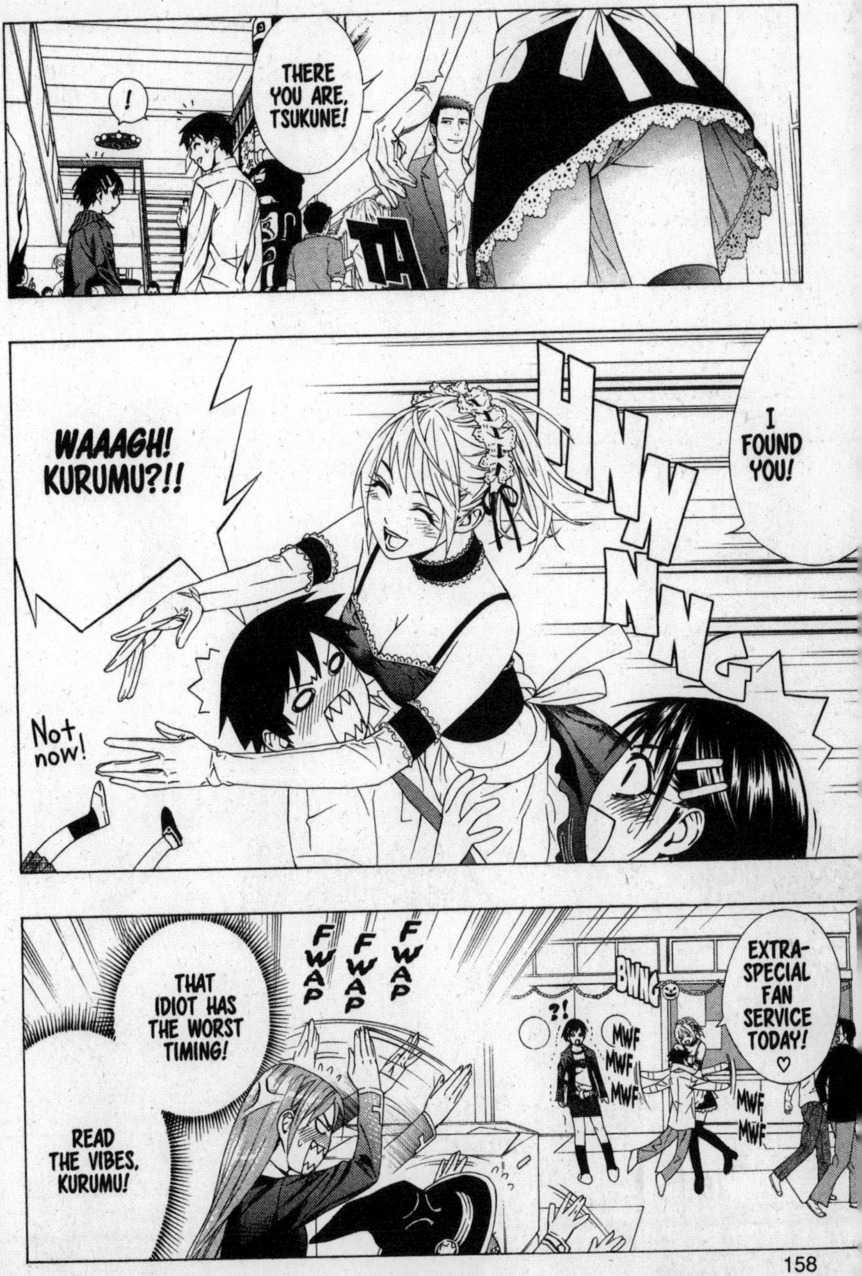

THERE YOU ARE, TSUKUNE!
TA
!
I FOUND YOU!
HNNNNG
WAAAGH! KURUMU?!!
Not now!
EXTRA-SPECIAL FAN SERVICE TODAY! ♡
MWF MWF
BWNG
MWF MWF MWF
?!
FWAP FWAP FWAP
THAT IDIOT HAS THE WORST TIMING!
READ THE VIBES, KURUMU!

READ THIS WAY

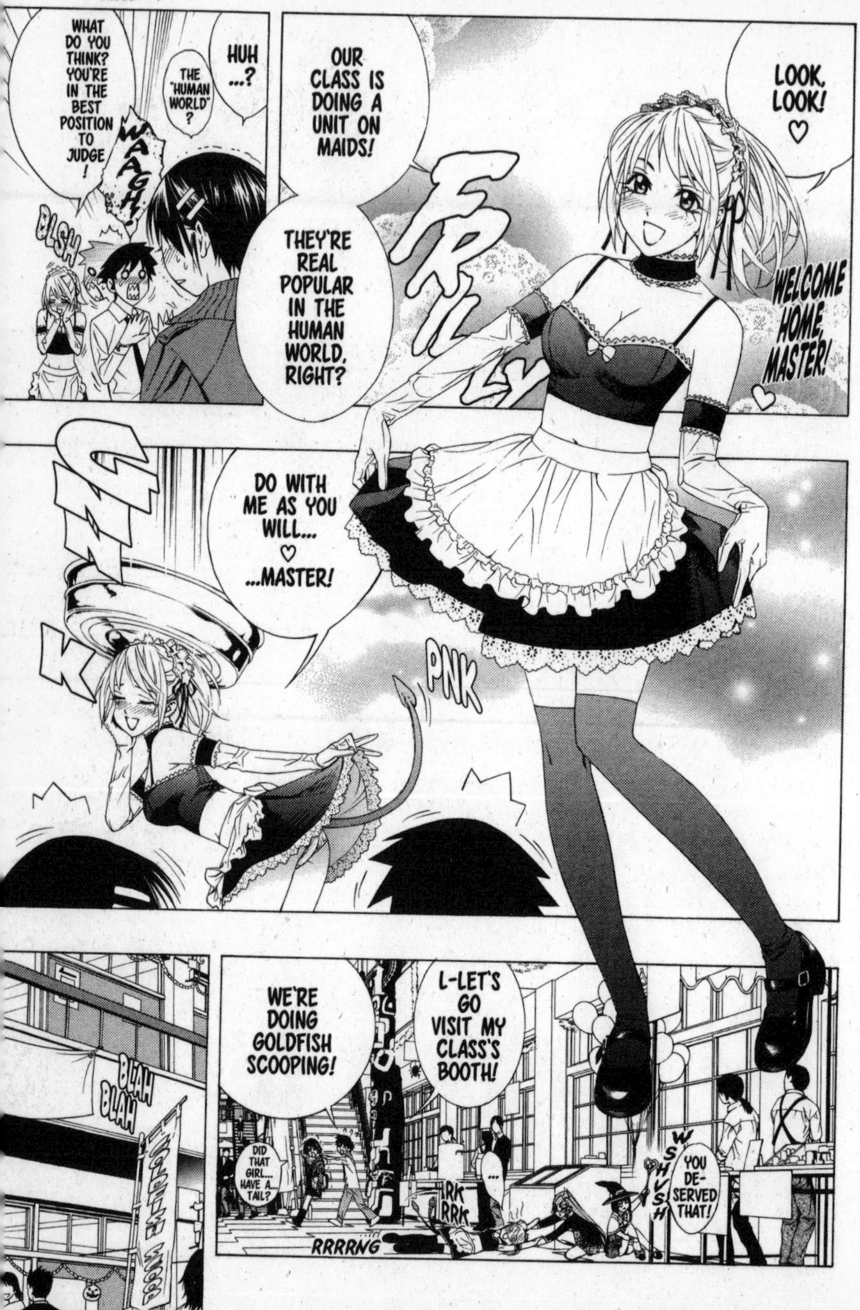
LOOK, LOOK! ♡
WELCOME HOME, MASTER! ♡
OUR CLASS IS DOING A UNIT ON MAIDS!
THEY'RE REAL POPULAR IN THE HUMAN WORLD, RIGHT?
HUH ...?
THE "HUMAN WORLD"?
WHAT DO YOU THINK? YOU'RE IN THE BEST POSITION TO JUDGE!
WAAGH!
BLSH
DO WITH ME AS YOU WILL... ♡ ...MASTER!
PNK
L-LET'S GO VISIT MY CLASS'S BOOTH!
WE'RE DOING GOLDFISH SCOOPING!
YOU DE-SERVED THAT!
WSHVSH
...
RK RRK
RRRRNG
DID THAT GIRL... HAVE A... TAIL?
BLAH BLAH

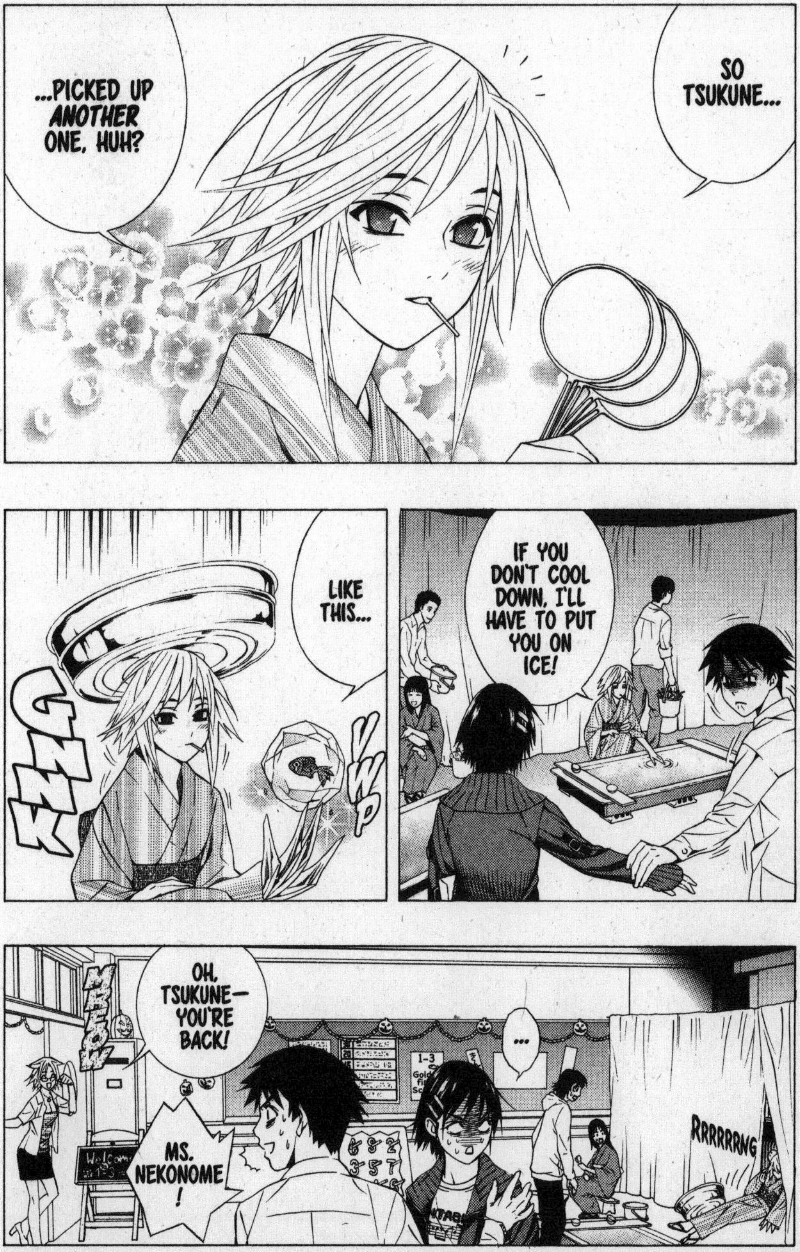
SO TSUKUNE...
...PICKED UP ANOTHER ONE, HUH?
IF YOU DON'T COOL DOWN, I'LL HAVE TO PUT YOU ON ICE!
LIKE THIS...
VWP
KNNG
RRRRRRNG
...
OH, TSUKUNE— YOU'RE BACK!
MEOW
MS. NEKONOME!

READ THIS WAY

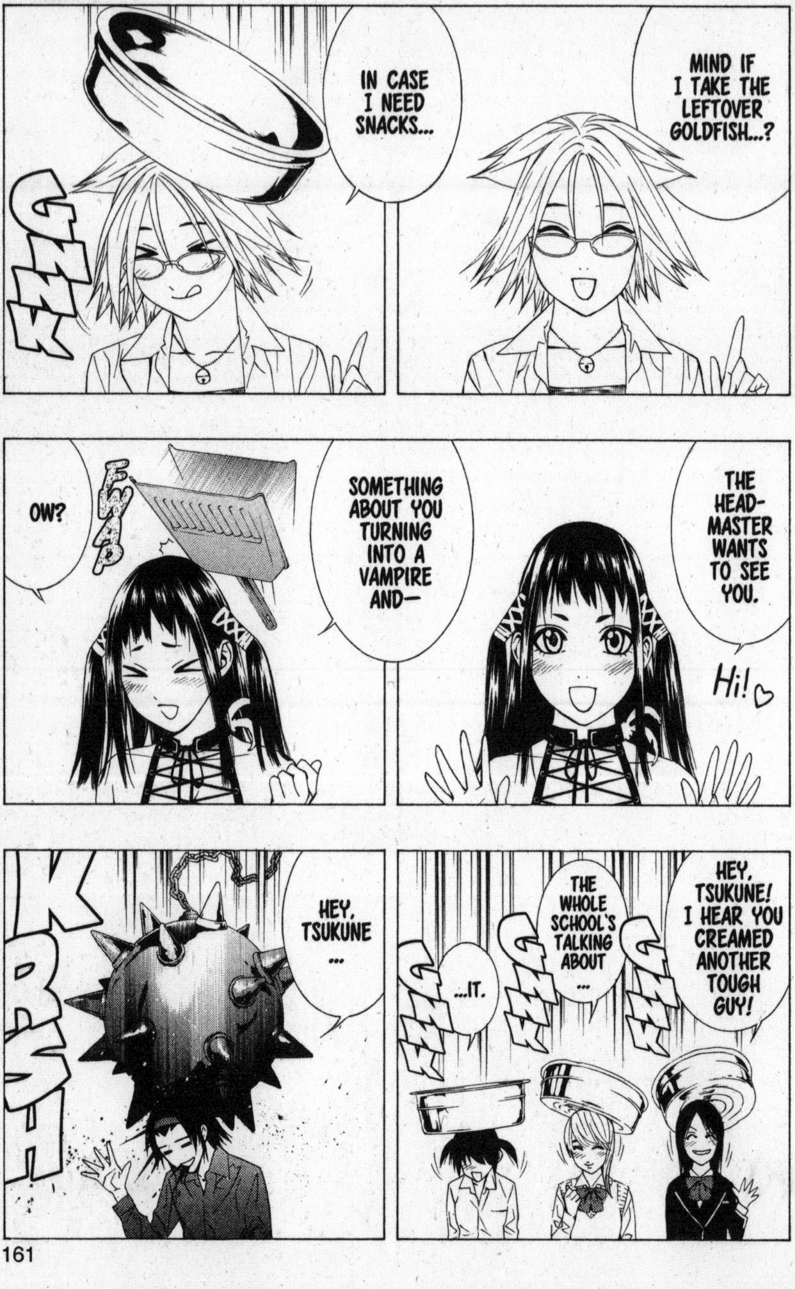
MIND IF I TAKE THE LEFTOVER GOLDFISH...?
IN CASE I NEED SNACKS...
GNNK
THE HEAD-MASTER WANTS TO SEE YOU.
Hi! ♡
SOMETHING ABOUT YOU TURNING INTO A VAMPIRE AND—
FWAP
OW?
HEY, TSUKUNE! I HEAR YOU CREAMED ANOTHER TOUGH GUY!
GNNK
THE WHOLE SCHOOL'S TALKING ABOUT ...
GNNK
...IT.
GNNK
HEY, TSUKUNE ...
KRSH

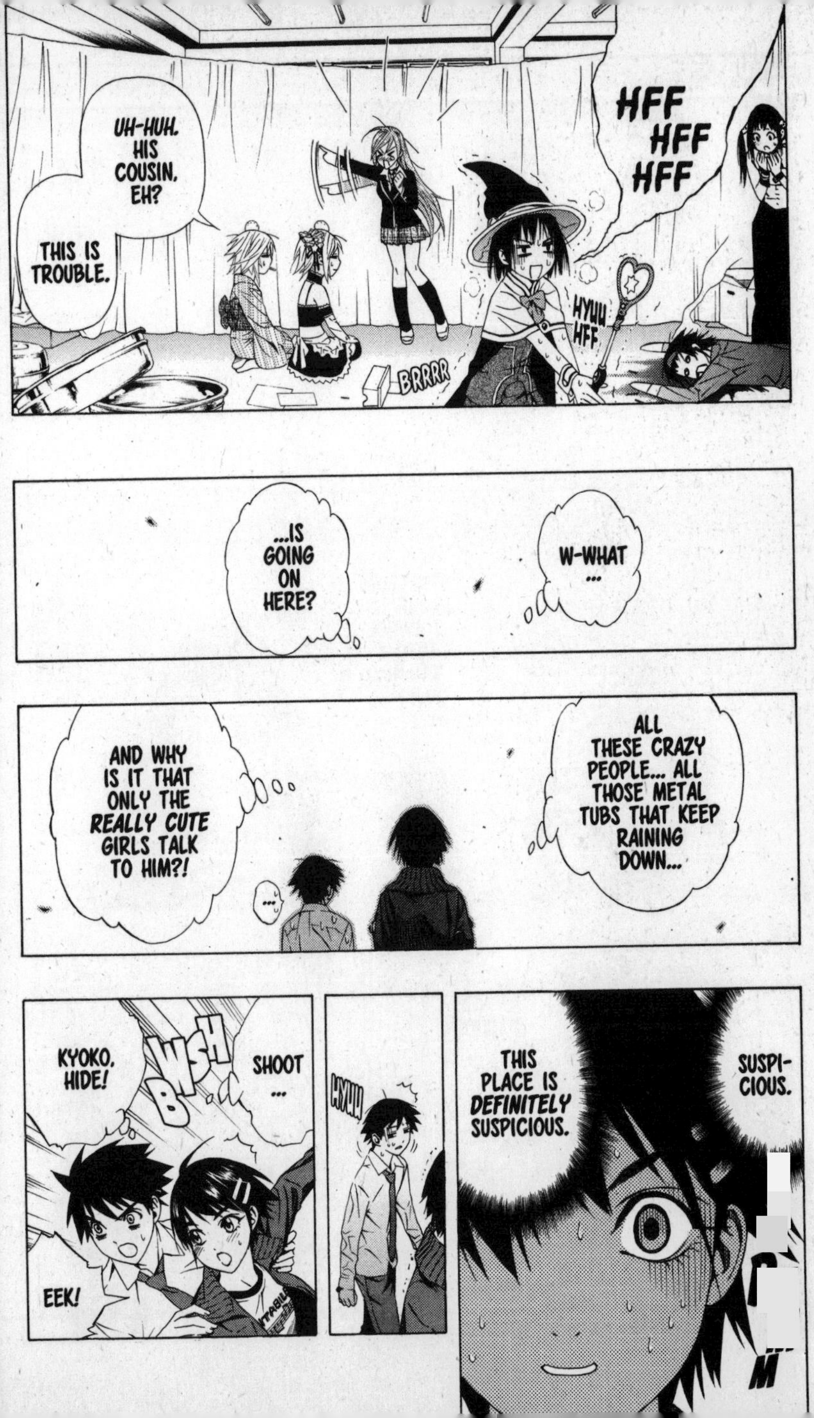
HFF HFF HFF
HYUU HFF
BRRRR
UH-HUH. HIS COUSIN, EH?
THIS IS TROUBLE.
W-WHAT ...
...IS GOING ON HERE?
ALL THESE CRAZY PEOPLE... ALL THOSE METAL TUBS THAT KEEP RAINING DOWN...
...
AND WHY IS IT THAT ONLY THE REALLY CUTE GIRLS TALK TO HIM?!
SUSPI- CIOUS.
THIS PLACE IS DEFINITELY SUSPICIOUS.
HYUU
SHOOT ...
BWSH
KYOKO, HIDE!
EEK!

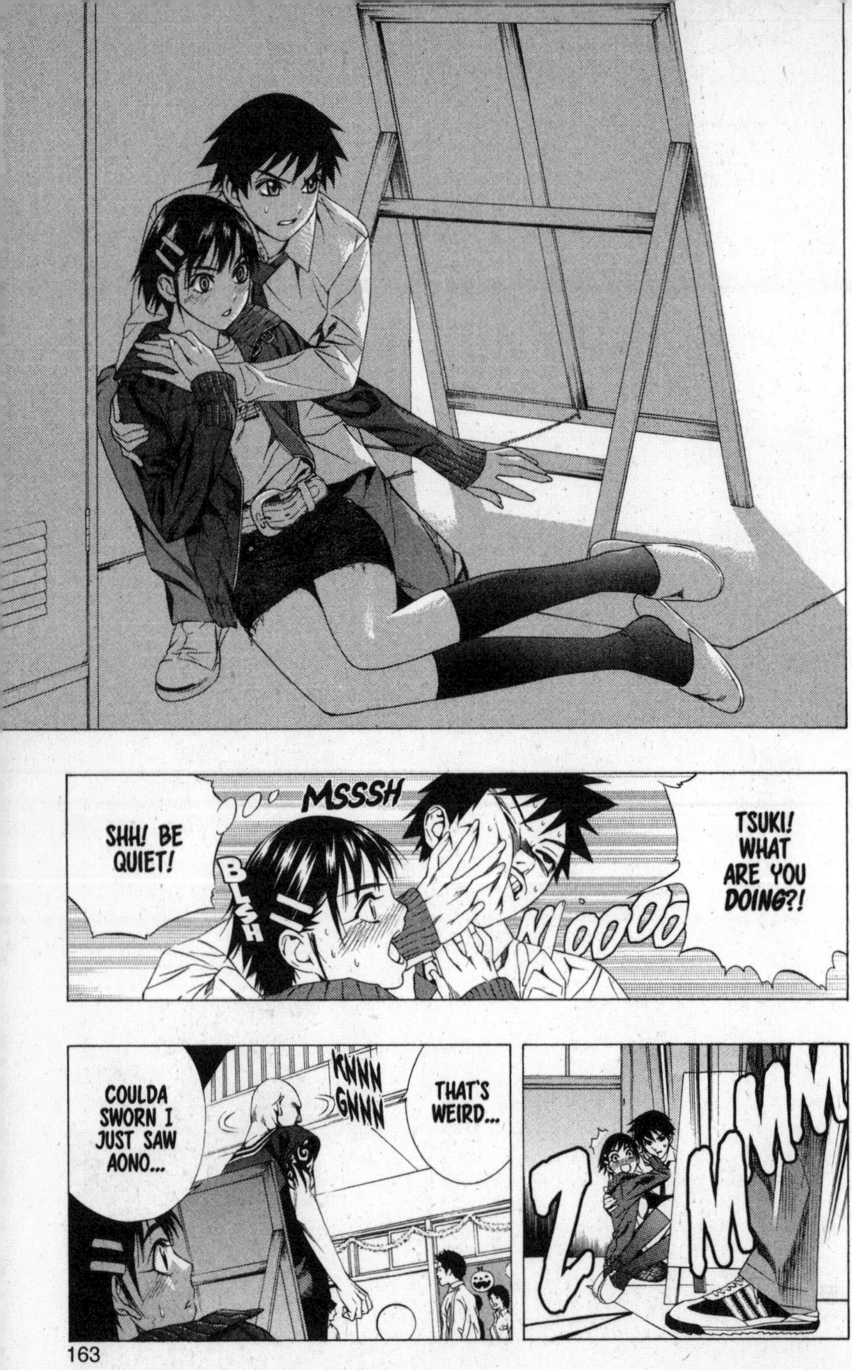
TSUKI! WHAT ARE YOU DOING?!
NOOOOO
MSSSH
BLSH
SHH! BE QUIET!
ZMMMM
THAT'S WEIRD...
KNNN GNNN
COULDA SWORN I JUST SAW AONO...

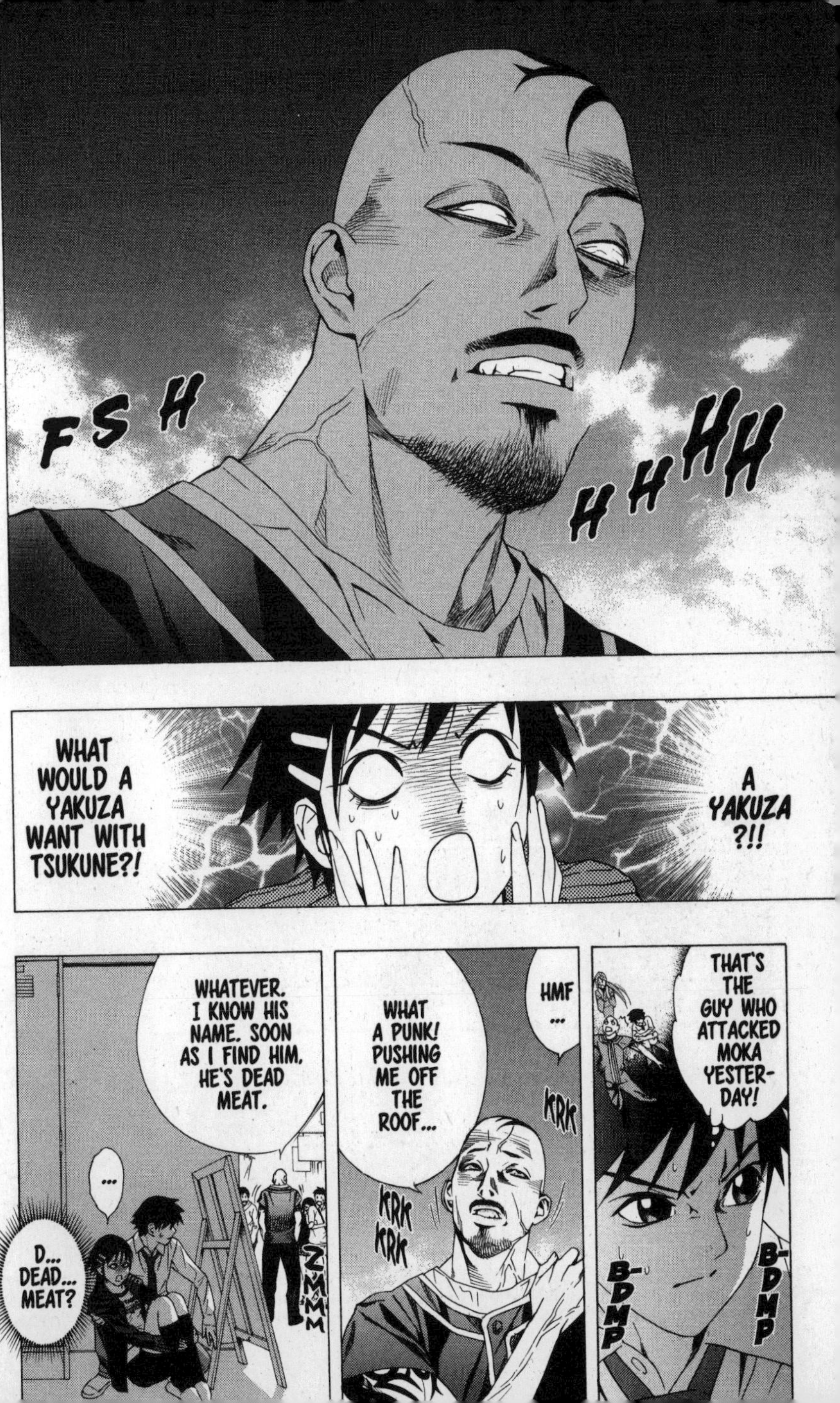
FSH
HHHHH
A YAKUZA?!!
WHAT WOULD A YAKUZA WANT WITH TSUKUNE?!
THAT'S THE GUY WHO ATTACKED MOKA YESTER-DAY!
B-BDMP
B-BDMP
HMF...
WHAT A PUNK! PUSHING ME OFF THE ROOF...
KRK
KRK KRK KRK
WHATEVER. I KNOW HIS NAME. SOON AS I FIND HIM, HE'S DEAD MEAT.
...
D... DEAD... MEAT?
ZMMM

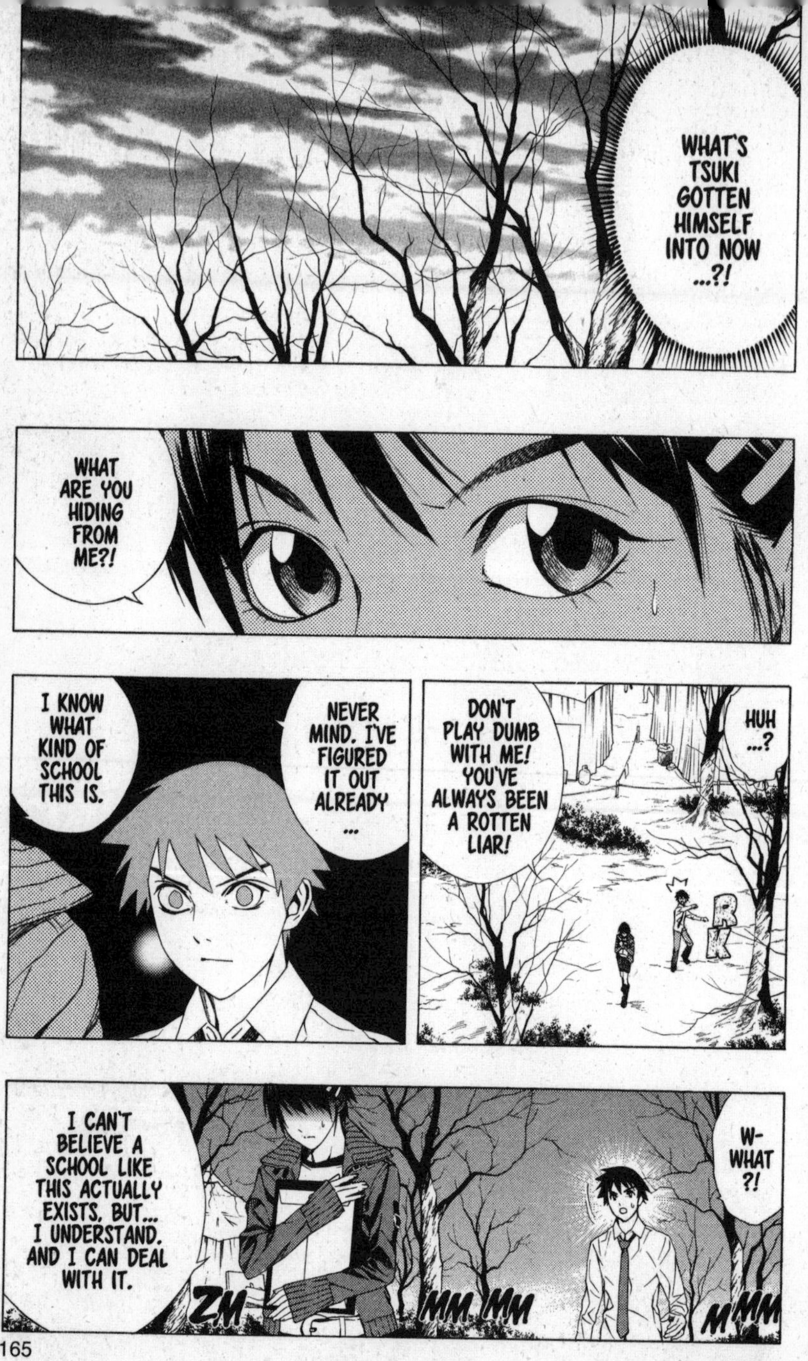
WHAT'S TSUKI GOTTEN HIMSELF INTO NOW ...?!
WHAT ARE YOU HIDING FROM ME?!
HUH ...?
DON'T PLAY DUMB WITH ME! YOU'VE ALWAYS BEEN A ROTTEN LIAR!
NEVER MIND. I'VE FIGURED IT OUT ALREADY ...
I KNOW WHAT KIND OF SCHOOL THIS IS.
W-WHAT ?!
I CAN'T BELIEVE A SCHOOL LIKE THIS ACTUALLY EXISTS, BUT... I UNDERSTAND. AND I CAN DEAL WITH IT.
ZM MM MM MMM

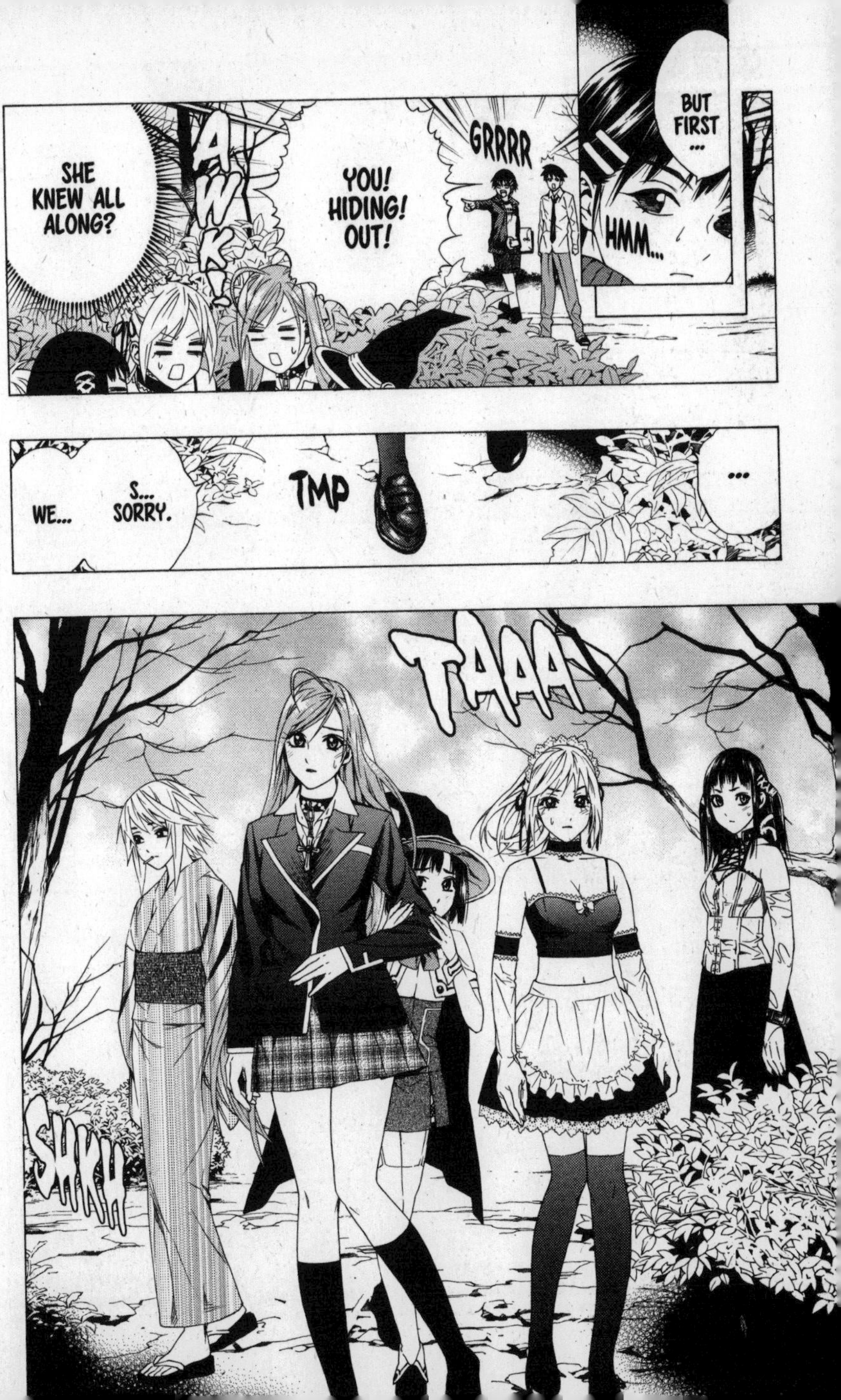
BUT FIRST ...
HMM...
GRRRR
YOU! HIDING! OUT!
AWK
SHE KNEW ALL ALONG?
...
TMP
S... SORRY.
WE...
TAAA
SHKH

READ THIS WAY

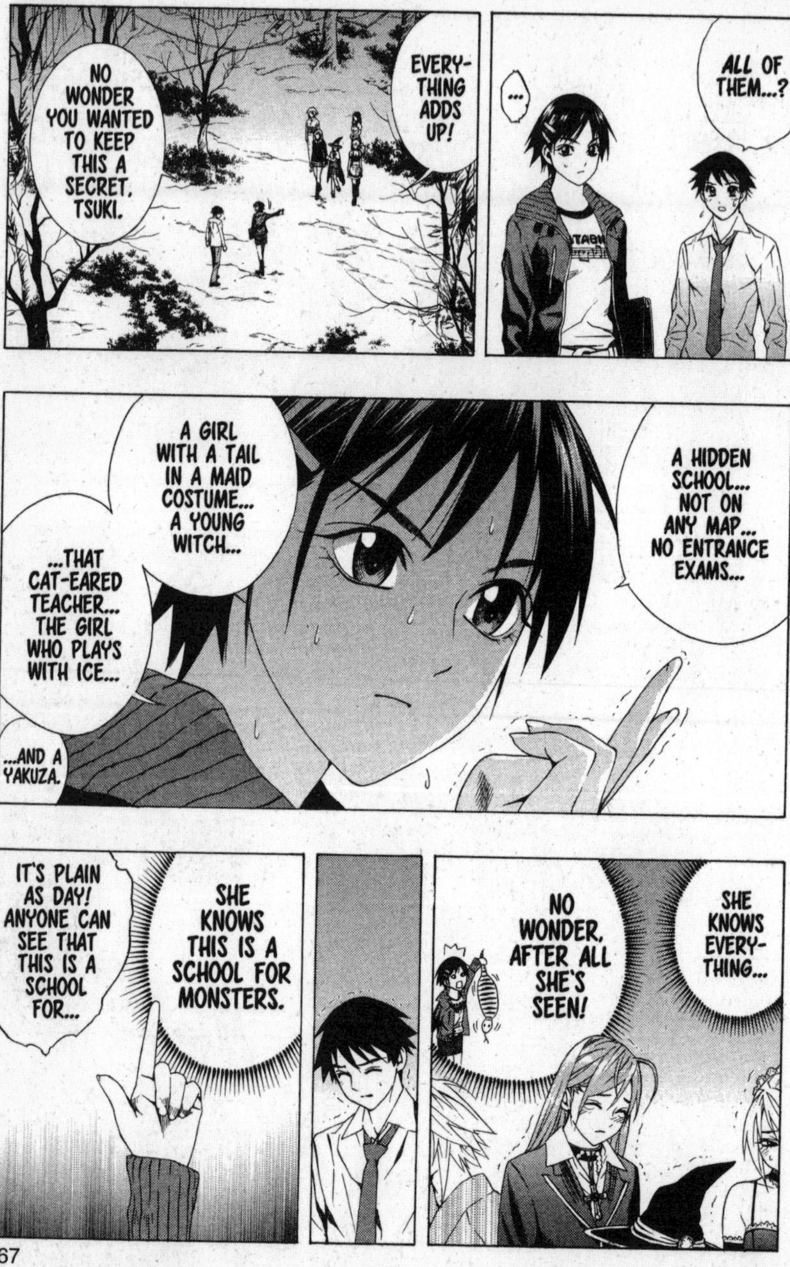
ALL OF THEM...?
...
EVERY-THING ADDS UP!
NO WONDER YOU WANTED TO KEEP THIS A SECRET, TSUKI.
A HIDDEN SCHOOL... NOT ON ANY MAP... NO ENTRANCE EXAMS...
A GIRL WITH A TAIL IN A MAID COSTUME... A YOUNG WITCH...
...THAT CAT-EARED TEACHER... THE GIRL WHO PLAYS WITH ICE...
...AND A YAKUZA.
SHE KNOWS EVERY-THING...
NO WONDER, AFTER ALL SHE'S SEEN!
SHE KNOWS THIS IS A SCHOOL FOR MONSTERS.
IT'S PLAIN AS DAY! ANYONE CAN SEE THAT THIS IS A SCHOOL FOR...

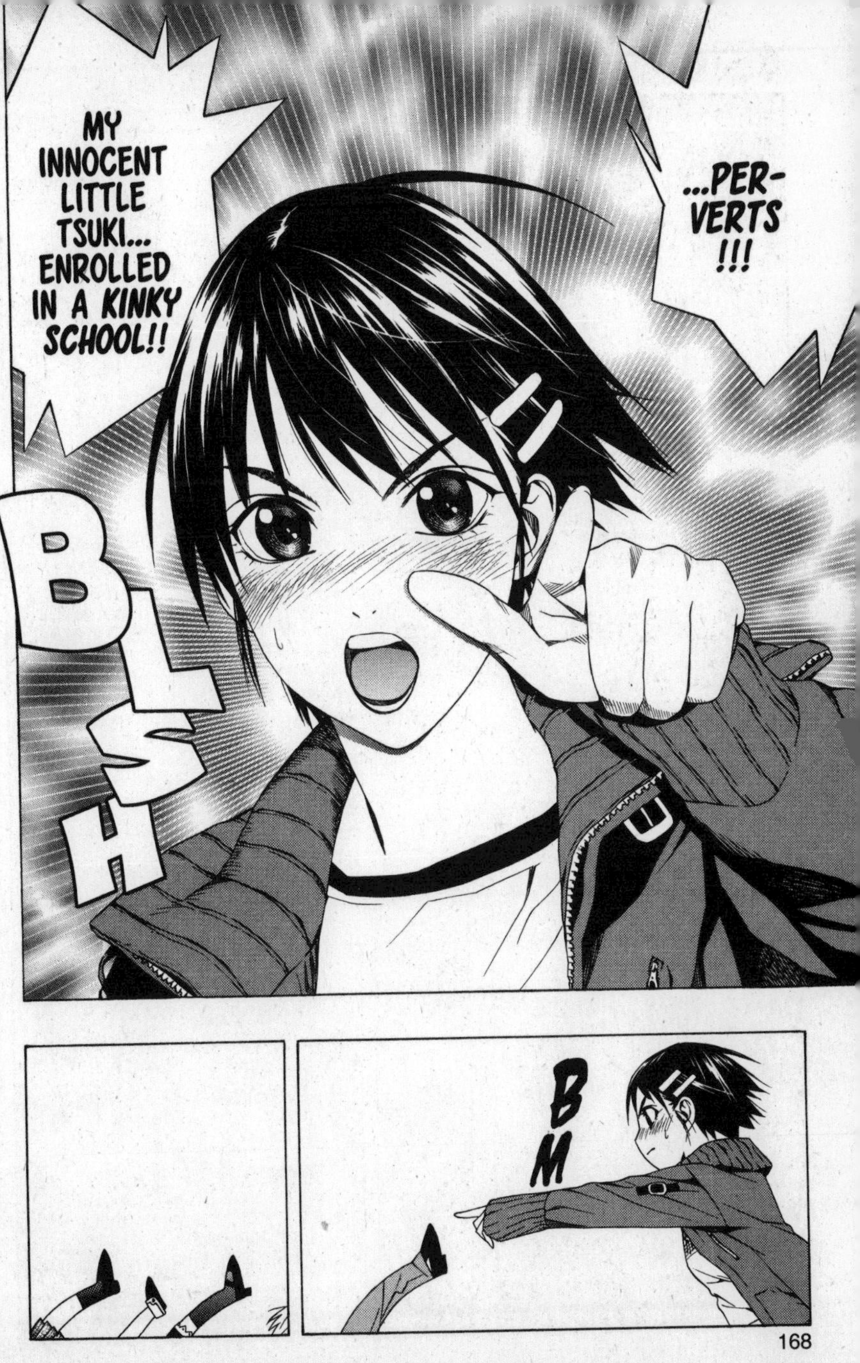
...PER-VERTS!!!
MY INNOCENT LITTLE TSUKI... ENROLLED IN A *KINKY* SCHOOL!!
BLSH
BM

READ THIS WAY

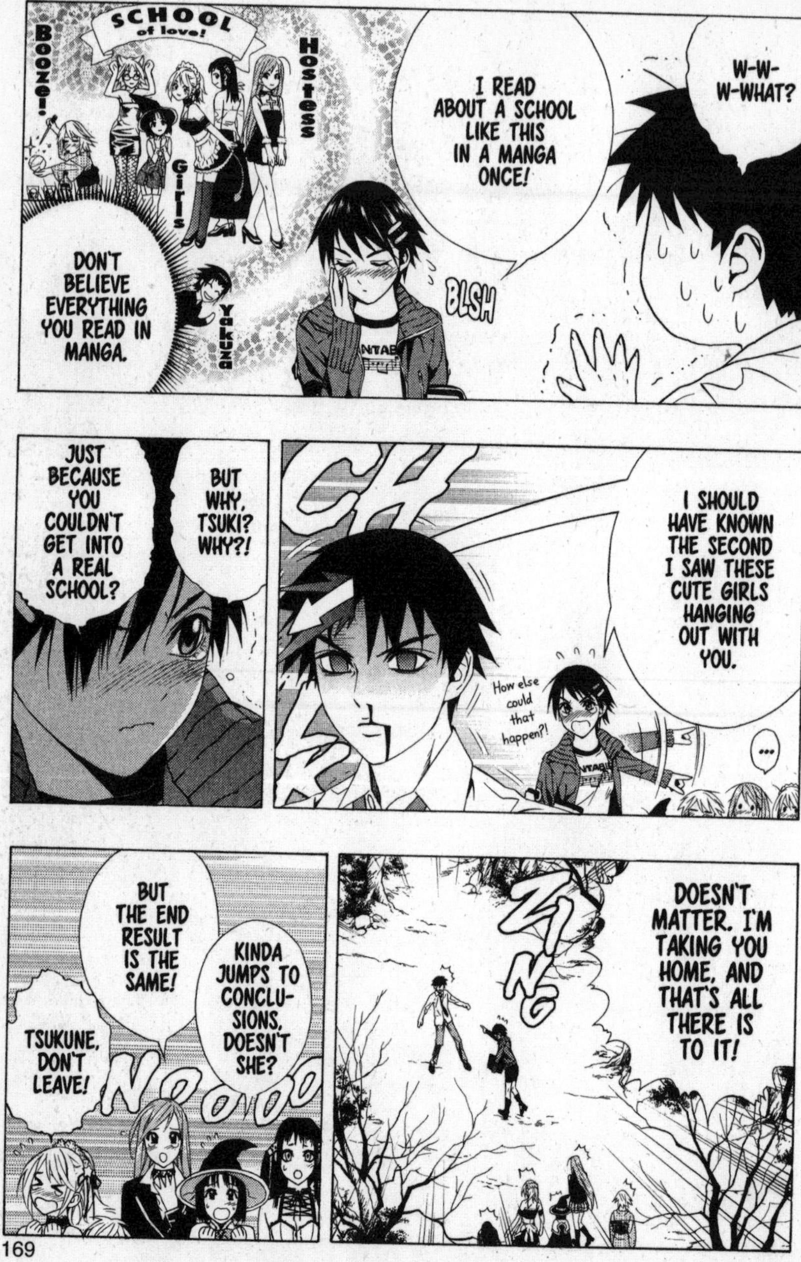

W-W-W-WHAT?
I READ ABOUT A SCHOOL LIKE THIS IN A MANGA ONCE!
BLSH
SCHOOL of love!
Hostess
Booze!
Girls
Yakuza
DON'T BELIEVE EVERYTHING YOU READ IN MANGA.
I SHOULD HAVE KNOWN THE SECOND I SAW THESE CUTE GIRLS HANGING OUT WITH YOU.
...
How else could that happen?!
CH
BUT WHY, TSUKI? WHY?!
JUST BECAUSE YOU COULDN'T GET INTO A REAL SCHOOL?
DOESN'T MATTER. I'M TAKING YOU HOME, AND THAT'S ALL THERE IS TO IT!
ZING
KINDA JUMPS TO CONCLUSIONS, DOESN'T SHE?
BUT THE END RESULT IS THE SAME!
TSUKUNE, DON'T LEAVE!
NOOOO

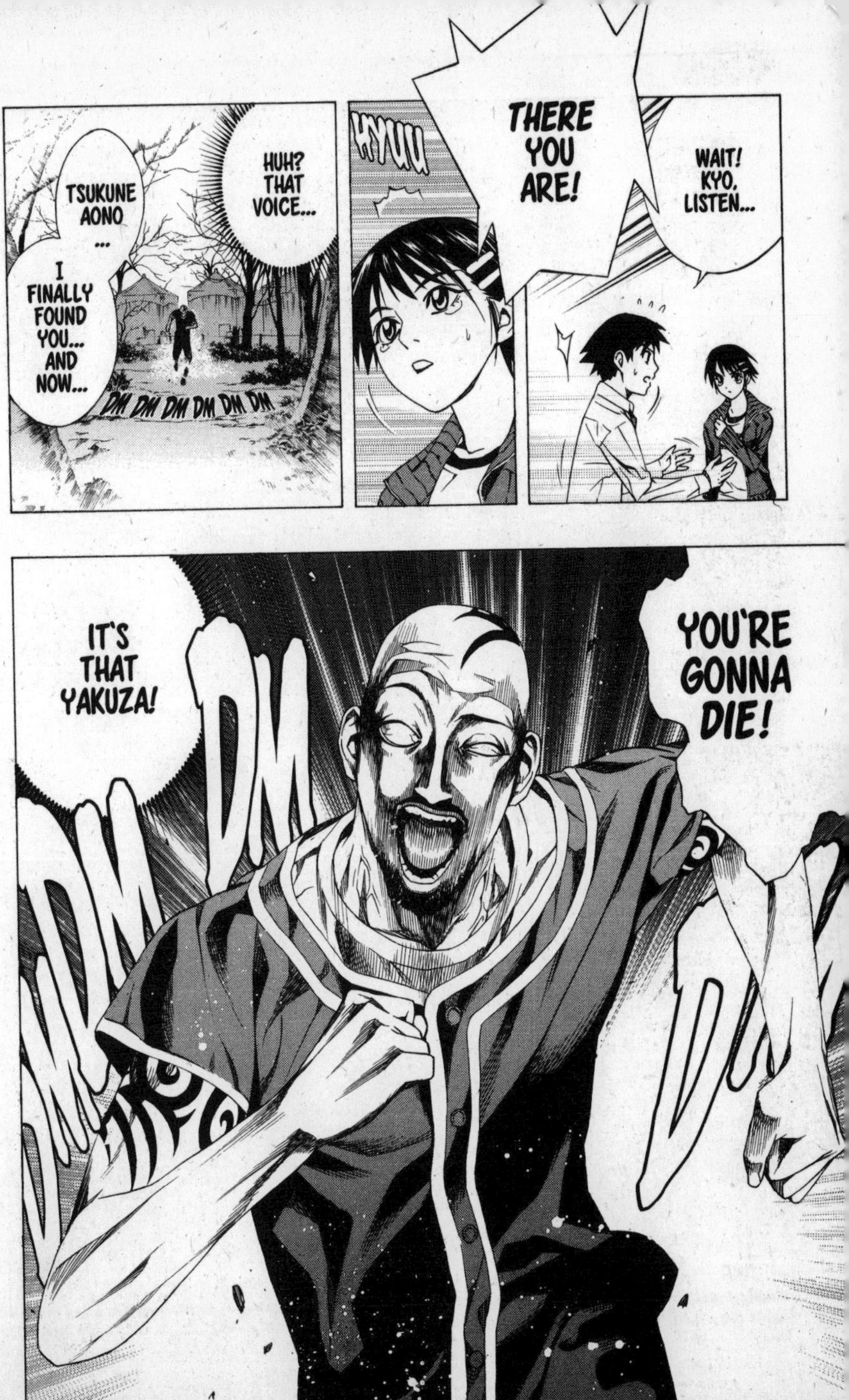
WAIT! KYO, LISTEN...
THERE YOU ARE!
HYUU
HUH? THAT VOICE...
TSUKUNE AONO ...
I FINALLY FOUND YOU... AND NOW...
DM DM DM DM DM DM
YOU'RE GONNA DIE!
IT'S THAT YAKUZA!
DM DM DM

READ THIS WAY

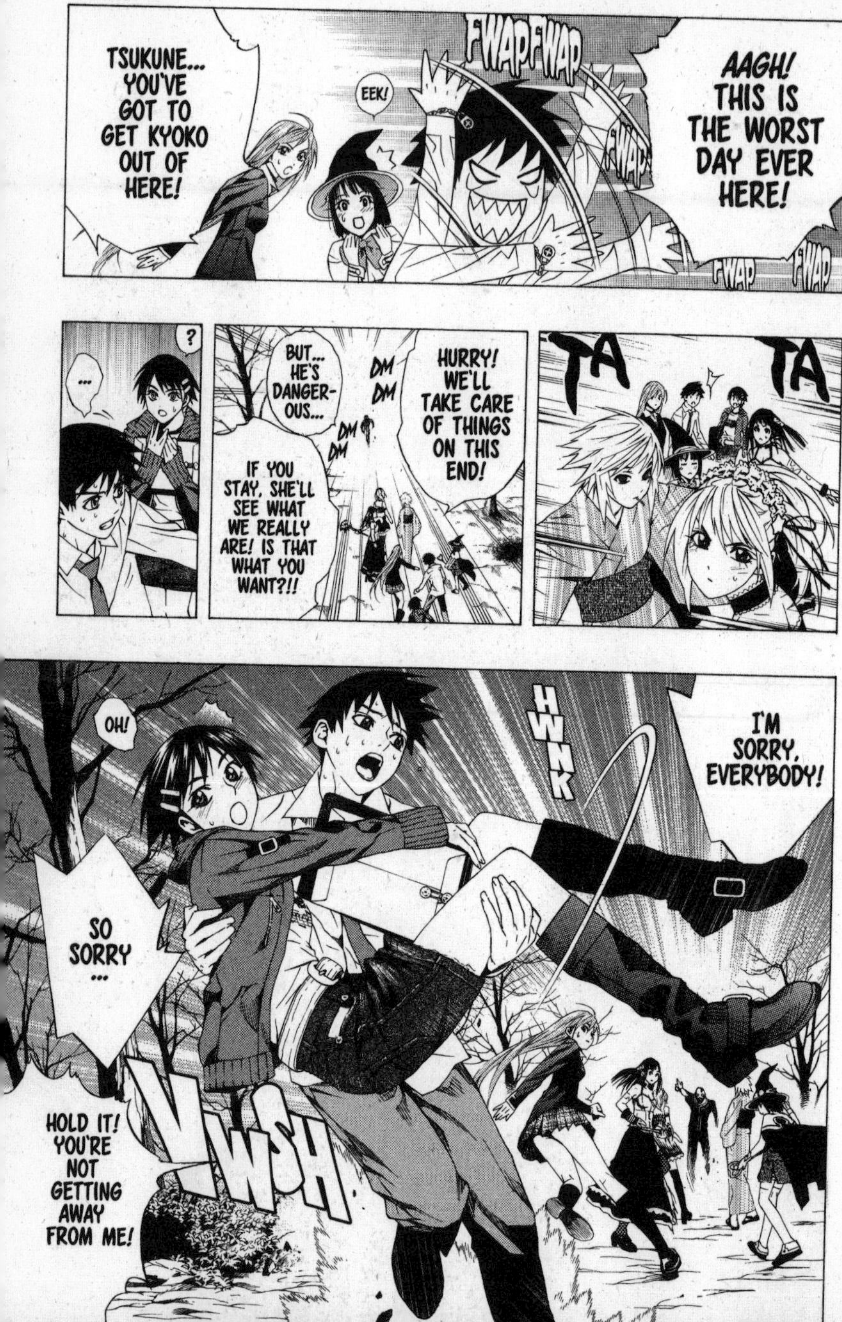

AAGH! THIS IS THE WORST DAY EVER HERE!
FWAPFWAP
FWAP
EEK!
TSUKUNE... YOU'VE GOT TO GET KYOKO OUT OF HERE!
FWAP
FWAP
TA
TA
HURRY! WE'LL TAKE CARE OF THINGS ON THIS END!
BUT... HE'S DANGER-OUS...
DM DM
DM DM
IF YOU STAY, SHE'LL SEE WHAT WE REALLY ARE! IS THAT WHAT YOU WANT?!!
?
...
I'M SORRY, EVERYBODY!
HWNK
OH!
SO SORRY ...
VWSH
HOLD IT! YOU'RE NOT GETTING AWAY FROM ME!

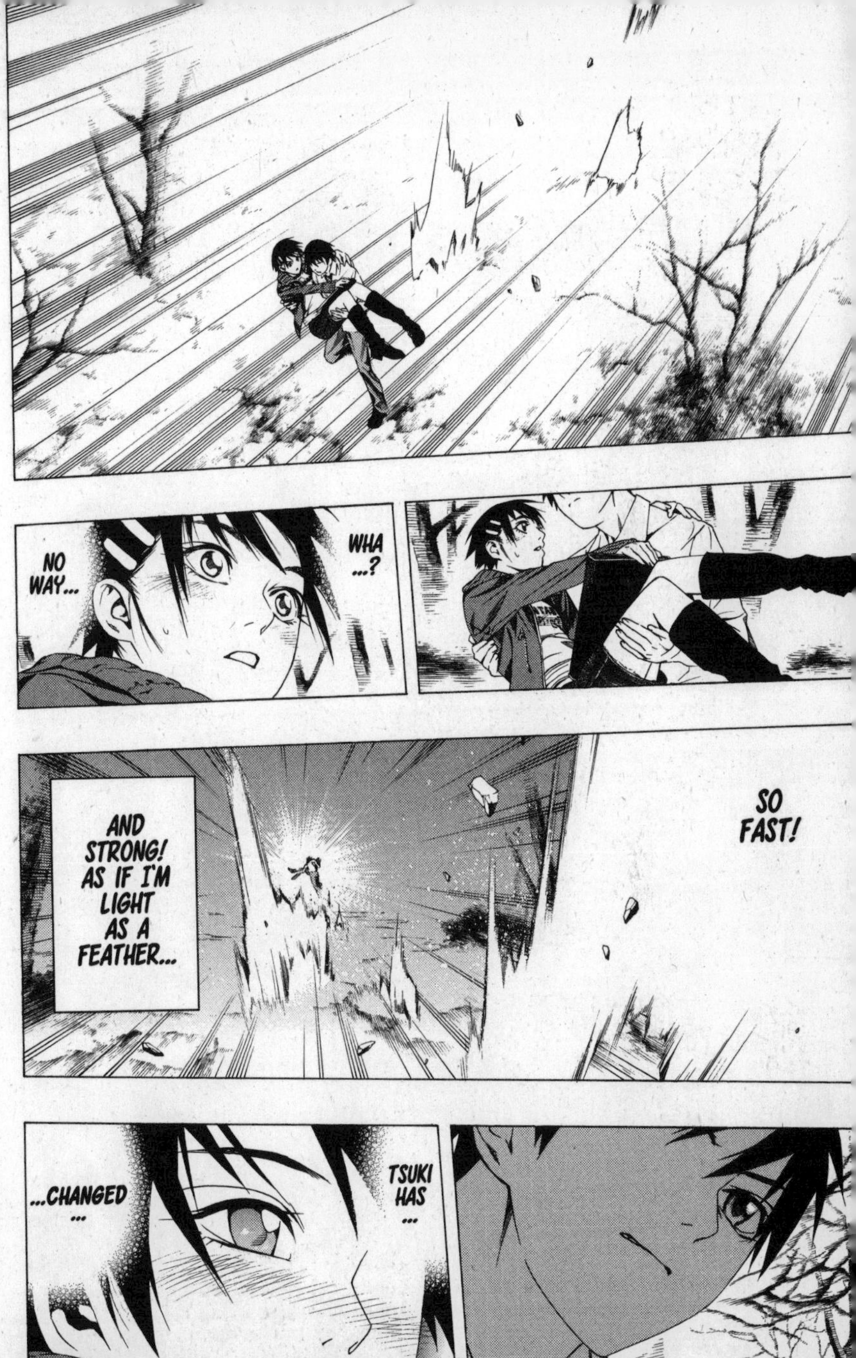
WHA ...?
NO WAY...
SO FAST!
AND STRONG! AS IF I'M LIGHT AS A FEATHER...
TSUKI HAS ...
...CHANGED ...

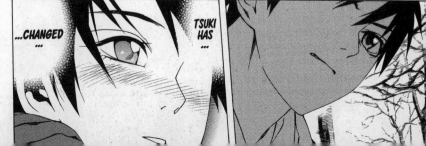

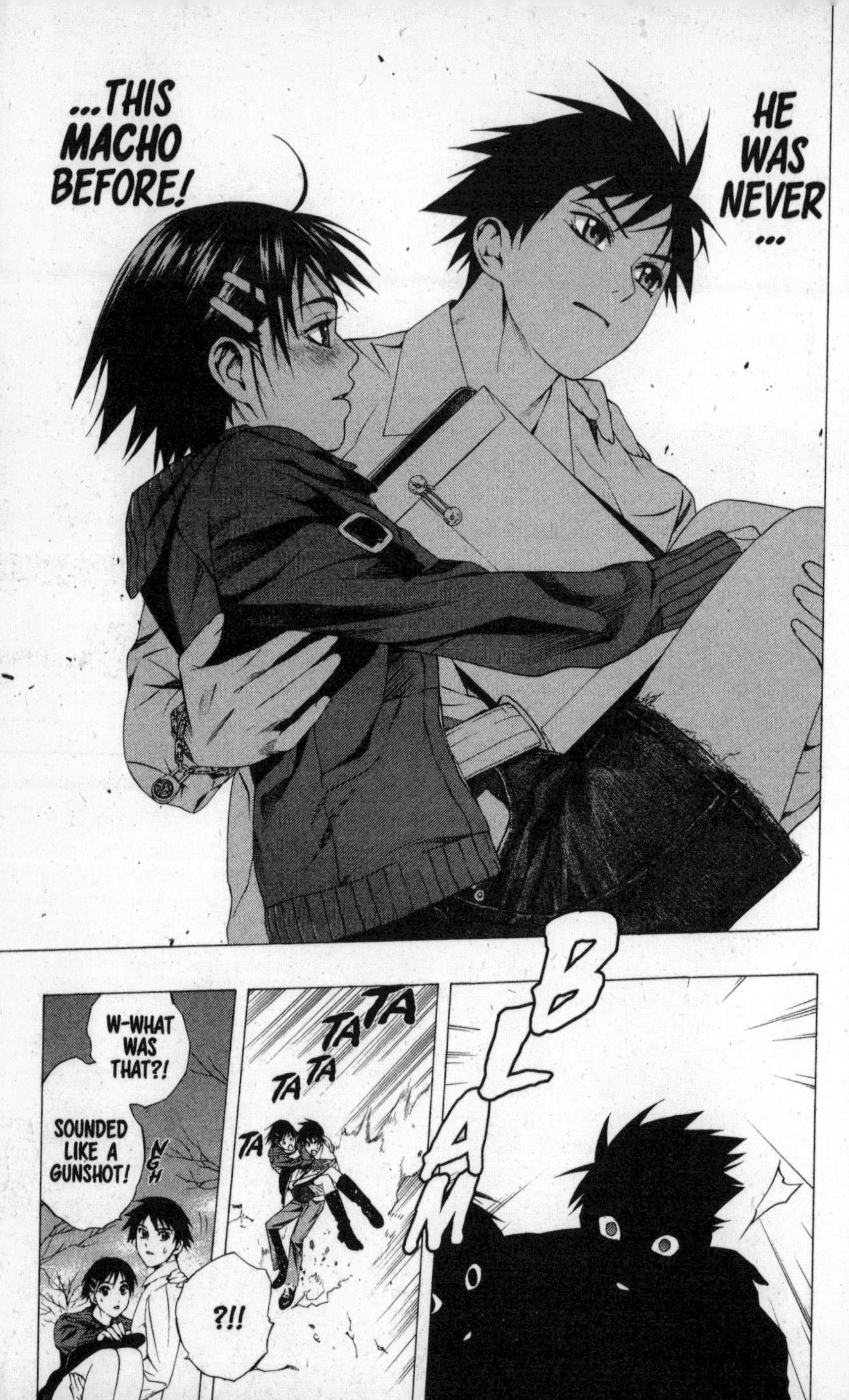
HE WAS NEVER ...
...THIS MACHO BEFORE!
BLAM
TA TA TA TA TA
NGH
W-WHAT WAS THAT?!
SOUNDED LIKE A GUNSHOT!
?!!

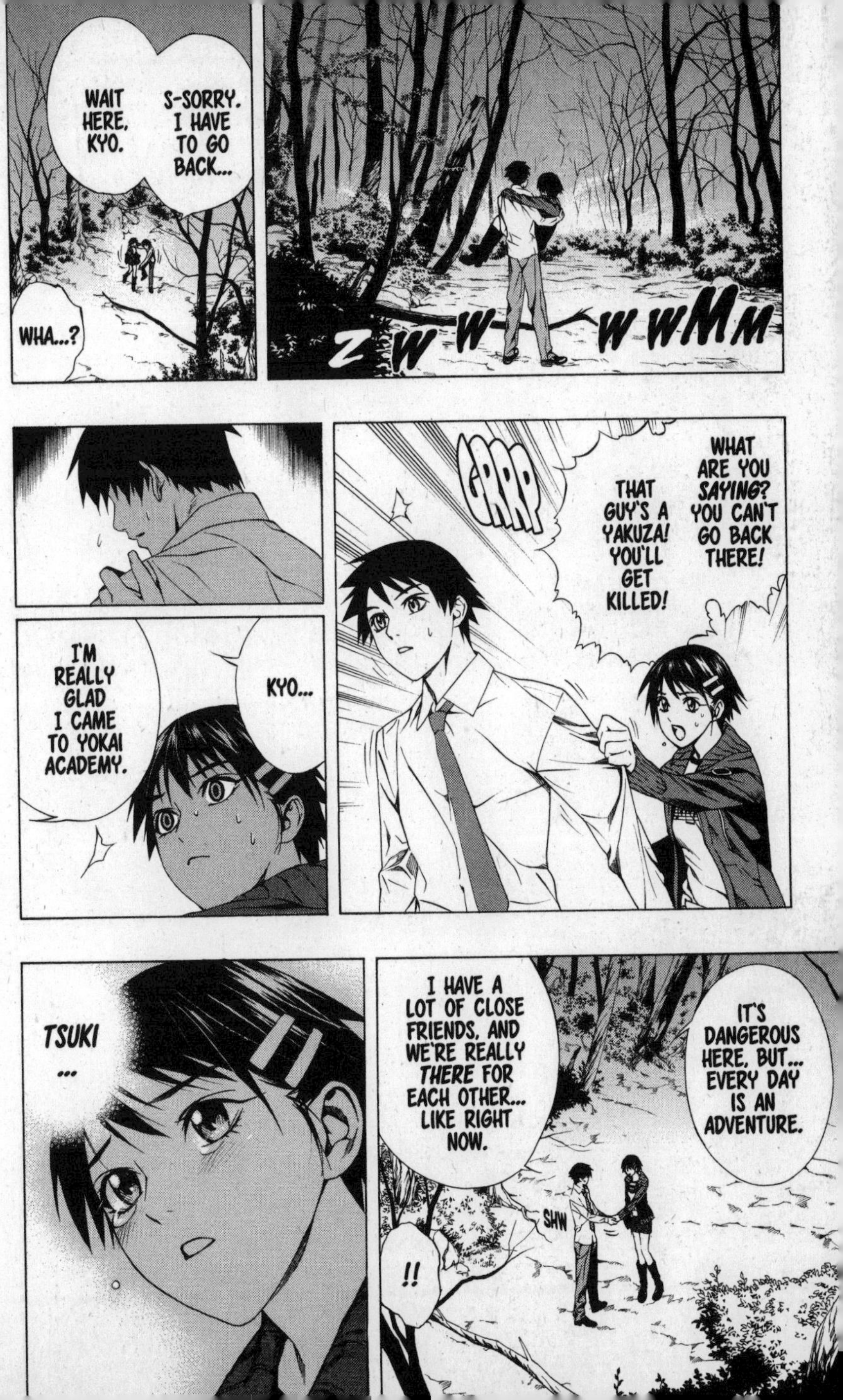
ZWWWWWMM
S-SORRY. I HAVE TO GO BACK...
WAIT HERE, KYO.
WHA...?
GRRP
WHAT ARE YOU *SAYING*? YOU CAN'T GO BACK THERE!
THAT GUY'S A YAKUZA! YOU'LL GET KILLED!
KYO...
I'M REALLY GLAD I CAME TO YOKAI ACADEMY.
IT'S DANGEROUS HERE, BUT... EVERY DAY IS AN ADVENTURE.
I HAVE A LOT OF CLOSE FRIENDS, AND WE'RE REALLY *THERE* FOR EACH OTHER... LIKE RIGHT NOW.
SHW
!!
TSUKI...

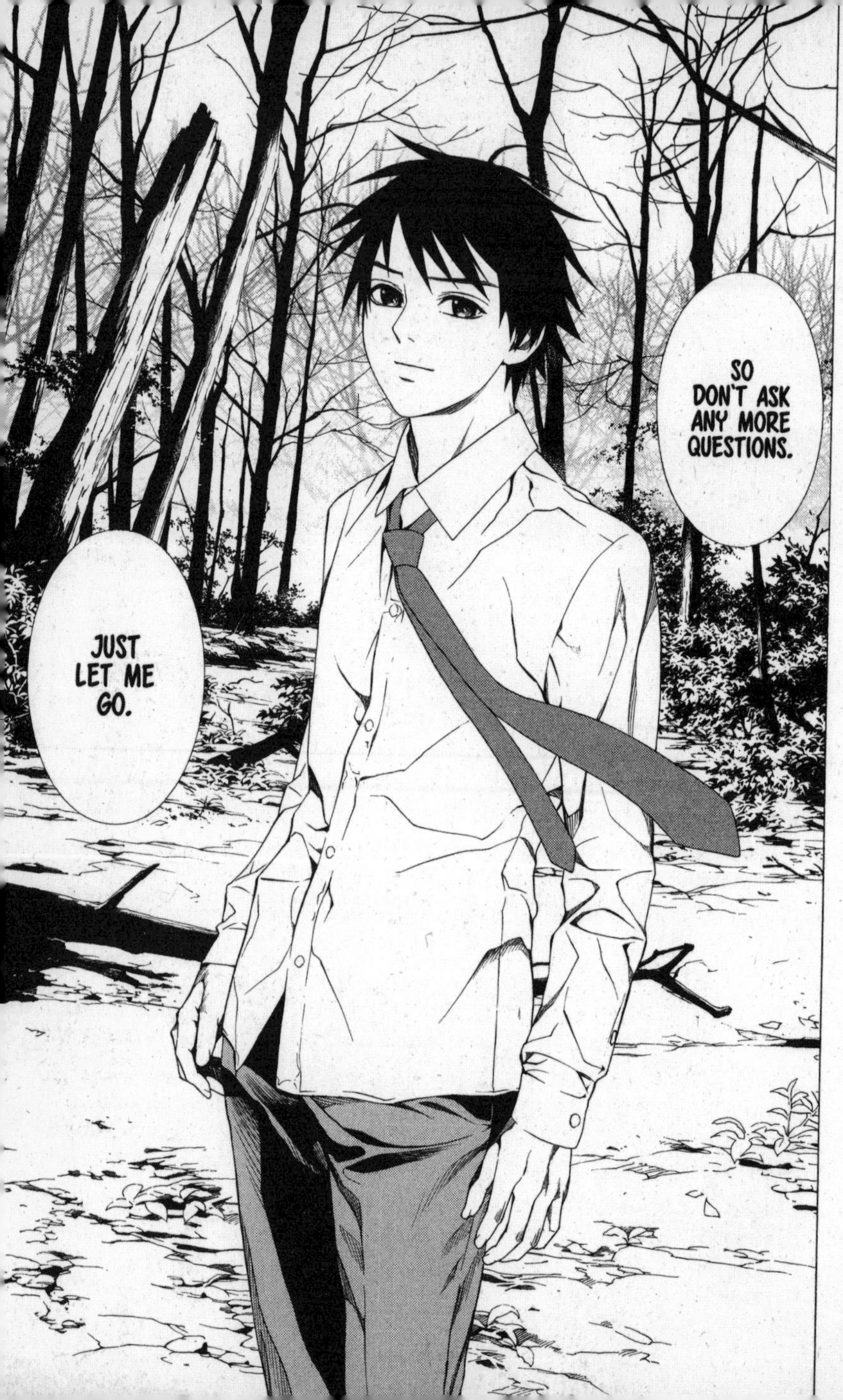
SO DON'T ASK ANY MORE QUESTIONS.
JUST LET ME GO.

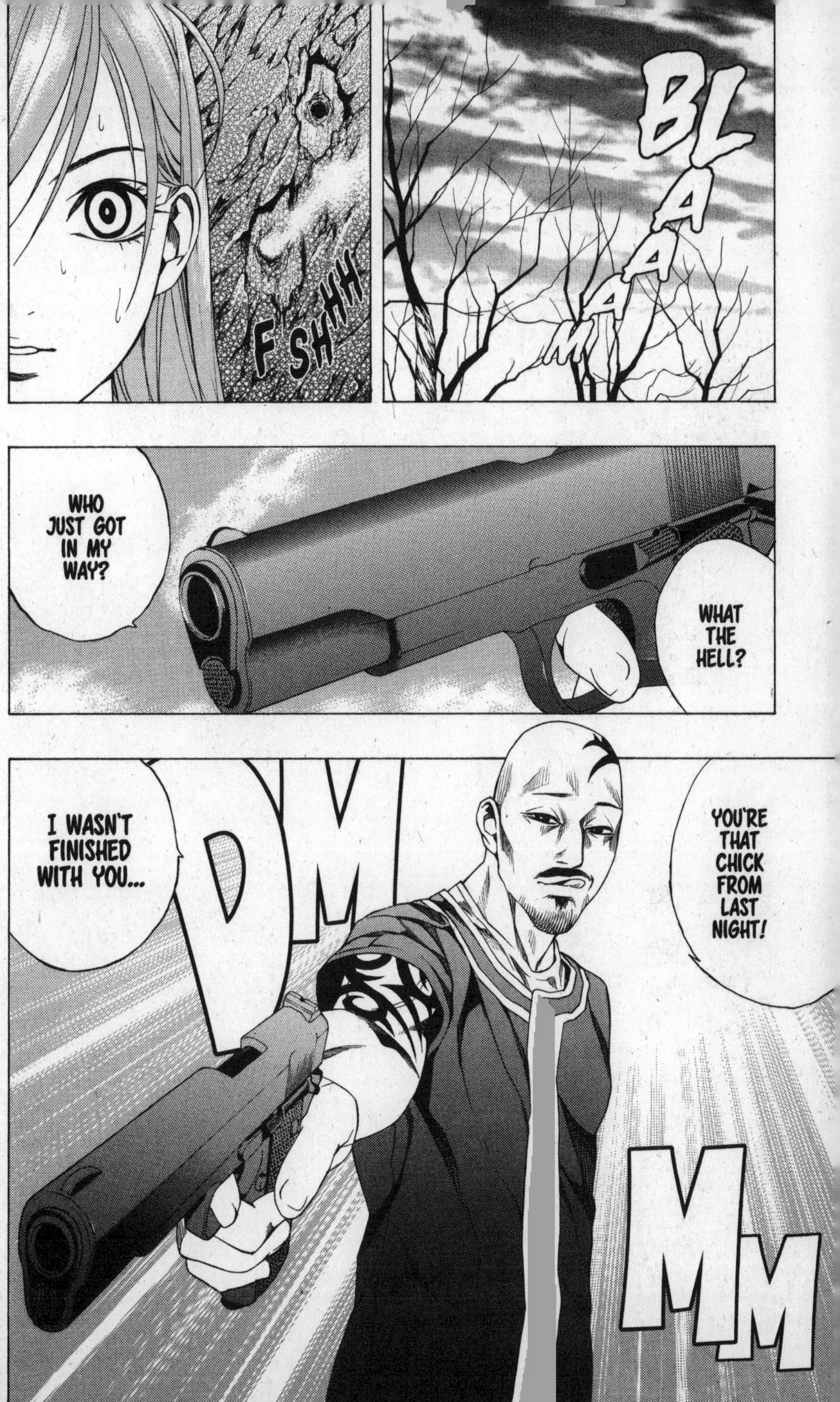
BLAAAM
FSHHH
WHAT THE HELL?
WHO JUST GOT IN MY WAY?
YOU'RE THAT CHICK FROM LAST NIGHT!
I WASN'T FINISHED WITH YOU...
DM
MMM

READ THIS WAY

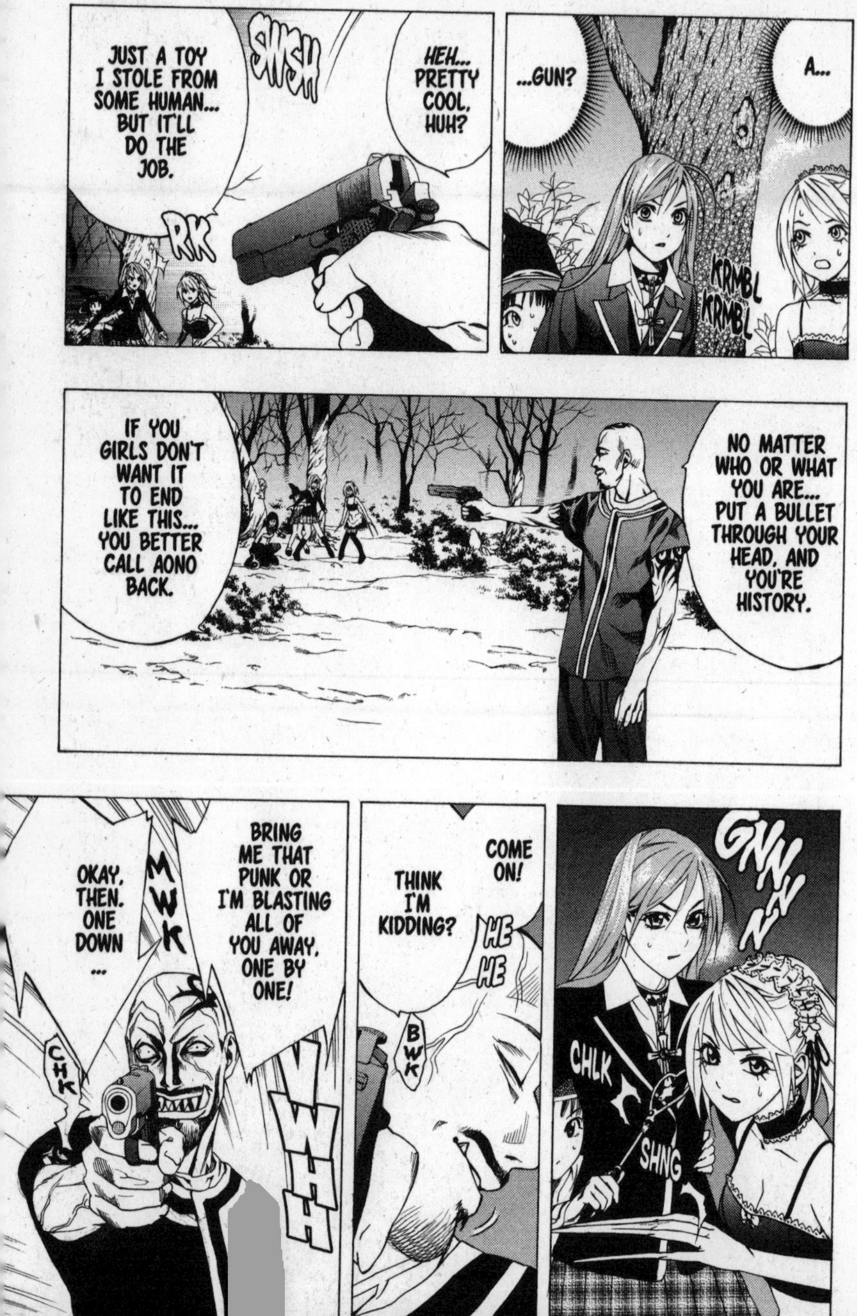
A...
...GUN?
KRMBL KRMBL
HEH... PRETTY COOL, HUH?
SWSH
JUST A TOY I STOLE FROM SOME HUMAN... BUT IT'LL DO THE JOB.
RK
NO MATTER WHO OR WHAT YOU ARE... PUT A BULLET THROUGH YOUR HEAD, AND YOU'RE HISTORY.
IF YOU GIRLS DON'T WANT IT TO END LIKE THIS... YOU BETTER CALL AONO BACK.
GNNNN
CHLK
SHNG
COME ON!
THINK I'M KIDDING?
HE HE
BWK
BRING ME THAT PUNK OR I'M BLASTING ALL OF YOU AWAY, ONE BY ONE!
MWK
OKAY, THEN. ONE DOWN...
CHK
WHHH

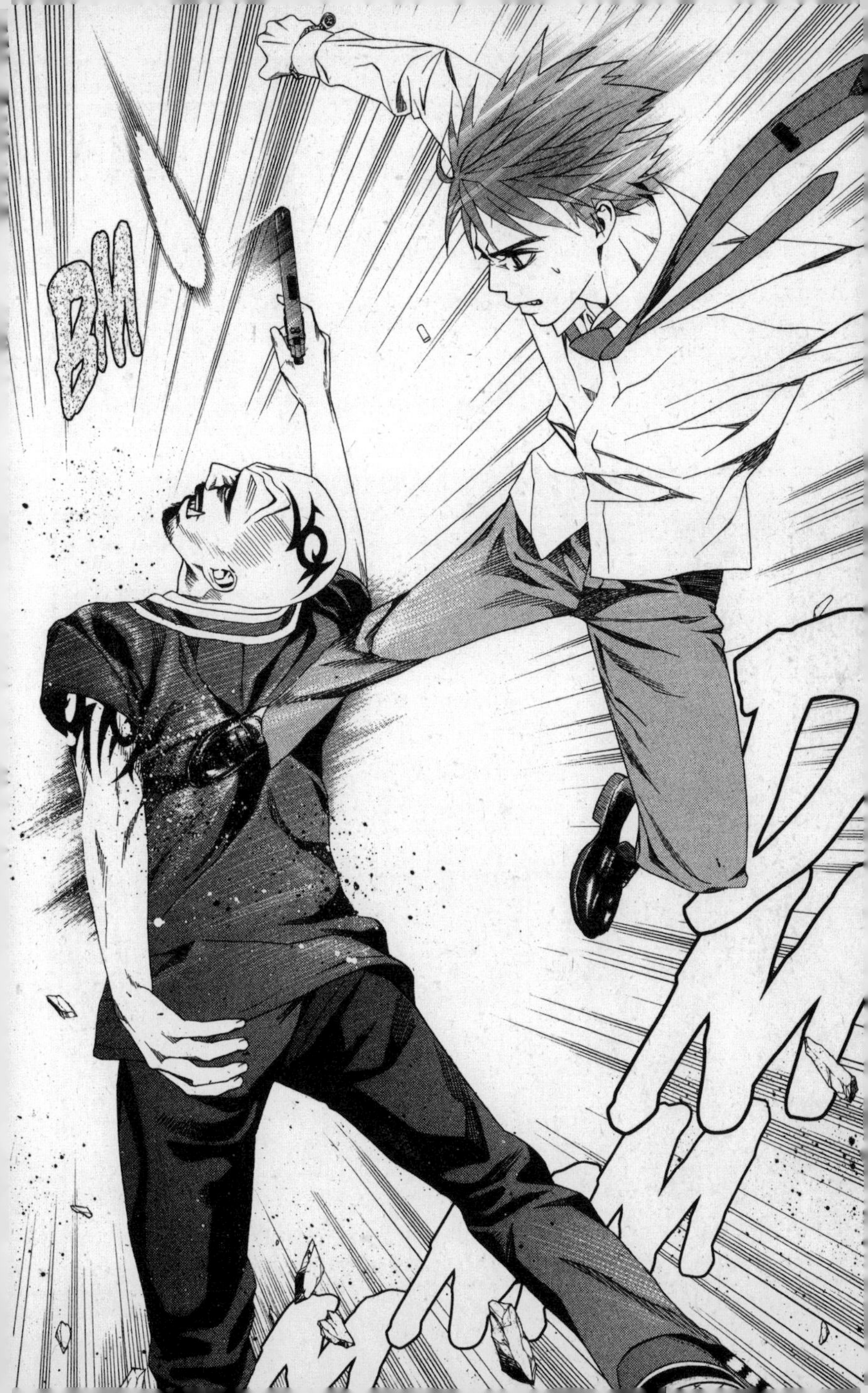
BM

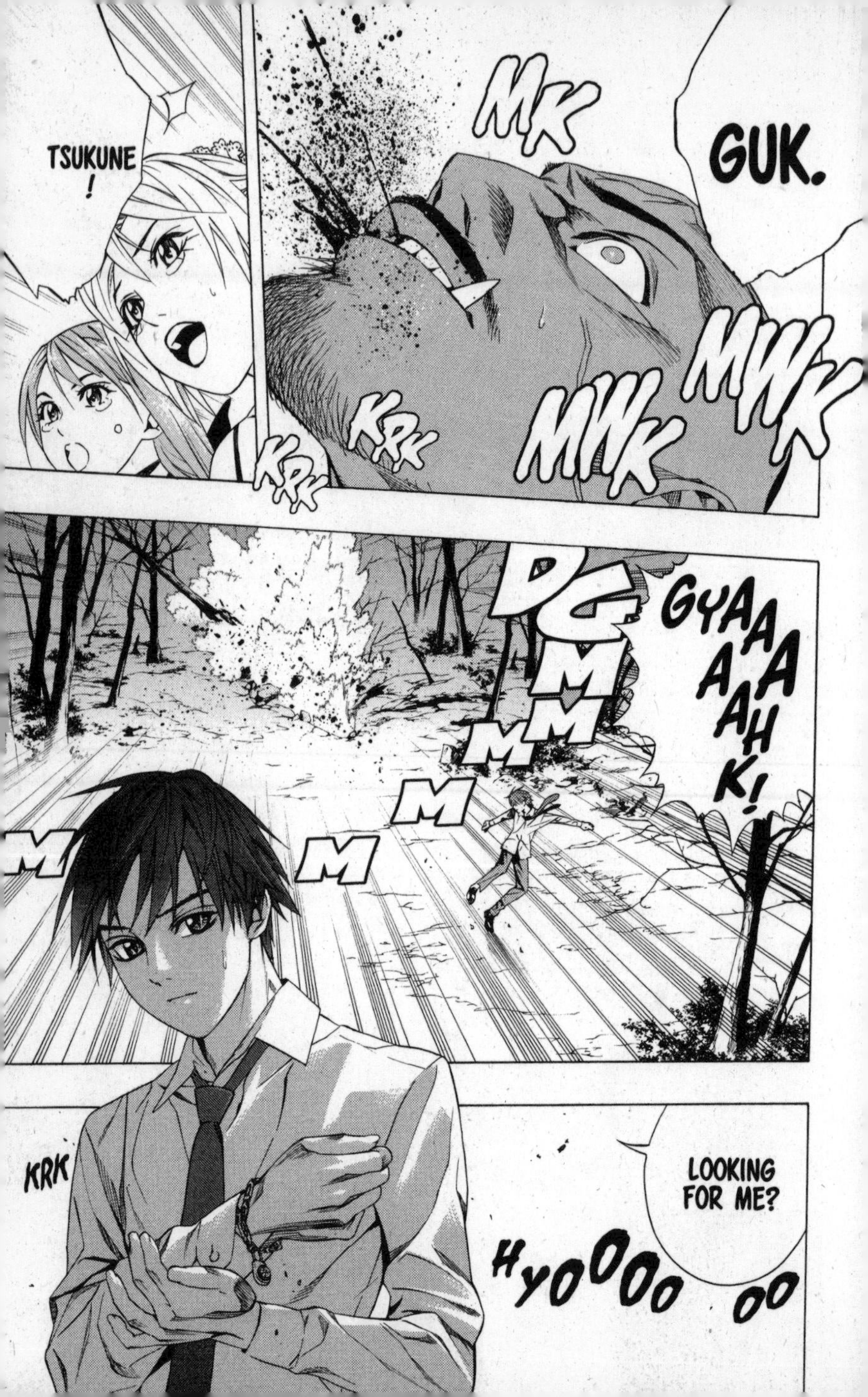
GUK.
MK
MWK
MWK
KRK
KRK
TSUKUNE!
GYAAAAAAHK!
DGMMMM
M
M
M
LOOKING FOR ME?
HYOOOO OO
KRK

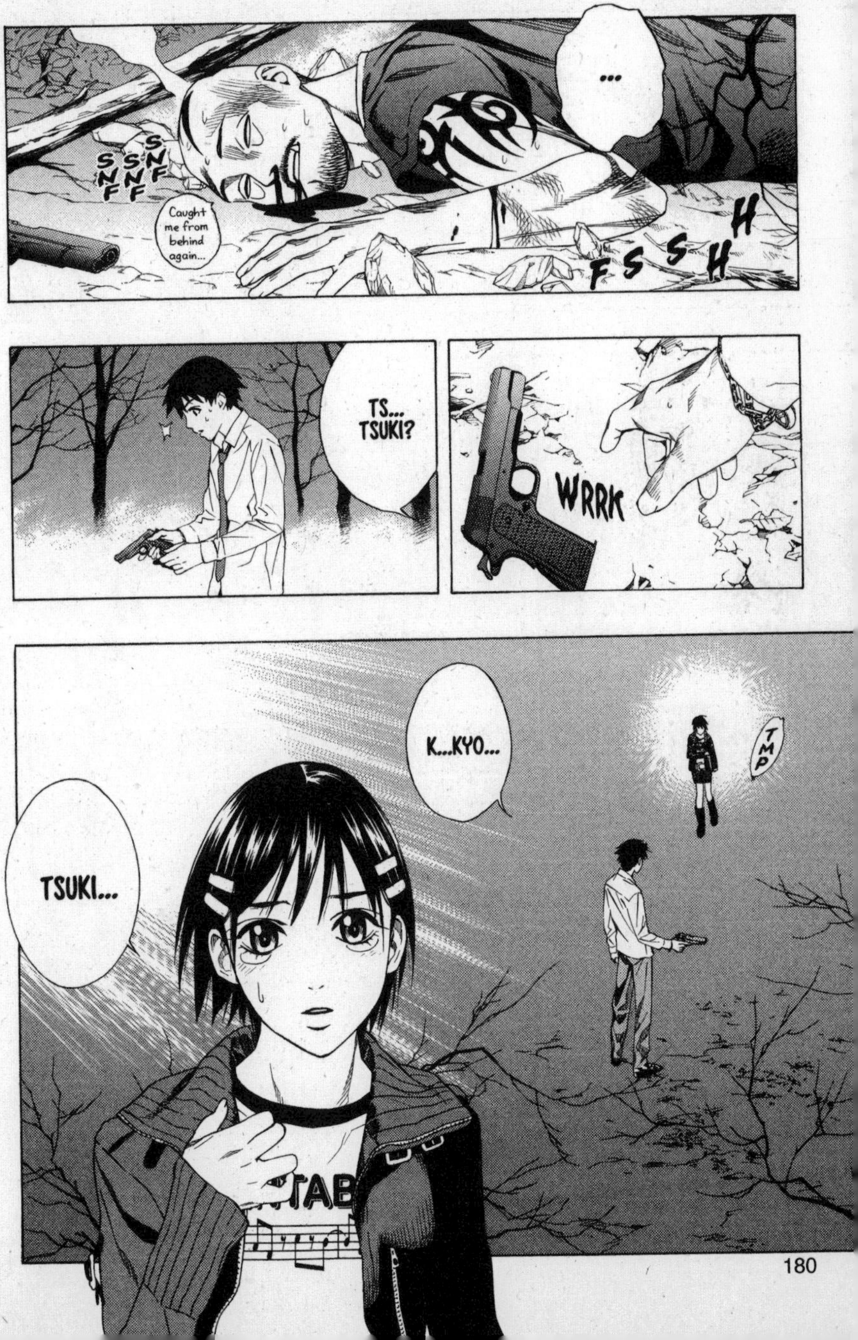
...
FSSHH
SNF SNF SNF
Caught me from behind again...
WRRK
TS... TSUKI?
TMP
K...KYO...
TSUKI...

READ THIS WAY

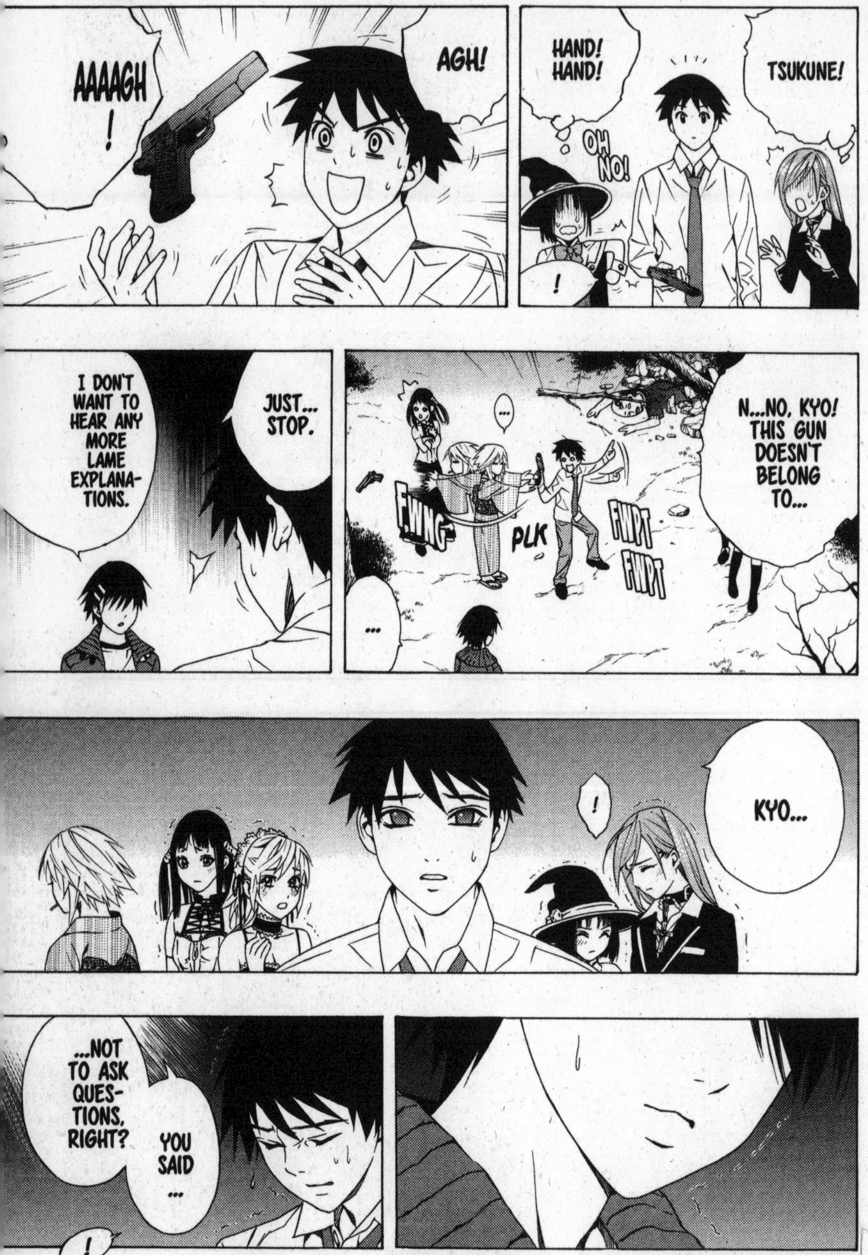
TSUKUNE!
HAND! HAND!
OH NO!
!
AGH!
AAAAGH!
N...NO, KYO! THIS GUN DOESN'T BELONG TO...
...
FWPT FWPT
PLK
FWING
...
JUST... STOP.
I DON'T WANT TO HEAR ANY MORE LAME EXPLANATIONS.
KYO...
!
YOU SAID...
...NOT TO ASK QUESTIONS, RIGHT?
!

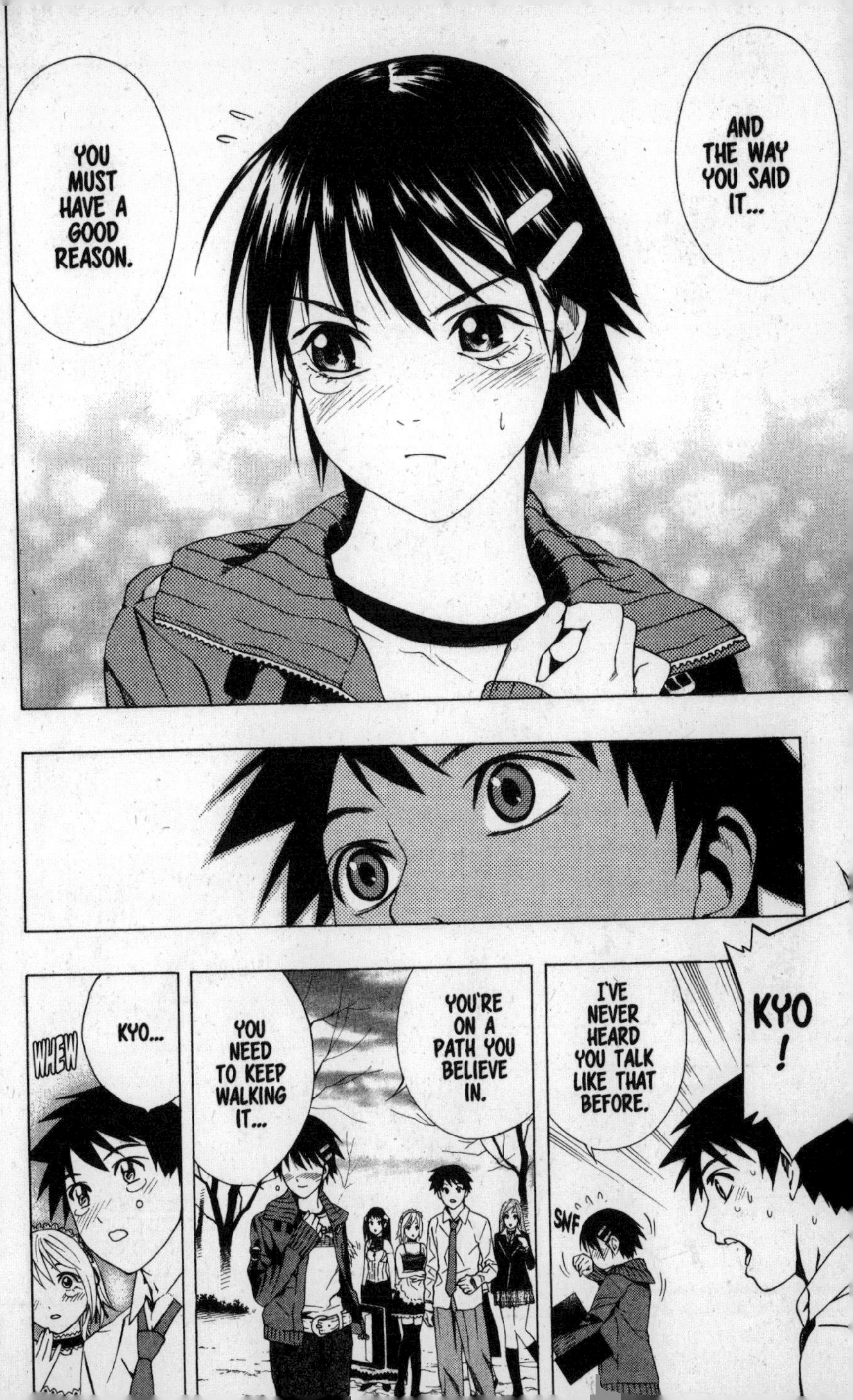
AND THE WAY YOU SAID IT...
YOU MUST HAVE A GOOD REASON.
KYO!
I'VE NEVER HEARD YOU TALK LIKE THAT BEFORE.
SNF
YOU'RE ON A PATH YOU BELIEVE IN.
YOU NEED TO KEEP WALKING IT...
KYO...
WHEW

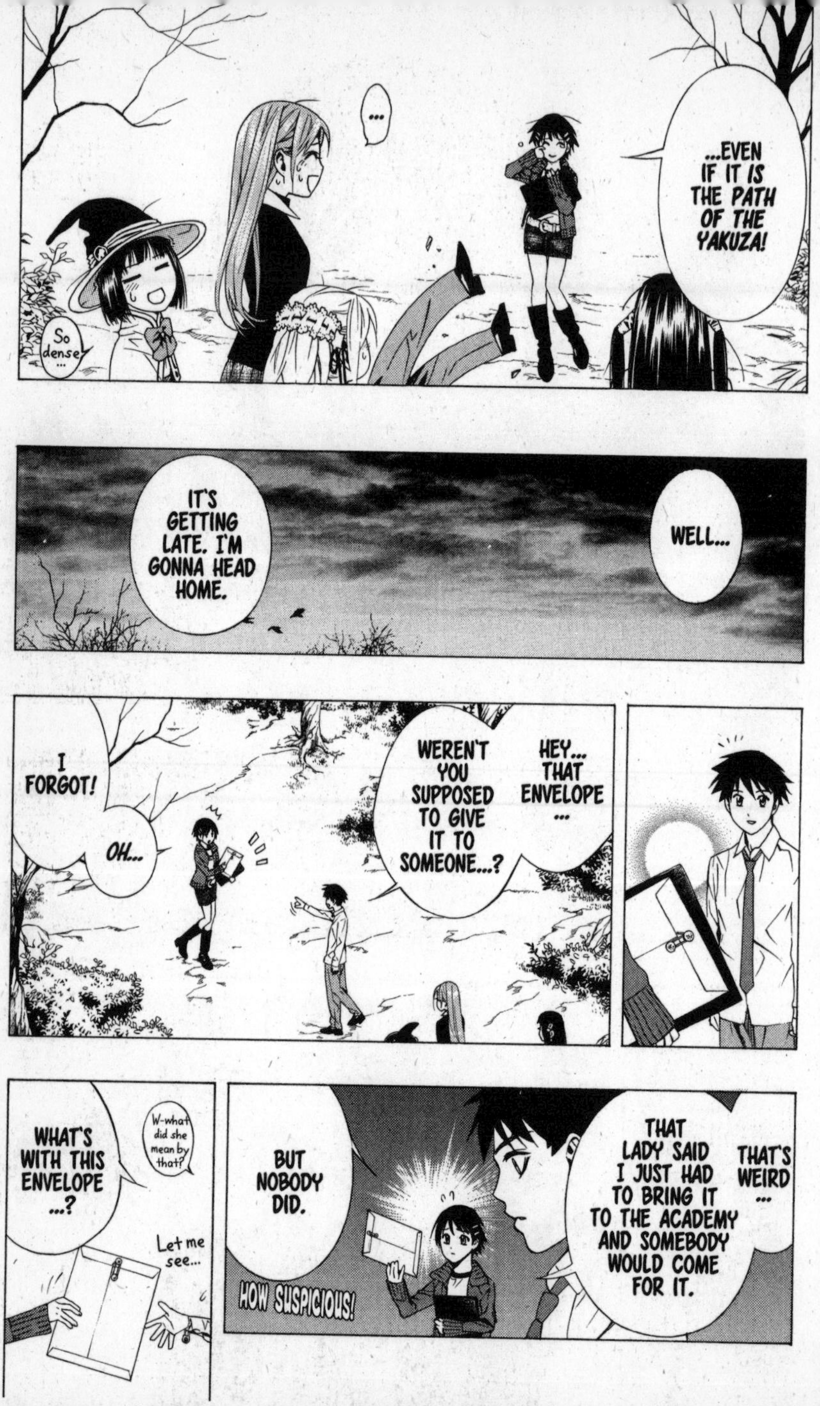
...EVEN IF IT IS THE PATH OF THE YAKUZA!
...
So dense...
WELL...
IT'S GETTING LATE. I'M GONNA HEAD HOME.
HEY... THAT ENVELOPE ...
WEREN'T YOU SUPPOSED TO GIVE IT TO SOMEONE...?
OH...
I FORGOT!
THAT'S WEIRD ...
THAT LADY SAID I JUST HAD TO BRING IT TO THE ACADEMY AND SOMEBODY WOULD COME FOR IT.
BUT NOBODY DID.
HOW SUSPICIOUS!
W-what did she mean by that?
WHAT'S WITH THIS ENVELOPE ...?
Let me see...

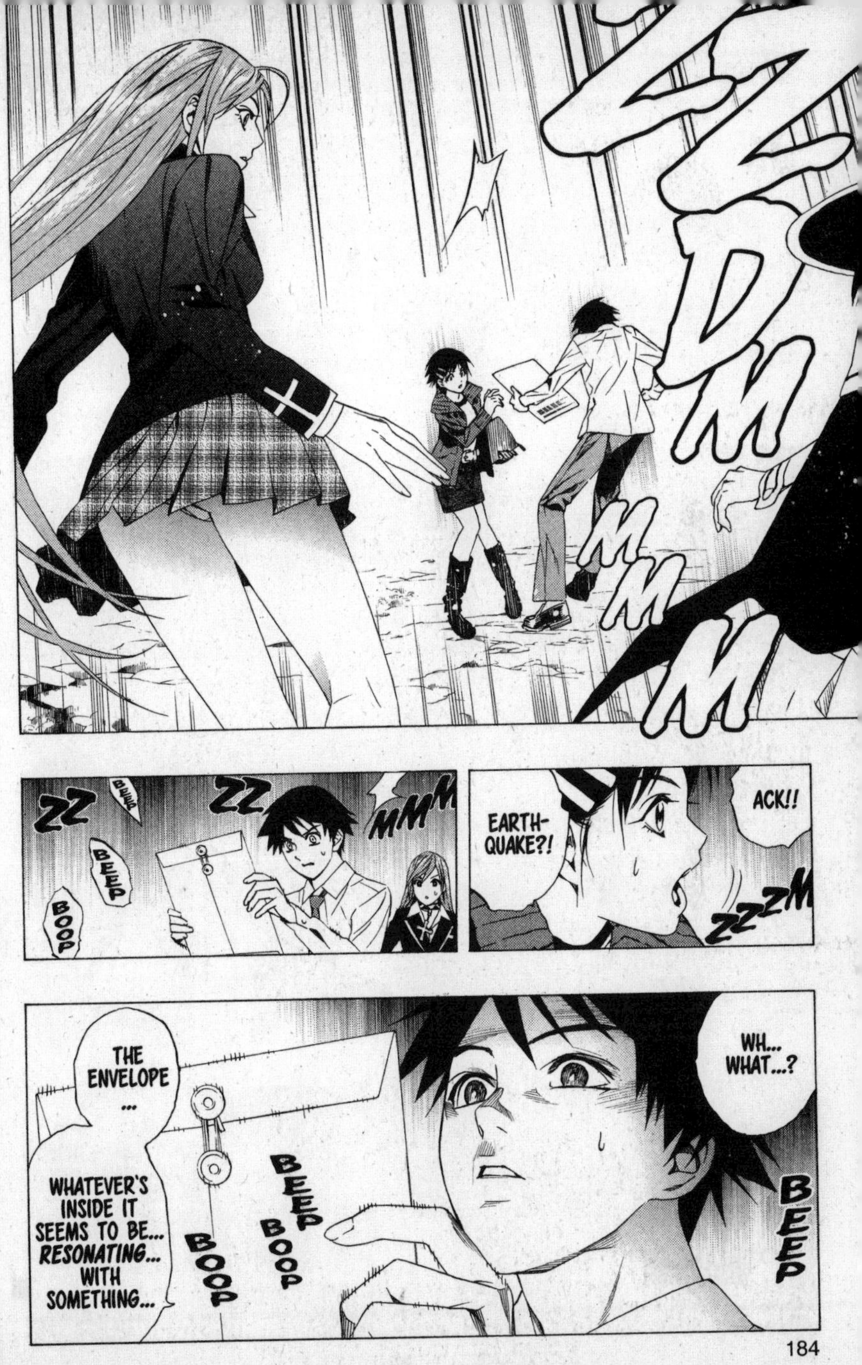
ACK!!
EARTH-QUAKE?!
ZZZZM
ZZ
BEEP
ZZ
MMM
BEEP
BOOP
WH... WHAT...?
BEEP
THE ENVELOPE ...
WHATEVER'S INSIDE IT SEEMS TO BE... RESONATING... WITH SOMETHING...
BEEP BOOP
BOOP

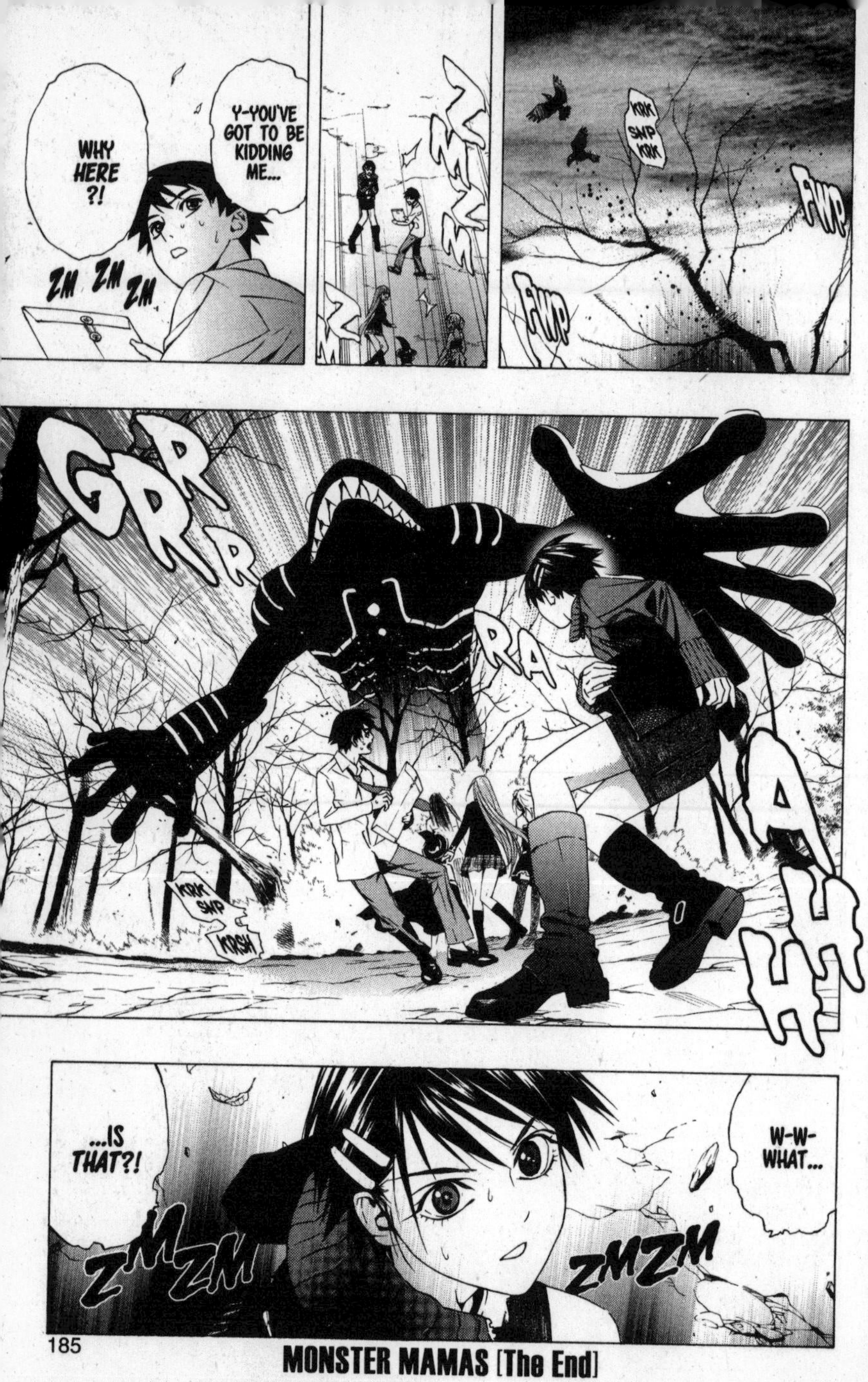
KRK
SNP
KRK
FWP
FWP
ZMMMM
ZM
Y-YOU'VE GOT TO BE KIDDING ME...
WHY HERE?!
ZM ZM ZM
GRRR
RA
AHHH
KRK
SNP
KRSH
W-W-WHAT...
...IS THAT?!
ZMZM
ZMZM

MONSTER MAMAS [The End]

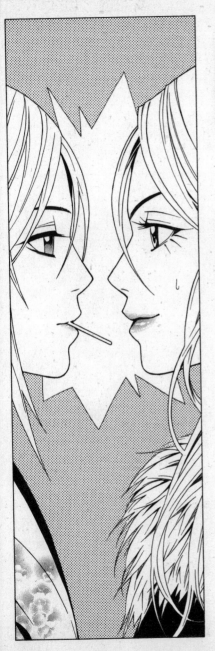

ROSARIO
+
VAMPIRE

Meaningless
End-of-Volume
Theater

IX

• Wicked Woman •

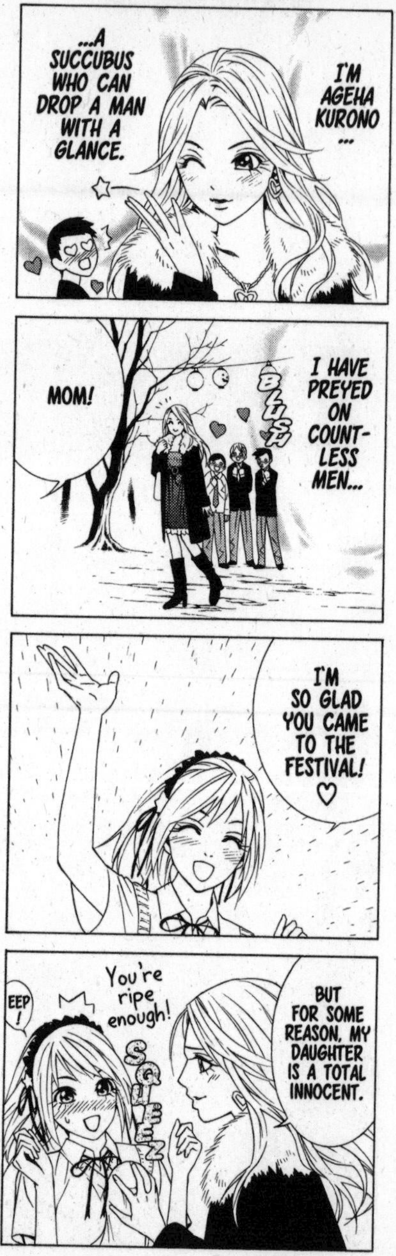
I'M AGEHA KURONO...
...A SUCCUBUS WHO CAN DROP A MAN WITH A GLANCE.
I HAVE PREYED ON COUNTLESS MEN...
BLUSH
MOM!
I'M SO GLAD YOU CAME TO THE FESTIVAL! ♡
BUT FOR SOME REASON, MY DAUGHTER IS A TOTAL INNOCENT.
You're ripe enough!
EEP!

• An Unhappy Woman •

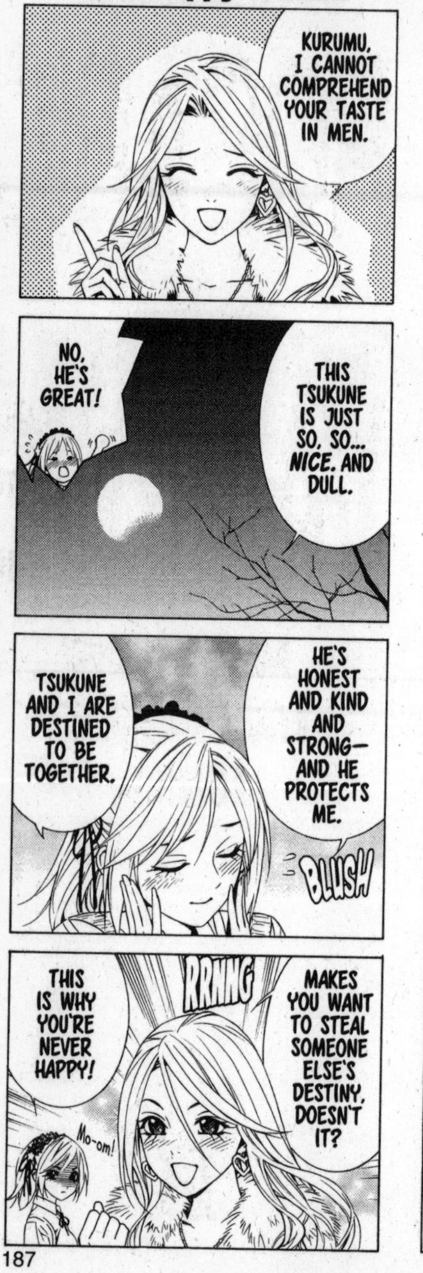
KURUMU, I CANNOT COMPREHEND YOUR TASTE IN MEN.
THIS TSUKUNE IS JUST SO, SO... NICE. AND DULL.
NO, HE'S GREAT!
HE'S HONEST AND KIND AND STRONG—AND HE PROTECTS ME.
BLUSH
TSUKUNE AND I ARE DESTINED TO BE TOGETHER.
MAKES YOU WANT TO STEAL SOMEONE ELSE'S DESTINY, DOESN'T IT?
RRNNG
THIS IS WHY YOU'RE NEVER HAPPY!
Mo-om!

•When the Time Comes•

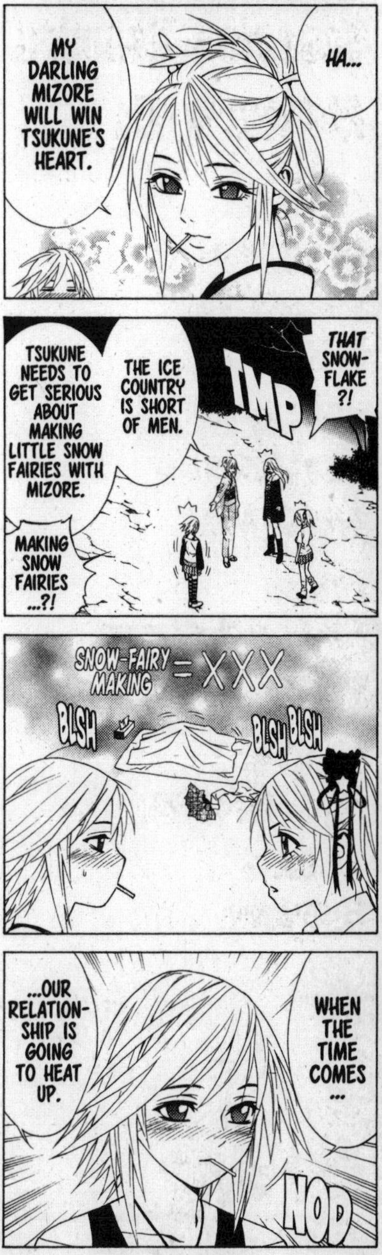
HA...
MY DARLING MIZORE WILL WIN TSUKUNE'S HEART.
THAT SNOW-FLAKE?!
TMP
THE ICE COUNTRY IS SHORT OF MEN.
TSUKUNE NEEDS TO GET SERIOUS ABOUT MAKING LITTLE SNOW FAIRIES WITH MIZORE.
MAKING SNOW FAIRIES ...?!
SNOW-FAIRY MAKING = XXX
BLSH BLSH
BLSH
WHEN THE TIME COMES ...
...OUR RELATIONSHIP IS GOING TO HEAT UP.
NOD

•Daily Special for Guys?•

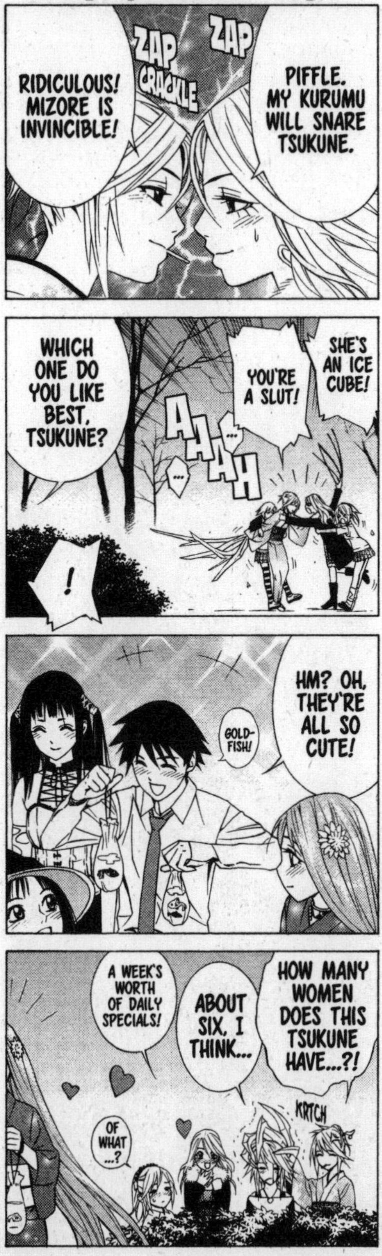
ZAP
PIFFLE. MY KURUMU WILL SNARE TSUKUNE.
ZAP
CRACKLE
RIDICULOUS! MIZORE IS INVINCIBLE!
SHE'S AN ICE CUBE!
YOU'RE A SLUT!
AAAAH
...
WHICH ONE DO YOU LIKE BEST, TSUKUNE?
...
!
HM? OH, THEY'RE ALL SO CUTE!
GOLD-FISH!
HOW MANY WOMEN DOES THIS TSUKUNE HAVE...?!
KRTCH
ABOUT SIX, I THINK...
A WEEK'S WORTH OF DAILY SPECIALS!
OF WHAT ...?

Please send questions and fan letters to ➡ Rosario+Vampire Fan Mail, VIZ Media, P.O. Box 77064, San Francisco, CA 94107

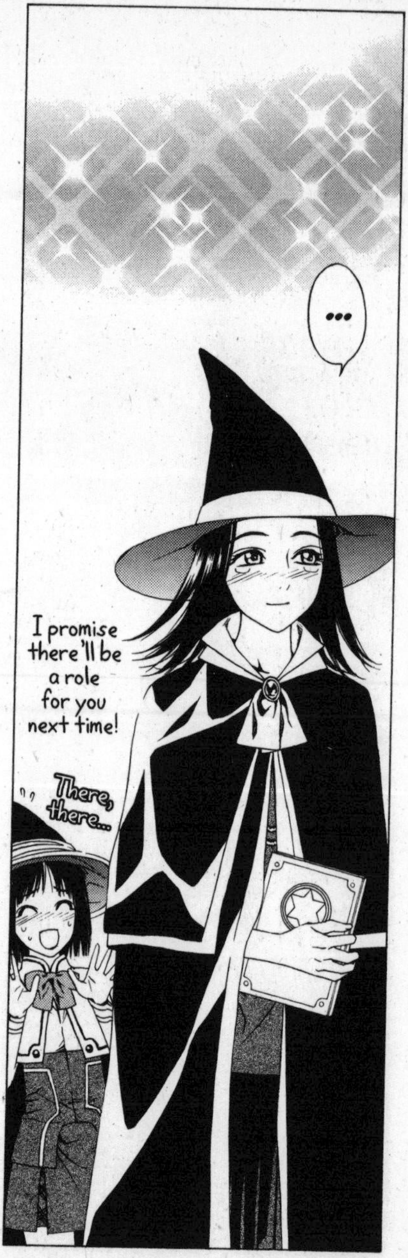
...
I promise there'll be a role for you next time!
There, there...

Rosario + Vampire

Akihisa Ikeda

• Staff •

Makoto Saito

Takafumi Okubo

Kenji Tashiro

• Help •

Yoshiaki Sukeno

Takeshi Toda

• CG •

Takaharu Yoshizawa

Akihisa Ikeda

• Editing •

Tomonori Sumiya

• Comic •

Kenju Noro

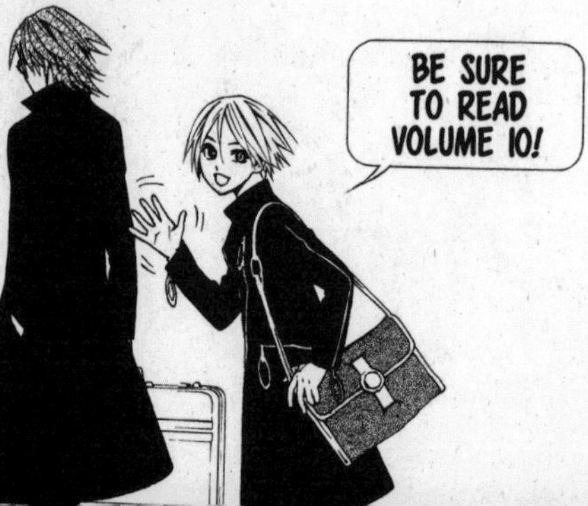
BE SURE TO READ VOLUME 10!

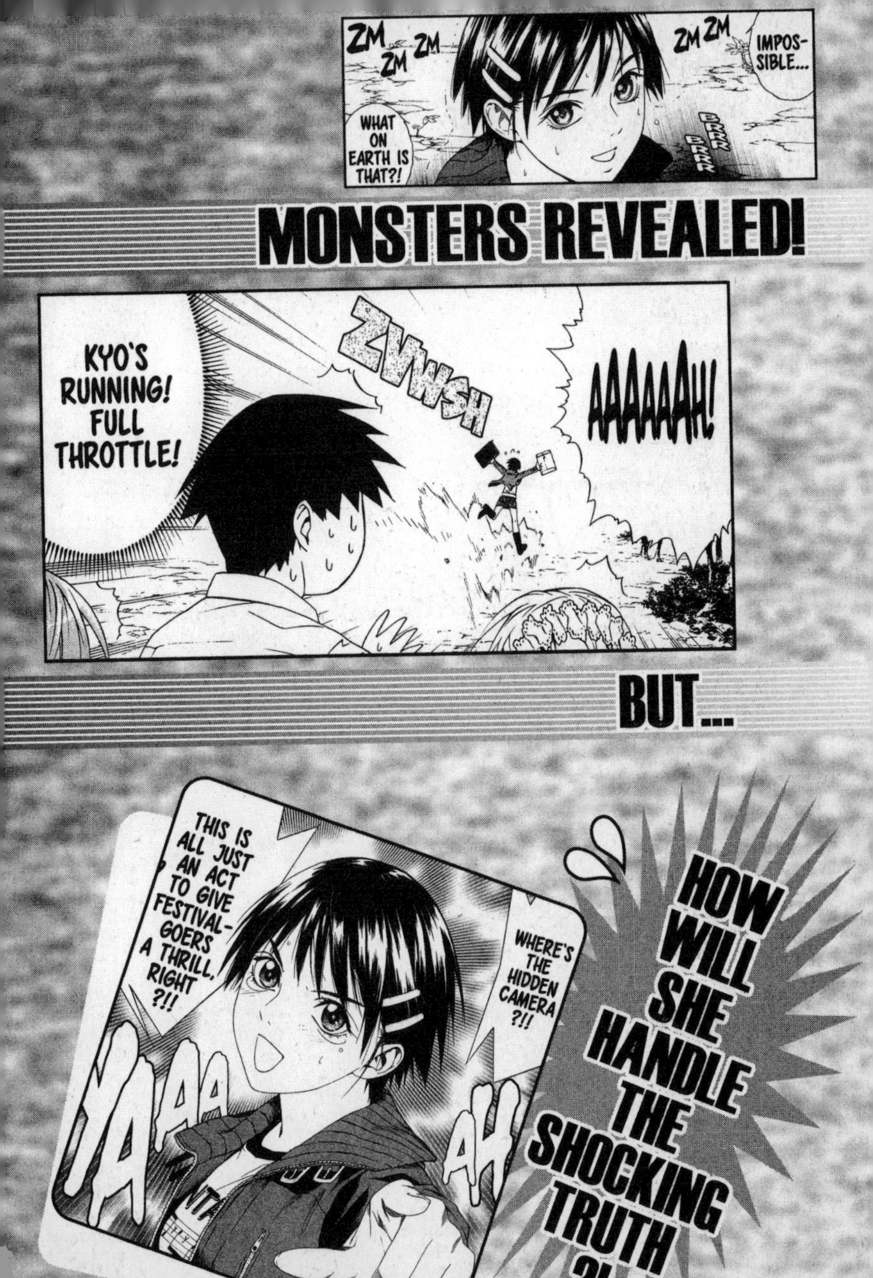
ZM ZM
IMPOSSIBLE...
BRRR BRRR
ZM ZM ZM
WHAT ON EARTH IS THAT?!
MONSTERS REVEALED!
AAAAAAH!
ZWWSH
KYO'S RUNNING! FULL THROTTLE!
BUT...
HOW WILL SHE HANDLE THE SHOCKING TRUTH ?!
WHERE'S THE HIDDEN CAMERA ?!!
THIS IS ALL JUST AN ACT TO GIVE FESTIVAL-GOERS A THRILL, RIGHT ?!!
YAAA-AH

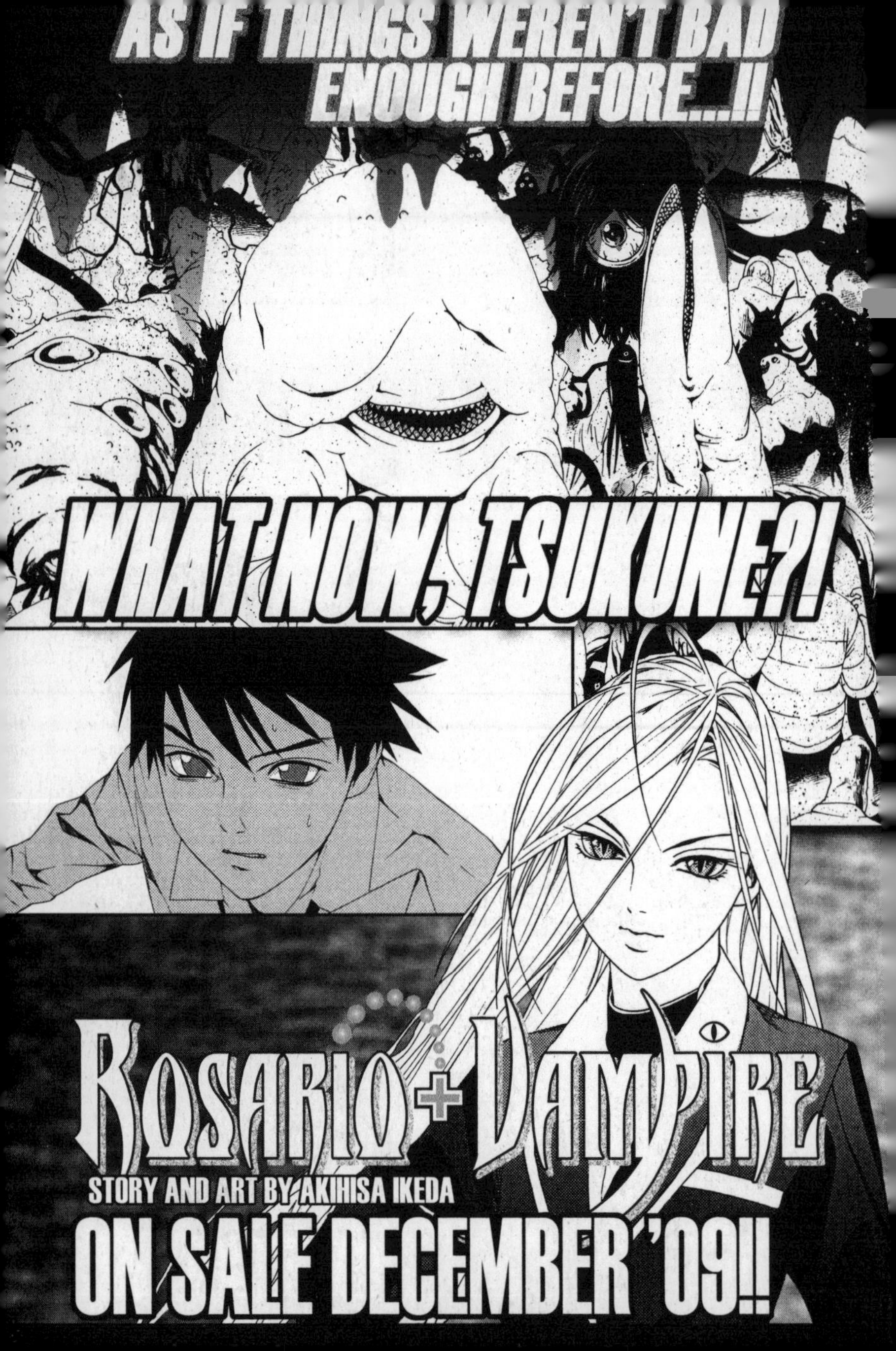

AS IF THINGS WEREN'T BAD ENOUGH BEFORE...!!
WHAT NOW, TSUKUNE?!
ROSARIO+VAMPIRE
STORY AND ART BY AKIHISA IKEDA
ON SALE DECEMBER '09!!

Crypt Sheet for Volume 10: Magic Mirror

QUIZ 10

A MAGIC MIRROR THAT REFLECTS THE TRUE NATURE OF WHOEVER LOOKS INTO IT IS BEST USED TO...

a. pop your zits

b. pick your friends

c. devour your soul

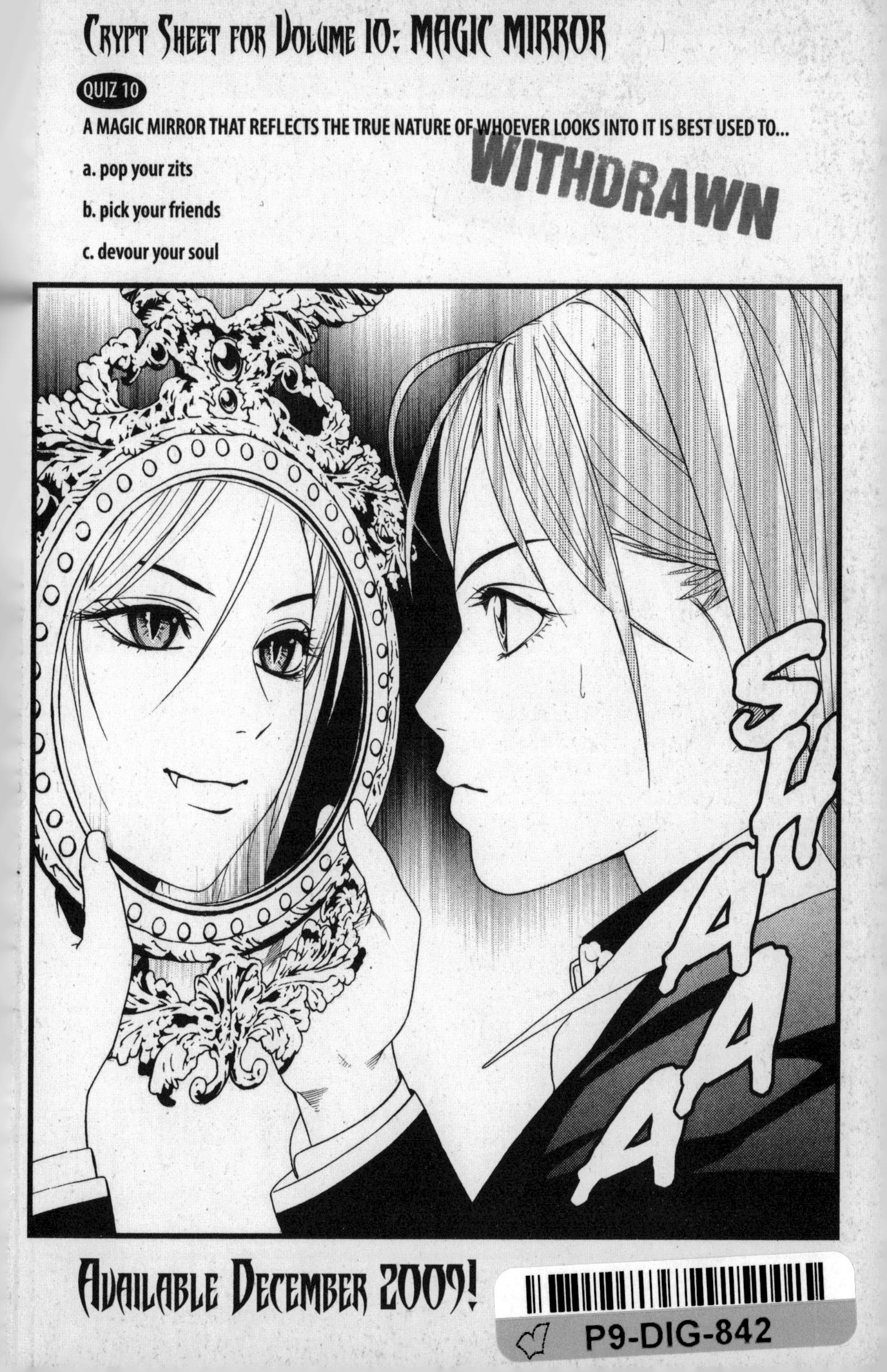
SHAAA

Available December 2009!